Arms and Armor Annual

Volume One

Edited by
Robert Held

Digest Books, Inc., Northfield, Illinois

Arms and Armor Annual Staff

EDITOR-IN-CHIEF *Robert Held*

ASSISTANT EDITORS *Stefano Solieri*
Allen Miller

STAFF PHOTOGRAPHER *Marcello Bertoni*

ART DIRECTOR *Mary MacDonald*

ASSOCIATE PUBLISHER *Sheldon L. Factor*

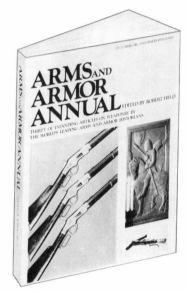

Our Covers

THE FRONT COVER: The illustrations chosen represent the chronological range of this volume's contents, which runs from about 1340 into the 1870's.

Motionless and timeless, the valiant knight Colaccio Beccadelli stands guard in effigy over his own tomb in the Church of Saints Nicolas and Dominick in the little town of Imola in Central Italy, where he was buried on the 13th of May 1341. For an exhaustive analysis of his armor, see our first article.

Rich in flavor of the American Western Saga is the unique trio of Winchester 1866 carbines produced in the late 1870's and engraved, nickeled and silver-wire inlaid shortly after. No similar triad seems to be known anywhere else—see page 315.

Crossbows have become inexorably associated with Switzerland, but in fact their evolution there only followed the styles and techniques of Austria and Germany. You'll find much worthwhile reading on this score beginning on page 56.

THE BACK COVER: Sotheby-Parke Bernet are holding, in their London and Los Angeles salesrooms, a series of sales from the William Goodwin Renwick Collection, which was one of the largest and most important collections of firearms ever in the U.S.A. Four sales in London and two in Los Angeles have already taken place, in the course of which new world record prices for a wide range of pieces have been established. These include 16th century English snaphaunce and French flintlock fowling pieces, 18th Century Italian flintlock magazine repeating pistols and 19th Century American flintlock duelling and officer's pistols. At least five more sales from this collection are planned.

On the back cover is shown a pair of holster pistols made about 1650 for Louis XIV when Dauphin of France by Pierre Bergier of Grenoble, with double waterproof locks firing two superimposed charges.

Also shown is the historic French flintlock fowling piece made about 1615/20 for Louis XIII of France. It bears his crowned cypher and the inventory number 134 from his Cabinet d'Armes and is signed by Pierre le Bourgeoys of Lisieux.

For all matters concerning the contents of the ARMS AND ARMOR ANNUAL, including communications to the various authors and offers of contributions to future issues, please contact the Editorial Office, Arms and Armor Annual, Piazza Santa Maria Sopr'arno 1R, Florence, Italy. Telephone 296-595 (Italian Area Code 055). Cable address: Acquafresca Florence.

ISBN 0-695-80407-3 (paper)
0-695-80435-9 (cloth)

Library of Congress
Catalog Card #73-83405

Foreword

Thoughtfully composed for people who never read forewords . . . and therefore brief. Not that there is much to say. The customary amenities are quickly disposed of: We wish to thank everyone who had the steely nerves and saintly patience to put up with us in the wakes of crises these past fifteen months that seemed time and again to have brought our cherished project to the edge of doom, and three times to have pushed it over; we thank the usual typists, the kind helpers with files and surly postmen and photos, the fetchers of coffee and the smokers who forebore in our virtuous presence, and Clara Gellerman who one day upped and silhouetted the gloomy background out of all of Dr. Hoope's photographs because she is good, brave and a wow with china-white. We thank all whom we haven't yet, and hope ruefully they'll bear up again under the strain of volume two in preparation.

That done, a micro-history of the ARMS AND ARMOR ANNUAL may prove bearable. About three years ago we mentioned over lunch to our good friend and colleague, Mr. Gun Digest, alias John T. Amber, how much a pity it was that good historical-weapons literature in America and in Europe seems to be fragmented into cells scattered throughout publications at times very difficult to come by even if excellent, or with unsatisfactory quality standards for illustrations reproductions, or very narrowly limited to specialized subject ranges, or overblown in graphic make-up to mask the paucity of substance in the comments, and so on.

For modern firearms and allied matters there were several noteworthy annual compendia here and abroad, conspicuous among them of course Mr. Amber's own inimitable Digest. Monthlies and bi-monthlies in the habit of dedicating some space to antiques were not rare, though with but two or three exceptions in America and two in Europe, the quality of scholarship and of literary as well as graphic presentation is usually mediocre. Why could there not be a species of Gun Digest dedicated exclusively to historical arms and armor and all that bears on these in any way worth setting down for serious study?—Any subject from stone age axes to, say, the advent of modern cartridge repeaters, treated by students of international stature and presented elegantly without ostentation, richly without silly (and costly) frills, scholarly but readable, meticulous but not tedious, and open to all viewpoints without prejudice or censure?

And the answers that rushed to mind were many and sad. We had been in publishing long enough to harbor no illusions about the hard realities of costs, break-even points, and the far greater probability of sending out for red ink than for black when the tallies were summed. Moreover, one could not really hope to persuade twenty or twenty-five (it turned out thirty) famous and overworked scholars to contribute generously to a non-existent, amorphous and probably a bit suspect shadow of a book in the first throes of embryo—should it ever get as far as that. Well-known authorities must answer more substantial claims upon their time. With no great odds for finding a publisher, and smaller ones yet for getting the sort of contributions one would need . . . the outlook was not bright. And yet—

One day we presented a rough outline to Digest Books' founder and President, Milton Klein, who took it all in thoughtfully. Let's think it over, he said; let's not rush; it may float; it may even soar—and then, it may gurgle down the drain. But we'll see what the others think and then . . .

A week later Digest Books was ready to try, a decision requiring no less courage than generosity, for the odds seemed against anything but a costly if prestigious contribution to arms study. And on that selfsame day, we set out to build it.

We shall spare you, reader, the moving, gripping and sometimes gruesome account of ARMS AND ARMOR ANNUAL's gestation. One dislikes thinking back on how many times defeat seemed snatched from the jaws of victory: the pessimists had been right, no worthwhile contributor could be budged or, if budged, rushed; postal strikes in Britian and Italy, with six-month repercussions everywhere, left manuscripts and unduplicatable photographs in forgotten boxcars on ungodly switchyard sidings, telexes to Northfield clicked off in a health resort in Peru, the designed and desired range of subject matter would not shape up and seemed incapable of being shaped. We flew hundreds of air hours all over Europe and America; we begged and bought, wheedled and frowned, laughed and growled, spoke softly and carried a big perseverance . . . and somehow it began to float. Eighteen months later it gave an airborne quiver. And now, judging by some initial responses, it seems to soar serenely on its maiden flight.

That's about all. The authors rest, the editors withdraw, and you, reader, will judge. We've left you two pages at the end of the book for that. We like to think, knowing that life is filled with illusions, that we have not done badly. To you the rest.

Robert Held
Florence, Italy
December, 1973

Contents

Colaccio Beccadelli: an Emilian Knight of about 1340

*by LIONELLO GIORGIO BOCCIA
and EDUARDO T. COELHO*

*Lionello Giorgio Boccia, architect, born 47 years ago in Cremona, Italy,
and Eduardo T. Coelho, book illustrator, born 54 years ago in Portugal, both
live in Florence. For many years they have collaborated in the study
of arms and armor, especially in the hitherto all but virgin field of Italian armor
and edged weapons. It is to their skills, wisdom and labor that world
collectordom owes the volume* L'Arte dell' Armatura in Italia, *one of the
precious few books in the field worthy of the abused adjective "monumental."
A companion work on edged weapons,* Armi Bianche Italiane, *is about to
appear. Their interest focuses especially on medieval armor; the present
observations on Colaccio Beccadelli and the already-published* L'Armamento
Misto di Cuoio e Ferro nel Trecento Italiano *are promises of more fine studies
to come. Lionello Giorgio Boccia, besides exercising his profession of architect,
is Supervisor of Arms and Armor in the National Museum at the Bargello
in Florence, and teaches a graduate seminar on arms and armor history
at the University of Pisa and in Florence. He is the author of many works[15],
and is co-author, with Robert Held, of a new two-volume social,
political and cultural history of arms and armor to be published by
Harper & Row, New York, 1975. Eduardo T. Coelho conducts organized
and systematic source research on problems of the 14th and 15 centuries;
he has amassed a unique treasure of documentation soon, it is hoped,
to reach the public.*

I. PRESENTATION OF THE CASE

Imola, a little town in Romagna in Central Italy, treasures in one of the side-chapels of the church of Saints Nicolas and Domenick a marble tombstone that may be reckoned among the most fascinating of 14th-century Italy (Fig. 1).

Usually, a monument of that time erected to the memory of an illustrious personage, in particular to a warrior, closely followed the rules of a precise iconography which symbolized the social condition and the fame of the deceased. A single stone or marble was generally inlaid into the church floor and represented the armed knight carved in bas-relief, lying with his hands clasped, his face showing through the opening of his coif or basnet; a Latin inscription incised along the margins of the slab briefly recalled his name, his titles and his dates. Sometimes—but mainly outside of Italy—the warrior was shown in a more life-like pose, perhaps holding his helmet and with the shield at his side, but always lying supine or "standing" (as though in a horizontal portrait), never in action. In Tuscany dominated the type of slab on which the effigy of the deceased is framed by a rich Gothic window with twisted columns and a flowery tympanum, whereas the typical Emilian specimen has a simple border.

A more elaborate memorial was the sarcophagus standing on the church floor or on corbels. In this case religious scenes and events from the life of the knight were carved on the face of the prism; the deceased's effigy in relief (more seldom in the fully-round) rested on the lid of the sarcophagus. Below, a more or less longish inscription, sometimes by a man of letters, told of the occupant's virtues (including a good many he never possessed). The sarcophagus could be enriched by architectural ornaments such as tympani, aedicule, pinnacles, open-work and figures, according to the degree of pomp and ostentation the family desired to lavish on the occasion by way of a social passport. A third and more complex sepulchre, still very rare in 14th-century Italy, was the equestrian monument sometimes added to a well-devised sarcophagus. Standing statues *in tondo,* i.e. fully round, were seldom used in Italy at this time, compared with the Northern countries. On the whole, and simplifying greatly, we may say that in Central Italy—roughly from Bologna to Rome—the slab set into the floor or wall dominated throughout the whole century; a few sarcophagi are found, but no equestrian monument. The names of some of the sculptors of the sarcophagi and of now-destroyed equestrian statues are known, but the authors of the tombstones can hardly ever be identified because they did not sign their work, having been for the most part only good lapidaries innocent of any ambitions of signing their daily routine labours.

To come back to our tombstone of Imola. It is an exceptional one: the warrior does not lie with his hands clasped but rides on a lively mount; he wears full armour, including his helm, and the horse too, is armoured; and finally, the sculptor has signed his work (Fig. 8).[1] It is now on the wall of the passage that leads to the chapel proper, but in the past it used

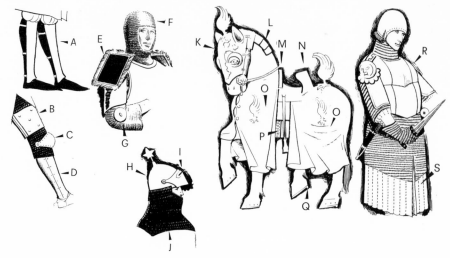

to be set in the floor; the expression *sub ista . . . arca,* "within this coffin," that appears in the inscription leads one to suppose that it might once have been the lid of a marble sarcophagus resting on the floor *more nobilium,* i.e. "in the manner of noblemen". In any case, it was moved when the chapel came under the patronage of the Vandini family, who tampered with it in favour of baroque ornaments that were removed in the course of the restoration of 1935-1938. The inscription incised around the border of the slab reads: CLAUDITUR SUB ISTA PRESENTI COLACIUS ARCA, QUI MIRA TANTA FECIT, QUOD SIBI MULTA SUBIECIT, QUEM GENUIT BONONIA, DANS BECHADELLI NOMINA, Q OBIIT ANNO D. MCCCXLI, INDICIONE VIIII DIE XIII MAGII, "Within this coffin, Colaccio Beccadelli, whom Bologna bore, lies ready for the call to judgment. He wrought many marvellous accomplishments because he excelled in many virtues. He died in the Ninth Indiction on May 13th, 1341." Between the legs of the horse we can read the signature BITINUS DE BONONIA ME FECIT, "Bitino of Bologna made me" (Fig. 8).

The Beccadelli were an illustrious Bolognese family named, so it is said, after a certain Beccadello degli Artenisi, who disassociated himself from the main lineage towards the end of the 1100's and was several times appointed to public offices by the *Comune* (township, city-state). They were *popolani* (i.e., they did not belong to Ghibelline stock of the "great") and were banished from Bologna in 1337 after having sided with the losing faction in a complex series of political upheavals. In 1350 they were granted permission to return to their homes in Piazza Santo Stefano, where we can still see traces of their coat of arms carved on the capitals of the columns; but meanwhile, in 1341, Colaccio (short for Nicolaccio) had died in exile at Imola. As early as 1305 Colaccio had fought against Guidinello Montecuccoli during the siege of Montese, near Modena, and in 1315 he had joined the allies of Florence in the bloody battle of Montecatini lost by the Guelphs. Ambassador in

Fig. 1—Tombstone of Colaccio Beccadelli, died 1341, in the church of Saints Nicolas and Dominick in Imola, by Bettino da Bologna. Mounted stance and full armour are unusual: generally, deceased warrior is shown lying or standing with his hands clasped. Only other 14th-century Italian tombstone showing a mounted warrior is in Bagnacavallo, a few miles from Imola, but it is later by some sixty years.

Padua and Ferrara in 1319, and elected an *Anziano,* i.e., an Elder, of the *Comune* several times between 1320 and 1335, he was one of the outstanding personalities of the political life in his city.[2]

His tombstone does him credit. His expression intent, he wears a basnet with ogival and centred skull; straps fitted over brass or bronze ringlets standing out from the skull (through which a leather thong runs to hold everything in place) support the hanging aventail all around, the upper part of which is turned down to form a fringe of mail as a further protection for the neck and cheeks (Figs. 2 and 3). The large helm can be thrown back over the shoulder, allowing the knight to breathe more easily, but remaining always ready to be donned again quickly. The sight and the vertical ridge of the visor are reinforced, whereas the cloth cap with mantle—partly functional and partly decorative—covers the high, oval skull (Fig. 2 insert). The crest is formed by two winged eagle claws, like those appearing on the knight's shield; and since we know that the coat of arms of the Beccadelli was azure with one gold winged claw, we may be sure that the material was azure and the crest gilt (Fig. 4). These must also have been the colors of the gown that covers the coat of plates, i.e. a gown of leather or canvas covered on the outside with silk or velvet, while its inside was lined with small tinned iron plates which protected the wearer's entire trunk. (Coats of plates could also be fashioned differently: open in front, at the sides or at the back, and variously shaped, while the rows of rivets that supported its metal parts could be left visible and gilded or silvered to form ornaments.) Colaccio Beccadelli's gown is short in front, where it is also scalloped so as to make riding easier, and longer behind, where it drops freely from the waist to the buttocks. The detail of the triangular shoulder defences—certainly armoured—that protect the shoulders and the top of the upper arms, decorated with heraldry, is very interesting. The attempt to protect the collarbones from blows had first led to the application of ailettes to the top of the shoulders (movable shields to mitigate or deviate cutting and thrusting blows); these were then abandoned in favour of small hemispherical shoulder-plates, hinged to the coat of plates proper. In Emilia, however—as in Tuscany and other places in Northern Italy—preference was still sometimes given to triangular shoulder-plates, pointed at the lower end and often also projecting beyond the line of the arms.

Colaccio's arms are otherwise protected solely by the sleeves of his mail shirt, worn over a gambaison which, in this period, reaches halfway down the thigh. It is not unusual to find arms still thus exposed without the protection of *cuir bouilli* (leather softened by soaking in boiling wax, shaped as desired around a form and hardened by the natural drying-out), more or less reinforced with metal. Only the hands are pro-

Fig. 2—Colaccio Beccadelli on foot, showing all the various elements discussed in this study. Some details must rest on conjecture in turn based on comparative experience: for example, the two exposed chains seem to come from the common central point of attachment, hence the one for the dagger must start from there, too. The sword is supported by the belt (and the quillons are level with the waist) when the knight is on foot, whereas it hangs from a special strap (and the quillons are level with the hip) when he is on horseback, the undone belt being then wrapped around the upper end of the sheath. Note relation of volume between basnet and helm.

13

Fig. 3—Face shown is an actual portrait of the deceased. Compact basnet ends in a centred apex; aventail overlaps where it hangs from the leather strap (a particularly Italian feature which lasted into the 1350's). Holes at regular intervals in the strap fitted over the pierced studs projecting from skull piece; a lace was then threaded through all the studs to secure the strap.

Fig. 4—Helm securing system: T-shaped grapple at extremity of chain fits into slit of the visor: T-grapple is then turned and weight of helm prevents it from re-turning and disengaging. At times a couple of chains were used, one over each shoulder. Crest and coloured mantle added pageantry.

Fig. 5—Triangular armouring and upper arm are of a Central- and North-Italian type in use around the 1340's. Heraldic decoration on them derives from family coats of arms painted on metal *ailettes* in use since the late 1200's to protect the shoulder but soon proved inefficient (last datable Italian ailettes are found on the effigy of Raimondo Cabanni, d. 1334, in the church of Saint Clara, Naples).

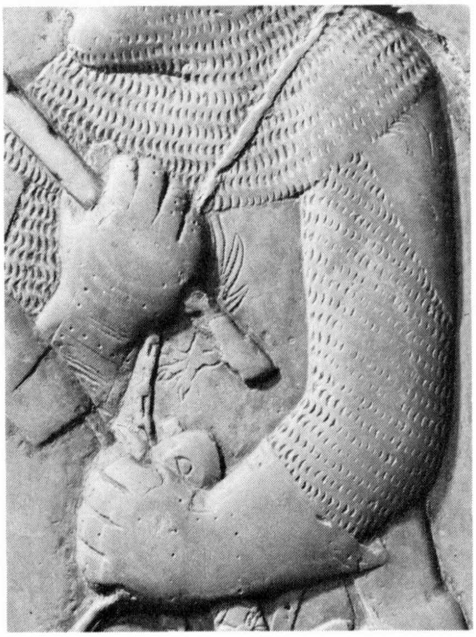

tected by leather gauntlets reinforced with metal on the cuffs and on the back of the hand, scales covering the separate fingers; armour evolution has not yet reached the stiff gauntlet, but the protection is fairly efficient (Fig. 5).

Leg protection is very developed and represents an important point of reference for the study of 14th-century armour. The mail breeches worn over leather reach almost down to the calf; over them in turn are worn leather or heavy canvas gamboised cuisses opened at the lower back to allow bending of the knee, and fastened below by a strap and buckle. The thigh is further protected by a cuisse plate and a poleyn, the latter being buckled on (the strap with the buckle is probably single-ended on the inside while forked or Y-ended on the outside: in this way

the hold is better and safer while the bending of the knee is rendered easier). The lower border of the mail breeches hangs over the leather jambers, thus defending the unprotected space below the poleyn; from this derived the later Italian custom of covering the space left between the poleyn and the greaves in 15th-century armour with a fringe of mail hanging from the lower plate of the poleyn.[3] The jambers are certainly leather, since they do not show the side-cut indispensable in hinged metal greaves; straps and buckles or strings fasten them together on the inside. A flap of soft leather reinforced with studs—like the one on the knight's shoes—covers the instep; this protects the joint better and also guards against the friction of the spur and its straps. Finally, the spurs have only slightly curved sides, pointed crests, short necks, and full rose rowels with fifteen points; their straps are reinforced with metal labels and plates (Figs. 6 and 16).

In his right hand Colaccio holds a long mace, and at his left side the sword hangs from a belt and is further secured by a chain; a second chain and a dagger are hidden by the warrior's right and by the neck of his mount.

The harness of the horse is interesting. The coverture is divided into two large panels, open at the level of the flank to allow for spurring, and buttoned in front down the neck and the chest; the housing, too, must have been azure with applied or embroidered gilt winged claws. The coverture was of *sàrgano* (canvas), sometimes wadded—"incamutato"— or lined with leather; it would protect the horse from ordinary blows and from arrows, and was reinforced with metal at least along the neck, on the loins and the crupper where cutting blows would prove most dangerous.[4] The shaffron of *cuir bouilli* and the armouring were usually hidden under the coverture; only a

metal protection along the nose running from the horse's forehead to its withers and—more rarely— another metal protection running from the back to the tail might be visible outside it. Colaccio's mount is unique in that it shows a real outer shaffron, complete with articulated crinet. It is probably of *cuir bouilli*, with protecting eye- and ear-guards, and is armoured crosswise to reinforce it; this reinforcement supports a winged claw, a further protective ornament. To the side margins of the shaffron are buckled the sideplates, probably also of *cuir bouilli;* on the other hand, the neck-lame and the three crinet-lames are certainly of metal, as there would be no reason for using any other material. There is no sign of a bridle, but the presence of the bit necessarily implies it. The cheeks are shaped like double cinquefoils and the reins act directly upon the bit without the help of branches; therefore, the bit is probably of the twisted snaffle type, whereas the reins—according to the custom of the time—are partly of chain and partly of leather (Figs. 7 and 21). The winged claw on the

Fig. 6—Colaccio wears much more developed leg than arm defences. For legs (see Fig. 16), protection is composed (going by layer from inside to outside) of leather or cloth breeches, mail breeches, gamboised cuisses and finally metal plates covering thigh and knee. Leg bending is not hindered by buckled leather straps holding different parts in place; jambers are of *cuir bouilli* and laced on inner side with thongs.

Fig. 7—Shaffron and its side plates are almost certainly of *cuir bouilli;* their articulation allows good adjustment over the horse's head, and blunted edges do not irritate or injure the animal's skin. But cross-shaped protection and four lames forming crinet (ancestors of the complete metal head and neck defence) are of iron. (See Fig. 21).

Fig. 8—Sculptor's signature, BITINUS DE BONOIA ME FECIT, is set between horse's hooves. Horse is powerfully shod: projecting nail heads and strong calcans on hind horseshoes are clearly visible, served on frozen ground as well as on soft to arrest running momentum.

15

Fig. 9—Evolution of the helm (pen rendition contemporary representations): (A) From a bas-relief panel once in the courtyard of the Bargello Palace in Florence, c. 1320-1325 (see Fig. 19). (B) From the Tarlati Mausoleum in the Cathedral of Arezzo, 1327-1330. (C) From the frescoes in the chamber of the bell-tower in St. Remigio, Florence (see Fig. 13-A). (D) Colaccio Becadelli's helm. (E) From the equestrian monument to Mastino II, Scaligere Ark, Verona (see Fig. 23). (F) From the tomb of the *gonfaloniere* (governor, head of state) Giovanni de' Medici in the church of Saint Reparata, Florence, 1353.

crupper reveals the presence of inside armouring under the coverture, otherwise this further protective ornament could not possibly stand upright.

The saddle is of the usual war type, with the sides of the cantle curved in at the top, and secured by a mail-covered surcingle to avoid its being cut; finally, the treadle of the stirrups is broader than the branches and the loop is protected by a bridge, anticipating the type that is going to develop throughout the 15th century. At first sight the stirrup leather seems also to be made of chain, at least in its lower part; but careful examination *in loco* shows that this is an optical effect of the regular surface fractures of the stone and leads us to exclude the possibility of chains in favour of the assumption that it was armoured (Figs. 6 and 16). The horse is very strongly shod, with at least ten

projecting nail-heads to a shoe, the hind shoes showing calcans (a custom still followed by some modern armies, and not only in winter); calcans kept the horse from slipping on soft ground, but served mainly to stop the animal short even if it had broken into a fast run, as its own weight, together with that of rider and equipment, gave it a quantum of inertia that could be very dangerous if not well under control (Fig. 8).

II. ANALYTICAL COMPARISONS

The defensive equipment of Colaccio Beccadelli and his horse allows some comparisons and precise specifications to be made within the sphere of experiences in Central Italy, mainly between those of Emilia and Tuscany, going from the 1330's into the 1350's.

The helm thrown over the knight's shoulder be-

Fig. 10—A figure in a bas-relief depicting stories of the life of Saint Victor, once in the Cathedral and now in the Museum of Sacred Art in Volterra, attributed to Agostino di Giovanni and Angelo di Ventura, c. 1325. Note the aventail and fringe of mail, fluted hemispherical shoulder guards, *cuir bouilli* protections of arms and small besagews at the elbows, gamboised cuisses worn over the mail breeches (which in turn are further protected by *cuir bouilli* poleyns), metal reinforcement applied to outside of jambers. Turned-over cuff of sleeve may conceal a muffler.

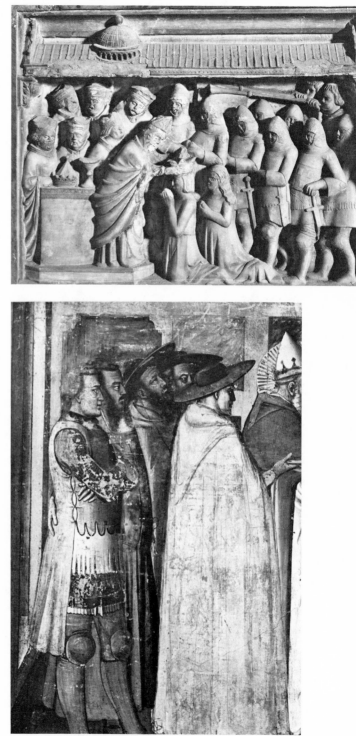

Fig. 11—*The Coronation of Ludwig the Bavarian,* by Agostino di Giovanni and Agnelo di Ventura, from the Tarlati Mausoleum, 1327-1330; Cathedral of Saint Donato, Arezzo. Armour of knights in retinue is very close to that shown in preceding illustration. Second knight from right wears gown rolled up to waist, clearly showing coat of plates underneath (note rivet heads, regularly disposed, securing inner metal plates).

Fig. 12—Detail of *Stories of Saint Sylvester,* frescoes by Maso di Banco, 1340 in the Church of Santa Croce, Florence. Armour of knight in foreground is composed of (from bottom to top) a gambaison, a mail shirt, a coat of plates with scalloped lower edges, and a gown with a scalloped short front and a long back panel (the back reaching down to bend of knees and fastened at the sides). Arms show only sleeves of mail shirt; legs are protected from thigh to ankle by *cuir bouilli* and simple globular poleyns at knees.

longs to a type that is already evolving new shapes. The head defence with the high and pointed skull, with or without visor, that had been used in the 1320's (and of which there is a fine and little-known example in Tuscany, worn by a knight on a bas-relief within a barbed quatrefoil frame [Figs. 9-A and 19] kept in the Museo Nazionale del Bargello in Florence[5]), was by now out of fashion in favour of a head defence of a more complex construction. An altered shape, appeared at the end of the 1320's. It was composed of several riveted plates which formed a brow piece with sight and visor in front and a neckshield and skull at the back; the apex of the skull was formed by an only slightly curved cop, ridged along the middle;

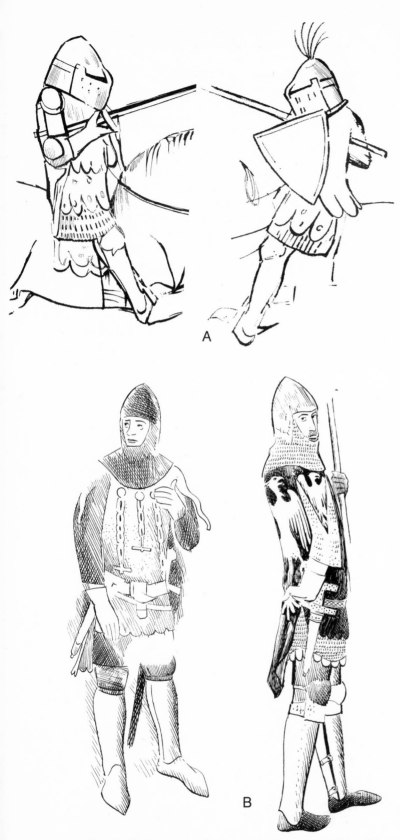

Fig. 13—Body armour, after contemporary representations: (A) From the frescoes in the chamber of the bell-tower in the church of Saint Remigio, Florence, c. 1325-1330 (see Fig. 9-C); note arm defences in *cuir bouilli* fastened so as to protect the inside of the biceps, a frequent usage in Italy in 1320-40. (B) From the frescoes by Matteo Giovannetti in the Palace of the Popes at Avignon, 1344; note triangular shoulder defences, three chains (for sword, dagger and helm) and mixed leg protections.

the whole was solidly riveted together and broadened at the lower margin, projecting in a frustum of cone from the sight downwards. This is the type which appears on the panels of Fronzola and Laterina in the Tarlati mausoleum in the Cathedral at Arezzo, datable between 1327 and 1330 (Fig. 9-B), but it represents only a step towards the headgear of Colaccio, which constitutes an improvement destined to last for many decades: closely-fitting in breadth, its visor-plate extending slightly downwards, the lower edge forming a cusp corresponding to the vertical medial ridge, and with a high and ovate skull, it is like those appearing on the equestrian statue of Mastino II in the Scaligere Arks in Verona, made while Mastino was still alive around 1345-1350, and on the tombstone of Giovanni di Alamanno de' Medici, who died in 1353 and was buried in Santa Reparata in Florence (Figs. 9-E and 9-F). Often, as for the joust, a reinforcing visor was added, which was secured to the apex of the helm by three cut-off appendices on its upper margin (two at the sides and one in the middle) and by a strap buckled at the nape of the neck, as shown on the sketched frescoes found in the little vault of the chamber at the foot of the belltower of the church of San Remigio in Florence, which can be dated around the end of the 1320's (Fig. 9-C). Jousting helms were bulkier than battle helms and also reached lower down in front and at the back; often they were decidedly long in front—a feature well-illustrated by the Mastino sculpture and the San Remigio frescoes.[6] It was not before the end of the 14th century that there appeared the first Italian helms with receding skulls with narrow slits for the eyes.[7] Colaccio's basnet still has a skull with a central ogive at the apex. A comparative specimen nearest to it in type may be found in the Tarlati Mausoleum on the panel by Laterina; this is coeval with one having a more ovate skull shown on the panels of Chiusi and the Coronation of Ludwig the Bavarian (Fig. 11). From the rounded and earlier shapes still in use (like that on the tombstone of Giovanni Castruccio Castracane, d. 1343, preserved in the church of St. Francis in Pisa, or that of Bernardino dei Baranzoni in the Museo Lapidario Estense in Modena) we progress to those with an ovate skull whose apex—in the older types always centered—tends to recede more and more; besides these, the ovate and pointed types, of which Colaccio's basnet is an example, already coexisted before his time. Both types are destined to converge and meet in the pointed basnet, the skull of which will descend at the back almost vertically, a typical feature of the end of the century.[8]

The fringe of mail that hangs from the leather strip fastened by the pierced studs of the basnet worn by our Bolognese knight is a detail almost exclusively Italian and one which we come across fairly often: for example, on a fragment of the Stories of San Vittore,

Fig. 14—Figure representing the planet Mars in a series of panels on Giotto's *campanile* (bell-tower) of the Cathedral of Florence, executed 1342-47, now in the Museo dell'Opera del Duomo. Helmet is in all probability a *crestuta*, a sort of reinforced Italian sallet with a medial crest and often ornamented with foliage. Armour is very close to that of Colaccio and of warriors on Tarlati Mausoleum, but armoured gauntlet is closer to known Emilian examples. Reins and harness are reduced to bare essentials.

sculpted around 1325 (Fig. 10), once in the cathedral of Volterra and now in that city's Museo d'Arte Sacra (some critics have attributed this work to the authors of the Tarlati Mausoleum); on the equestrian statue of Cangrande of Verona, who died in 1328, but the statue is later by several years; on the basnets of the Tarlati Mausoleum (Fig. 11), and on that worn by Bernardino dei Baranzoni; and on a *Crucifixion* of the Italian school kept in Paris at the Louvre, datable about 1355. Thus we see that this feature remains in use from the middle of the 1320's to the middle of the 1350's, for approximately thirty years, and has few similars or followers outside the peninsula.

Colaccio's coat of plates, short at the hips and hidden under a close-fitting scalloped gown, corresponds to other examples in Italy, mainly in Tuscany: in the stories of San Vittore referred to in the preceding paragraph, on the bas-reliefs of the Tarlati mausoleum (mainly the Rondine and Caprese panels), and on that of the Coronation of the H.R. Emperor Ludwig of Bavaria (Fig. 11); on the frescoes of San Remigio (Fig. 13-A); in the Stories of San Silvestro, frescoes by Maso di Banco in Santa Croce in Florence, datable 1340 (Fig. 12); in the frescoes painted in 1344 by Matteo Giovannetti in Avignon (France), in the Chapel of San Marziale and San Giovanni of the Papal Palace (Fig. 13-B); finally, worn by Mars on the Campanile of Giotto, now in the Museo dell'Opera del Duomo in Florence, datable between 1342 and 1347 (Fig. 14).[9] The shoulder defences, on the other hand, are more of a Northern type, as can be seen on the tombstone of Bernardino dei Baranzoni, on the Avignon frescoes and on the standing St. George in the fresco on the left wall of the church of San Zeno in Verona, painted around 1350.

Fig. 15—Evolution of arm defences (after contemporary representations). In Italy, this development was slower than that for the legs because preference was given to the reinforcement of shoulder, elbow and hand, in order to preserve the lightness and agility of the upper limbs. (A) On the tombstone of Filippo dei Desideri, by Arriguccio da Treviso, 1315, now in the Civic Museum, Bologna. (B) On the tombstone of Colaccio Beccadelli, 1341. (C) On the tombstone of Bernardino dei Baranzoni, c. 1345-1350, now in the Este Lapidary Museum, Modena. (D) In the *Coronation of the Virgin* by Simone dei Crocifissi, c. 1340-1350, now in the Pinacoteca Nazionale, Bologna.

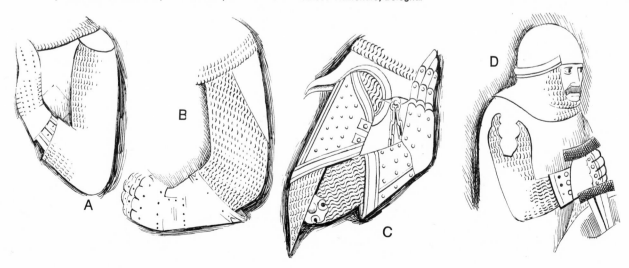

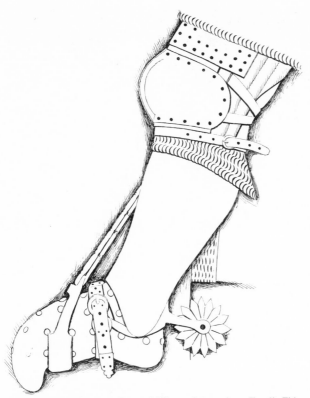

Fig. 16—From Colaccio Beccadelli's tombstone (see Fig. 6). This drawing (like all the others) was made from direct observation, not from photographs. Wherever some discrepancy between the photograph and the drawings should appear, the drawings rather than the photos should be accepted as definitive, since they take into account and carefully balance many elusive variables, e.g. the general state of conservation of the original, natural marble veining, fractures, optical changes under different angles of lighting, palpability of bas-relief, parallaxes and perspective distortions, etc.

We have already noticed the inadequacy of the protection of Beccadelli's arms; there are no hemispherical shoulder-plates like those appearing on the fragments of Volterra (Fig. 10), in the Tarlati mausoleum or as worn by Mars, no *gombitini*—ancestors of the *cowters*—like those of St. George in Verona. The armoured gauntlets are more Emilian, and we can see similar ones on the tombstone of the Bolognese Filippo dei Desideri, d. 1315, kept in the Museo Civico in Bologna.[10]

The leg-harness, and in particular the poleyns, deserve special attention. We are in a period where the shortening of the coat of plates had to be reconciled with the need for better protection of the thigh and knee, one exigency conditioning the other. The solution adopted by Colaccio is very important (always of course within the limits of mixed-leather-and-metal armour) and represents a definite improvement over those seen on the Volterra and Arezzo bas-reliefs, even though the basic idea is similar. In the Volterra and Arezzo examples, the poleyn is applied directly over the breeches or mail breeches; the greaves are of *cuir bouilli* and the thigh is sometimes protected by a cuisse made of this same material, also placed over the mail (Figs. 10 and 11). The protection of Colaccio's legs is far more complex and functional, and finds an almost exact correspondence in that of Mars in Giotto's Campanile (Figs. 14 and 17-A)—though it is even better than Mars' (which is a little later)—because it is completed by the mail breeches that better defend the unprotected stretch

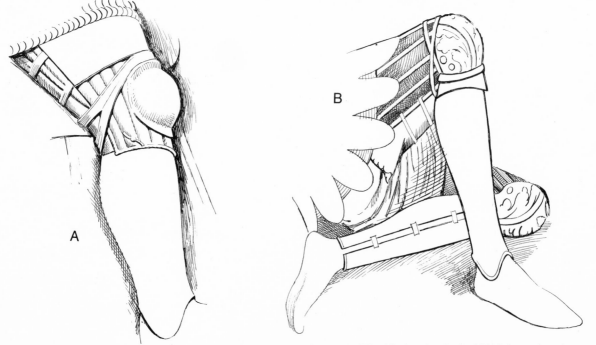

Fig. 17—Two other leg defences: (A) From Mars on Giotto's Campanile (Fig. 14); functional ensemble is very close to Tuscan examples in Volterra and Arezzo (Figs. 10 & 11). (B) From the *Crucifixion* by Vitale da Bologna, c. 1350-1355 (von Thyssen Collection, Lugano, Switzerland; note metal bars which armour the cuisses, a system just then—mid-14th century—beginning to assert itself on the peninsula.

20

Fig. 18—Miniature in Codex 1538 in the Biblioteca Riccardiana, Florence, c. 1320-1330, illustrating a battle between Caesar and the Saxons. Saxon chief wears a *crestuta* with projecting nasal (not new in North Italian iconography) and rides a horse with a stitched coverture reinforced by a trellis of leather strips studded with metal at the crossings; from this are suspended an armoured peytral and a crupper with scalloped lower margin (similar to margins of coats of plates in vogue twenty years later). Helmet shows decidedly pointed apeces.

Fig. 19—Bas-relief of a knight, c. 1320-25, once in the courtyard of the Bargello Palace, Florence. Helm with visor pivoting at sides and the heraldic ornament are already outdated, as is scaled leather or canvas shirt (not seen here but confirmed by Florentine documents) and scaled right gauntlet (scaled shirts and scaled gauntlets for the right hand only were used in Florence in the late 1200's). But leg defences show a developing movement towards more complex armour: the reinforced poleyn and the shynbald are placed over the mail and fastened by leather straps.

under the knee. In the *Crucifixion* by Vitale da Bologna, c. 1350-1355, now in the von Thyssen Collection in Lugano, the soldier who is throwing dice for Christ's robe shows very similar, if more developed, leg-protection: leather beeches defend the legs and over these the thighs are further protected by true *cuir bouilli* cuisses fastened by straps and splinted with metal bands: other straps, partly attached also to the cuisse and crossing over the bending of the leg, secure a *cuir bouilli* poleyn which reaches down with a small flap that covers the unprotected part above the jambers, these last being open and laced along the inside (Fig. 17-B). Within less than a decade, the application of metal plates and the true metal poleyn pivoting at the sides were to carry the mixed-leather-and-metal armour to its ultimate functional limit. Leather sabatons, reinforced with studs, are also found among the examples already mentioned (viz., Bernardino dei Baranzoni, St. George in Verona); it was a solution destined to endure into the 1360's.

During that same span of time, horse harness suffered only minor variations, but it is worthwhile to compare Beccadelli's horse with the mounts of some other illustrious personages. A miniature from Sallustio preserved in Codex No. 1538 at the Riccardiana in Florence, which is of the Bolognese school and datable in the 1320's, illustrating a battle between Caesar and the Saxons, shows the chief of the latter (who wears a nasal helm with spiked crest) mounting a horse protected by a shaffron of *cuir bouilli* with projecting eye-and-ear-pieces covered by a canvas hood, while a peytral and the lower part of the crupper—cerainly armoured—are suspended from a quilted coverture reinforced by a system of leather bands forming a trellis studded at the crossovers (Figs. 18 and 22-C, E). This is a very interesting solution, which partly anticipates leather or metal bardes and which appears superior to a few later ones, as for example to the Bargello knight (Figs. 19 and 22-A), where real progress is reflected only in the armoured shaffron. Or again, the horse of Guidoriccio da Fogliano, painted by Simone Martini in 1328 in the Palazzo Pubblico in Siena (Fig. 20), shows only the addition of the cheeks to the bit and the false reins; but the upper edge of the saddle's cantle is still curved in and reaching forward, though on the other hand the decorative and protective elements for the head and crupper of the horse are missing, and in this Guidoriccio is more modern than Beccadelli. As to Cangrande, the shaffron and coverture do not present any relevant differences from those of Guidoriccio (both covertures are longer than those of the other examples cited up to now), but the saddle shows a mighty development of the front arson. Beccadelli's horse, on the other hand, shows innovations in the well-organized shaffron and the articulated crinet (Figs. 7 and 21), whereas Mastino della Scala's horse is fitted with a rather decorated but clearly outdated shaffron and coverture (Figs. 23 and 22-B). Quite impressive, on the other hand, is his tall jousting saddle, its seat reduced to a mere rounded bar raised above the horse's back. The front arson is very high and extends downwards on either side to protect thigh and leg—the first step towards the large 15th-century saddles—whereas two bars, reaching from front to cantle, curve round the knight's hips. In the *Crucifixion* by Vitale da Bologna re-appears (as it had been depicted thirty years earlier in the miniature shown in Fig. 18) a quilted coverture fitted with a trellis of studded leather strips, but the leather shaffron is independent (even if not articulated like that worn by Beccadelli's horse); a similar coverture and shaffron may be seen in the *Crucifixion* by Jacopino da Bologna (Fig. 22-D). The horse defences showing on Beccadelli's tombstone are therefore exceptional for their time—quite advanced for an ensemble whose articulated shaffron and crinet-lames represent fundamental progress, even though some smaller details, such as the heraldic ornaments on the shaffron and crupper (already disappeared from Guidoriccio's horse and from the few horses wearing covertures shown on the panel of Bucine in the Tarlati Mausoleum), do not correspond.

In conclusion, the tombstone to Colaccio Beccadelli shows armour of a definitely Tuscan bent as well as of course an Emilian one, quite different from Northern and mainly the Venetian examples. Florence was of the Guelph party, like practically the whole of Tuscany, Bologna and all of Emilia. United by many common social, mercantile, political and military interests, Tuscany and Emilia not surprisingly shared common characteristics in armour, too. These represent a peninsular core where French-Angevine fashions did not strike root, and the influences coming from beyond the Alps or the sea were less felt here than in Lombardy and the Venetian area (even though Florence was in those years one of the greatest centres of the international arms trade, supplying especially England and France). But all this does *not* mean that Colaccio's armour was exclusive to the Tuscan-Emilian area, nor that it was the only type adopted there; a variety of species were used in the same zone, and war apparel similar to Colaccio's was known outside Italy (for example, on the little statue of St. George and the Dragon, about 1334, once in the Stefankirche in Vienna and now in the Metropolitan Museum of Art in New York; in the groups of the Centurion with the two soldiers carved in alabaster, formerly in a church at Huy on the Meuse, datable around the 1340's and this now, too, in the Metropolitan; on the effigy of Ulrich de Tréyvaux, who died around 1351, once in the Convent of Hauterive in the Canton of Fribourg, now in the Schweizerisches Landesmuseum in Zurich (where

Fig. 20—Guidoriccio da Fogliano, painted in 1328 by Simone Martini, Siena, Palazzo Pubblico. Horse's coverture hides *cuir bouilli* shaffron, but signs of armouring can be seen on the crinet and along the back and the crupper. Projecting heraldic ornaments have disappeared. Note high mail *gorgiarino* (collar), ample poleyn set over the mail breeches, and spurs, which are among the first in Italy shown with rowels instead of spikes.

the warrior also wears the basnet with the fringe of mail and the fluted hemispherical shoulder pieces).[11] In Italy, however, this type of armour tends to show up more frequently in the Tuscan-Emilian territory than elsewhere, and it differs from the one then dominant in other parts of Europe.

In England, the tomb brass of Sir William Fitzralph, in Pebmarsh, Essex, shows a knight, d. 1323, with an already well-developed metal defence for the limbs. The brass of Sir John de Creke, d. 1325, in Westley Waterless, Cambridgeshire, shows an armour with the scalloped coat of plates reaching down to the hips, a gown short in front and long at the back, and metal defences for the limbs including closed vambraces; a similar type is shown on the brass of Sir John d'Aubernoun the Younger, d. 1327, at Stoke d'Abernon, Surrey, and the same type (with less developed arm defence) can be seen on the brass to Sir John de Northwood, d. 1330, in Minster, Sheppey. Therefore, it can be generally said that in England the shortened coat of plates and the gown—opened in the front, or short in front and long at the back— are accompanied by a defence for the limbs that is more efficient than contemporary Italian specimens,

23

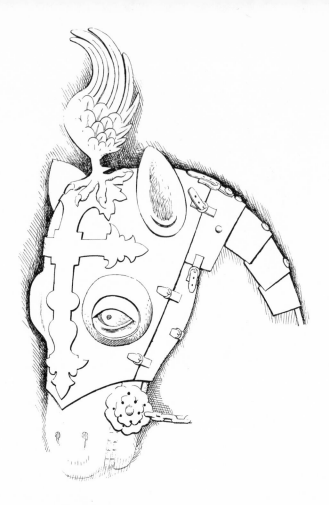

Fig. 21—From Colaccio Beccadelli's tomb-stone (see Fig. 7). Articulation of shaffron to crinet lames is assured by a neck-lame buckled to its strap. Lames are locked to one another along top ridge by means of sliding rivets (working freely in rectangular slots) in order to allow head and neck movement in all directions.

and already in metal.

In the sphere of German influence, broadly speaking, besides the long gown open at the sides worn by the already-mentioned Ulrich de Tréyvaux, we may note: the shortened coat of plates and the long gown opening in the front worn by the statue of Gottfried von Bergheim, d. 1335, in the church of Münstereifel in the Rhineland; the shortened coat of plates and the deeply dagged gown (with armoured shoulders and leather defences for the forearms and knees) on the tombstone of Albrecht von Hohenlohe-Möckmühl, d. 1338, in the Convent of Schönthal on the Jagst; and, finally, the shortened coat of plates together with a longer gown (and a defence for the limbs consisting only of mail, except for the knees) on the tombstone of Ulrich de Werdt, d. 1344, in the church of St. Guillaume in Strasbourg.[12]

Generally speaking, therefore, it appears that in this sphere and within these years, the shortened coat of plates was often associated with a long gown, and the adoption of metal and leather protection for the arms and legs was still not very developed. On the other hand, great steps forward had been made towards a metal defence of the trunk around the 1340's, one made of metal bands fitted horizontally across the breast and vertically down the back, at first hidden by a gown or by a cover in leather or textile, but afterwards exposed to view.[13]

Summing up, one can say that between 1325 and 1350 a coat of plates of leather and metal was adopted all over Europe, short at the hips and generally combined with a gown of dagged panels. In England, and also in France—although nothing certain is known about pre-1550 French armour*—a very rapid evolution of the metallic defences of the limbs took place; it was to continue right up to the time when arms and legs were at last perfectly protected by metal all around. In the German-speaking world, the interest centered more on a metallic protection for the torso, somewhat neglecting the limbs; this new protection survived in essentially its primordial structure for many years. The Italian mixed defences of leather and iron, for the torso as well as for the limbs, developed rapidly, reaching a high point from both the decorative and functional points of view in the armour of Lorenzo Acciaioli, d. 1353, (tombstone, Certosa di Valdema, near Florence), and in that shown in the effigy of Galeotto Malaspina, d. 1367, in the Propositura di San Remigio in Fosdinovo.[14] But the Italian armourers did not stay deaf to the experiences accrued by their colleagues North of the Alps, and between 1355 and 1365 integrated much of extra-peninsular origins with their own production. The next phase was to be the beginings of that "sacred monster" of arms history: the all-plate white armour.

---

*See the introduction to Dr. Bruno Thomas' article in this Volume.—Ed.

Fig. 22—Development of some shaffrons: (A) From the bas-relief panel in the Bargello, Fig. 19, c. 1320-1325. (B) From the equestrian monument to Cangrande della Scala in the Arche Scaligere, Verona, datable some years after the death of the knight in 1329. (C) and (D) From the *Crucifixion* by Jacopino da Bologna fn. 8, a little after 1350. (E) From the *Crucifixion* by Vitale da Bologna, c. 1350-1355 (von Thyssen Collection, Lugano, Switzerland).

25

Fig. 23—Equestrian monument to Mastino II della Scala, c. 1345-1350 (erected during his lifetime), Verona, Arche Scaligere. The noble is represented in his complete tournament armour: note elongated helm reaching down in a point at the front; shield with a semicircular cutout for the lance; very tall saddle with raised seat and long extensions of front arson for leg protection, and with side bars which secure hips from front to cantle. Shaffron is of embossed and probably painted *cuir bouilli;* heavy coverture shows a trellis of cross strips which frame the embroidered *camerelle* (i.e., squares).

NOTES

1. We have knowledge of only two other Italian tombstones in the 13th and 14th centuries showing the warrior on horseback: one in the Chiostro dei Morti in the church of Santissima Annunziata in Florence, erected to Guglielmo di Dufort, killed at Campaldino in 1289; and another in the church of S. Francesco in Bagnacavallo, a few miles from Imola, erected to Tiberto Brandolini, d. 1397. We know of only one other signed tombstone in Emilia, that of the Bolognese Filippo dei Desideri, d. 1315, in the Museo Civico of Bologna, which bears the name of the lapidary Arriguccio da Treviso.

2. The Beccadelli were perpetuated in two branches that still exist: in Bologna, the Beccadelli-Grimaldi, who bear azure one gold-winged eagle claws, and as a crest a demi-elephant, winged and crowned; and in Palermo the Beccadelli di Bologna, Princes of Camporeale, who bear partly Aragon-Sicily per dexter, azure per sinister with three gold-winged eagle claws in fesse.

3. The frescoes of hunting scenes and tournaments decorating the Sala del Consiglio in the Palazzo Comunale of San Gimignano in the Province of Siena, painted between 1288 and 1292 by Azzo da Siena, show the thighs already protected by leather breeches reaching slightly above the shin, cut out at the bend of the leg and reinforced with poleyns of *cuir bouilli.* See: R. Davidsohn, *Forschungen zur Geschichte von Florenz,* Berlin, 1900, II, nn. 2353-2358; L.G. Boccia, *L'armamento in Toscana dal Millecento al Trescento,* in *Atti del Convegno sulla Civiltà delle Arti Minori in Toscana,* Arezzo, 1971.

4. *Sàrgano, sàrgane* and *sàrgine* was the name given to a sort of very strong canvas used for covering carts, mules' backs and such. From Giovanni Villani we learn that—evidently when sewn together in several layers—it was arrow-proof: at Crecy, in 1346, the English archers shot "from carts and from under carts covered with sargane and cloth that guaranteed them from the quarrels" (of the Genoese crossbowmen). See: G. Villani, *Cronica,* XII, 67. The term *coverta* (coverture) was also used for the covering of the war-horse, which was said to be "coverto" or "covertato;" this was compulsory for the milites (whose gown was of silk, cloth or "baracame"—also "bucherame"—interwoven with wool and goat's hair). "Incamutata" meant "quilted" or "wadded," and perhaps referred to covertures decorated with squares (*incamerata, a camerelle*) outlined by stitching and further sustained by crossed leather strips. Villani, though writing all his *Cronica* between 1308 and 1348, is very precise when using terms referring to different times; this is of considerable help for the study of 14th-century armour and its nomenclature.

5. Another bas-relief of a knight shown in the head of

a mullioned window on the outside of the Bargello accompanies it. This can be dated after 1322 but shows a much older armour, though with a closed helm; this is another instance of the irregularity of armour developments. See L.G. Boccia, *op. cit.* fn. 3; L.G. Boccia-E.T. Coelho, *L'Armamento di cuoio e ferro nel Trecento italiano,* in "l'Illustrazione Italiana," 1974.

6. The church of Santa Reparata was the primordial cathedral of Florence over whose foundations the present *duomo,* Santa Maria del Fiore, was built after the demolition of Santa Reparata in 1375. The recent excavations, which are still in course, have brought to light, among other things, some swords, spurs and tombstones with heraldic decoration (everything of course antedating 1375). See: P. Bargellini-G. Morozzi-G. Batini, *Santa Reparata, la Cattedrale Risorta,* Florence, 1970. The frescoes of San Remigio came to light during the Great Flood of 1966. They consist of simple, linear sanguine drawings and show hermits weaving baskets, hunting scenes and tournaments.

7. For instance: on the tombstone of Nicolò di Bindaccio dei Benedetti, d. 1403, once in Volterra and now in the Museo Bardini in Florence; or in the frescoes in the Sala di Balìa of the Palazzo Pubblico in Siena, painted in 1407 by Spinello Aretino, showing the victory of the Venetians over Barbarossa's fleet at Punta Salvore.

8. See: L.G. Boccia-E.T. Coelho, *op. cit.,* fn. 5. A large head defence which appears in the Crucifixion of a polyptych painted by Jacopino da Bologna a little after 1350, now preserved in the Pinacoteca Nazionale in Bologna, is worn on a warrior's back but hanging from a buckled strap, not from a chain; it is fairly bulky and pointed, and has a visor without appliqué work. It represents, at that date, a spurious shape that is evolving atypically toward the basnet proper.

9. See: L.G. Boccia-E.T. Coelho, *op. cit.,* fn. 5.

10. The Tuscan gauntlet is mainly protected by scales, as in the two old examples in the Bargello, already mentioned in the text and in note 5, and that on the tombstone to Giovanni di Castruccio Castracani, d. 1343, preserved in the church of San Francesco in Pisa; it is very interesting to note the ancient Florentine use of wearing the gauntlet only on the right and a leather glove on the left (late 1200's to about 1325). The Emilian gauntlet, instead, seems to have favoured horizontally plated cuffs and backs. See: L.G. Boccia-E.T. Coelho, *op. cit.,* fn. 5.

11. See F.O. Leber, *Sale Catalogue,* 1925; H. Nickel, *Warriors and Worthies,* New York, 1969, p. 52; H. Dürst, *Rittertum,* Aargau, 1960, p. 180.

12. See M. Clayton, *Brass Rubbings,* London, 1903, p. 14; J.G. Mann, *Monumental Brasses,* Harmondsworth, 1957, p. 14; H. Trivick, *The Craft and Design of Monumental Brasses,* London, 1969, p. 58; J.H. von Hefner-Alteneck, *Waffen,* 1903, p. 16 (with erroneous dating); B. Thordeman, *Armour from the Battle of Wisby 1361,* Uppsala, 1939, pp. 298 sg.; P. Martin, *Armes et Armures,* Paris, 1967, p. 55.

13. Excellent examples are those found in the miniatures by the Flemish Jean de Grise, made between 1338 and 1344 on the manuscript of a Roman d'Alixandre, now in the Bodleian Library in Oxford; in the statue of Otto von Orlamünde the Younger, d. 1340, in the Convent of Himmelkron in Upper Franconia; in the tombstone of Walter Bopfinger, d. 1359, in the Parochial Church of Bopfingen in Württemberg. See J.H. von Hefner-Alteneck, *op. cit.,* pp. 16, 18; B. Thordeman, *op. cit.,* pp. 305, 307. The term 'armadura' used by Villani (see end of note 4) must therefore refer to this new protection splintered with broad metal bands (horizontal and vertical), so very different from the usual coat of plates. In 14th-century Italian, the term indicated everything that formed a solid whole either for one's own or else for another's or some object's support; or: a complex of equipment or material destined for war; or: a little-used or foreign arm. Therefore also the new-style armour could easily be fitted into these various definitions. As to the contemporary Italian "metallic current"—*filone metallico*—we must mention at least the "armadure" with large plates shown in the frescoes in the apse of the church of Saint Abbondio in Como, datable 1330-1335. See L.G. Boccia-E.T. Coelho, *art. cit.*

14. See: L.G. Boccia, *op. cit.,* fn. 3; L.G. Boccia-E.T. Coelho, *op. cit.,* fn. 5.

15. Among Boccia's many publications in periodicals and in brochure–, catalogue– and book form, the following are the most important: *Nove Secoli di Armi da Caccia,* Florence, Editoriale Edam, 1967; *L'Arte dell'Armatura in Italia* (with E.T. Coelho), Milan, Bramante Editrice, 1967; *Gli Acquafresca di Bargi,* in "Physis", Florence, 1967; L'Armadura de' *Gattamellà* in "Armi Antiche," Turin, 1972; *L'Armamento in Toscana dal Millecento al Trecento,* in "Atti del Primo Convegno sulla Civiltà delle Arti Minori in Toscana, dal Romanico al Gotico," Arezzo, 1973; *Catalogue* of the arms and armor section of the Poldi-Pezzoli Museum, Milan; 1972.

Further Notes on the Origins of the Wheellock

by CLAUDE BLAIR

*Claude Blair, Keeper of the Department of Metalwork (which includes one of the
world's fine arms collections) at the Victoria & Albert Museum, London,
was born in Manchester, England, in 1922. After service in the Royal Artillery
during World War Two, he studied history at Manchester University,
where he graduated in 1950. In 1951 he joined the staff of the Tower of London
Armouries, moving from there in September 1956 to become Assistant Keeper
of Metalwork in the Victoria & Albert. He is a Fellow of the Society of Antiquaries
of London and a member of a number of European arms societies, including the
Arms & Armour Society of London (of whose* Journal *he has been Honorary Editor
since its foundation in 1953). He is married and has a son. His many publications
on arms and armor include* European Armour *(1958, reprinted 1972),*
European and American Arms *(1962),* Pistols of the World *(1968),* The Silvered
Armour of Henry VIII in the Tower of London Armouries *(1965),* A Royal
Swordsmith and Damascener: Diego de Cais *(1971), &c.*

I.

The familiar story of the invention of the wheellock in Nuremberg in 1517[1] is by no means a modern one. It seems to have been printed for the first time by J.C. Wagenseil in his history of Nuremberg, published in 1697, where he states that in a certain manuscript Nuremberg chronicle one can read that "Firelocks for guns were first invented in Nuremberg in the year 1517."[2] Unfortunately, Wagenseil gives no indication of the date of the chronicle, and I am informed by Dr. Hirschmann of the Nuremberg State Archives that neither he nor the authorities at the Germanisches Museum are able to identify it. Though the value of the statement in the chronicle cannot, therefore, be assessed, the information given by another early writer on the subject suggests that it must have been based on a tradition already current not later than the beginning of the 17th century. The writer in question, Johann Guler von Weineck, gives a brief history of firearms in a work published in Zürich in 1616. After discussing the alleged invention of gunpowder and guns by Berthold Schwarz, he goes on to say that "Thereafter in the year 1517 the ingenious firelock was introduced in Augsburg and Nuremberg."[3]

On the other hand, the equally familiar statement that the inventor of the lock in 1517 was a Nuremberg gunmaker named Johann Kiefuss does not seem to go back any further than Moritz Thierbach's great work on the history of firearms, which appeared in 1886.[4] So far as I can discover, no maker of this name has been traced in the Nuremberg archives,[5] nor is he known from any other source. Thierbach gives no indication of where he obtained his information and it is not improbable that his statement is a garbled version of Johann Gabriel Doppelmayr's account of the Nuremberg gunmaker Georg Kühfuss (ob. c. 1600), published in 1730. Doppelmayr says that Kühfuss was famous for making firelocks and in a footnote gives the traditional story of the invention of the lock.[6] Thierbach, who was less concerned with documentation than with technical development, may have made a careless note of this entry when preparing the material for his book and so produced a final version of it quite different from the original. Whether this is so or not, the fact remains that we cannot accept Thierbach's account of the origin of the wheellock, nor can we accept even that it was invented in 1517 in Nuremberg.

II.

The evidence for the use of the wheellock prior to 1517 given by the most recent writers on the subject before the publication of this article in its earlier version is, briefly, as follows:[7]

1. Wheellocks are shown among Leonardo da Vinci's sketches of military devices in the *Codex Atlanticus,* which are believed by some authorities to be products of the artist's period of service with Lodovico il Moro, Duke of Milan, that is from about 1482 to 1499.

2. A MS volume of drawings of mechanical devices, formerly in the Staatsbibliothek, Berlin, exe-

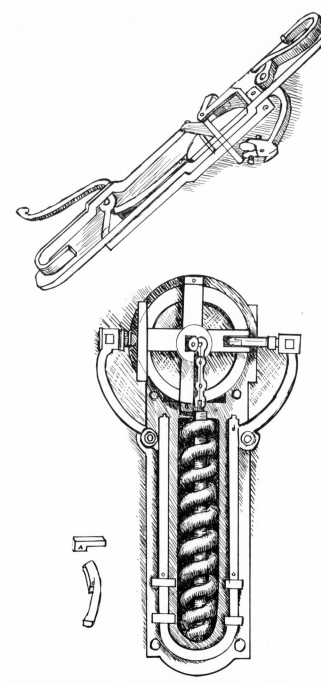

cuted by or for Martin Löffelholz of Nuremberg and dated 1505, contains illustrations of wheellock tinder-lighters.

3. The rules of the shooting range at Geislingen an der Steige, Württemberg, drawn up in 1506, state that nobody is to use a "self-igniting gun" [*selbst zündende Buchse*], presumably a wheellock, on the range.

4. The *Tafelamtbücher* of the town of Goslar, Hanover, record a payment made to one Hans Luder, "wheellock and gun-maker" in 1509.

5. The epic poem *Theuerdank,* written for the Emperor Maximilian I and first printed in 1517, contains that statement that the "pernicious fire-lock . . . has now become common."

The evidence of Leonardo da Vinci's sketches and of the Löffelholz MS. can be accepted, though with certain reservations discussed below; but the other references, when traced back to their sources, prove to be quite worthless. In view of the fact that they have been so widely accepted for so long, it seems desirable to discuss the reasons for rejecting them fairly fully here. They are as follows:

The Geislingen Shooting-Range. The reference to the banning of the *selbst zündende Buchse* at Geislingen in 1506 was apparently first made known to students of arms and armour by Artilleriemajor D. Toll in an article published in 1866.[8] Toll gives as the source of his information a work on medieval Swabian towns by Carl Jäger, published in 1831, which contains the following passage: "In the countryside likewise there were preparations for the practising of military affairs, for example a shooting-lodge was erected in Geislingen in 1406 [sic], and it was ordered that nobody was to carry a self-igniting gun [*selbst zündende Busche*] there."[9] In a footnote Jäger gives his source for the above as *Veit Marchtalers Chronik.*

Toll apparently assumed that the date 1406 in the above passage was a misprint of 1506, but this is clearly not so, for the earlier date is the only one that fits into the chronology of the paragraph containing it.[10] But it is highly improbable that the wheellock could have been in use as early as 1406—indeed it is not even likely that an organized shooting-range for firearms would have been in existence at that date[11] —and one can only conclude therefore that Jäger's information about the Geislingen range is either completely incorrect or very garbled. This view is confirmed by Dr. Schmolz, *Stadtarchivar* of Geislingen, who writes as follows in reply to my letter asking for information on this point:[12]

The municipal archives of Geislingen (Steige) include no ordinances for the Geislingen shooting-association dating from this early period. The passage you quote from Jäger's "Schwäbisches Stadtwesen des Mittelalters" occurs also in the Oberamt Survey for the Geislingen

Fig. 1—Two wheel-principle firestriking mechanisms drawn—and almost surely invented—by Leonardo da Vinci *(Codex Atlanticus, Folio 56 v.b.),* the one above being a wheellock for a firearm, the other a household or general-purpose firemaker. Function of gunlock is explained in captions to Figs. 2-5. Function of other device is carefully detailed in Leonardo's notes, though no specific purpose is mentioned. Wheel is wound counter-clockwise so that bicycle-type chain and long rod pull up and compress coil spring; sear connected to quadrant arm projecting on upper right snaps into a recess in wheel's raised rim (under toggle-effect of long right arm of U-spring held to lockplate by four staples) and locks wheel in cocked position. Pyrites is held in head of left quadrant arm, secured by a square-headed cross bolt, and pressed against wheel's periphery (which protrudes through shallow, coverless flashpan) by toggle-effect of long left arm of U-spring. Upon right quadrant arm—actually a trigger-*cum*-sear—being pressed inward to free sear from engagement in recess on rim, coil spring snaps downward, wheel performs a lightning-fast turn, friction with pyrites engenders sparks and priming or tinder in pan takes flame. Note four holes in lockplate (lower l. and r. corners, and l. and r. below wheel), presumably for screws for securing mechanism on some base.

administrative area of the year 1842. Unfortunately, up to now the question of the truth of this statement has not been investigated.

I suspected that there would be more information in the Stadtarchiv of Ulm-Donau (the town of Geislingen belonged to the former Imperial town of Ulm from 1396 to 1803), so I addressed an enquiry to the Director of this Archiv, Herr Oberarchivrat Dr. Huber. I enclose a copy of the reply received from the Ulm Stadtarchiv. Unfortunately, Dr. Huber's investigations have produced no result, or rather they have shown clearly the faultiness of Jäger's statement.

The relevent portions of Dr. Huber's reply are as follows:

> I can find no entry in our Council Minutes that refers to a regulation of 1406 or 1506 for the shooting-lodge in Geislingen. All that are noted there during the 16th century are repeated awards by the Ulm Council to the Geislingen marksmen of webs of cloth for prizes in competition-shooting. In 1596 a contribution was made out of official funds towards the repair of the shooting-house of the *Pürschrohr-Schützen-Gesellschaft* in Geislingen and in 1599 a payment for the same purpose was made to the *Stahlschützen* there.

> The revised regulations of the *Pürschrohr-Schützen-Gesellschaft* in Geislingen dating from the 1st May, 1642 are preserved here but they do not contain any reference to "self-igniting guns."

I am unfortunately unable to confirm Carl Jäger's reference . . . in the Chronicle of Veit Marchtaler the Elder (1565-1641), nor in the supplement produced by his son Veit Marchtaler the Younger. Presumably Jäger made a mistake in this matter or he relied on the extracts of Prälat von Schmid[13], which are no longer at our disposal. If you would like to go to the trouble of searching through the Marchtaler Chronicles I shall be very pleased to place a copy at your disposal. Veit Marchtaler the Elder was a member of the Privy Council in Ulm and he wrote a Chronicle which extended to the year 1640. This was expanded by his son of the same name.

Dr. Schmolz was kind enough to borrow the Marchtaler Chronicles from Ulm and to search them personally on my behalf, but he was unable to find anything that throws any light on Jäger's statement. He concludes his letter with an assessment of the situation that must be accepted as the final word until further evidence is discovered:

> Our investigations have thus at least produced one certain piece of information: if Jäger's statement cannot be definitely rejected as false it can

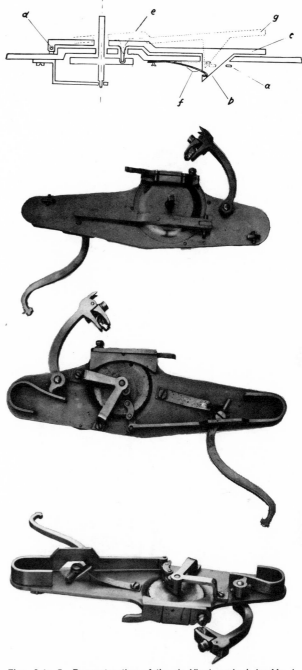

Figs. 2 to 5—Reconstruction of the da Vinci gunlock by Mr. J. Hart of Guernsey. Bottom photograph shows lock from exactly the same angle of view as in the da Vinci drawing. Arrangement of wheel, spindle, chain, mainspring, bridle, dog (or cock) and flashpan is fundamentally that of all wheellocks to come; absent is the self-opening flashpan cover and the later standard wholly-internal double-sear release device. Leonardo's lock has an external sear: a long horizontal bar hinged at the right of the wheel (d in the diagram) with a prong (e) that passes through a hole on the wheel cover and fits into a recess in the wheel when this is fully wound. A flat spring (f), riveted or screwed against the inside of the lockplate, keeps the sear pressed against the wheel. At the end of the sear a flat triangular lug projects through a slit in the lockplate. Behind and below this is hinged the trigger, whose upper end (i.e. above the pivot) moves forward when the lower, external arm is pulled upward, forcing the wedge-shaped lug of the sear outwards and hence the prong out of the recess in the wheel; the wheel is then snapped through a full or three-quarters rotation by the downward pull of the mainspring on the chain. Shooter would have had to open flashpan by hand before firing. Dog, or cock, has ear-like projections, a play on the resemblance of jaws and rivet "eye" to an animal's head. Spring acting on spur of dog is a closed U and internally-placed in Leonardo's lock—in later wheellocks it is conventionally external and a flat V.

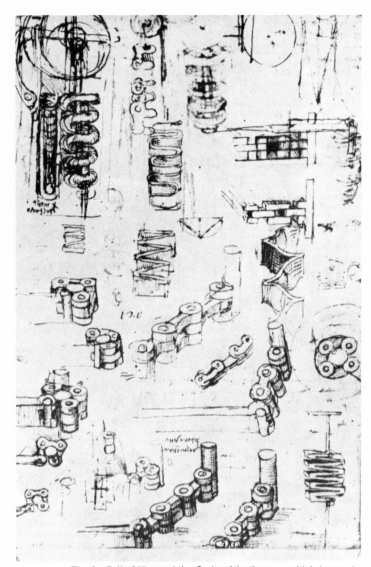

Fig. 6—Folio 357 r.a. of the *Codex Atlanticus,* on which Leonardo sketched out a variety of springs, wheel-spindles and transmission chains; note links of three different shapes, two methods of attaching chain to spring, sectional views of chains, chains in wound-up position.

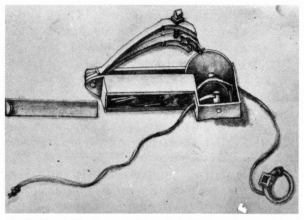

Fig. 7—One of the two wheel-type tinderlighters shown on Folio 27 of the Loffelholz manuscript, almost certainly executed before 1505. Simple device is operated by pull string; small rectangular box with sliding lid holds spare tinder.

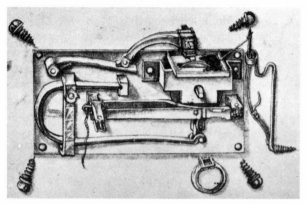

Fig. 8—Other tinderlighter from Folio 27 of the Loffelholz Manuscript. Rectangular baseplate is pierced by four screw holes for securing to some wooden surface. Wheel is wound by projecting square lug (note ring-shaped winding key, lower right) against force of mainspring, to which it is connected by chain. Sear is horizontal bar hinged by a vertical pin at right of wheel; it has an incorporated flat return spring held on by a rivet to keep sear's lug—not visible in drawing but presumably a projection working in an inclined groove in the wheel's side—engaged with the wheel. Dog is a split iron bar terminating in a cubical head with transverse screw for holding pyrites; flat feather spring works on dog's heel to keep pyrites pressed down on wheel. "Trigger" is piece of string seen dangling from sear's left end: pulling it removes sear's lug from wheel recess and frees wheel to snap. Tinder in flat, tray-like flashpan appears connected to a small wax taper in a bracket by a fuse: a pull of the string produced a light for lighting the candles in the house. Similarity between this device and Leonardo's is striking—see text.

only be accepted with great caution. The extracts of Prälat von Schmid would probably have furnished the only possible test of its accuracy, but these no longer exist in the Ulm Stadtarchiv.

Hans Luder of Goslar. The existence of this alleged "wheellock and gun maker" in Goslar in 1509 was first brought to the attention of students in an article, "Waffenschmiede im Dienste der früheren Reichsstadt Goslar," by F.W. Mathias, which appeared in the *Zeitschrift für historische Waffenkunde* in 1915 (Vol. VII, p. 26). The article takes the form of a calendar of references to armourers and weaponsmiths in the municipal account-books *(Tafelamtbücher)* of Goslar from 1450 to 1664. The original wording of the various entries is given in only a few instances and these do not include the reference to Luder which Mathias published simply as follows:

1509 Hans Luder Radschloss- und Büchsen-macher.

The original wording of the entry, however, is *xix marc Hans Luder rade und bussen beschlagen,* that is: "19 marks to Hans Luder for mounting wheels and guns". The wheels were presumably for artillery as the record of this particular payment is included in the section of the account-book headed "Arrows, Guns, Artillery" *(Pfyel, Bussen, Geschutte).*[14]

32

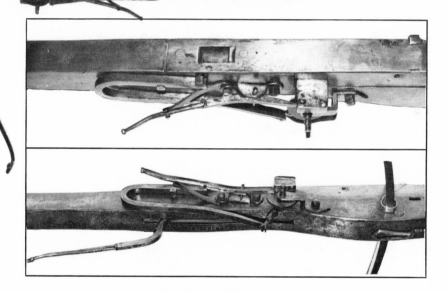

Fig. 9—Elaboration of etched ornamentation of crossbow Q2, Doge's Palace Armoury, Venice (see text and Figs. 10 & 11). Work is typical of that found on Italian armor of middling quality from the end of the 15th century to about 1520. Shown with mechanism removed.

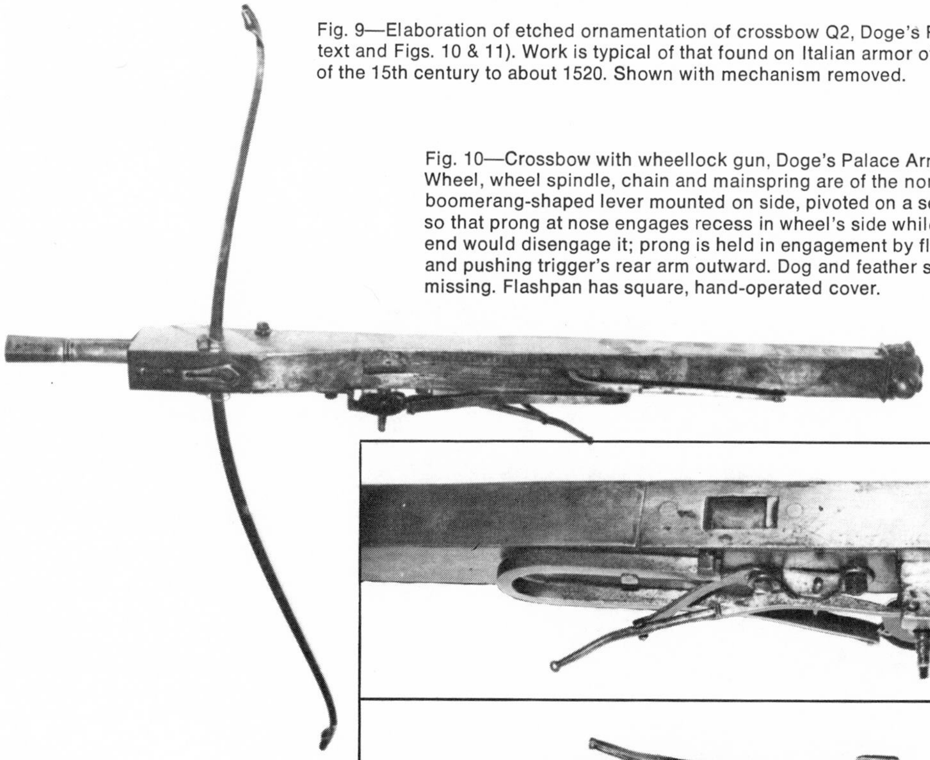

Fig. 10—Crossbow with wheellock gun, Doge's Palace Armoury, Venice, No. Q3. Wheel, wheel spindle, chain and mainspring are of the normal sort; trigger is long boomerang-shaped lever mounted on side, pivoted on a see-saw vertical pin at its belly so that prong at nose engages recess in wheel's side while an inward push on its other end would disengage it; prong is held in engagement by flat spring secured to side of lock and pushing trigger's rear arm outward. Dog and feather spring of this specimen are missing. Flashpan has square, hand-operated cover.

Theuerdank. Artilleriemajor Toll seems again to have been the first person to draw attention to the passage in *Theuerdank* in which reference is made to the firelock. The full text as quoted by Toll[15] is:

> Denn zu den Zeiten war die Sitt
> Bein Büchsen trug man Zündstrick mit.
> Mit eim Feureisen, Schwam und Stein
> Hielt man Feur bei Geschütz insgemein,
> Die schädlich Feurschloss noch nit waren
> Wie jetzt gemein in selben Jahren.

That is: "For in those times it was customary to carry matchcord with a gun. Artillery was generally ignited with fire-steel, flint and tinder. The pernicious fire-lock, which has now become common in recent years, did not then exist."

Toll gives as his source for the above Folio 49b of the Frankfurt edition of *Theuerdank,* but implies that the passage also occurs in the first edition, published in Nuremberg in 1517. In fact, it is one of the "merry rhymes" interpolated by Burkard Waldis in his revised version of the poem published in Frankfurt in 1553[16], and it does not occur in any of the earlier editions, all of which are more or less exact copies of the first one, and all of which mention only matchlock guns.[17] The passage is thus, if anything, evidence *against* the use of the wheellock in 1517.

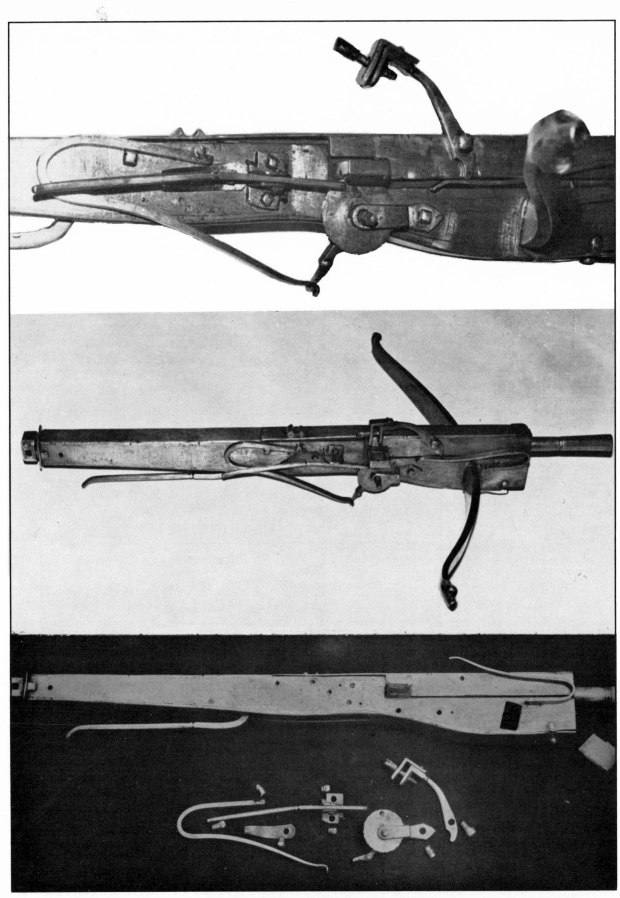

Fig. 11—Crossbow with wheellock gun, Doge's Palace Armoury, Venice, No. Q2. Mechanism is same as that of Crossbows Q1 (not shown here) and Q3, Fig 10. Upper jaw is made of a flat piece bent 90° to form a vertical tail which is slotted and secured to stem by a small screw.

Burkard Waldis is a notable figure in the history of 16th-century German literature, though he has been much critized for his "improved" edition of *Theuerdank*.[18] Born in c.1490 at Allendorf, Hesse, he was for a time a Franciscan friar at Riga but, having gone over to the reformed faith, he subsequently became a pewterer and then a protestant pastor. In 1544 he was appointed to the living of the parish church at Abterode, Hesse, where he died late in 1556 or early in 1557. During his somewhat chequered career Waldis travelled widely in Europe and it is interesting to note that he visited Nuremberg, the traditional birthplace of the wheellock, as early as 1524 with a deputation from the Archbishop of Riga to the Emperor. His comment that "in those times", when *Theuerdank* was first published, the firelock did not exist cannot therefore be dismissed lightly. It must be remembered, however, that before the advent of modern journalism the spread of information about such minor events as the invention of the wheellock was very much influenced by the accidents of personal contact and experience. All that can reasonably be deduced from Waldis's remarks about the firelock, therefore, is that examples must have been comparatively uncommon until shortly before the publication of his new edition of *Theuerdank* in 1553.

III.

Though the Geislingen, Goslar and *Theuerdank* references must be discarded, there is, in fact, documentary evidence to show that the wheellock was in use long prior to 1517. This is contained in a book of accounts for the year 1507 of the steward of the Cardinal Ippolito d'Este I (1479-1520), Archbishop of Zagreb (Agram), a city which was then in Hungary:

> Item ivit quidam Gaspar Bohemus servitor castri ad sanctum farkas ad Halemaniam pro devotione cui fece dare pro suis servicijs florenos quatuor cum medio ed iterum alios quatuor ut emeret pro Reverendissimo domino meo unam piscidem de illis qua incenduntur cum lapide et emit et misi Reverendissime dominationi sue ferrariam per petrum Lardum castellanum agriensem et in toto faciunt florenos octo cum medio ff.8 D.50.[19]

That is:

> Also, a certain Caspar the Bohemian, castle servant, went to St. Farkas[20] in Germany on a pilgrimage, to whom I caused to be given four and a half florins for his services, and also another four for him to buy for my most reverend Lord *a gun of that kind that is fired with a stone*, and he bought it and sent it to Ferrara to his most reverend lordship by the hand of Petrus Lardus, castellan of Zagreb, making in all eight and a half florins. Florins 8 Denarii 50.

The passage in italics in the translation might conceivably refer to some form of snaphaunce. In view of the very early date, however, it seems more likely that the gun sent to the cardinal was a wheellock, though we shall never know whether it was desired because such mechanisms were still rare or perhaps even unknown in Ferrara and in Italy generally, or whether, being frequent and widely known, a German specimen was interesting for comparison.

Another pre-1517 reference to a gun with a self-igniting lock is contained in a revealing story related by the Augsburg chronicler Wilhelm Rem in his *Cronaca newer geschichten* (1512-1527):

> How Laux Pfister shot a whore at Constance
> In the year of Our Lord 1515,[21] on the day of the Three Holy Kings [6th January], there was at Constance a certain young citizen of Augsburg, who invited a handsome whore. And when she was with him in a little room, he took up a loaded gun in his hand, the lock of which functioned in such a way that when the firing-mechanism was pressed, it ignited itself [*so schlug es selb feur auff*] and so discharged the piece. Accordingly he played around with the gun and pressed the firing-mechanism and shot the whore through the chin, so that the bullet passed out through the back of her neck. So he had to compensate her and give her 40 florins and another 20 florins per annum for life. He also paid the doctor 37 florins, and the other costs amounted to some 30 or 40 florins.[22]

Quite clearly Pfister's gun must have been fitted with either a snaphaunce or a wheellock, presumably with an automatic pancover. The former is not out of the question but the latter is more probable at this early date.[23]

The way in which Wilhelm Rem describes Pfister's gun suggests that in 1515 it was regarded as something unusual. But only two years later "self-igniting" guns had become common enough to make the Emperor Maximilian decide that they were a public danger and ought therefore to be prohibited. On the 3rd November, 1517, he addressed a letter-patent to all his subjects in his Archdukedom of Styria,[24] saying:

> Inasmuch as certain persons in our territories of Lower Austria are in the habit of carrying self-striking hand-guns that ignite themselves [*die selbschlagenden hanndtpuchssen, die sich selbs zundten*] which we are on no account prepared to allow, for various reasons that we have arrived at ourselves and also in consultation with our excellent Council. And accordingly we recommend most earnestly to all and sundry that none of you should carry the self-striking hand-guns referred to, and that our nobles, stewards, administrators, chief justices, mayors and judges should under no circumstances permit such guns to be carried.

The letter states that nobody, irrespective of nationality, is to be exempted from the order and continues with a list of punishments for its infringement. It concludes with the following rider:

> Further it is our earnest command that no craftsman or other person shall make any more self-striking guns that ignite themselves, and any person that shall be found to be making such hand-guns shall be punished with a fine of 30 Rhenish guilders.

One reason for the banning of self-igniting guns is revealed in a letter sent to the Emperor on the 16th March, 1518, by the *Ausschuss Landtag* of the Austrian hereditary lands meeting at Innsbruck.[25] This contains a list of recommended laws dealing with all types of offences, one section being directed against highwaymen and other similar criminals [*muetwilligen strassenrauber austreter und abseger*], including certain persons who "carry guns secretly under their clothing" [*haimlich puchsen under den Klaidern tragen*]. This section concludes with the recommendation that the Emperor should make it illegal "to carry or bear guns that ignite themselves, and to make the locks anywhere".[26] The second recommendation clearly follows from the previous one, for, by obviating the need for a lighted match, the invention of the wheellock made possible the production of a gun that could be carried concealed ready for instant use.

On the 28th July, 1518, the Emperor addressed a mandate to all rulers and subjects in the Empire[27] saying:

> Since notable and considerable damage has happened and is daily happening through the self-igniting guns which it is now the use and practice to carry both mounted and on foot, we have prohibited under pain of severe penalties their manufacture or their use or carrying, either when mounted or on foot, in all our hereditary Principalities and lands, as also in the kingdom of Bohemia and the Margravate of Moravia. Furthermore, we find many excellent reasons that would justify the extension of this prohibition to the Holy Empire and we do accordingly recommend you all and sundry and earnestly request you not to permit in future the manufacture of small or large self-igniting guns [*klein noch gross Püchssen, die sich selbst zünden*], or the use thereof on horseback or on foot.

How strictly the Emperor's ban was enforced is at present unknown, though a search in German legal records of the period might provide the answer. It must have had some effect on the manufacture of the lock in Germany, and this perhaps accounts for the apparently complete absence of actual examples of German wheellocks dating from before the third decade of the 16th century. After Maximilian's death on the 12th January, 1519, we must assume that the ban was eventually lifted, or allowed to lapse,[28] for his successor Charles V, judging from the number of wheellock firearms he owned in later life,[29] clearly approved very much of the mechanism.

IV.

We can now consider the drawings of wheellock mechanisms in the *Codex Atlanticus* of Leonardo da Vinci and in the Löffelholz manuscript.

The Leonardo da Vinci drawings.

The two most important of the Leonardo drawings (Fig. 1), both of which are on Folio 56 v.b. of the *Codex,*[30] have been illustrated and discussed in many publications on firearms.[31] Their function is explained in detail in the captions of Figs. 2-5. The second of these drawings (upper illustration) is undoubtedly the earliest representation of a wheellock for a gun yet recorded, but, unfortunately, it is not at present possible to say precisely how early it is. The *Codex Atlanticus* comprises about four thousand sheets of varying sizes and dates covered with notes and drawings relating to every conceivable subject and, for all practical purposes, arranged in no sort of order. The view that the drawings on folio 56 v.b. date from Leonardo's period of service with Lodovico *il Moro* (i.e. from c. 1482 to 1499) seems to be based on nothing stronger than the fact that he is known to have made military devices for the Duke,[32] and the latest writer on the dating of the various folios in the *Codex Atlanticus,* C. Pedretti,[33] ascribes this particular one to about the year 1508. His dating is based largely on a study of the changes in Leonardo's handwriting, a method that does not seem to be by any means foolproof, and can only be accepted with caution. While the drawings on folio 56 v.b. do probably date from c. 1508, or even earlier, all that can be said with absolute certainty therefore is that they must have been executed before 1519, the year of Leonardo's death.

The drawings present yet another problem. Are they original designs by Leonardo or do they simply show objects drawn "from life" or copied from other manuscripts? There can be little doubt that the device with a spiral spring was an original invention, for a number of preliminary sketches for it appear on folios 357 r.a. (Fig. 6) and 357 v.b. of the *Codex,* both of which are dated by Pedretti to c. 1500. In addition, related sketches of similar devices operated by flat helical springs, worms and pinions occur on folios 217 r.a., 217 v.a., and 353 r.c., all dated by Pedretti about 1500-5.

It is less easy to come to any definite conclusions about the drawing of the gun-lock. Nevertheless, there is good evidence to suggest that it, too, is a design. On folio 357 r.a. (Fig. 6) of the *Codex*—dated by Pedretti, as already said, about 1500—are several sketches of transmission-chains,[34] mostly attached to

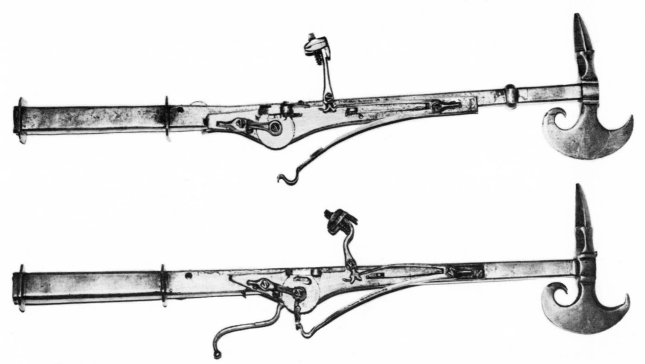

Figs. 12 & 13—Two of a group of war axes combined with wheellock pistols, Doge's Palace Armoury, Venice. Dating is difficult: 1520 would seem right for so simple a mechanism, but a similar one, only barely more evolved and dated 1552, is known.

springs and wheel-spindles of the type shown on the lock under discussion. Chains with links of three different shapes are shown, also two different methods of attaching the chain to the spring, while one group of drawings illustrates in some detail the appearance of the chain, the end of the spring and the wheel-spindle both before and after the lock is wound. Against this group Leonardo has written *per dare una volta intera,* that is, "for giving a complete turn," a remark that clearly refers to the length of transmission chain required to make the wheel turn a complete revolution. The general impression given by all the drawings taken together is that they do not represent details of existing mechanisms but are preliminary designs for the gun-lock under discussion.

Further evidence in favour of the view that the drawing on folio 56 v.b. is a design has been provided by practical experiment. Mr. J. Hart of Guernsey, a skilled amateur gunsmith, very kindly undertook to try to make a reproduction of the lock shown in the drawing. He agreed that in doing this he should not attempt to alter the original design in any way, except where is was absolutely essential to make the lock work. The result of his experiment (Figs. 3-5) has been to show that a lock made exactly as in the drawing would not operate, chiefly because the mainspring and wheel-spindle are impossibly thin. But by rectifying these faults and making a number of minor adjustments, Mr. Hart was able to produce a lock that works satisfactorily, though the curious shape of the mainspring is a serious weakness.

Mr. Hart's remarks on the problems he encountered while making the lock are of very considerable interest. He writes as follows in a letter to me of August 4th, 1960:

The only big difficulty has been, as I foresaw, the main spring. The design with its sharp corners and curious shape asks for trouble during the hardening and tempering process. I made and broke two although I constructed an electric furnace specially for the job. They both broke in the same place, the angle nearest the curve. Then my good friend Arthur Hamon volunteered to try his hand with his little coke fire. I made another and passed it on to him. The first attempt was too soft, but the second, although on the soft side, works the lock except I cannot get sparks because there is not enough zip. I have tried both pyrites and flint. For my own satisfaction I put a few cross grooves which may not have been intended in the original design. They did not improve matters, possibly due to increased friction.

You will have noticed that there are two holes for the release pin in the wheel, one in the uncocked and one in the cocked position. If it were not for the former the lever would be sticking out except when the lock is cocked. To cock, therefore, it is necessary to first lift the trigger. This could be obviated if one made an inclined groove in the wheel but you ordered I should not try to improve on Leonardo unless it was

37

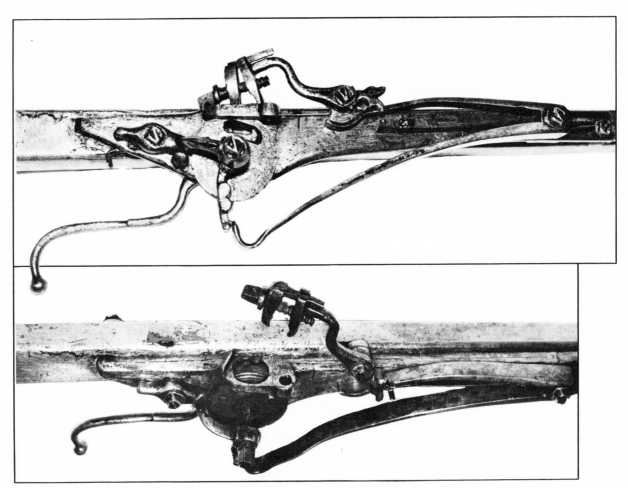

Fig. 14—Lock of lower of the two axes in Figs. 12 & 13. An upward pull on the trigger lever forces a wedge between sear prong and wheel engagement to release wheel to snap. Flashpan cover missing.

vital. In my model the pin does not always drop into this hole. It might be satisfactory if the spring was very strong or if there was a stop of some kind as one often sees on a wheellock.

By the way I freely accept any blame for any misunderstandings on my part of the design and any sheer bad workmanship of which I fear there are examples.

The design of the vice on the pyrites holder is not very good because the screw is too near the hinge. I had to waist the screw where it passes through the upper jaw in order to obtain even reasonable movement of the jaws.

In spite of the wheel being inset in the plate it is still required that a double bend or joggle be made in the arm of the holder to bring the jaws in line with the pan. The latter is of course pure imagination on my part as is the cover. I now wish I had hinged it differently.

I had quite a bit of bother over the perspective one way and another but you may put that down to me. I suppose it would be impudent to suggest it may be slightly wrong in parts!

The position of the spindle of the pyrites holder and those of the release lever and wedge piece give me trouble. The latter rather gets in the way of the main spring when cocked. The trigger screw position I found by trial and error as I could not get it to work nicely as it appears to be in the sketch. Its final position meant altering the position of the kink in the main spring. I found it necessary to increase the diameter of the wheel spindle which is shown as if there were no squares on it to drive the wheel and to take the spanner.

I am quite convinced that the sketch was a design and not a picture of an existing lock. Leonardo was thinking with his pencil just as I do in a more humble way when trying to work something out. Slight modifications would in my opinion produce a first-class practicable lock.

(Since this was written, the reproduction lock has passed into the collection of Mr. A.C. Carpenter, who has been able to make it function perfectly by increasing the hardness of the wheel. This does not, of course, make any difference to Mr. Hart's conclusions that an exact replica of the lock drawn by Leonardo would be unworkable.)

In the light of the foregoing, it seems virtually certain that the drawing under discussion was a design. But the features that it has in common with nearly every existing wheellock could hardly all have arrived at independently by someone else. It seems highly probable, therefore, that Leonardo was the inventor of the wheellock and that the drawing in the *Codex Atlanticus* is the prototype from which all locks of this type stemmed.[35] If this view is correct the drawing must, for reasons given below, date from before 1505.

The Löffelholz Manuscript.

This interesting manuscript was until the last war kept in the Staatsbibliothek, Berlin *(Codex german., quart.* 132). I am informed that it was not among the objects returned a few years ago to East Germany by the Soviet Union and its present whereabouts, if indeed it survives, are unknown.[36] It was a quarto volume of seventy-six paper folios of which the first fifty-five bore line and wash drawings of technical devices of all kinds, many accompanied by notes on their operation, and the remainder various recipes. The frontispiece consisted of the arms of the Nuremberg patrician Martin Löffelholz (ob. 1533) and of his first wife Anna Haugin, together with the date 1505.

Whether the manuscript was executed by Löffelholz himself or by someone working for him is uncertain. The problem is not one of great importance, for quite clearly the volume was not a book of designs for inventions by one individual, but a record of existing devices culled from various sources, presumably mainly in Nuremberg, on the lines of the "Book of Secrets" that were then starting to become popular. What is of importance is the question of whether the date 1505 referred to the compilation of the whole book or merely to the binding together of a set of blank sheets of paper on which drawings were made over a period, possibly extending up to Löffelholz's death in 1533. In fact, there seems to be little doubt that it referred to the former, for the drawings were arranged in groups covering devices of a similar type with no blank pages for additions between the groups. The only parts that had apparently been added later in Löffelholz's life were the recipes at the end.

On folio 27 of the manuscript were drawings of two wheellock tinder-lighters, which, fortunately, were illustrated in an article by the late Baron Rudolph Cederström of Stockholm published shortly before World War II.[37] One of these (folio 27 v.) (Fig. 7) consists simply of an L-shaped box in which is mounted a narrow wheel, rotated manually by a thong wrapped round its axle, and a pair of screw-operated jaws, pivoted at the bottom, to hold the pyrites. Attached to one side is an oblong container, fitted with a sliding cover, for spare tinder. The other device

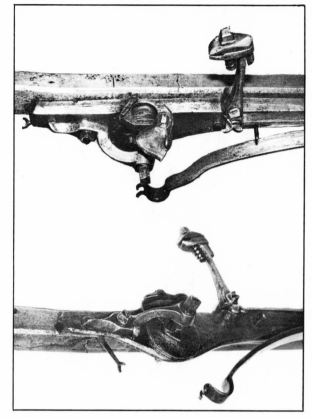

Fig. 15—Lock of upper axe in Figs. 12 & 13. Trigger bar and chain are missing.

(Fig. 8) is more complex. It consists of a flat, oblong plate with screw-holes at the corners for attaching it to a support of some kind. Its function is explained in the caption to Fig. 8; it seems quite clear that it is closely related to the drawings in the *Codex Atlanticus*. The transmission-chain and the method of linking it to the mainspring are exactly as shown by Leonardo, while the transverse sear-lever could well be an adaptation of the one on his gun-lock. Most significant, however, is the fact that the tray-shaped pan and the cock, with its curious cubical head and transverse screw, are identical to those on Leonardo's tinder-lighter. It seems reasonable to suggest, therefore, that the device illustrated by Löffelholz was a direct development from Leonardo's designs, possibly imported into Nuremberg from Italy. If this is correct the drawings in the *Codex Atlanticus* must date from well before 1505.

V.

The earliest surviving wheellocks.

Support for the view that the second Löffelholz tinder-lighter was Italian in origin is provided by an examination of a group of three wheellock guns combined with crossbows preserved, along with other remnants of the Doge's armoury, in the Palazzo Ducale in Venice (Nos. Q1, Q2 and Q3; Figs. 10 and 11).[38] These seem to have escaped the notice of writers prior to the publication of the first version of the present article, though they have a considerable claim to being regarded as the earliest surviving wheellock firearms.

They are made entirely of steel and are all exactly similar form and construction, though one (Q2) varies from the others in decoration and in certain other very minor details, for example the shape of the screws holding the parts of the lock-mechanism. In each case the bow is held in a slot in the forward end of the tiller by a steel wedge and is operated by a nut and lever-trigger mechanism of the type found on most crossbows of the 15th and 16th centuries. The tiller terminates at the rear in a lion mask of cast bronze (missing from Q2) secured by a transverse bolt to the head of a long screw running longitudinally into the tiller and probably originally forming part of a device for spanning the bow. A gun-barrel with a slightly flared muzzle projects forwards from the front end of the tiller and extends back into it, above the bow, for rather more than a third of its length. The mechanics of the locks are explained in the captions to Figs. 10 and 11.

Apart from the fact that the cock is mounted in front—or to the right—of the pan, and that the trigger-spring pushes the sear-lever outwards instead of inwards, the basic construction of the locks on the Venice crossbows is exactly the same as that of the more complex of the two tinder-lighters in the Löffelholz manuscript. All clearly belong to the same line of development, though the modifications that have taken place on the Venice locks, notably the improved form of cock, suggests that they are rather later in date than the tinder-lighter. Unfortunately, the question of how much later is not an easy one to answer. The director of the Archivio di Stato at Venice informs me that he has been unable to trace any reference to the crossbows among the records under his care, and I know of no comparative material upon which an accurate estimate of date might be based. The fact that only one other lock of this type is recorded—on a combined gun and bill at Vienna[39]—does, however, suggest that the construction was in use over only a limited period. On the basis of the evidence provided by the Löffelholz manuscript it can perhaps, therefore, be dated tentatively to the period round about 1510.[40]

A certain amount of support for such a dating is provided by the decoration on the most complete of the three crossbows (Q2). This, unlike the other two, which retain traces of rather indeterminate scrollwork damascened in gold, is etched in a somewhat scratchy manner with bands and panels containing trophies of pseudo-Classical armour, scrollwork and grotesques against a ground of diagonal lines (Fig. 9). This type of etching is characteristically Italian and is commonly found on Italian armours dating from

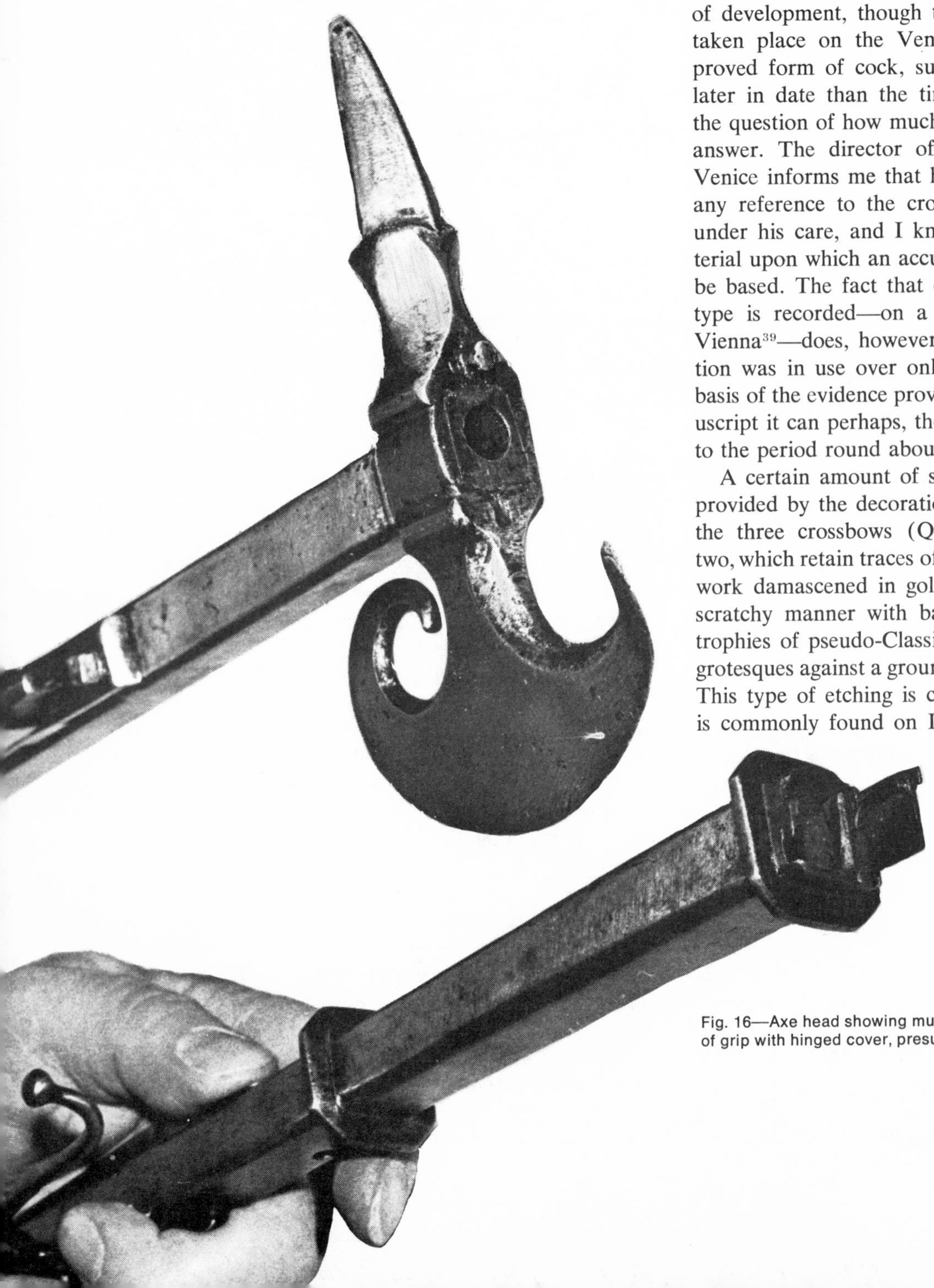

Fig. 16—Axe head showing muzzle of barrel, and hollow end of grip with hinged cover, presumably for storing pyrites.

the end of the 15th century to about 1520. The style of the etched decoration on a Milanese armour of c. 1510 in the Musée de l'Armée, Paris (No. G.8), for example, is particularly close to that on the crossbow, though the actual execution is very much better.[41] Unfortunately, etching of not dissimilar character is recorded on a few armours dating from well into the second quarter of the 16th century,[42] so its occurrence on the crossbow is by no means conclusive evidence of an early date.

But the style of the etched decoration on Q2 does point to an Italian origin for the crossbows, and it is even possible to suggest a precise locality. Also preserved at Venice is another combined wheellock gun and crossbow (No. Q4)[43]—unfortunately lacking its lock—of much more advanced design than the ones under discussion, which is signed and dated *Renaldo de Visin da Asolo 1562.* The tiller and bow on this are sufficiently close in form to those on the earlier crossbows to suggest that perhaps they too were made in Asolo, a small town in the Veneto, 19 miles N.W. of Treviso.

The subsequent history of the wheellock in Italy is outside the scope of this note. It should be mentioned, however, that a developed form of the lock found on the crossbows apparently remained in use there until after the middle of the 16th century. A number of examples of this type of lock exist in various collections but, as yet, no satisfactory chronology has been worked out for them. An example of the difficulties involved in attempting to do this is provided by a group of war-hammers and axes combined with wheellock guns, of which two specimens are preserved at Venice. (Figs. 12-16).[44] The lock-mechanisms on these are mounted on separate plates and certain details—notably the developed form of the cock and of the mainspring which acts on both the cock and the wheel—show that they must be somewhat later in date than the locks on the crossbows. On the other hand, many of them have simple hand-operated pan-covers and very elementary sear- and trigger-mechanisms. The sear-lever is a flat spring mounted on the inside of the lockplate through which the sear itself projects on to the back of the wheel. The trigger is simply a lever, like that on a 15th-century crossbow or on Leonardo's gunlock, pivoted vertically to the inside of the lockplate and with a wedged-shaped lug on its upper edge. When the trigger is pulled upwards the lug catches behind the end of the sear-lever so forcing it outwards and withdrawing the sear. One would at first sight be inclined to date this very simple mechanism as early as about 1520 if it were not for the fact that a double-barrelled pistol in the Musée d'Art et d'Histoire, Geneva, which is dated 1552 on one barrel, is equipped with locks of only slightly more advanced construction, a button acting directly on the sear-

lever being substituted for the lever trigger.[45]

A few of these later wheellocks have associations with Hungary, or were actually found there.[46] They may all have been imported from Italy, but in view of the close links that existed between Hungary and the Venetian Republic through Dalmatia,[47] it is likely that some at least were made in Hungary under Italian influence. This second view is supported by the fact that the form of wheellock with external mainspring found on the distinctive type of 17th-century birding-rifle known as a *Tschinke,* which was apparently made exclusively in Central Europe,[48] is clearly derived from the group of locks under discussion.[49] A later version of the Italian lock was also used in the Iberian Peninsular in the last quarter of the 16th century and in the 17th century.[50]

The form taken by the first wheellocks made in Germany is uncertain. The earliest known example, and also the earliest dateable wheellock recorded, occurs on a combined gun and crossbow in the Bayerisches Nationalmuseum, Munich (Fig. 17). It bears the arms of the Archduke Ferdinand, later Emperor Ferdinand I, as used before he became King of Bohemia in 1526, together with the initials F.A., which could stand either for *Ferdinandus Archidux,* or *Ferdinandus* and *Anna,* the latter being his first wife, whom he married in 1521 when he was eighteen years old. The piece must, therefore, date from before 1526 and possibly from as early as 1521 or a little before.[51]

The lock of the Munich crossbow belongs to a distinctive group with sickle-shaped cock-springs, discussed in some detail in an article by Dr. Arne Hoff published in 1940, and in which he suggested that its origins were to be sought in Nuremberg. More recently, however, Dr. Erwin Schalkhausser has suggested that the Munich crossbow may have been made in Italy.[52] It is a much more sophisticated piece of work than anything we have considered thus far. The greater part of the mechanism is concealed behind the lockplate, the pan has an automatic sliding cover and the sear-lever, which is operated by a press-button release, is made of two interacting bars. Nevertheless, the large U-shaped mainspring and the slender curved cock, which unfortunately lacks its jaws, are still very reminiscent of those found on the early Italian locks.

Probably more-or-less contemporary with the Munich crossbow is a carbine, unfortunately undated and unmarked, in the Musée de l'Armée, Paris (No. P.O. 194, ex-Pauilhac collection) (Fig. 18).[53] It has a stock of similar form to the wheellock of 1530 referred to below, but with a lock of more primitive construction. This has an almost square lockplate carrying the wheel and cock, the cock-spring, which has a very long upper arm and a very short lower one, being attached directly to the wood of the stock

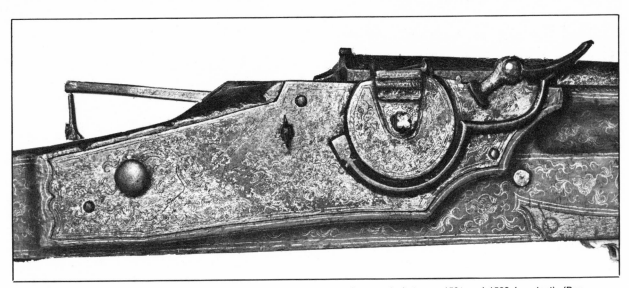

Fig. 17—The earliest known datable wheellock: on a German crossbow made between 1521 and 1526 (see text). (Bayerisches Nationalmuseum, Munich)

in front of the plate, as on some of the earliest recorded snap-matchlock guns.[54] The cock is similar in shape to that on the Leonardo lock and has its jaws pivoted together at the back in a similar manner. A safety-catch is mounted on a separate plate behind the bottom of the rear edge of the lockplate. The mainspring, instead of being attached to the lockplate, is mounted independently inside the stock, a construction that from at least as early as the middle of the 16th century onwards was confined almost exclusively to France. The gun may, therefore, be French in origin, though in view of its apparently very early date, it is impossible to be definite.

The earliest dated wheellock recorded, a carbine in the Real Armeria, Madrid (No. K.32) (Fig. 19) which belonged originally to the Emperor Charles V, is undoubtedly German in origin. It bears on the barrel the mark of Bartholomaeus Markwart of Augsburg, together with the date 1530, and has a lock that has already achieved the basic construction that was to remain the usual one for the wheellock for the remainder of its history. The cock-spring is of similar form to that on the Paris gun mentioned above, but this time mounted on a tongue-like extension of the lock-plate.[55] This gun, the first of a long dated series of German examples, marks the beginning of the period in the history of the wheellock that has been examined in some detail by other writers. There is thus no need to take the present study further. But, in conclusion, some brief references must be made to the "Monk's Gun", now happily restored to the Historisches Museum in Dresden.

VI.

The Monk's Gun

This device (Fig. 20) derives its name from a tradition, already current in 1606, that it was the invention of the monk Berthold Schwarz, legendary discoverer of gunpowder.[56] Made of blued iron, it consists of a barrel of circular section, 11 in. long, with a bore 7/16 in. in diameter, resembling in shape the barrels on the Venice crossbows. It is thickened over the breech and the last three inches flare out slightly to form the muzzle; at the point where the flare commences it is encircled by a groove between a pair of incised lines. The front and rear of the muzzle and the breech are each encircled by an incised band formed of close-set Gothic I's, while between the muzzle and the breech are two encircling rows of widely-spaced slipped trefoils, also incised.[57] On top of the breech is punched a mark, possibly that of the maker, consisting of three addorsed crescents. Its function is explained in the caption of Fig. 20. The Monk's Gun cannot be dated precisely at present. It may well have been made as early as the third quarter of the 15th century, but all that can be said with certaintly is that the Gothic letters used in the decoration indicate that it is not likely to be later than the middle of the 16th century.[58] In all probability it antedates the invention of the wheellock, but this does not necessarily mean that it was the latter's direct precursor, as was suggested by Thierbach.[59] The only evidence of a possible relationship between the Monk's Gun and the early wheellock is provided by the pivoted cock-jaws, which are exactly similar to those on Leonardo's gun-lock, though, so far as I can discover, no other instance of the use of jaws of this type to hold pyrites is recorded, apart from the French carbine mentioned above.[60] But it would be unwise to deduce too much from this, for the lock of the Monk's Gun appears otherwise to be unique in all its details.[61] Until further evidence is available, therefore, it must be regarded as an experimental arm outside the main line of development of the pyrites-lock.[62]

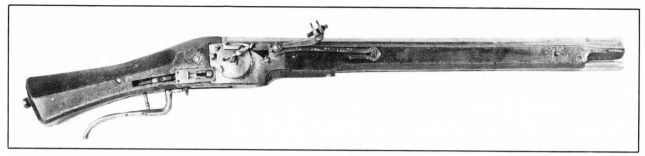

Fig. 18—One of the earliest wheellock arms known, a carbine more or less contemporary with the weapon in Fig. 17. (Musée de l'Armée, Paris)

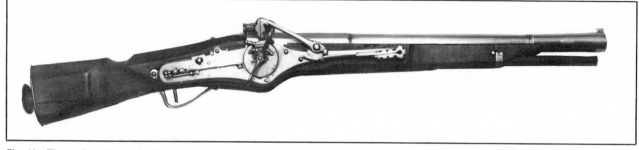

Fig. 19—The earliest dated wheellock known: a German carbine bearing the mark of Bartholomaeus Markwart of Augsburg and the date 1530. (Real Armeria, Madrid)

VII.

Conclusion

The two articles here combined were originally written with the intention of bringing together all the evidence then available about the origins and early history of the wheellock, in the hope that this would provide a firm basis for further research. Regrettably, this hope has not yet been realised and, so far as I am aware, no new information on the subject has been published since the second article appeared in 1964. My conclusions that the system was invented in Italy by Leonardo da Vinci—which merely elaborated those reached by previous writers—have, however, been questioned by Freiherr Alexander von Reitzenstein in a review of the first volume of John F. Hayward's *Art of the Gunmaker* published in 1965 in *Waffen- und Kostümkunde*. In this, he pointed out that all the early documentary evidence, commencing with the Löffelholz manuscript of 1505, seems to indicate that it was in Germany that the wheellock was first widely manufactured and used, while the earliest known written records of the manufacture of wheellocks in Italy, dating from 1536 onwards, mention that the craftsmen responsible were German. In his opinion the *Codex Atlanticus* drawings can only be regarded as evidence that Leonardo was acquainted with wheellock mechanisms, and not that he was the inventor of the system, and he therefore concluded that the traditional view that the lock originated in Germany was the one to which most credence ought to be attached.

Freiherr von Reitzenstein's conclusions are, of course, perfectly valid if one accepts his views on the evidential value of Leonardo's drawings. Any discussion of these is bound to be speculative in the absence of any means of dating them firmly, and in my own I merely attempted to demonstrate that there are good reasons for regarding them as designs rather than sketches of existing mechanisms. Where the gun-lock is concerned, in particular, Mr. Hart's experiment appears to me to demonstrate conclusively that it would not have worked as represented without considerable modification. One can only conclude, therefore, that if the sketch was made from an actual lock it must be very inaccurate: this is by no means impossible but, in view of Leonardo's remarkable skill as a draughtsman, is not very likely.

The fact that in 1507 Cardinal Ippolito d'Este, then residing in Ferrara, ordered what was presumably a wheellock gun to be sent to him from Germany suggests, as already noted, two opposed conclusions: one, that the wheellocks were so little known in central Italy at that time that it was necessary to procure one from Germany; and the other, that a German specimen was desired for comparison with the Italian ones already in the princely gun-room. Both pictures may be drawn from the given facts with equal persuasiveness, and hence the claim for Leonardo is unaffected. As to the absence of published references to wheellocks in Italy prior to the Duke of Ferrara's ordnance of 1522, we must remember that the enormously rich archives of Italy, both public and private, have been searched only superficially and sporadically for information about firearms: the German archives, on the other hand, have been the subject of

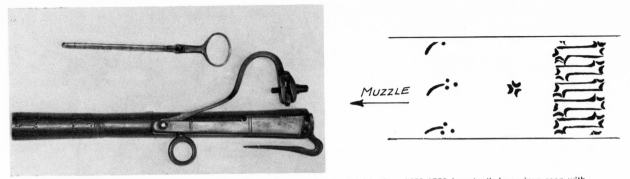

Fig. 20—The famous "Monk's Gun" of Dresden, not more closely datable than 1450-1550 (see text). Long iron rasp with oval ring handle was inserted from rear into long (5½ in.) box riveted to piece's side, priming was heaped into box's rearmost flashpan-like section, pyrites was lowered onto hasp by screwing arm downward by means of ring-headed tension screw, and hasp was then rapidly pulled rearward to engender sparks and fire charge. Note belt-hook. Line drawing shows engraving around barrel. (Historisches Museum, Dresden)

MUZZLE

continuous study by arms students for well over a century. Moreover, because of Italy's turbulent and disrupted history, only a few 16th century Italian firearms have survived, in contrast to the many thousands of German specimens still to be found in their original armouries. The impression of total German domination of the early history of the wheellock may, therefore, be an illusion produced by the accidents of survival and the vagaries of research, though obviously evidence not yet known or no longer knowable cannot be adduced in proof of anything. A number of Italian scholars are, however, not at work, but it is likely to be many years before any definite conclusions about the early use, or lack of use, of wheellocks (or snaphaunces or flintlocks) in Italy is likely to be possible.

In the meantime, the *Codex Atlanticus* drawings must, in my opinion, be regarded as providing strong *prima facie* evidence that the system was invented in Italy by Leonardo da Vinci.

ACKNOWLEDGEMENTS

In addition to the people whose assistance I have acknowledged in the text, I should like to express my thanks to the following: Prof. Dr. Carlo Castiglioni of the Ambrosiana, Milan, for information about the *Codex Atlanticus*; Prof. Arch. E. Trincanato, Director of the Plazzo Ducale, Venice, and Signor Apollonio, a member of his staff, for searching, unfortunately unsuccessfully, for records relating to the crossbows and axes; Herr J. Schöbel, Director of the Historisches Museum, Dresden, for permission to examine and photograph the Monk's Gun; Mrs. B. M. A. Ellis, for making the drawing reproduced in Fig. 9 from a photograph; Mr. E. A. Mornard for making the drawing reproduced in Fig. 20 from rubbings of the decoration on the Monk's Gun; Dr. Bruno Thomas and Dr. Ortwin Gamber of the Vienna Waffensammlung, and Prof. Hans Schedelmann of Salzburg for help on various problems connected with the preparation of this article; Dr. T. T. Hoopes of St. Louis for permission to reproduce the drawing shown in Fig. 2. I am especially grateful to Mr. J. Hart for devoting so much time and trouble to the copy of Leonardo da Vinci's gun-lock, and to Mr. J. F. Hayward, who, apart from giving much help in other ways, very kindly made all the translations of the 16th-century German texts.

NOTES

1. See F.M. Feldhaus, *Die Technik*, Leipzig and Berlin, 1914, 445-6. Some writers say that it was invented in 1515, for example A. Demmin, *An Illustrated History of Arms and Armour*, London, 1877, p. 487. I have been unable to trace the source of this statement, but it does not seem to have appeared before the 19th century.
2. J.C. Wagenseil, *De Sacri Rom. Imperii Libera Civitate Norimbergensi etc.*, Altdorf, 1697, p. 150: " . . . cum in Chronico quodam MS. legatur: *Die zu den Schiess-Rohren gehörigen Feuer-Schlösser sind erst A. 1517 zu Nürnberg erfunden worden.*"
   It appears to be reasonably certain that *Feuerschloss* was synonomous with *Radschloss* in the 16th century: See, for example, T. Hampe, "Eine Notiz über Feuerschloss-(Radschloss)macher, Büchsenmacher, Büchsenfasser und Pulverflaschenverfertiger in Nürnberg, 1536", *Zeitschrift für historische Waffenkunde*, V, (1909-11), pp. 125-6, 154-5.
3. J.G. von Weineck, *Raetia: Das ist Aussführliche*

vnd wahrhaffte Beschreibung Der dreyen Loblichen Grawen Bündendten vnd anderer Retischen Völcker etc., Zürich, 1616, p. 152: "Die kunslichen feuwr-schloss seynd hernach Anno MDXVII zu Augsburg vnd Nüremberg auffkommen. Solche erfindung were ein sinnreich werk vnd schön kleinot gewesst, wann der missbrauch nit hinzü geschlagen were . . .".

4. M. Thierbach, *Die geschichtliche Entwicklung der Handfeuerwaffen,* Dresden, 1886-7 (reprinted Graz, 1965), p. 29: "Als eigentlicher Erfinder des Rad-schlosses wird Johann Kiefuss in Nürnberg genannt, und zwar soll er dasselbe im Jahre 1517 gleich voll-ständig fertig hergestellt haben."

5. He is not mentioned, for example, in any of the documents relating to 16th-century Nuremberg gun-makers quoted by the following: Josef Baader, "Beit-räge zur Kunstgeschichte Nürnbergs", *Zahns Jähr-bücher für Kunstwissenschaft,* I, Leipzig, 1868, pp. 255-257; Hans Bösch, "Nürnberger Büchsenmeister, Büchsenschmiede und Feuerschlossmacher des 16 Jahrhunderts", *Mitteilungen aus dem germanischen Nationalmuseum,* Jahrgang 1890, Nürnberg, 1890, pp. 70-72; T. Hampe, *loc. cit.*

6. J.G. Doppelmayr, *Historische Nachtricht von den Nürnbergischen Mathematicis und Künstlerin,* Nürn-berg, 1730, p. 294.

I am grateful to Freiherr Alexander von Reitzen-stein of the Bayerisches National Museum for the information that a Georg Kühfuss, presumably the gunmaker, was buried in the St. Johannis burial ground, Nuremberg, in 1594. See *Norischer Chris-ten Freydhöfe Gedächtnis,* Nuremberg, 1682, p. 103.

7. See, for example, J. Alm, *Arméns Eldhandvapen Förr och Nu,* Stockholm, 1953, pp. 30-35.

8. Artilleriemajor D. Toll, "Die ersten Büchsenchüt-zen die an der Wange abschossen", *Anzeiger für Kunde der deutschen Vorzeit. Organ des German-ischen Museums,* Neue Folge, 13, Nürnberg, 1866, columns 172-3.

9. Carl Jäger, *Schwäbisches Städtewesen des Mittelal-ters,* Vol. I, Löslund und Heilbronn, 1831, p. 422: "Auf dem Lande waren ebenfalls Anstalten zur Ein-übung des Kriegswesens getroffen, z.B. in Geislin-gen wurde 1406 eine Schiesshütte errichtet, und verordnet, dass niemand auf derselben eine selbst-zündende Büchse tragen dürfe."

10. This deals with the events leading up to the forma-tion of the Swabian League in 1488.

11. See P. Sixl, "Zur Geschichte des Schiesswesens der Infanterie", *Zeitschrift für historische Waffenkunde,* Vol. II (1900-02), pp. 327-37.

12. The original letter is in German, as is the following one from Dr. Huber of Ulm.

13. I am informed by Dr. Schmolz that Prälat von Schmid (1756-1827) was a local historian.

14. *Tafelamts-Rechnung* for 1509, p. 161. I am indebted to Dr. Bruchmann, Staatsarchivdirektor of Goslar, for a transcript of the original entry.

15. *Loc. cit.*

16. [M. Pfintzing] *Die Ehr vnd manliche Thaten, Ges-chichten vnd Gefehrlichaitenn des Streitbaren Rit-ters vnnd Edlen Helden Tewerdanck zu Ehren dem Hochloblichen Hause zu Osterreich . . . New züger-icht, Mit schönen Figuren vnnd lustigen Reimen volendet,* Frankfort, 1553. The passage quoted by Toll occurs on folio XLIX, in the section headed "Wie Teurdanck solt in ainem Kriegschiff von dem

pulver verdorben sein."

17. The 1517 edition of *Theuerdank* was reproduced in facsimile in the *Jahrbuch der Kunsthistorischen Sammlungen in Wien,* Vol. 8 (1888).

18. The following information about Waldis is taken from Georg Buchenau, *Leben und Schriften des Bur-card Waldis,* Marburg, 1858. See also *Allgemeine Deutsche Biographie,* Vol. 40, Leipzig, 1896, pp. 701-09.

19. Archivio di Stato, Modena: *Archivio Segreto Es-tense, CASA—Amministrazione, Cardinale Ippolito I d'Este—Vescovado di Agria—Registro di Spese No. 8—Anno 1507—Busta 91/7084.* I am greatly indebted to the Director of the Archivio di Stato, Modena, for a transcript of the passage. It was pre-viously published by Albert Nyàry in his article "A modenai Hippolit codexek," *Szàzadok* 1870 (Buda-pest), p. 679. See also Janos Kalmàr, "Die Tschinke oder Teschner Büchse," *Folia Archaeologica,* Vol. X, Budapest, 1958, pp. 179-80.

20. Dr. Arne Hoff identifies this in *Feuerwaffen* (Vol. I, Brunswick, 1969, p. 47) as St. Wolfgang in Upper Austria.

21. This was 1515 New Style also. See Grotefend, *Hand-buch der historischen Chronologie des deutschen Mittelalters und der Neuzeit,* Hanover, 1872, pp. 25*ff.*

22. I am grateful to Dr. H.F. Deininger, Director of the Augsburg city archives for drawing my attention to this passage.

I am indebted to Professor Dr. Lieb, Director of the Augsburg museums for the information that Laux (Lukas) Pfister was a son of the Augsburg merchant Lukas I Pfister (1451-1500) and Eliza-beth Welser (d. 1509). He was born in 1493 and in 1515 married Walburga Neidhart at Memmingen in Bavaria. He later returned to Augsburg.

23. The earliest recorded reference to a snaphaunce is contained in a Swedish document of 1547. See Ake Meyerson, *Stockholms Bössmakare,* (Stockholm, 1936), p. 10, n. 21.

24. I am indebted to Dr. O. Posch, Director of the Steier-markisches Landesarchiv, Graz, for a transcript of this document made from the original in his charge.

25. See *Archiv für Kunde österreichischer Geschichts-quellen,* Vol. XIII (Vienna, 1854), pp. 236-39. *Cf.* F. Pischler, *Das Landes-Zeughaus in Graz,* Leipzig, 1880, Part 1, p. 111, n. 1.

26. *Desgleichen sollen die puchssen, so selbst fewr slagen, meniglich zufurn oder zu tragen, vnd den Slossen an allen orten zu machen verpotten werden.*

27. It should be emphasized that this mandate was a general one affecting all parts of the Empire. The copy addressed to Nuremberg (Staatsarchiv, SIL 77, No. 21) has been known for many years and has led to the erroneous belief that it concerned that city alone. The wording of the mandate makes it quite clear that this was not the case. Another copy, ex-actly similar to the Nuremberg one is preserved in the Augsburg Stadtarchiv (1518 28/7); a note on the back of this shows that it was received by the city on the 14th October, 1518. A search in the archives of other cities of the Empire would no doubt reveal further copies.

I am indebted to Dr. Hirschmann of the Nurem-berg State Archives and Dr. H.F. Deininger, Direc-tor of the Augsburg City Archives for information about the two copies of the mandate referred to and for microfilms of them.

28. It was still nominally in force as late as 1532, though apparently not regarded very seriously. In that year the Markgraf Georg of Ansbach (1484-1543) wrote to the Nuremberg City Council, requesting that, in view of depredations in his game-preserves, they should prohibit their citizens from carrying "fire-striking or other guns" [*feuerschlagende oder andere Büchsen*] in the countryside. The Council replied, in a letter of the 6th May, 1532, that a general ban on such guns was already in force in the Empire, but that despite this they were the favourite weapons of the marauders who made the roads unsafe for travellers. This being so, the enforcement of the ban on the citizens of Nuremberg would be unfair as it would render them defenceless against these marauders. The Council therefore agreed only to forbid their citizens to shoot game in the Markgraf's preserves. See J. Baader, "Markgraf Georg zu Ansbach will den Nürnbergern die feuerschlagenden Büchsen verbieten," *Anzeiger für Kunde der deutschen Vorzeit*, N.S., Vol. XII (1856), columns 237-39.

Pischler *(loc. cit.)* refers to an order of the Emperor Ferdinand I (1556-64) directed against robbers who carry "short self-igniting guns" [*kurtzn selbszundend Büchsen*] under their clothes.

29. Many of these are preserved in the Royal Armory, Madrid.

30. These and all the other drawings from the Codex referred to here are reproduced in the full-sized facsimile of the manuscript: *Il Codice Atlantico di Leonardo da Vinci . . . ripridotto e pubblicato dalla Regia Accademia dei Lincei*, Milan and Rome, 1894-1914. This also includes transcripts of all the notes.

31. The most important of these are as follows: F.M. Feldhaus, "Das Radschloss bei Leonardo da Vinci," and "Handfeuerwaffen bei Leonardo da Vinci," *Zeitschrift für historische Waffenkunde*, Vol. IV, (1906-08) pp. 153-4, and Vol. VI (1912-14); pp. 30-31; T. T. Hoopes, "Radschlösser nach Leonardo da Vinci?", *ibid.*, Vol. XIII, pp. 225-7; R. Cederström, "Ha Gevärslåsen Uppstått ur Elddon?" *Liv Rust Kammaren*, Vol. I (Stockholm, 1937-39), pp. 65-76; A. Gaibi, "Appunti sull'origine e sulla evoluzione meccanica degli apparecchi di accensione delle armi da fuoco portatili," *Armi Antiche: Bollettino dell'Accademia di S. Marciano—Torino*, Anno III (1956), pp. 81-120.

32. See Gaibi, *op. cit.*, pp. 90-91.

33. C. Pedretti, *Studi Vinciani*, Geneva, 1957, pp. 264-89.

34. These are apparently the earliest recorded evidence for the existence of chains of this type.

35. This conclusion is reached, for similar reasons, by Gaibi in the article referred to in Note 31.

36. My information about the manuscript is derived from the following: F.M. Feldhaus, "Eine Nürnberger Bilderhandschrift", *Mitteilungen des Vereins für Geschichte der Stadt Nürnberg*, Vol. 31 (Nuremberg, 1933), pp. 222-26; E. Reicke, "Martin Löffelholz der Ritter und Techniker (gest. 1533). Enthüllungen über den Verfasser der Handschrift," *Ibid.*, pp. 227-39; F.M. Feldhaus, "Waffentechnisches aus der Nürnberger Löffelholz-Handschrift von 1505," *Zeitschrift für historische Waffen- und Kostümkunde*, Vol. XV (1937-39), pp. 123-25; Cederström, *op. cit.* A microfilm copy is available in the Victoria and Albert Museum Library.

37. *Op. Cit.*, Note 31.

38. See M. Morin, "La 'ruota' arcaica," *Diana Armi*, Anno V, No. 3, Florence. May/June 1971, pp. 88-91.

39. Quirin von Leitner, *Die Waffensammlung des Österreichischen Kaiserhauses im K.K. Artillerie-Arsenal Museum in Wien*, Vienna, 1866-70, Pl. XLVII, Fig. I. The piece is now numbered A.1046 in the Waffensammlung of the Kunsthistorisches Museum, Vienna.

40. The earliest recorded written evidence for the use of the wheellock in Italy is contained in an ordinance issued by the Duke of Ferrara on the 14th November, 1522, forbidding the carrying of arms in the streets of Ferrara. Among the arms enumerated are "stone or dead-fire guns" [*scoppeti . . . da pietra o da fuoco morto*], which must have been snaphaunces or wheellocks, the latter being the most likely at so early a date. The ordinance refers to previous edicts about the carrying of this type of gun, but I am informed by the Director of the Archivio di Stato of Ferrara that he is unable to trace copies of these. The only other earlier ordinance of this type, dated 31st July, 1513, merely mentions guns [*schioppeti*] without qualification. See A. Angelucci, *Documenti Inediti per la Storia delle Armi da Fuoco Italiane*, Vol. I, Part 1, Turin, 1869, pp. 304-09; *idem., Catalogo della Ameria Reale*, Turin, 1890, pp. 420-21; C. Bosson, "Contribution à l'étude des armes à silex," *Armes Anciennes*, Vol. 1, No. 2, Geneva, 1954, pp. 31-40.

41. See Sir James Mann, "Notes on the Armour of the Maximilian Period and the Italian Wars," *Archaeologia*, Vol. LXXIX (1929), Pl. LXIX, a. See also L.G. Boccia and E.T. Coelho, *L'Arte dell'Armatura in Italia*, Milan, 1967, Nos. 151, 188-204, 216-22.

42. For example, on portions of an armour of c. 1540 in the Historisches Museum, Vienna. See *Das Wiener Bürgerliche Zeughaus*, Historisches Museum der Stadt, Wien, 1960, p. 41, No. 56.

43. de Lucia, *Op. cit.*, pp. 125-7. See also M. Morin, "L'opera di Renaldo di Visin da Asolo," *Diana Armi*, Anno V, No. 6, Florence, Nov./Dec. 1971, pp. 20-23.

44. de Lucia, *op. cit.*, p. 127, where it is suggested that one of the axes can be identified with the "semozza con schioppo in el manego" mentioned in the 1548 inventory of the Doge's armoury. See also M. Morin, "La 'Semozza con schioppo in el manego'," *Diana Armi*, Anno IV, No. 4, Florence, July/Aug. 1970, pp. 88-91. Cf. fn. 38.

45. C. Bosson, "Quelques Armes du Musée d'Art et d'Histoire de Genève," *Armes Anciennes*, No. 1 (Geneva, 1953), p. 20, No. 36. I am indebted to M. Bosson for additional information about this pistol.

46. These are: An all-steel pistol from the collection of Graf Festeticz, now in the Germanisches Museum, Nuremberg; two pistols found in a bog at Komorn (Komarno) on the Hungarian-Czechoslovak border, formerly in the Wilczek and Thill collections respectively; two detached locks "found in Hungary," one in the Hungarian National Museum, Budapest, and the other in the Waffensammlung, Vienna, (No. A2221); and four of the Danube locks in Kalmar, *op. cit.*, Pl. XXVIII. See also J. Kalmar, "A Kerék-lakatos Puskàrol," *Annuales Musei Miskolciensis de Herman Otto Nominati*. Vol. III, Miskolk, 1963,

pp. 63-8. The locks of the first three examples are illustrated and described with others of the same type in Thierbach, *op. cit.*, pp. 37-39, Figs. 80-84. The pistol at Nuremberg is illustrated in A. Essenwein, *Quellen zur Geschichte der Feurwaffen*, Leipzig, 1872 and 1877, Vol. II, Plate XVI-a.

Thierbach gave a further account of these locks in an article, "Die ältesten Radschlösser deutscher Sammlungen," published in *Z.H.W.K.*, Vol. II (1900-02), pp. 138-42. To the examples he mentions there and those at Venice and Geneva can be added the following: (1) A pistol exactly like that at Nuremberg in the F.E. Bivens Collection, U.S.A. See F. Theodore Dexter, *Half Century Scrapbook of Vari-Type Fire-arms*, Santa Monica, Cal., 1960, Plate 9, No. 292. I am indebted to Mr. W. Reid for the information that this pistol is also illustrated in the same author's *Forty-two Years Scrapbook of Rare Ancient Fire-arms*, Los Angeles, 1954, p. 239. (2) A combined axe and pistol in the same collection, Dexter, *Half Century Scrapbook*, Plate 19, No. 707. (3) A combined war hammer and pistol, parcelgilt, at the Castle of Konopiste, Czechoslovakia. (4) A combined wheel- and snap match-lock fitted to a mid-17th century Italian gun in the same collection. (5) Several muskets in the Zeughaus, Graz, at least one of which is dated 1558 on the barrel. See Pischlee, *op. cit.*, Part II, Plate XXXVII, Fig. 1, and Alm, *op. cit.*, p. 34, Fig. 17. (6) A gun in the Artillery Museum, Turin (No. 2716-M.5). Gaibi, *op. cit.*, pp. 104-5. This appears to be a very late version of the lock. (7) A double-barrelled pistol, resembling that at Geneva, in the Royal Armoury, Turin.

47. See S. Gigante, *Italia e Italiani nella storia d'Ungheria*, Trieste, 1933; C. Budinis, *Gli Artisti Italiani in Ungheria*, Libreria dello Stato, Italy, 1936; A. Mihalik, "L'Origine dello Smalto Filogranato," *Corvina*, Vol. XXI-XXIV (1931-32), R. Accademia Ungherese di Roma, Rome-Budapest, 1933.

A parallel case to that of the locks is provided by the swords carried in the 15th century by the *Schiavoni* (Slavs), the Dalmatian troops in the service of the Venetian Republic. These are of a distinctive type, with square pommel and horizontally recurved quillions, of which a few examples have been found in Hungary. The type may, in fact, be Hungarian in origin but the vast majority of surviving specimens, nearly three hundred in number, are preserved in the Doge's Palace at Venice, many with Italian "twig" marks on their blades. See de Lucia, *op. cit.*, Nos. G289-586; also J. Szendrei, *Ungarische Kriegsgeschichtliche Denkmäler*, Budapest, 1896, Nos. 156, 555, and 567, and J.V. Kalmàr, "Säbel und Schwert in Ungarn," *Z.H.W.K.*, Vol. 14 (1935-6), pp. 150-55.

48. The term appears to be the German form of the Polish *cieszynka*, which is derived from the Polish name for Teschen in Silesia—*Cieszyn*—where many, perhaps even all of these rifles were made. See Z. Stefanska, "Tschinke—Cieszynka," *Muzealnictwo Wojskowe, Vol. I*, Warsaw, 1959, pp. 257-61; Kalmàr, *op. cit.*, in note 19, above; Viktor Karger, "Neue Teschiner Beiträge zur Herkunftsfrage der Teschinken," *Waffen und Kostümkunde*, Vol. VI, Munich & Berlin, 1964, pp. 29-46.

49. This connection has already been noted by Thierbach and, more recently, by Gaibi, *Loc. cit.*

50. See W. Keith Neal, *Spanish Guns and Pistols*, London, 1955, Figs. 15 and 16. J. Florit y Arizcun,

Catalogo de las Armas del Instituto de Valencia de Don Juan, Madrid, 1927, No. 164: J.D. Lavin, *A History of Spanish Firearms*, London, 1965, pp. 66-7.

These later locks were also probably made in Italy. One of several detached specimens in the Artillery Museum, Turin, for example, is combined with a snap-lock that has every appearance of being Italian (Gaibi, *op. cit.*, Plates II-IV bis). In addition, a gun fitted with one of the locks in the Musée de l'Armée, Paris (M394), has a barrel signed by the Brescian maker Venturi Cani. Too much significance must not be attached to this last, however, in view of the extensive Brescian export trade in barrels. See M. Morin, "Alcune considerazioni sui sistemi arcaici di accensione meccanica," *Diana Armi*, Anno VI, No. 8, Florence, August 1972, pp. 18-23, where doubts are expressed both about the Italian origins of these locks and the early date that is usually ascribed to them.

51. T.T. Hoopes, "Das frühste datierbare Radschloss im National-museum in München," *Z.H.W.K.*, Vol. XIII (1932-34), pp. 224-5; E. Schalkhausser, "Die Handfeuerwaffen des Bayerischen Nationalmuseums," *Waffen un Kostümkunde*, Vol. XI, Munich and Berlin, 1967, pp. 1-2.

52. A. Hoff, "Hjullaase med seglformet hanefjer," *Vaabenhistoriske Aarbøger*, Vol. III, Copenhagen, 1940-42, pp. 68-89; Schalkhausser, *loc. cit.*

53. See Hoff, *Feuerwaffen*, Vol. I, pp. 60-62; R.J. Charles, *La collection Georges Pauilhac au Musée de l'Armée*, reprinted from *La Revue Francaise*, No. 182, Paris, Nov., 1965, pp. 6-7.

54. For example, a gun at Graz illustrated by Hoff in *Feuerwaffen*, Vol. I, p. 15, Abb. 13.

55. For a discussion of this form of lock see *ibid.*, pp. 58-60.

56. In the 1606 inventory of the *Pistolenkammer* in Dresden it is stated:: "Diese Büchse soll die Invention seyn von dem bekannten Erfinder des Pulvers, Berthold Schwarz, womit derselbe den Effect des Pulvers probiren wollte." (Thierbach, *Handfeuerwaffen*, p. 28). A. Erbstein in his guide to the Historisches Museum, Dresden (2nd edition, Dresden, 1892, p. 54) suggests that the gun can be identified with one described in 1567 "als ein alt Rohr mit einer Ruchbüchse oder Feuereisen."

57. Wendelin Boeheim's statement that the decoration is oriental in style is quite incorrect, as is his drawing of the gun (*Waffenkunde*, Leipzig, 1890, pp. 474-5).

58. It was already regarded as old in 1567. See note 56.

59. *Handfeuerwaffen*, p. 29.

60. Matchlocks with match-holders in the form of animals' heads are however illustrated in a number of early-16th-century German engravings. See A. Essenwein, *op cit*, fn 46, Plates B.VII, B.XIII and XIV.

61. Thierbach (*Handfeuerwaffen*, pp. 37-39, Figs. 80-84) describes and illustrates a number of 17th century locks using a spring-actuated rasp in place of a wheel. There seems to be no reason for thinking that these are connected with the Monk's Gun.

62. The gun, like many pieces at Dresden, is in almost mint condition and shows no obvious signs of use. It is possible, though, that some part of the pan is missing, for as it exists at the moment it would hold an amount of priming considerably in excess of that normally required. Furthermore, there is no arrangement to prevent a very serious blow-back through the aperture for the fire-steel.

A Wheellock Dagger for the Court of the Medici

by STEPHEN V. GRANCSAY

Dean of arms and armor scholars the world over, respected and held dear by all who know him, Stephen Grancsay enjoys global fame as researcher, cataloguer, teacher of three generations of writers and scholars many now famous in their own rights, and prolific author (over two hundred important articles in The American Rifleman, The Journal of the Walters Art Gallery, *the* Bulletin *of the Metropolitan Museum of Art and other organs, plus the well-known books* American Engraved Powder Horns *and* Master French Gunsmiths' Designs). *Born in 1897, Mr. Grancsay joined the Metropolitan Museum in 1914 (he was a student of Bashford Dean) to become first Assistant Curator, then Curator of Arms & Armor from 1930 to 1960. Energetic, ambitious, intellectually restless and insatiable, he is now busy on half a dozen new projects, the most important of which are his forthcoming* Biographies of Gunmakers *and* A Bibliography of Firearms. *He lives in Brooklyn, N.Y.—when he isn't girdling the globe in pursuit of source materials and study subjects.*

The aim of this article is to describe in detail a rare combined wheellock pistol and dagger, to make comparisons with a few related combined weapons, and to comment on its probable origin. First of all, it should be noted that this combined wheellock pistol and dagger is an unusual as well as a complicated weapon. The difference between it and the more usual wheellock-and-blade weapons is that its mechanism is contained in the interior of the hilt, not mounted on one side of the blade, this latter type being much more common. Furthermore, the mechanism of spanning and releasing the wheel differs from the normal wheellock.

The piece is described in a horizontal position ready to shoot. The principal elements of the weapon are (1) the hilt, (2) the wheellock mechanism, (3) the hollow blade that also serves as the barrel, and (4) the removable tip that also functions as an arrow and as a spanner for winding the wheel.

The entire weapon is of iron and steel. The pommel is chiseled in relief with cartouches enclosing reclining figures, caryatids and foliage. The weapon is mercury-gilded except part of the barrel-blade and, judging from the areas rubbed by use, the gilding is apparently original. The grip is etched with a shallow design of foliate motifs. The upper part of the blade is etched with foliage, birds, shells and masks on an irregular stippled background that was executed with the needle in the Italian manner.

The hilt comprises five elements, namely: (1) grip with quillons and extended ricasso area, (2) the pommel, (3) the enclosed wheel-lock mechanism, (4) the pivoted ring guard that holds the pyrites, and (5) a pivoted plate opposite the ring guard (explained below).

The grip is cylindrical and tapers towards the pommel. It was wrought from a shaped flat piece of iron, with a small prop brazed on the interior to support the proximal end of the spiral spring, and lap welded. The pommel has a cylindrical opening in the center extending for its entire length. Its lower end is threaded to screw into the grip. In addition, there are the quillons, each of which terminates in a horse's head. The pan cover is a narrow rectangular iron strip 3¾ in. (4.5 cm.) long, with a stop on the underside that prevents it from sliding too far in. The ring guard is pivoted on each side and hollowed in the center for inserting a piece of pyrites, which was held by a screw. When ready to use, the pyrites is placed in contact with the serrated wheel. To hold the pyrites securely against the turning wheel, a pivoted curved loop on the reverse of the hilt is pressured against the sides of the ring guard.

While the wheellock mechanism is different from the normal wheellock, the operative principle is the same. The axis of the normal wheellock is disposed transversely; the axis (shaft) of the wheel in the present piece is parallel to the barrel. The mechanism for spanning the wheel is unusual. The wheel axis, or iron shaft, roughly 7⅛ in. (18 cm.) over-all, passes through the grip. Its rounded spindle at the distal end fits into a bearing in the breechblock. At the proximal end, which protrudes from the pommel, the spindle is square to fit the spanner. The pommel may originally have had a removable apical button to give it a finished appearance. A spiral spring, 2¾ in. (7 cm.) long, fits over the central area of the shaft. The shaft is slightly thicker in the area adjacent to the proximal end of the spiral spring, and at the junction of the thick area and the spring is a transverse perforation, apparently for a pin to stabilize the shaft and thus prevent the spindle at the distal end from slipping out of the breechblock. At its distal end the spiral spring is fastened securely into a stop (arrêt) that is brazed on the shaft. As already noted, on the interior of the grip (right hand side) is a prop for holding the proximal hooked end of the spiral spring. When turned clockwise with the spanner, the shaft winds the wheel, and the proximal end of the spiral spring rests on the prop in the interior of the grip. Thus the spiral spring turns with the shaft, being expanded when it is wound.

Near the distal end of the shaft is brazed the priming pan, the upper end of which has a rectangular channel with access to the touch-hole which is on top of the breech end of the barrel. The trigger is pivoted on a wire that passes transversely through it and the wire ends are flattened on the exterior. On the interior, to the left of the trigger, is a spring with

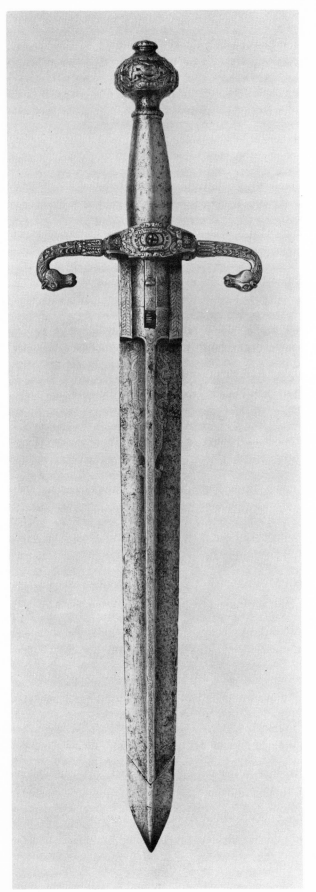

Fig. 1—Combined wheellock pistol and dagger, Italian, late XVI century, now in the Metropolitan Museum of Art, N.Y.

a screw for regulating trigger tension. The trigger has a pin (scear) on the end which fits into a notch on the shaft below the priming pan. The pressure of the scear locks the shaft securely when wound. When the trigger is pressed, tension is removed from the shaft and the proximal end of the spiral spring is released, compressing the spring. This compression supplies the energy to turn the shaft which simultaneously revolves the wheel against the friction of the pyrites which rests on the wheel to generate the sparks that ignite the priming powder. The ignited priming passes through the touch-hole. Apparently the priming charge was very fine as it was expected to burn quickly, for the priming pan, *being an integral part of the shaft,* turns with it. The expansion and contraction of the spiral spring takes the place of the cam and chain that bend the main hairpin spring in the normal wheellock mechanism.

The barrel-blade and the breech are wrought in one piece, including the opening that fits over the serrated wheel when assembled. The blade is hollow in the center along its entire length, bored to .39 caliber, and the proximal end is lap-welded for 2¾ in. (7 cm.). It is double-edged with flattened mid area extending full length on each side. The top of the breech end has a small grooved inclined area leading to the touch-hole. The breech has a female thread on each side for screwing the barrel-blade to the ricasso side extensions. In addition to the two screws, a peg extends from each ricasso extension and fits into a corresponding hole in the proximal end of the blade. This construction is intended to make a tight fit to prevent gas leakage. The area below the wheel is, when assembled, threaded on the interior to correspond with the ridges of the wheel. The arrow is held securely in the muzzle end by means of a projection cut in the side of the tang. The tang of the arrow is hollow and acts as the spanner. A wheellock pistol of the Emperor Charles V in the Royal Armory in Turin, made about 1530, retains its metal arrows, not unlike the arrow mentioned here.

There are extant several other combined weapons with concealed wheellock mechanisms that are related to our piece. Four extant cutlasses are combined with concealed wheellocks—two in the Waffensammlung in Vienna (A 2248, A 2249), one in the Musée de l'Armée in Paris (Pauilhac collection) and one in the Russell B. Aitken collection in New York City. All of these weapons are cutlasses, the upper part of the blade being hollow to form a pistol barrel. This specialized type of blade with integral hollow barrel forming the back edge is illustrated in the Petrini manuscript (Fig. 6). At the base of the grip is housed the concealed wheellock mechanism. These four combined weapons apparently have similar design and structural features. A combined mace, with concealed wheellock mechanism that corresponds with that of the four swords mentioned above, is in the Musée de l'Armée in Paris, and a similar mace is in the Metropolitan Museum of Art. All six of these combined weapons are considered to be of French origin, are associated with the court of Henry II, and are dated in the mid-sixteenth century. The Pauilhac combined cutlass as well as the combined mace in the Musée de l'Armée are both recorded in the inventory of the collection of Louis XIII of France (nos. 286 and 279). Here we may recall that many Italian artists were in the service of the French court and that the French royal family throughout much of the sixteenth century were associated by marriage with the Medici.

Axes were popular weapons when firearms were first used. There is a concealed wheellock pistol axe in the Bargello Museum, of which the grip and concealed wheellock mechanism are related to the combined weapons mentioned above. This weapon has a Medici origin since the Medici collection of arms and armor is housed in the Bargello, and it is richly damascened in gold. We shall presently see that Antonio Petrini in his *Arte Fabrile* speaks of the skill in damascening of the Brescian gunmaker Giovanni Antonio Gavacciolo who was in the service of Antonio de Medici. Another combined wheellock pistol axe, damascened in gold and silver, is in the Historical Museum in Dresden. The Dresden weapon is of particular interest, since its release mechanism has a spiral spring. (I am arbitrarily referring to a spiral spring as an elongated twisted wire, a coil spring as a roll of wire.)

All the pieces referred to above are widely scattered and only the Dresden combined wheellock pistol axe has been published in detail. These weapons are recorded here because they have rare features, namely a concealed wheellock mechanism and a hollow barrel that is integral with the blade. It is suspected, however, that a coil spring, rather than a spiral spring, is housed in their restricted mechanism area. With this in mind, we should also mention here some other firearms that may be related to our subject. In the Palazzo Ducale, Venice, is an unusual three-shot wheellock gun with coil springs on the interior of the lockplates, dating about 1580, and signed by the inventor Giorgio Bergamini. Letters patent were granted in 1635 to the Grenoble watch- and gunmaker Pierre Bergier, who made specialized superimposed-load waterproof guns and pistols with completely enclosed wheels and coil springs, a construction that saved space. Also with enclosed locks and coil springs are a pair of pistols bearing the Medici arms and signed "Fait a Mouges par la Fontaine, 1642," in the Army Museum in Prague.

It is safe to conclude that the Metropolitan Museum's combined piece is an experimental model since in its combined details it is unique. The spiral spring was hitherto known only in two extant wheellock

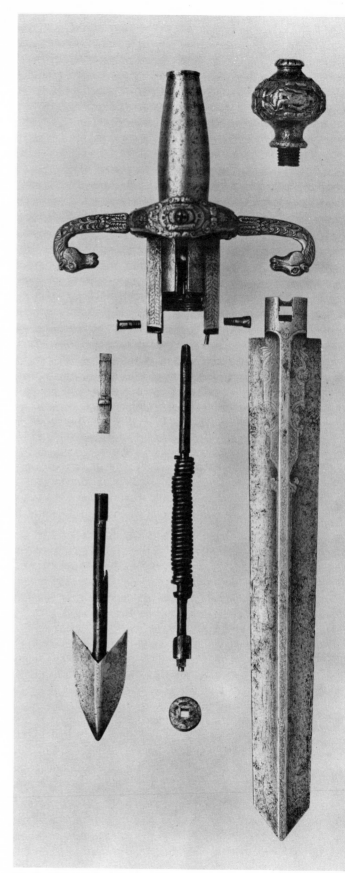

Fig. 2—Dismantled piece showing: pommel, hilt with extended ricasso with pins and screws for securing blade; pan cover; shaft with priming pan and spiral spring; wheel; hollow blade and combined arrow and spanner.

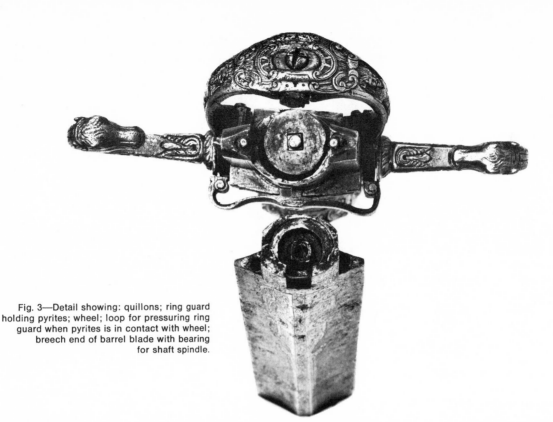

Fig. 3—Detail showing: quillons; ring guard holding pyrites; wheel; loop for pressuring ring guard when pyrites is in contact with wheel; breech end of barrel blade with bearing for shaft spindle.

firearms, namely a carbine in the Royal Armory in Madrid (K 63) and a combined axe wheellock pistol in the Historical Museum in Dresden, both dating from the mid-sixteenth century. Our illustration (Fig. 7) shows that Leonardo da Vinci's drawing of a wheellock mechanism could have served either as a tinder lighter or as a firearm mechanism. Leonardo's wheellock used both types of springs; the hairpin spring to press the pyrites holder against the wheel and also to hold the sear in the wheel depression before trigger release; the spiral spring, which is combined with the chain construction, served as the mainspring. This drawing cannot be dated precisely, but we know that Ludovico Sforza, the Duke of Milan, seriously considered Leonardo's recommendation of himself as an expert designer of military devices, and it has been noted that some of Leonardo's drawings of military equipment were made for the duke's armorer, Gentile dei Borri, about 1483-1485. Count Galeazzo Arconati purchased the major part of the Leonardo manuscripts which he bequeathed to the Ambrosian Library at Milan in December, 1636, and it is known that extensive copies of the manuscripts were made. The spiral mainspring in firearms was revived by the Florentine gunmaker Antonio Petrini, and it is probable that he had access to the Leonardo wheellock drawings.

Before the Industrial Revolution, all crafts had their secret methods, the so-called "mysteries" not to be divulged. So long as the crafts continued as closed corporations the mysteries had not been disclosed. Antonio Petrini, who worked for the Medici court, failed to adhere to this tradition, for in a manuscript entitled *Arte Fabrile** he proceeds to explain with text and drawings the practical weapons conceived and manufactured by himself in conjunction with various other inventor-smiths, such as locksmiths, bowmakers, archers, clockmakers, cutlers and others. The use of spiral springs, instead of the normal flat mainspring, apparently reflects the influence of clockmakers and locksmiths· It was normal procedure for locksmiths and clockmakers to work also as gunmakers. It was therefore natural that spiral and coil springs should pass into gunsmithing. Pocket watches which used steel springs in the driving mechanism appeared towards the end of the fifteenth century, so similar progress was apparently made with time pieces and firearms. In the Munich archives Peter Pech is mentioned as *Uhrmacher,* clockmaker. Pech made and signed with his mark the wheellock pistol of the Emperor Charles V that is in the Metropolitan Museum of Art. It may be of interest to note that Charles' collection of clocks was famous in his day.

Antonio Petrini, whose writing is a generous mixture of fact and fiction, described some of the outstanding objects in the grand-ducal armory. He gave a silly account of the armor of Guidobaldo II della Rovere-Montefeltro, Duke of Urbino (1514-74), parts of which are today in the Bargello Museum in Florence, in the Hermitage Museum in Leningrad, in the Wallace Collection in London and in New York's

*See "Literature" at the end of this article.

52

Fig. 4—The etched motif on barrel blade has the irregular dotted ground which was made with a needle on acid-proof varnish in the Italian manner.

Metropolitan Museum of Art, saying that it originally belonged to Hannibal the Carthaginian! We can excuse this lapse from accuracy, for Petrini names several armorers and gunmakers who were famous in their day, and whose work survives today. He describes Lazarino Cominazzo as one of the greatest masters who ever lived. He mentions a pupil of Battistino Paratici whose new ideas and inventions of wheellocks and works of bas relief and damascening iron "will never be surpassed." His name is Giovanni

Antonio Gavacciolo. There is in the Metropolitan Museum of Art (47.110.12) a pair of wheellock pistols, the barrels of which are inscribed Lazarino Cominazzo and the inside of the locks bear the mark of Gavacciolo. Petrini attributes the invention of the segment lock to Raffaele Verdiani (c. 1580-1630). A signed example of his lock is on a gun in the Tower of London Armouries and is signed and dated inside RAF. VERD. F. 1619. The segment lock, like the wheellock mechanism of our piece, was apparently experimental, since it is a unique example of its period. Other artists mentioned by Petrini are Cinatti of Florence and Frassinelli, who lead all the rest in the making of fine dagger blades. Petrini was obviously referring to the combined hollow blade-barrels that he illustrates, a type that forms part of the combined weapon that is the subject of this article.

By the time Petrini wrote his treatise in 1642, the old Medici line was nearly spent, and so was the great era of Tuscan creativity. The sciences were young and only just beginning to flower, and this made them more attractive than the arts. The second part of Petrini's manuscript deals with inventions, particu-

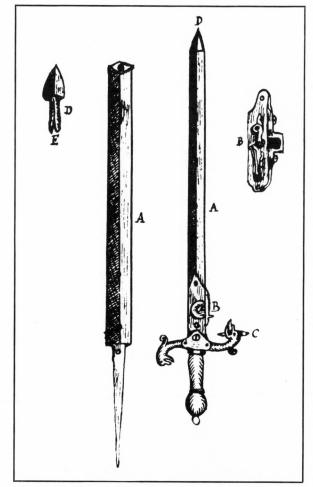

Fig. 5—Drawings from Petrini manuscript showing combined wheellock pistol dagger; pivoted cock holding pyrites; blade barrel hollow along its center; removable arrow tip of blade.

larly of combined weapons. One of his descriptions with drawings reads in translation: "How to make a weapon that serves both as dagger and as pistol." While the Petrini combined pistol dagger represents the more common type of combined firearm-and-blade weapon, and while the spiral springs illustrated by Petrini are for spring-driven pistons in air guns, it is clear that the materials for making our type of combined weapon were available to him. Another of Petrini's descriptions with drawings read in translation: "Method of making an arquebuse that shoots without powder." The spiral springs illustrated by Petrini are for spring-driven air guns, one of which, he tells us, was made for King Charles I of England. Petrini even made a grinder for grinding grain concealed in the hilt of a sword (some readers will recall that 220 years later several examples of Sharps' carbine were furnished with coffee mills in the butt!).

In 1632 the Medici Armory of Don Antonio de

artistic works of great merit. The Medici family were Petrini's patrons, and the Petrini manuscript is dedicated to Don Lorenzo de Medici. We have already mentioned that a combined axe with concealed wheellock mechanism, that forms part of the Medici heritage, is still in the Bargello Museum (M.1224). Furthermore, the provenance of our piece favors a Florentine origin. It was one of thirty daggers acquired by the Duc de Dino (whose collection is in the Metropolitan Museum of Art) from Constantin Ressman (1832-1899), formerly Italian Ambassador in Paris. Ressman's remarkable collection of selective historical arms and armor was willed to the Bargello Museum. It is easy to believe that Ressman, who knew of the early sale in Florence of the Medici Armory, would have had a special interest in locating pieces which, because of their construction and fine quality and workmanship, apparently had a Medici provenance.

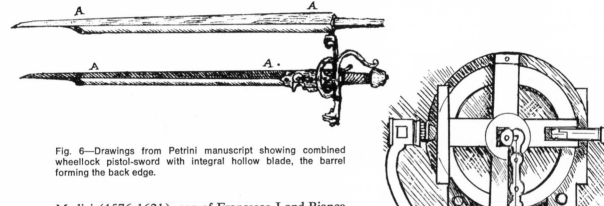

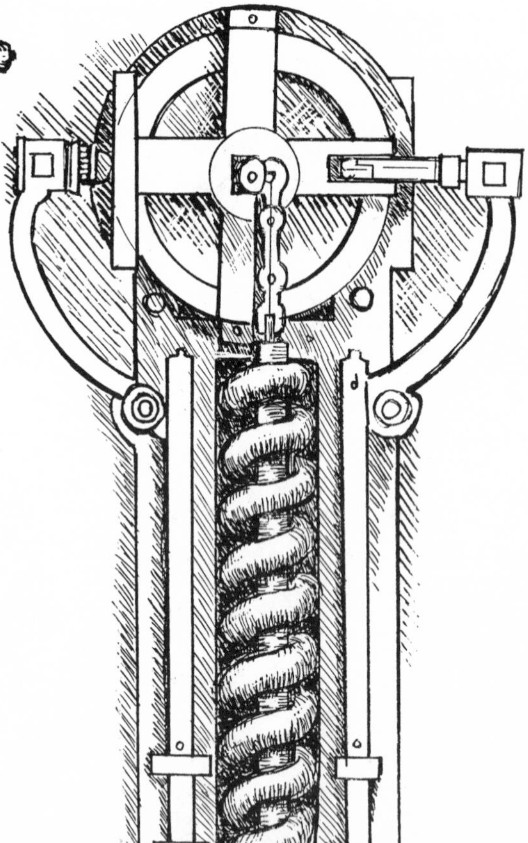

Fig. 6—Drawings from Petrini manuscript showing combined wheellock pistol-sword with integral hollow blade, the barrel forming the back edge.

Medici (1576-1621), son of Francesco I and Bianca Capello, was increased following the death of Francesco Maria II della Rovere, last Duke of Urbino. All of his possessions were inherited by his niece Vittoria, wife of the Grand Duke Ferdinand II de Medici. In the following years, the Armory, which comprised almost ten thousand items, was moved from the Pitti Palace to the workshop of Giuseppe Petrini, uncle of Antonio. By the Treaty of Vienna in 1735 the Medici estates and possessions were annexed to those of the House of Austria. The Medici art treasures were bequeathed to Florence in 1743 by the Archduchess Anna Maria Ludovica, the sister of the last Grand Duke, Gian Gastone. The Medici collection of arms and armor was sold at auction in 1776 as old iron. A very few pieces, esteemed to be of great importance, were preserved in Florence, and now form part of the Nation Museum.

There are several considerations that favor a Medici provenance for our combined weapon. The most favorable point is that there was a gunsmith shop in Florence that was devoted to experimental work in developing combined weapons, supervised by the said Giuseppe Petrini, uncle of Antonio. Antonio boasted that his uncle conceived and made many

Fig. 7—Design for wheellock mechanism by Leonardo da Vinci. Taken from Codex Atlanticus, folio 56 v.b. Ambrosiana, Milan.

LITERATURE

Blair, Claude. "Further Notes on the Origins of the Wheellock." *The Arms & Armor Annual,* Northfield, Ill., 1973.

Buttin, Charles. "Pistolets de Louis XIII par Pierre Bergier de Grenoble et P. Chabrioux de Montelimar." *Armes Anciennes,* Geneva, 1957, vol. II, no. 10, pp. 75-83, pl.

(Waterproof two-shot wheellock pistols with coil springs, made by Bergier in Grenoble, about 1635 for Louis XIII, in the Musée de l'Armée, Paris).

de Cosson, C.A. "Notizie su diversi pezzi d'armatura provenienti dall'antica armeria medicea esistenti nel Museo nazionale di Firenze." *L'Arte,* 1914, vol. 17, pp. 387-392, ill.

Gaibi, A. "Un manoscritto del '600: *L'Arte Fabrile,* di Antonio Petrini. Primo Libro. Arte Fabrile overo armeria vniversale dove si contengano, tutte, le qvalita, e natvra del ferro con varie impronte che si trovano in diversi arme cosi antiche come moderne et vari segreti et tempere fatto da me Antonio Petrini. 1642. Serenis'imo Prencipe Don Lorenso, Medici.
Armi Antiche, Torino, 1962, pp. 111-139, ill.

Libro Secondo dove si contengano diverse inventioni fatte in diversi fucile e canne. Novamenti messe in luce da me Antonio Petrini firmano. Con le regole e operatione di esse e sua dichiaratione. Fatte l'anno 1642 in firenze.
Armi Antiche, Torino, 1963, pp. 141-168, ill.

Gaibi, A., & Gay, P.
"Terzo Libro dove si contengano diverse regole e capitoli da Bombardieri et varij instrumenti non piu usati, con altri segreti e regole da carricare Archibusi nouamenti retrouati et inventati da me. Antonio Petrini Archibusiero et Armaiolo Firmano. Fatte nell anno 1642 in Firenze."
Armi Antiche, Torino, 1964, pp. 67-109, ill.

(The Petrini manuscript, which is dedicated to Don Lorenzo dei Medici, is in the Magliabechi Library in Florence. Similar Petrini manuscripts are in the Tower of London Armouries Library and in The Metropolitan Museum of Art. The script of the Manuscript in Florence is set in type in the above articles. Petrini had the precedent of two great Florentine-artists who left a record of their work and he was apparently emulating them—at a respectable distance. We have already referred to the Leonardo manuscripts and drawings that were apparently available to Petrini. Petrini was no doubt familiar with the activities of Benvenuto Cellini, who tells us that he made his own bird gun complete, lock, stock and barrel. We may also mention that Cellini had a keen appreciation of fine firearms, for he tells us that he coveted the fowling piece that was sent from Germany to Duke Alessandro dei Medici).

Grancsay, Stephen V. *Master French Gunsmiths' Designs of the XVII-XIX Centuries.* New York, Winchester Press. 1970. 208 pp. ill.
(The combined mace and wheellock pistol in the Metropolitan Museum of Art [04.3.39] and the combined sword and wheellock pistol in the Russell B. Aitken collection, which are referred to in this article, are illustrated on pages 148 and 149 respectively).

Hoopes, Thomas T. "Radschlösser nach Leonardo da Vinci?" *Zeitschrift für Historische Waffen- und Kostümkunde,* Berlin, 1934, new series vol. 4 (vol. 13), pp. 225-227, 2 pls.

Koetschau, Karl. "Studien aus dem Königl. Historischen Museum und der Königl. Gewehrgalerie zu Dresden. I. Ein Axthammer mit Schiessvorrichtung." In: *Beiträge zur Geschichte der Handfeuerwaffen. Festschrift zum achtzigsten Geburstag von Moritz Thierbach.* Dresden, 1905. pp. 117-123, 8 figs.
(Describes in detail a combined axe and concealed wheellock with spiral spring).

Notes on the Crossbow in Switzerland

by EUGEN HEER

Eugen Heer, born in 1941, is one of Switzerland's leading arms experts, best known for his book Geschichte und Entwicklung der Militärhandfeuerwaffen in der Schweiz von 1800 bis zur Gegenwart *(History and Development of Military Small Arms in Switzerland from 1800 to the Present), of which Volume I is dedicated to Pistols, 1850-1956. In 1970, after extensive experience in research, restoration and museum organization, Mr. Heer became Director of the* Schweizerisches Waffeninstitut *(Swiss Institute for Weaponry) at the Castle of Grandson, an international Center for the dissemination of information and assistance in all that pertains to arms and armor studies, restoration, exhibition, etc.*

Crossbows are often associated with Switzerland. The legend of William Tell—which is really of Scandinavian origin—has forever stamped the crossbow as the Swiss national weapon: in recent years a tiny crossbow has even become the official mark on Swiss export products! But this arm was by no means a Swiss invention; in fact, its development, many phases of which are still obscure, was little influenced by the Swiss. Nevertheless, it is true that crossbows enjoyed an unusual degree of popularity in our country up to the early 17th century. Towards the end of the 19th century, attempts were even made to re-introduce updated, specially-constructed crossbows in the Swiss army for "sharp-shooting" detachments! Needless to say, this project never got beyond the drawing-board. Crossbow shooting with sophisticated modern weapons is still practised today in the German-speaking part of Switzerland.

Some authorities consider that the idea of the crossbow may have originally come from using ordinary bow traps for hunting purposes. This supposition is quite convincing if we examine the hunting crossbows used in South-East Asia today. These large wooden bows are basically nothing but longbows to which very small and short tillers are affixed; used as traps for hunting and warfare, such weapons are very effective, as the Americans learned in Vietnam—the poisoned arrows are deadly. The earliest sources showing fully developed crossbows are Chinese tomb reliefs dating to the Han Dynasties (206

B.C. to A.D. 220). We know from contemporary detailed drawings of crossbow locks that these were already equipped with advanced release mechanisms of bronze and that no springs were used in them; one manuscript, the *Shih Chi,* written in about 100 B.C., reports the extensive use of crossbows in a certain battle of Ma-ling in 381 B.C. We also find a reference to crossbow man-traps, built to defend the tomb of the Emperor Ch'in Shih (died 210 B.C.).

The Romans were familiar with a type of heavy siege crossbow called *arcabalista.* A lighter hand-weapon was also used, to judge by the Greek historian Arrian, who at one time held a command in the Roman army. Pictorial evidence dating from between A.D. 300 and 400 can be seen in a Roman funerary sculpture at the Musée Crozetier, Puy, France (Fig. 1). But despite these and a few other sporadic documentations, reliable information remains scant throughout the first thousand years of the Christian era. A 10th-century copy of the Book of Ezekiel written by a certain monk Haimo, of Auxerre, France, contains several representations of fully developed medieval crossbows (Fig. 2). After the 10th century, information about crossbows becomes more frequent. Although the Bayeux Tapestry does not include cross-bowmen, the biographer William of Poitier mentioned them as being part of the Norman army at the battle of Hastings in 1066. Probably crossbows reached England (where in time they became rather popular) with the Normans. During the 12th century cross-bows seem to have been widely used throughout

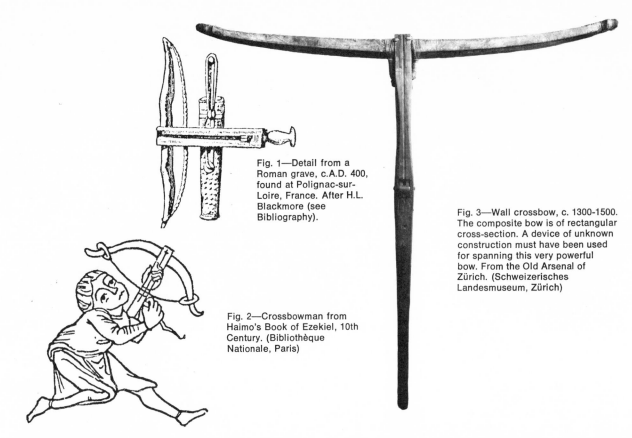

Fig. 1—Detail from a Roman grave, c.A.D. 400, found at Polignac-sur-Loire, France. After H.L. Blackmore (see Bibliography).

Fig. 2—Crossbowman from Haimo's Book of Ezekiel, 10th Century. (Bibliothèque Nationale, Paris)

Fig. 3—Wall crossbow, c. 1300-1500. The composite bow is of rectangular cross-section. A device of unknown construction must have been used for spanning this very powerful bow. From the Old Arsenal of Zürich. (Schweizerisches Landesmuseum, Zürich)

Europe. In fact, they came to be considered insidious because of their power and silence; they were feared more than longbows, a fact demonstrated by a decision of the Second Lateran Council under Pope Innocent II (1130-1143) to ban crossbows as hateful to God and unfit for use among Christians; this ban had, of course, no effect. During the 12th and 13th centuries, Genoese crossbowmen achieved a widespread reputation for their deadly skill. Richard I (1189-1199) was an expert marksman with his crossbow, and when he was killed by a crossbow quarrel during the siege of the castle of Chaluz in France in 1199, it was considered a judgement from Heaven for having had crossbowmen in his service.

It was most likely during this period that the inhabitants of the central part of what was to become Switzerland had their first contact with the crossbow. The explanation for its striking deeper roots in primitive Switzerland than in other parts of Europe is probably to be found in the fact that after the St. Gotthard Pass had become a main trade route toward the end of the 12th century, the peoples of what were to become the Cantons of Uri, Schwyz and Nidwalden were brought into steady contact with great numbers of merchants, pilgrims and soldiers traveling between Italy and the lands north of the Alps, and many adventuresome youths went to seek their fortunes as mercenaries in Italy and France; it was probably they who brought the art of the crossbow back home to their native soil. Political factors, too, favoured the entrenchment of crossbows. For example, the people

of Schwyz and their neighbours enjoyed many privileges under the reign of Frederic II, Holy Roman Emperor. When he was excommunicated in 1245 by Pope Innocent IV they rebelled against their new master, Duke Rudolph of Habsburg; the Pope promptly retaliated by excommunicating the rebels, who in turn sacked and plundered monasteries and occupied Church lands. Quite naturally, this unstable situation prompted swift development of local military affairs. But Rudolph of Habsburg chose not to attempt to punish his subjects; instead he guaranteed them a fair measure of independence, but also imposed heavy taxes because he needed money from the flourishing Gotthard-Pass trade for his ambitious projects. Moreover, he needed good soldiers. In his campaign against Count Othon of Burgundy in 1289, over 2000 men from Schwyz served in his army, many of them—though we do not know exactly how many—crossbowmen. Two years later, on July 15th, 1291, Rudolph died, and leaders of the peoples of Uri, Schwyz and Nidwalden signed a pact at the beginning of August to insure their independence and mutual help in case of danger (hence Swiss National Day is celebrated on August 1st). Being by then no longer peaceful shepherds but well-trained and organized fighting men, though unfortunately with no cavalry whatever, the weapon on which they naturally relied as a counterforce against mounted troops (which formed the main force in every medieval army) was the crossbow. Steel-tipped quarrels could penetrate armour, and at the same time crossbows were less

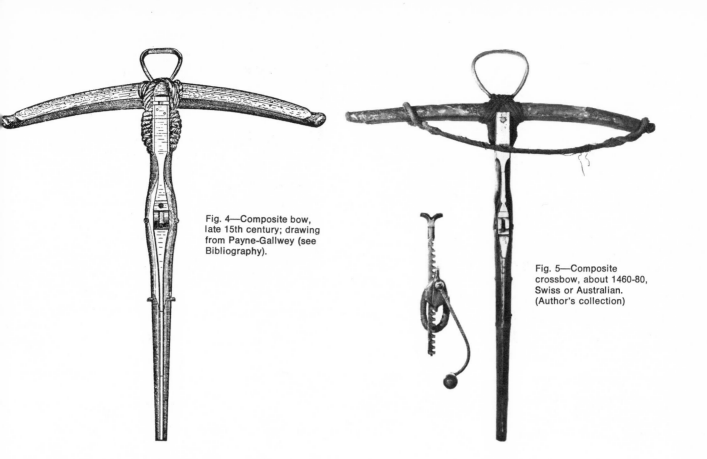

Fig. 4—Composite bow, late 15th century; drawing from Payne-Gallwey (see Bibliography).

Fig. 5—Composite crossbow, about 1460-80, Swiss or Australian. (Author's collection)

cumbersome than longbows. Crossbows were widely used as hunting weapons as well. They were locally made, like the halberds which were the main arm of Swiss troops, and indeed these two weapons led to the introduction of new tactics which earned the Swiss a pan-European reputation as a military power in the 15th century. By the end of that century about two-thirds of the soldiers were also equipped with still a third basic weapon, viz. the long pike which had already started to appear three generations earlier.

The Crossbow, like the halberd, was a personal arm and was kept at home. Every male citizen was pressed into the army at age sixteen and remained on the call-up list until age sixty. When he was called under the banner he carried with him enough food for several days, supplied by his family or neighbors. If he was not wealthy enough to acquire his personal weapon, one was lent to him by some richer citizen. Although we have little information about what constituted a man's complete equipment in the 13th and 14th centuries, we know that throughout most of the 15th a crossbowman was usually equipped with his crossbow, a short sword or so-called *Schweizer Degen* in a leather scabbard (in some cases an axe which could be used as a tool or arm), a quarrel quiver hung from his belt on the left and a spanning rack or *crannequin* on the right. Contemporary documents show him very often with a half armour and a sallet-type helmet. The present writer has not been able to establish any details about the bag or sack in which

Fig. 6—Crossbowman hooking his belt claw onto string prior to spanning by force of straightening back; from Payne-Gallwey (see Bibliography), after a manuscript of about 1370 in the Bibliothèque National, Paris.

59

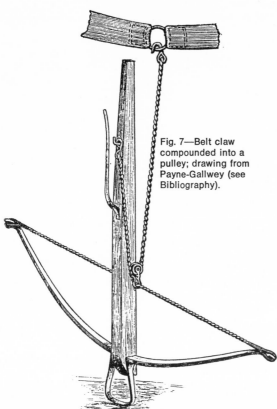

Fig. 7—Belt claw compounded into a pulley; drawing from Payne-Gallwey (see Bibliography).

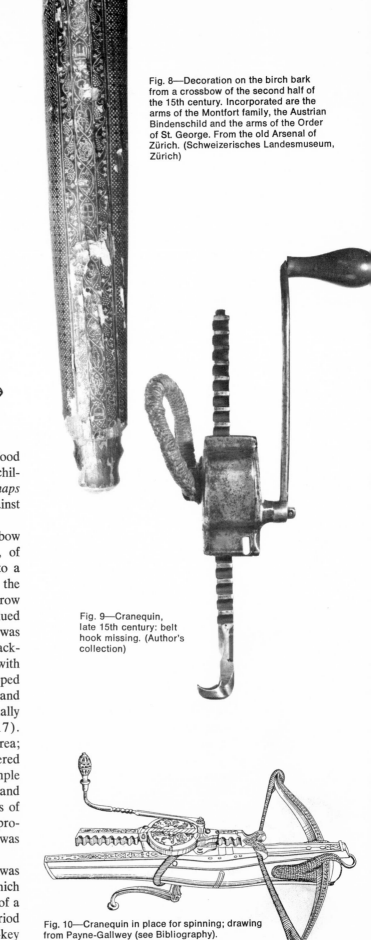

Fig. 8—Decoration on the birch bark from a crossbow of the second half of the 15th century. Incorporated are the arms of the Montfort family, the Austrian Bindenschild and the arms of the Order of St. George. From the old Arsenal of Zürich. (Schweizerisches Landesmuseum, Zürich)

Fig. 9—Cranequin, late 15th century: belt hook missing. (Author's collection)

Fig. 10—Cranequin in place for spinning; drawing from Payne-Gallwey (see Bibliography).

personal belonings like spare shoes, clothes, and food were carried. A contemporary author (Diebold Schilling of Bern) advised the carrying of *Schnaps* (brandy), of which "one nutshellful is better against thirst than a bucketful of water".

Up to the beginning of the 16th century, the bow was of the composite type: laminated, that is, of long horn plaques glued in upright position onto a base consisting of a strip of oak. The sides of the horn lames and the oak base were fluted with narrow grooves, which gave the total lamination, once glued and pressed, greater strength. The resulting piece was then surrounded or paralleled lengthwise by a packing of thick shredded ox or cow sinews mixed with glue; this new resulting piece was in turn wrapped in pigskin and, to protect the whole from rain and dampness, covered with birch bark which was usually decorated with attractive designs (Figs. 8 and 17). The tiller was made of woods varying with the area; oak and maple were common. Its top was veneered with bone, and the sides often worked in a simple inlay motif of horn. Bow and tiller were fixed and tightened together with hemp or flax cords; strips of leather braided around this joint seem to have protected the binding from wearing. The bowstring was made of sinew.

The release mechanism of the early crossbows was simple. There is no evidence that the system in which a pin pushes the cord out of a groove on the top of a tiller was used in Switzerland during the early period —on surviving pieces we always find the nut-and-key

Fig. 11—Crossbowman spanning his steel bow; mid-19th-century drawing of a figure in a Holbein painting dated 1519.

Fig. 14—Spanning device with belt hook, probably early 14th century. (Schweizerisches Landesmuseum, Zürich)

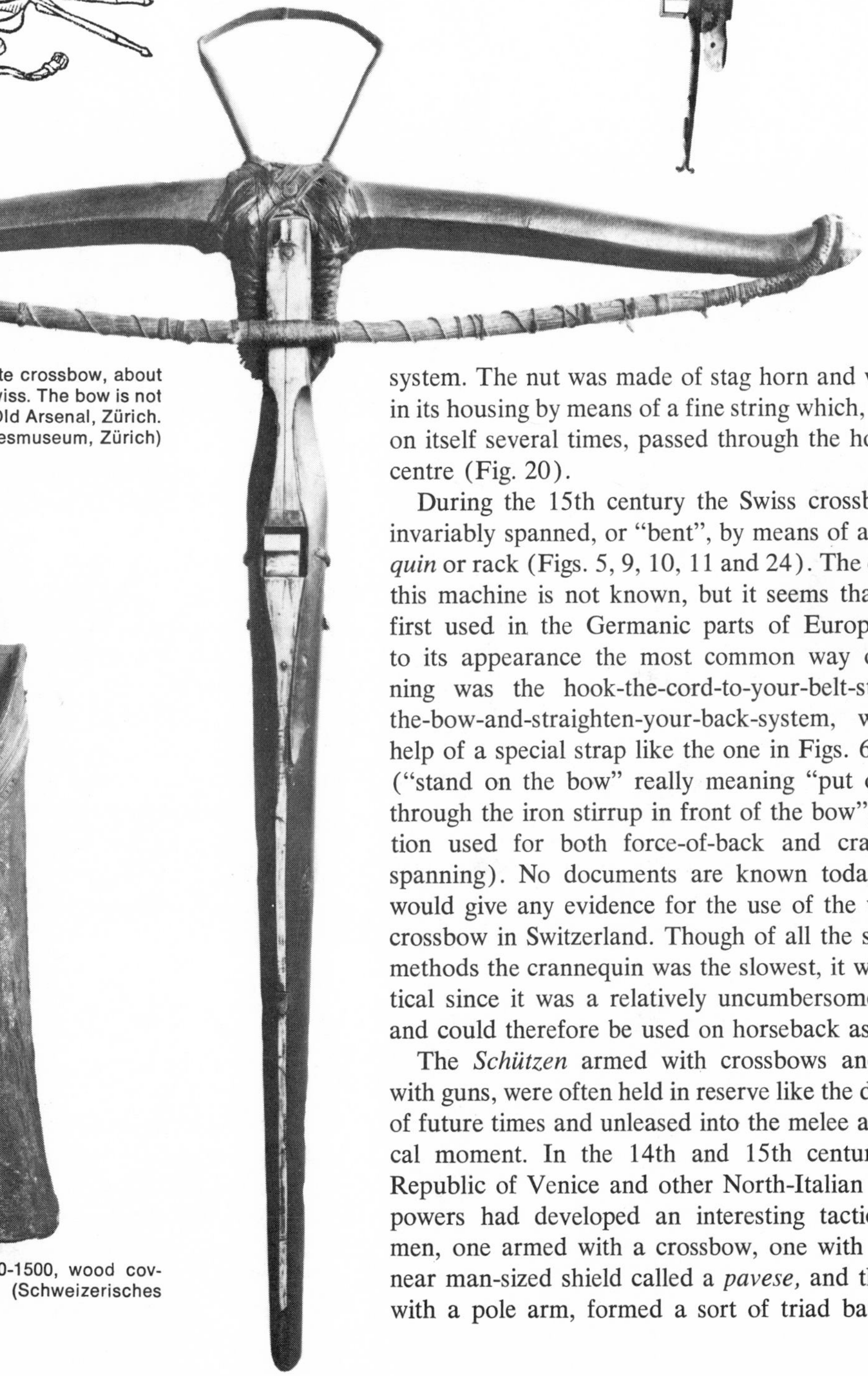

Fig. 12—Composite crossbow, about 1490-1500, probably Swiss. The bow is not decorated. From the Old Arsenal, Zürich. (Schweizerisches Landesmuseum, Zürich)

Fig. 13—Bolt quiver, 1450-1500, wood covered with badger skin. (Schweizerisches Landesmuseum, Zürich)

system. The nut was made of stag horn and was held in its housing by means of a fine string which, doubled on itself several times, passed through the hole in its centre (Fig. 20).

During the 15th century the Swiss crossbow was invariably spanned, or "bent", by means of a *crannequin* or rack (Figs. 5, 9, 10, 11 and 24). The origin of this machine is not known, but it seems that it was first used in the Germanic parts of Europe. Prior to its appearance the most common way of spanning was the hook-the-cord-to-your-belt-stand-onthe-bow-and-straighten-your-back-system, with the help of a special strap like the one in Figs. 6 and 14 ("stand on the bow" really meaning "put one foot through the iron stirrup in front of the bow", a position used for both force-of-back and crannequin spanning). No documents are known today which would give any evidence for the use of the windlass crossbow in Switzerland. Though of all the spanning methods the crannequin was the slowest, it was practical since it was a relatively uncumbersome device and could therefore be used on horseback as well.

The *Schützen* armed with crossbows and, later, with guns, were often held in reserve like the dragoons of future times and unleashed into the melee at a critical moment. In the 14th and 15th centuries, the Republic of Venice and other North-Italian military powers had developed an interesting tactic: three men, one armed with a crossbow, one with a large, near man-sized shield called a *pavese,* and the other with a pole arm, formed a sort of triad battle cell;

61

Fig. 15—Three quarrels (point of left one missing), 15th-16th centuries. (Castle Museum, Grandson, Switzerland)

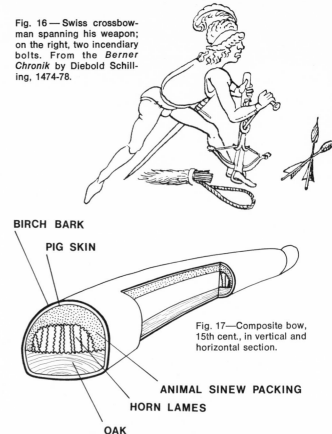

Fig. 16 — Swiss crossbowman spanning his weapon; on the right, two incendiary bolts. From the *Berner Chronik* by Diebold Schilling, 1474-78.

BIRCH BARK

PIG SKIN

Fig. 17—Composite bow, 15th cent., in vertical and horizontal section.

ANIMAL SINEW PACKING

HORN LAMES

OAK

while the crossbowman was spanning, one companion protected him with his shield and the other warded off attackers. Sometimes the crossbowman carried a small targe (shield) on his back which he turned towards the enemy while loading. But Swiss tactics were different: documentary evidence shows that the *Schützen* rushed forward to discharge their weapons at the enemy and, as soon as pressed by the opponent, returned in a quick movement back to both flanks of their own infantry. Targes would have been too cumbersome for this kind of swift surprise manoeuvre.

During the Burgundian Wars of 1474-1477, one-third of the Swiss troops consisted of pikemen, forming the famous square called a "hedgehog". At Grandson, on March 2nd, 1476, two hundred *Schützen* opened the battle with a hail of bolts and bullets but were forced back rapidly by the charging Burgundian cavalry. Instead of moving to the sides, they retreated to the feet of the pikemen and knelt down; under the protection of the fifteen-foot pikes the reloading and firing could not be prevented by the cavalry.

In spite of the crossbow's popularity in Switzerland, firearms are mentioned as early as the close of the 14th century. A hundred years later, half of the *Schützen* carried handguns. During *Freischiessen,* i.e., shooting competitions, which were regularly organized ever since the 14th century, separate ranges were built for crossbows and firearms. It was here that the differences between these two weapons were

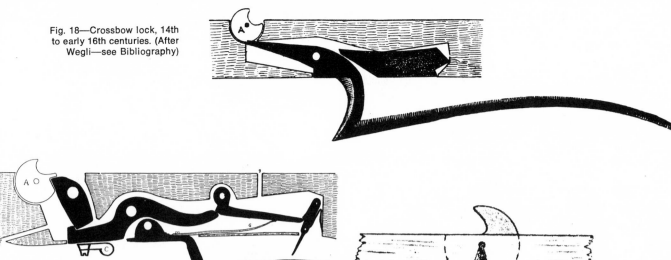

Fig. 19—Crossbow lock, middle 16th century, probably Swiss.

Fig. 20—Nut held by thin twine turnings; from Payne-Gallwey (see Bibliography).

brought sharply and objectively into evidence. The accuracy of the crossbow could not be matched by firearms until well into the 16th century, and as fire-arms were improved, so were crossbows. *Freischies-sen* were international events, with contenders arriving from Germany, Austria and many other parts of Europe. The winners of the first seven prizes at the crossbow competition in Zürich in 1504 were all Germans.

As to the power of crossbows, we know from many sources that no armour of the time could withstand the force of a steel-pointed crossbow quarrel at ranges as great as 150 yards, and indeed, modern trials have proved that the power of early 16th century military crossbows was far greater than his-torians had hitherto imagined.

Steel bows, as already mentioned, were introduced fairly late in Switzerland. The chronicler Edilbach records that the Swiss competitors on the *Freischies-sen* of Zürich in 1504 used composite crossbows, perhaps prefered because they could be manufac-tured locally whereas metal bows almost certainly had to be imported. Moreover, not only was it diffi-cult to forge steel bows, but these had a tendency to break in very cold weather (the Burgundian army in the wars of 1474-77 used a great number of steel bows, but needed to bring along a considerable sup-ply of spares). Emperor Maximilian I, an expert marksman with the crossbow, preferred composite bows in the 1510's for chamois hunting. The earliest known document relating to steel bows for military

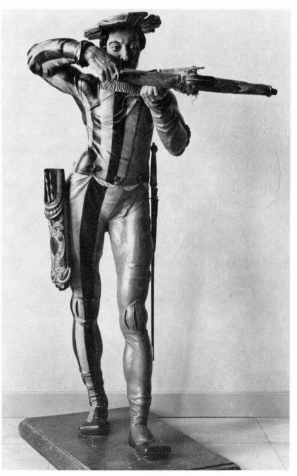

Fig. 21—Life-size wooden figure of William Tell, early 16th cent.; crossbow later. (Historisches Museum, Bern)

63

Fig. 23—A *Freischiessen*, i.e. shooting match, held in Zürich in 1504. Not hour glass for limiting shooting time. From the *Züricher Chronik* by Gerold Edlibach, 1506.

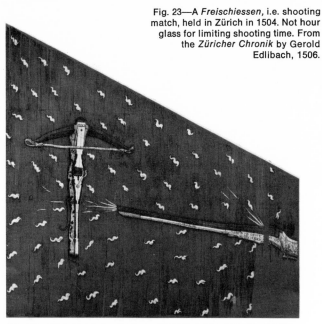

Fig. 22—Banner of the Bernese *Schützen* (marksmen) of 1531, showing steel-bowed crossbow with a bolt holder and a matchlock arquebus. (Historisches Museum, Bern)

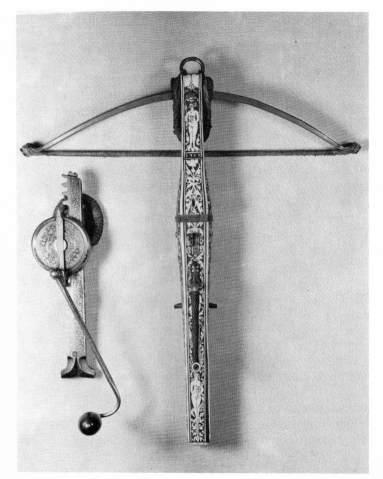

Fig. 24—Sporting crossbow, dated 1565, probably Swiss. (Historisches Museum, Basel)

purposes is dated 1426: an entry of payment for a number of steel bows for crossbows in the Burgundian military accounts—in fact, the Burgundians seem to have played a rather important role in the development of the steel bow, and to have introduced the Swiss to it in the course of the 1474-77 war. In time, the Swiss adopted it; a general change-over from composite to steel bow must have taken place over the span from about 1500 to 1525. The banner of the *Schützen* of Bern of 1531 shows unmistakably the short-tillered, steel-bowed crossbow typical for the rest of the 16th century (Fig. 22). The trigger mechanism had been improved during the same period. In the absence of documentary evidence which would attribute these improvements to a particular individual or even nation, it seems likely that they were inventions of necessity, come upon by many and promulgated, refined and diffused at the international shooting competitions. Development must have progressed apace and along very similar lines in Germany, Switzerland and Austria, much as was the case with firearms during the first half of the 19th century.

Reliable information about the trade of Swiss crossbow makers in the 15th and 16th centuries is very scant; we must judge many accepted "facts" carefully. Generally speaking, the crossbow maker was an important man; every town had one or several at its service, and some working contracts have survived. Until the middle of the 1500's, when crossbows ceased to be military equipment, not only were these craftsmen exempted from watch duty on the town

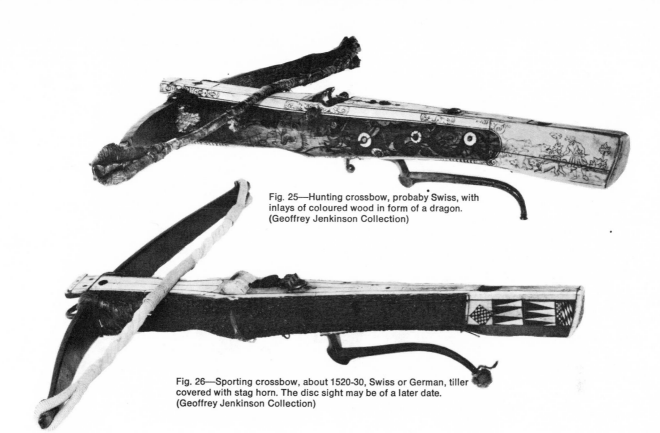

Fig. 25—Hunting crossbow, probaby Swiss, with inlays of coloured wood in form of a dragon. (Geoffrey Jenkinson Collection)

Fig. 26—Sporting crossbow, about 1520-30, Swiss or German, tiller covered with stag horn. The disc sight may be of a later date. (Geoffrey Jenkinson Collection)

walls but also from paying taxes, and, if foreigners, citizenship was bestowed on them as a gratuity—but in exchange, whenever the troops were called under the banner they had to join them, for theirs was the responsibility of the maintenance of the crossbows. Later on, crossbows seem to have been made in gunmakers shops as well: for example, a boy's crossbow in the Schweizerisches Landesmuseum in Zürich bearing the initials *I W* on the tiller can be attributed to the gunmaker Ioachim Waltert of Luzern. Swiss crossbows were usually less decorated than those made in Germany, but there are exceptions; it is difficult and sometimes impossible to distinguish a German from a Swiss specimen of the 1500-50 era. Despite identifiable coats of arms found on many crossbows, the maker is not necessarily of the same nationality as the owner. Of all the marks that can be found on steel bows, not a single one can be attributed to a maker—steel bows were traded all over Europe like gun barrels or sword blades and hence are often as much and as confusingly marked. Finding a fully signed Swiss crossbow is still one of the present writer's unfulfilled ambitions. In the second half of the 16th century, decoration closely followed the fashions in firearms design, so that attributions to individual schools or makers on a stylistic basis is sometimes possible. But we are only at the beginnings of such studies—only the systematic comparison of all known crossbows will in due time lead to valid conclusions.

BIBLIOGRAPHY

Commissariat Central de Guerre: *Histoire Militaire de la Suisse,* Bern, 1915.

Howard L. Blackmore: *Hunting Weapons,* Barrie & Jenkins, London, 1971.

Charles Brusten: *L'Armée Bourguignonne de 1465 à 1468,* Editions Fr. van Muysewinkel, Bruxelles, 1953.

Vladimir Denkstein: *Pavezy,* in "Sbornik Nàrodniho Muzea V Praze," Prague, 1962-64.

Sir Ralph Payne-Gallwey, Bt.: *The Crossbow,* first published in 1903, reprinted by The Holland Press, London, 1958.

Dr. Rudolph Wegeli: *Inventar der Waffensammlung des Bernischen Historischen Museums in Bern, Vol. IV, Fernwaffen,* Bern, 1948.

Othmar Gurtner: *Schweizer Schützenbuch,* Zurich, 1943.

Walter Schaufelberger: *Der Wettkampf in der Alten Eidgenossenschaft,* Bern, 1972, Verlag Paul Haupt.

Emanuel v. Rodt: *Geschichte des Bernischen Kriegswesens,* Bern, 1831.

Dr. Johannes Häne: *Militärisches aus dem alten Zürichkrieg,* Zürich, 1928.

Hugo Schneider: *Altschweizerische Waffenproduktion,* in "Neujahrsblatt der Feuerwerker-Gesellschaft," Zürich, 1964.

Stone Bows in the Old and New Worlds

by HELMUT NICKEL

Dr. Nickel, born in Dresden, Germany, in 1924, is Curator of Arms & Armor of the Metropolitan Museum of Art, New York. After having earned his doctorate in art history and ethnology in Berlin, he assumed assistant directorships of several German public arms, costume and ethnological collections, and accepted the nomination to his present post in 1960. His arms and armor studies cover all aspects and phases of weaponry, well into the percussion period in firearms, and know no geographic confines— but his first loves are medieval armor and heraldry. He is the author of many internationally respected and often-cited articles.

The two basic missile types developed from the hurled stone and the thrown stick are the bullet and the dart, each of them best suited for a specific way of propulsion. If propelled by a mechanical device it was most efficient for the *bullet or ball* to be thrown by a lever, such as the sling or the trebucket, which released the projectile from a fully or partly rotary motion, and for the *dart or arrow* to be launched by a force directed straight forward, such as is the case with bow or a catapult. This difference is caused by the unlike ways these missiles are supposed to strike: the dart is effective only if it hits point forward to penetrate, but with the bullet the particular point of impact on its surface striking the target is immaterial.

There is, however, a deep-rooted tendency in man to experiment with different uses for a given object or with different objects for a given purpose, in order to find new and better ways to achieve perfection. Frequently—as is the case with most combination weapons—the result is considerably less than a success, but sometimes an unlikely method fares remarkably well. One of these unlikely but workable ideas is the substitution of the missile component of the classic bow-and-arrow combination (i.e., the arrow) by a ball-type missile or pellet. At the first glance it seems an impossible feat to fit a pellet to a bow and propel it forward without hitting the bowstave or the holding hand. By means of several modifications of the basic design of the bow, however, this adaption was in fact achieved quite successfully.

The first and obvious change was to create a pouch or cradle on the bowstring in which the pellet could be safely fitted. For this the bowstring had to be doubled and equipped with a pair of braces or spacers (little wood or ivory rods) that would hold the two strings apart at the necessary width. The pouch itself could be made of any suitable material: leather, fabric or woven cord, solid or openwork; in some cases there were small bucket-shaped containers of wood or ivory instead of pouches, which would be wedged between the strands of the double string, making the braces superfluous.

The other important element was to find a device to let the pellet fly clear of the bowstave. This could be achieved most simply by turning the horns of the bow slightly outward to the right, and pulling the string with a slight slant to the left. When the pellet was released, it passed to the right of the bowstaff. The effectiveness of this method was greatly increased by fixing the double string in such a way that it had a permanent twist to the right, and still more by shaping the bow in such a way that its ends were listing to the right. Finally, the bow could be constructed asymmetrically, with the upper arm considerably more flexed than the lower one; the greater flexibility of the upper arm gave the pellet an upward jerk, which helped it to stay clear of the endangered thumb. Because of the necessary twist in spanning the bow, it was all-important that the hand should get a good grip on the bowstave—therefore all of the bows of this type have a specially reinforced handgrip, either carved in one piece with the bow or attached separately.

The alternative method was to construct a "window" within the bow so that the pellet might be driven straight forward, right through the bow itself. This type of pellet-bow was presumably easier to handle, but presented considerable difficulties in construction. If it was to be made of two parallel bowstaves to form the "window," the flexibility of the two staves had to be carefully coordinated; if it was to be fashioned with a single staff, the only material strong enough to hold the "window" was steel, a commodity obtainable only in an advanced technology.

The pellet-bow was a special-purpose weapon used for hunting, particularly birds with precious feathers. Here the round pellet that only struck a crushing blow without penetrating the skin was much better suited than the pointed, piercing arrow, which would have spilled blood and spoiled the plumage. (An alternative would be the use of arrows with a blunt, clublike head, which was, in fact, the solution preferred in a large part of the world). Interestingly enough, the areas of distribution of pellet-bows are also areas where feathers played an important role in costume and decor. Such is the case in the southern half of Brazil and in the adjacent areas of Bolivia, Argentina, Paraguay, and Uraguay. From South America, incidentally, comes the only reference that pellet bows were used in warfare: the German gentleman-explorer, Maximilian Prinz zu Wied-Neuwied, writing from South America in 1815-1817, reports that the

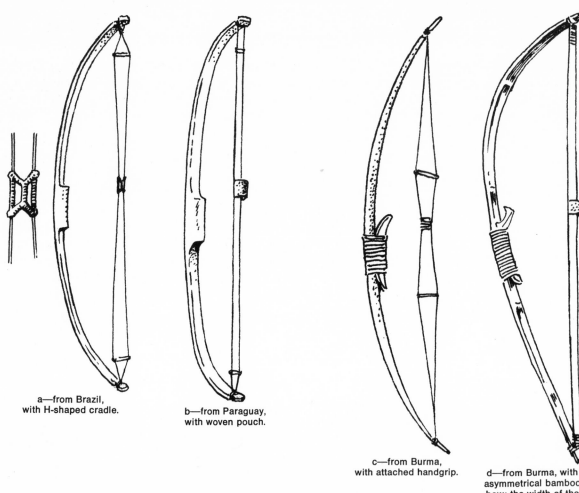

a—from Brazil, with H-shaped cradle.

b—from Paraguay, with woven pouch.

c—from Burma, with attached handgrip.

d—from Burma, with asymmetrical bamboo bow; the width of the bamboo staff serves as a spacer for the double string.

Fig. 1—Pellet-bows of differing constructions (after Antze).

Indios at the Rio Doce used their pellet-bows to keep the neighboring warlike Botocudes off their territory. He and other travellers never failed to be impressed by the deadly accuracy of the archers, who could hit a hummingbird in flight and who "always bring back as many birds of considerable sizes as they took clay pellet with them when they went forth on a hunting trip." The South American pellet-bows are the most primitive in construction, the bow being fashioned with the reinforced handgrip carved from a single piece of wood. The double strings of fiber are spaced apart by short sticks, and the pouch can be just a small square of leather or woven fibers, though Brazilian tribes used a sort of net shaped like a letter **H** set between the two strings (Figs. 1a and b). The Abipones of Patagonia in the early nineteenth century (1822) were observed using a pellet-bow of particularly primitive stamp, with a "string" made of a three-inch-wide strip of tough bark. Because of the air resistance against this ribbon, most other tribes chose the more sophisticated double-string with pouch.

The pellet-bow was to be found until recent times in the southern part of Asia, encompassing India (Gulail), Nepal, Burma, Thailand, Indochina and southern China. There it was used for the hunting of birds, too, with the notable exception of the guards of the royal palace in Bangkok, who were armed with pellet-bows in order to inflict prompt and painful punishment on passersby who failed to offer proper reverence. Most of these Old World pellet-bows were of the same basic construction as these from South America, but their handgrips were always carved and attached separately. Some, such as a type from Burma, had their bows quite asymmetrically curved, no doubt to give the pellet an additional uplift that would help it clear the holding hand. The same asymmetry and stronger curvature of the upper arm of the bow can be found in bows from China and Cochinchina. Here the material is often bamboo, but composite pellet-bows of the same structure as the regular arrow bows can be found too (Figs. la, d and e). East Asian pellet-bows have the peculiarity of a partially rigid bowstring; Chinese strings are made of two strips of wood, bamboo, or rattan, with a short center part of double cords braced apart by two short spacers to form the rest for the pellet; often the rigid parts are

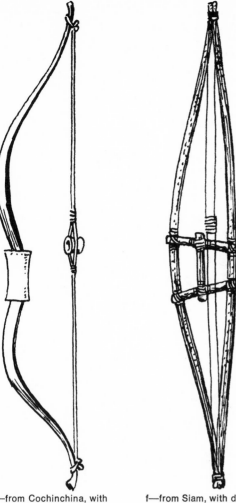

e—from Cochinchina, with asymmetrical reflex bow, and ivory cradle wedged into the split rattan string.

f—from Siam, with double bow and "window" construction.

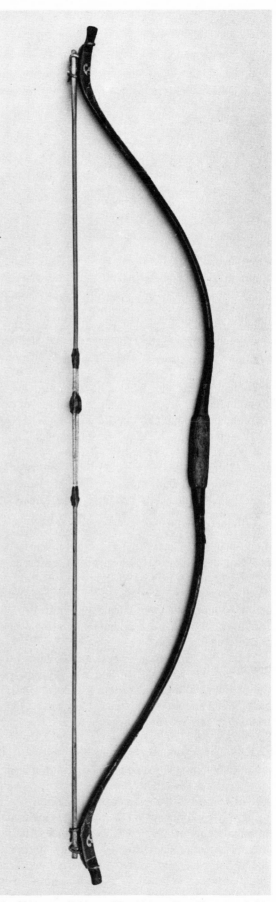

of a distinct spoon- or paddle-shape (Figs. 2 and 3). In Cochinchinese specimens the rattan bowstring is divided in its central part, and an hourglass-shaped receiver of ivory for the pellet is wedged between the double strings. The string divided in the central part holding the bullet pouch or container is just another variation of the double string with pouch.

The danger of hitting the bowhand with pellets veering too far to the left presented a major problem, and various ingenious devices were employed to avoid this peril. Persians and Turks adapted the *majra*—a trough-like guiding device tied to the bowstring to hold arrows too short for the span of the bow—by attaching to its tip a conical or cylindrical pellet-holder called the *midfa mudawwar,* by which means the pellet always stayed in front of the holding hand (in short, the *majra* and *midfa mudawwar* were elaborate and improved pellet-pouches requiring only a single string because the pellet was always propelled to the right side of the bow).

Bowstaffs forming a window are much more rarely found. Bows of this type were used in what is now Thailand, though side by side with the regular solid

Fig. 2—Chinese pellet-bow. (The Metropolitan Museum of Art, bequest of George Cameron Stone, 36.25.2505)

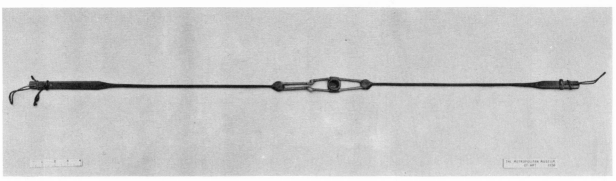

Fig. 3—String of a Chinese pellet-bow. (The Metropolitan Museum of Art, bequest of George Cameron Stone, 36.25.2690)

bows: two bowstaves were united at their ends, but braced apart in the middle, and the braces again were bridged by another piece that formed the handgrip. The double string with a fiber-woven pouch threw the pellet through the opening just above the grip. By placing the grip slightly off-center, the danger of hitting the holding hand was diminished even further (Fig 1f).

Though pellets shot from a bow are already mentioned in the Vedas, pictorial representations of pellet-bows are not frequently found. Perhaps the earliest is the blazon of Ala ad-Din the Bowman, Mamluk emir and governor of Egypt (1216-1285), which shows two addorsed pellet-bows, gold on red, and is painted on a mosque lamp destined for his mausoleum in Cairo. The emphasized handgrips and clearly indicated pellet-pouches leave no doubt as to the nature of these bows, though the painter gave them only single strings (Fig. 4).

Howard Blackmore has given a comprehensive account of the European pellet- or stone-bow from the fourteenth century onward in his recently published *Hunting Weapons;* his single illustration is of 1609, which is of extraordinary interest because of this late date.

The earliest European representation known to the author is in The Book of Hours of Catherine of Cleves, painted in the Netherlands around 1440, now in the Pierpont Morgan Library, New York (Fig. 5). In the framing margin of the page for the feast day of Saints Fabian and Sebastian (January 20), bows, crossbows, bolts and other accessories are illustrated. Among the bows is one pellet-bow with double string and square pellet-cradle carefully rendered, while a special feature is the portrayal of a central brace of steel with a round eye for the passage of the pellet. The two arms of the bow are separately fitted into sockets on either side of the eye. Since with this type of bow the pellet did not have to be shot with a twist to circumvent the bowstaff, there was no need for a special reinforced handgrip. The double-pouches of white and blue shown above and below this bow are carrying-pouches for pellets (on the upper one the painter took pains to draw tiny circular shadows to indicate the bumps made by pellets pressing against the fabric); the different colors of the pouches were presumably to indicate pellets of different material, such as clay and lead.

For curiosity's sake it might be mentioned that in Heinrich Aldegrever's engraving "Jupiter" (1533) a boy is aiming a bow that has a strange U-shaped central element, a derivation of the Netherlandish pellet-bow as seen in the miniature just mentioned. The entire bow seems to be fashioned out of steel, and the U-shaped element—open to the left side—is located immediately above the handhold. Unfortunately Aldegrever indulged in one of the popular draughtsman's jokes by letting the boy aim directly into the eye of the viewer: therefore the missile held back by the hand at the string and hovering in front of the aiming eye of the boy cannot be made out. It could be a pellet—it shows only as a round dot—but it might also be an arrow in total foreshortening. The fact that the boy is holding the bow in his right hand, pulls back the string with his left, but aims with his right eye is somewhat less than reassuring about Aldegrever's knowledge of archery. In other engravings by Aldegrever, bows are shown of the regular composite form, but in "Hercules slaying Nessus" (1550), Hercules holds the same strange bow with the U-shaped middle-element, but has clearly shot an arrow into the hapless man-beast.

The one continent where the pellet-bow was not known was black Africa. In 1623 an English traveller reported "with considerable glee" that he had brought the natives of River Gambia, West Africa, into a state of "wonderful admiration" when he with his "stone or pellet bow, in two hours, killed twenty pigeons." The "pellet-bow" mentioned, though, might possibly have been a pellet crossbow; if it was a true bow, then it would be the only case on record where a European was admired for his shooting skill with this instrument by "primitives," and not the other way around.

Fig. 4—Mosque lamp, with blazon of the Mamluk emir Alā' ad-Dīn the Bowman (1216-1285), governor of Egypt, showing two pellet-bows addorsed, gold on red. (The Metropolitan Museum of Art, gift of J. Pierpont Morgan, 17.190.985)

Fig. 5—Miniature for the feast day of Saints Fabian and Sebastian, from The Book of Hours of Catherine of Cleves, Netherlands, ca. 1440. (The Pierpont Morgan Library, New York, M. 917)

BIBLIOGRAPHY

Antze, G.—"Einige Bemerkungen zu den Kugelbogen im Städtischen Museum für Völkerkunde zu Leipzig," *Jahrbuch des Städtischen Museums für Völkerkunde zu Leipzig,* 3 (1908/09); pp. 79-95, ill.

Blackmore, H.L.—*Hunting Weapons,* Arms and Armour Series, London/New York, 1971/1972; pp. 129, 164-169, fig. 70.

Egerton of Tatton, Lord—*A Description of Indian and Oriental Armour,* new edition, London, 1896; cat. nos. 304-5, 368, 599-600.

Hansard, George Agar—*The Book of Archery,* London, 1845; p. 239.

Nickel, Helmut—"A Mamluk Axe," *Islamic Art in the Metropolitan Museum of Art,* New York, 1972; pp. 213-235, fig. 5.

Plummer, John—The Book of Hours of Catherine of Cleves, New York, 1966; pl. 123.

Schmitz, Carl A.—*Technologie frühzeitlicher Waffen,* Museum für Völkerkunde, Basel, *Führer durch Sonderausstellung vom 1. Juni bis 31. Dezember 1963;* pp. 38-39, ill.

Stone, George C.—*A Glossary of the Construction, Decoration and use of Arms and Armour,* Portland, Maine, 1934; entries: Bow, Bow String, Gulail, Pellet Bow.

Anton Peffenhauser, Last of the Great Armorers

by Freiherr ALEXANDER von REITZENSTEIN

Baron von Reitzenstein, born in 1904 in Germany, received his degree in Art History in 1928 and has dedicated his career to public service and to arms-historical literature. After several years on the staffs of the Deutsche Akademie and the Bayerische Denkmalpflege, he joined the Bayerisches Armeemuseum in 1936 and the Bayerisches Nationalmuseum in 1948, and was Director of the newly-constituted Bayerisches Armeemuseum from 1965 to 1969. In addition to many essays and studies, he has published books on the art of the armorers of Augsburg, Nuremberg and Landshut, i.e. Der Waffenschmied *and* Rittertum and Ritterschaft. *Since 1958 he has been editor of the arms part of the* Zeitschrift für Kostüm- und Waffenkunde.

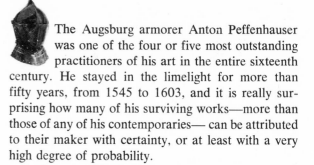

The Augsburg armorer Anton Peffenhauser was one of the four or five most outstanding practitioners of his art in the entire sixteenth century. He stayed in the limelight for more than fifty years, from 1545 to 1603, and it is really surprising how many of his surviving works—more than those of any of his contemporaries— can be attributed to their maker with certainty, or at least with a very high degree of probability.

In the second half of the sixteenth century, the art of the armorer lost much of its vigor, and celebrated masters like Desiderius Helmschmied and Matthäus Frauenpreis could not long struggle against the decline; only Anton Peffenhauser was not swept along —on the contrary, his position grew stronger, probably more because of his dealings in the foreign trade, i.e. export business, than in the home market. But everywhere, also of course at home, his works remained in high esteem until his death, and for a long time after.

The Correr Museum in Venice possesses an etched and figured iron plate, once the lower part of an epitaph on a tomb in an Augsburg church (Fig. 1). On it are shown "Master Anthonius Peffenhauser," his two wives and his fourteen children. Next to him is his coat of arms, the figure of which—a triquet, i.e. three legs revolving about a common center, at which they join—was also his mark as armorer. In fact, this device definitively indentifies his work, and in the absence of it an attribution would have to be supported by documentary evidence.

Peffenhauser's stylistic range varies from lush ornamentation to extreme simplicity. One of the most remarkable bas-relief armors known, believed to have been property of King Sebastian of Portugal (1554-78, killed in Morocco at the Battle of Alcazarquivir), now in the Real Armeria, Madrid, bears his mark (Fig. 2). At this point a question arises quite naturally: did he, Peffenhauser, himself do the bas-relief chiseling, or did he provide a fine armor in the white for elaboration by an independent artist? The answer is that of the independent artist. We know, for example, that another chiseled suit in the Real Armeria, once property of King Philip II of Spain (1527-98), made by the master Desiderius Helmschmied in about 1549-50, was ornamented by the goldsmith Jörg Sigman, no doubt on direct solicitation of Helmschmied. In terms of their structures and architectures, these two suits are so similar that the student is led to suspect that one served as the model for the other, King Phillip's probably following King Sebastian's. But the chiseling on the Peffenhauser suit reaches a level of artistry and refinement far above that attained by Jörg Sigman on the Helmschmied armor: its plasticity is more robust and vigorous, the play of light and shadow is far richer, more colorful, and the spaces to be ornamented are generously and fluidly treated in grand style, without little patches of frills and geegaws. However good the work of Jörg Sigman, its author was a goldsmith—while the creator of the Peffenhauser ornaments would seem to have been a sculptor, an artist. Nevertheless, surface ornamenta-

tion, be it ever so ingenious and praiseworthy, always remains subordinate to the iron underbody wrought by the armorer. Even if the ornamentation were, hypothetically, eliminated, there would remain the splendid sculpture of the armor itself, a work of art in its own right.

In fact, very few suits were ever so lavishly, so royally chiseled—for obvious economic and social reasons—and indeed, these perfections fall outside the normal artistic province of the armorer. The far more standard ornamental technique used throughout the sixteenth century was acid etching; this, too, was but rarely carried out by the armorer, but the designs for it were planned by him and carefully tailored to the spatial requirements of the suit in question. How beautifully the results of this technique and this working hand-in-hand could be is exemplified by the suit shown in Figs. 3-5, made by Peffenhauser in about 1580 (as Hans Stöcklein was able to show) on orders of the Duke of Bavaria and worn in the annual Corpus Domini procession in Munich by the knight representing Saint George. The white breastplate in Fig. 6, almost surely worn by one of St. George's squires, is

73

Fig. 1 — Part of an engraving executed about 1600 after an iron epitaph which must once have been in an Augsburg church but is now preserved in the Correr Museum in Venice. Shown here are Master Anton Peffenhauser and three of his fourteen children. Note the triquet coat of arms, which became the Peffenhauser armorer's mark. (Berlin, Kupferstichkabinett).

Fig. 2 — Wing of the right pauldron of the Peffenhauser suit said to have been made for King Sebastian of Portugal in about 1550. This designation is a little doubtful: although the ornamentation incorporates in several places the arms of Portugal and those of Spain, these would be heraldically as correct for Philip II of Spain as for Sebastian of Portugal. (Real Armeria, Madrid)

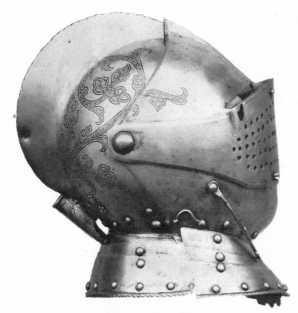

Fig. 3 — Helmet of the suit made in about 1580 in the Italian style on orders of Duke William V of Bavaria and worn by the knight representing St. George in the annual Corpus Domini procession in Munich. (Schlossmuseum, Berchtesgaden)

an example of pure functional form in the armorer's art, sufficiently strong to create its own canon of aesthetics for appraisal and judgment, without need of ornamentation. But when even such a form is well treated by the etcher, as is that in Fig. 7, its structure and fluidity can be splendidly accentuated (one must imagine this specimen as it was before rust attacked it—the broad bands finely etched in bright relief against a gilt ground, the central rib dominating the composition). Another example of fine etching, also

74

Figs. 4 & 5—Details of the suit described in Fig. 3.

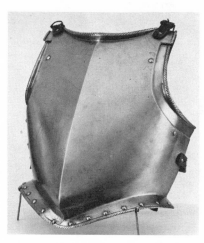

Fig. 6—White breastplate. It is marked with the Augsburg pinecone poinçon, exactly as the St. George armor in Figs. 3-5, and was probably worn by one of the St. George-knight's six squires. (Schlossmuseum, Munich)

surely of the Augsburg school but not quite so surely attributable to Peffenhauser, is the gold-on-blue specimen in Fig. 9; the treatment is very similar to that on a Berlin suit marked "HR" (Hieronymus Ringler?), ex-property Johann Georg von Brandeburg-Jägerndorf. The foot-jousting armor in Fig. 8 is one of twelve made in 1590 on orders of the Electress Sofia of Saxony as a Christmas present for the Elector Christian I; here the gold-on-blue theme is used to emphasize the frontal rib of the breastplate.

Fig. 7—Breastplate, white with broad etched and gilded bands. It is older than that in Fig. 6, dating from about 1550-60. (Bayerisches Nationalmuseum, Munich)

Fig. 8—Foot jousting armor, gold etched designs on blue ground, executed with eleven others on the orders of Sofia, Electress of Saxony as a Christmas present for the Elector Christian I. (Germanisches Museum, Nuremberg)

But *pure* armor—that is, undecorated iron body covering combining maximum protection with maximum mobility, existing solely toward a functional end and relying for artistry on the perfection of its execution—is the final proof of an armorer's worth. Such a work is shown in Fig. 10: a suit destined for the so-called "royal joust"; while not signed by Peffenhauser, careful comparison with similar specimens in Paris and in London, all known and signed Peffenhauser products, makes the attribution a safe

one. The structure of heavy, smooth steel plates dispenses with all ornament—and indeed, there is no need of any, for the work is an organic whole complete within its own volumetrics and enobled by the clear fulfillment of the purpose for which it was created.

For these notes we have chosen but a very few of the great number of surviving works by the Augsburg master. But even these are sufficient for showing the wide range his art embraced: from the richest of

Fig. 9—This more delicate style of gilt on blue ground is another good example of how etched designs could be used to emphasize the plasticity of any armor component. (Bayerisches Nationalmuseum, Munich)

Fig. 10—Armor for the Royal Joust (arms and legs missing). Though not signed, the Peffenhauser hand is easily established by comparison with similar suits in Paris and London (Fig. 11). (Bayerisches Nationalmuseum, Munich)

parade armors to the simplest jousting suit. When he set out in his long career, barely twenty years old, in the middle of the sixteenth century, the Augsburg school was still in vigorous flower; in his old age he saw it languishing into oblivion without hope of revival. He was one of the few who knew how to survive in the age of armor's decline and fall, and to keep the Great Tradition alive until the very closing years of the century.

Fig. 11—Armor for the Royal Joust by Peffenhauser, one of four in the Musée de l'Armée, Paris, and very similar to another two of the same series now in the Wallace Collection, London. The Paris specimens probably were taken from the Munich arsenal to Paris by Napolean, the London ones in turn by the victorious British from Paris.

An Introduction to Japanese Sword Guards

by GRAHAM GEMMELL

Graham Gemmell, born in Scotland 23 years ago, is Assistant Cataloguer of Japanese Art for Sotheby & Co., specializing in swords and their fittings. His enthusiasm for, and knowledge of, the subject he has chosen for his contribution to these pages have often proved infectious, having "converted" more than one devotee of purely European weaponry to the appreciation of Japanese. At the time of our going to press, Mr. & Mrs. Gemmell are awaiting the arrival of their first child.

The Japanese sword—blade, scabbard and furniture—falls more into the higher realms of art and mysticism than into those of technology and military science. It is difficult for a Westerner (and for most modern Japanese) to grasp the cultural significance, to say nothing of the macabre but hypnotic beauty, of the great classics of bladesmithing in the Golden Age, of works of swordsmiths like Masamune, Sadamune, Nobutane, Muramasa and their colleagues and heirs. A very important component of every weapon was the *tsuba*, the guard which protected the hand that wielded the blade: a more or less flat plate, usually of circular, oval or quatrefoil shape (but frequently also square, lozenge or completely irregular) located at the upper termination of the cutting edge of the blade and immediately before or below the braid-and-ray-skin-bound hilt. Its function was that of any sword-guard anywhere, anytime: to protect the user's hand while he parries the cut of an opponent. But beyond this, tsuba (the plural and singular forms are identical) constituted the objects of an entire epicycle of Japanese art, ranging—as do all art objects—from the banal to the sublime, and accruing in their wake through the centuries a mystique, a body of canons, unlike those of any comparable metalwork elsewhere.

The story of the tsuba is the story of the sword and, despite the independence of the tsuba-maker from the swordsmiths, the development of the two arts was of course closely associated. The earliest

known sword-guards are those that have been excavated from burial dolmens and can only be dated vaguely to the period between the second century B.C. and the sixth century A.D. These *Hoju* tsuba were either bronze or copper, often gilded, in the form of thick, oval plates lightened by a ring of trapezoid openings but otherwise undecorated. With the spread of Buddhism in the sixth century came the Chinese sword with its relatively ineffective type of guard: the so-called *shitogi* guard (from its resemblance to shinto rice-cakes), a short quillon or cross-bar decorated on the outer face only. The ninth century brought with it a rise in the power of the military class, the celebrated *Samurai,* and at the same time a return to the discoid form of tsuba achieved by the filling of the loops of the *shitogi* tsuba as an attempt to provide better hand protection for the warrior in a time of rapidly increasing civil disorder and clan wars. The tsuba of this period were predominantly made of iron, though a surprisingly adequate alternative was lacquered leather reinforced with thin iron plates or an iron rim. Decoration was subdued, the monotony of the plain disc relieved only by piercing with usually simple geometric designs. The absence of more dramatic decoration does not, of course, mean that they were unattractive: textural and visual appeal was wrought through the use of high-quality iron and asymmetric positioning of the pierced design; many early-period tsuba are highly desirable collector's pieces.

The Mongol invasions of Japan in the late 13th century and the accompanying switch in military tactics from the use of mounted cavalry to armoured foot-soldiery created the need for larger and stronger guards, made of very fine wrought iron and steel and often forged by swordsmiths and armourers as well as by those craftsmen specialised in making tsuba. These tsuba (through the 14th and 15th centuries) bore decorations of rather primitive inlays in copper or brass on the flat iron plate.

Toward the end of the 15th century the attitude toward the minor crafts, and in particular toward metalworkers, underwent profound change through the influence of Zen Buddhism. The artist became free to elaborate his tsuba in more complex designs and to enrich them with inlays and applications of softer metals, gold, silver, brass, copper, various alloys, *sentoku* (a type of brass—see Glossary) and in particular two alloys called *shakudo* and *shibuichi* (see Glossary). These last-mentioned three are peculiar to Japan; their chief virtue lay in the muted, harmonious colouring they assumed when patinated or "pickled" in a special solution (raw, bright metal was considered an anathema of good taste).

In 1601, following centuries of internal strife and civil war, the regime of the Tokugawa clan commenced the begining of a dynasty which ruled Japan until 1868. This period of two and a half centuries was an era of almost uninterrupted peace; with it, the necessity for strictly functional sword-mounts diminished, and artistic expression was given ever-greater impetus. Indeed, within a short time

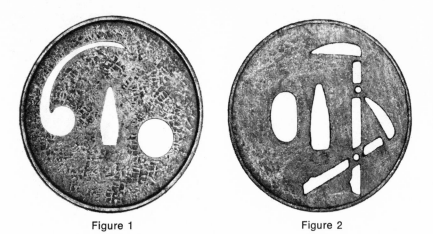

Figure 1   Figure 2

the sword's *raison-d'être* slipped from its almost religious status of terrible death-dealer to that of a fine weapon, yes, but one serving also as masculine ornament in the flamboyant costumes of the 17th and 18th centuries (not unlike contemporary European rapiers). Many fine blades were made during this *Shinto* ("new sword") period, but assessment of sword quality was moving ever more away from its former concentration on the blade alone. Now the tsuba and the other mounts, and the quality of the lacquer work of the scabbard, were not only taken into consideration but measured against high and complex levels of criticism.

In 1868 an imperial edict was issued banning the carrying of the sword, that immemorial symbol of the soldier, the gentleman, the Samurai. This was part of an overall policy to bring the old Japan into step with modern Europe, but its effects were of course devastating to swordcraft. Not only did it destroy the ancient warrior class intentionally but thousands of swordsmiths, tsuba-makers and others of the Art were left breadless and hence forced to turn their hands to snuff- and cigarette-boxes, pouch-clasps, netsuke and inro. There are some modern authorities who claim that this disintegra-

tion of the tsuba industry came only just in time to save it, mercifully, from imminent descent into decadence and over-elaboration. Indeed, many mid-nineteenth century tsuba, flamboyant and even garish, were never made as real hand-guards but as just decorative pieces of *virtuoso* bric-a-brac.

The study of tsuba is an involved and at times confusing discipline. Perhaps understanding of basic definitions can be facilitated by listing the major schools. These usually take their titles from the name of the province or town with which they are most closely associated, or, less frequently, from the name of the master who is credited with originating the style or technique for which the school is noted. But some are not easily attributable to a person or a place, having been made in many parts of Japan over long periods; in such cases students make use of some other identifying factor for valid classification.

The following section, then, is a survey of the major schools and their salient characteristics. They are arranged in chronological order so far as possible; in some cases, where the active life of a school extends over several centuries, the dates of the working life of the generally-accredited founding

Figure 6   Figure 7   Figure 8

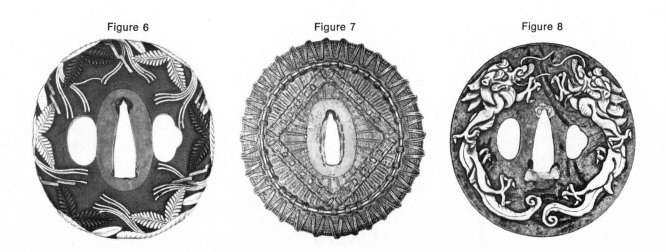

80

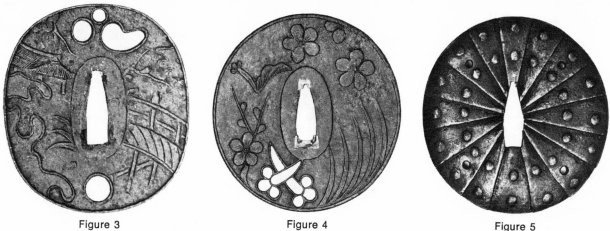

Figure 3   Figure 4   Figure 5

master has been used as the school's starting period. The following Table and Glossary will be useful:

JAPANESE ART PERIODS AND THEIR CHRISTIAN CALENDAR EQUIVALENTS	
Early Muromachi	1392 - 1450
Middle Muromachi	1451 - 1510
Late Muromachi	1511 - 1567
Momoyama	1568 - 1615
Early Edo	1615 - 1703
Middle Edo	1704 - 1800
Late Edo	1800 - 1867
Meiji	1868 - 1912

GLOSSARY OF BASIC TERMS

Bori *Carving.*

Hira-zogan *Flat inlay, flush with the surrounding host metal.*

Mokko *Of quatrelobe or quatrefoil shape.*

Mon *Crest, badge, coat-of-arms, emblem of a family or feudal clan.*

Nunome *Gold or silver foil hammered onto an iron base to heighten details of design; approximately like damascening, not truly inlay work.*

Sentoku *An alloy imitating Chinese bronze consisting of copper, tin and lead; has an appearance much like brass.*

Shakudo *A species of bronze consisting of varying quantities of gold, copper and antimony, which, when treated with a "pickling" solution, produces a velvety blue-black patina.*

Shibuichi *An alloy of silver, copper, lead, zinc and tin, in varying proportions to give subtle differences of colour tone.*

Sukashi *Piercing, open-work carving, fretwork.*

Zogan *Inlay, usually in bas-relief and sculptured or engraved; see Hira-zogan.*

Figure 9   Figure 10

81

Figure 11   Figure 12

THE MAIN SCHOOLS OF TSUBA-MAKING

HOJU
This is the earliest of tsuba (200 B.C.-600 A.D.) of which we have extant examples; see preceding section.

SHITOGI
Produced between the sixth and ninth centuries A.D.; exceedingly rare and perhaps of greater interest to archeologists than to collectors of Japanese sword fittings.

TOSHO (Fig. 1)
These are tsuba made by swordsmiths simply as presentation gifts to complete the mounting of a newly-made blade; always made from a thin iron plate, the only decoration being a simple, stylised pierced design. Example shown: plain forged iron, 16th century.

KATCHUSHI (Fig. 2)
Armour-makers' guards. Made from iron, usually similar in appearance and style to Tosho tsuba, the plate however being a little thinner. This division

includes Kabutoshi Tsuba (Fig. 5), i.e. guards made by specialist helmet makers and often used as promotional objects to demonstrate skills in iron forgings to a potential customer. Example shown: iron, pierced with two adzes.

KAMAKURA (Figs. 3 and 4)
These thin iron guards derived their name from the similarity of the carving technique used to the lacquer wares of Kamakura; generally round or of mokko form and decorated in low relief with landscapes and floral designs. The iron usually bears a dark patina but is of only mediocre quality. Examples shown: No. 3, iron with relief landscape pierced with a stylized radish; No. 4, an unusually good specimen of this school·

KABUTOSHI (Fig. 5)
See Katchushi, of which school Kabutoshi is a part. Example shown imitates the manner in which helmet plates overlapped.

GOTO (Fig. 6)
This school, founded by Goto Yujo (1453-1512), worked in *shakudo* and developed a technique of a dotted relief ground (*nanako*) with gold or relief designs. This style of mount for a sword was the

Figure 15   Figure 16

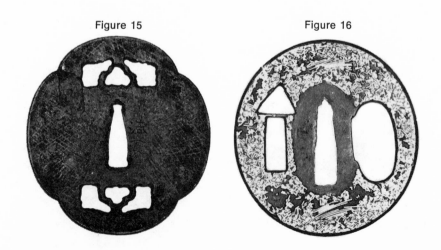

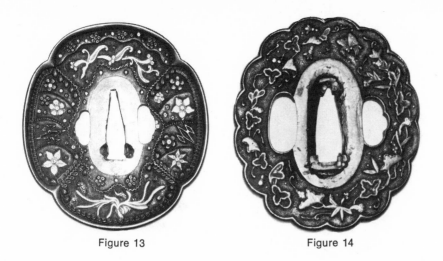

Figure 13   Figure 14

only correct one for court ceremonial wear right down to 1868. In the late eighteenth and early nineteenth century, several of the Goto artists deviated from the production of this classical style and developed individual techniques of their own, founding new schools to perpetuate their particular styles. The work of the various members of the Goto family is a complex study, beyond the reach of the present introduction. (For further reading see: *"The Sword Ornaments of the Goto Shirohei Family"* by Alexander G. Mosle in the Transactions of the Japan Society of London, Volume VIII.) Example shown: a good *shakudo nanako* guard, with gilt details of New Year's decorations.

SHINGEN (Fig. 7)

Popular in the late sixteenth century, this style of work derived its name from the warrior Takeda Shingen (1521-1573), who extolled the virtues of the strength and lightness of these tsuba. Their construction is an iron web decorated with brass and copper wires either woven through piercings in the web or applied to the surface. Also in this section are Mukade ("centipede") tsuba, a stylized form of this creature forming the basis of the decoration. Example shown: unusually good and complex.

YOSHIRO-ZOGAN (Fig. 8)

"Zogan" means inlay, and Koike Yoshiro is reputed to have worked in the early sixteenth century and to have originated this style of high relief inlay of brass or *sentoku,* as well as a parallel style sometimes termed *Mon-Sukashi,* i.e. "with family crests" or badges, in open work and flat brass inlay. Example shown: iron, good quality, beautifully carved brass dragons in relief.

ONIN (Figs. 9 and 10)

Plain or pierced thin iron plate with decorations applied in relief in brass "pin-heads", brass wire or larger pieces. The earliest examples of this particular style of inlay dates back to the first half of the sixteenth century. Examples shown: No. 9, "pin-heads", early 16th century, exceptionally good; No. 10, same period, wire inlay.

TACHIKANAGUSHI

These were amongst the earliest tsuba produced in soft metals. They were made from *shakudo* and *yamagane* and were used on *tachi* (slung swords). Most can be dated to the sixteenth century.

KANEIYE (Figs. 11 and 12)

Kaneiye is credited as being the first man to use

Figure 17   Figure 18

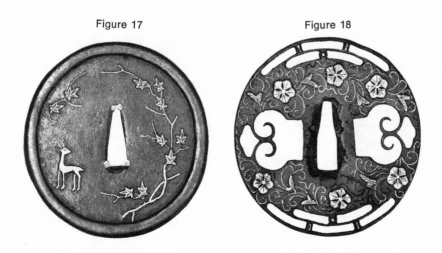

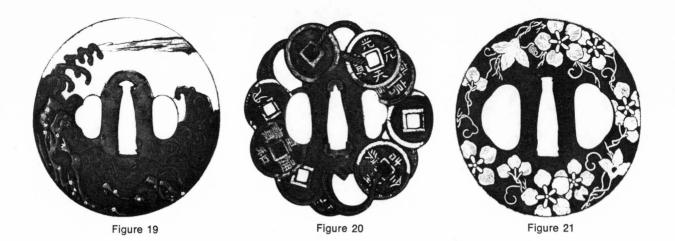

Figure 19   Figure 20   Figure 21

graphic designs on tsuba. He worked at Fushimi in Yamashiro province during the middle and late sixteenth century and produced finely tempered, thin iron guards of rounded, square and *mokko* shape decorated in relief and sometimes with inlays of copper, brass or gold to form landscapes, human and animal figures, and Taoist and Buddhist divinities. There is controversy as to whether only one or several people worked in this style and signed their work "Kaneiye", but no irrefutable resolution has been put forward to date. Examples shown: both typical; the *mokko* one signed "Kaneiye of Fushimi in Yamashiro Province".

NOBUIYE
Tsuba by Nobuiye, the seventeenth Master of the Miochin family working in the sixteenth century, are much prized by collectors and indeed have been sought after for several centuries. They are of iron of the finest, best-hammered quality, and extremely simple, delicate and refined in decoration. He favoured surface textures of light hammer marks *(tsuchime),* radiating lines *(amida-yasuri)* and an hexagonal diaper design *(kikko).* His works have been much imitated (in good faith and in bad), and genuine examples are extremely rare.

KO-KINKO (Figs. 13 and 14)
These are again soft metal tsuba, usually of *shaku-*

do but examples in copper and other alloys are known. They are elaborately decorated and frequently of irregular, lobed form. Although more refined in workmanship and quality of materials, Ko-Kinko tsuba are contemporary with those of the Tachikanagushi style. Examples shown: No. 13, very fine *shakudo* guard with gilt seaweed and shells, late 15th century; No. 14, another similar, possibly the work of an earlier Goto master.

HOAN (Fig. 15)
Living in Owari province in the late sixteenth century, the first Hoan was a swordsmith who turned his hand to tsuba making at the request of his *daimyo* (feudal lord). His works show greatly the influence of Nobuiye in the thick, well-hammered iron and the use of the *amida-yasuri* ground. Hoan I never signed his work but later generations, of which there were seven, not only attested their work but eventually changed the style completely. Example shown: iron, with typical cross-hatched ground, signed "Hoan", early 17th century.

YAMA KICHIBEI
Yamasaka Kichibei, like Hoan, was working in the Owari province about the middle of the sixteenth century and he, too, fell under the influence of Nobuiye; his decoration of the iron plate was done

Figure 23   Figure 24

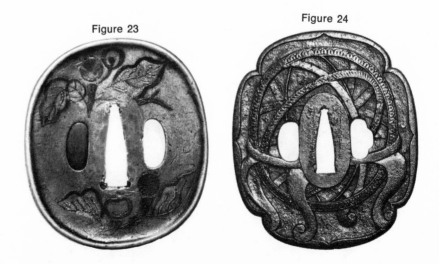

Figure 22

chiefly in large perforation, often in the form of a wheel.

GOMOKU-ZOGAN (Fig. 16)

The title translates literally as "dirt" or "rubbish" inlay, and the decoration of these late-sixteenth-century guards was achieved in precisely this way: by scattering scraps of brass wire and filings over the iron plate and then hammering them in. In addition, the guard might also be pierced with a stylised design. Example shown: small but typical, pierced with a gate-post, late 16th or early 17th centuries.

HEIANJO (Figs. 17 and 18)

Taking its name from the town of Heianjo (modern Kyoto), this style bears a great similarity to the Onin school: an iron plate, quite thick, decorated in relief and with applied brass, silver or *yamagane* in floral designs and stylised geometric patterns. Less common are landscape-decorated tsuba of this type; illustration No. 17 shows a particularly good and rare example. The earliest Heianjo-school tsuba are attributable to the late sixteenth century or early seventeenth century. Examples shown: No. 17, very rare iron with brass inlays showing deer and maples, early 16th century; No. 18, somewhat later and more typical, floral brass inlays.

SHOAMI (Figs. 19-22)

The Shoami schools originated with the *Ko Shoami* ("Old Shoami") group active in Kyoto in the middle and late sixteenth century. Their work was in iron, almost invariably circular and decorated by piercing and with gold, brass or silver inlay of the "lightning" and similar geometric designs. From this school in the early seventeenth and the eighteenth centuries developed a number of sub-schools in Awa, Akita, Edo (modern Tokyo), Bizen, Kyoto and other localities throughout Japan. The range of styles and materials used covers a wide area, but a detailed study of these unfortunately is beyond the scope of the present article. Examples shown: No. 19, Akita Shoami work in iron with a gilt and *shakudo* representation of waves; late 17th or early 18th centuries. No. 20, Kyo Shoami work from Kyoto, the iron carved in the form of a string of coins; late 17th century. No. 21, Awa Shoami, iron plate with gold *nunome* design; 18th century: No. 22, iron finely inlayed with gold streams, water-lillies.

UMETADA (Figs. 23 and 24)

Umetada Myoju (1558-1631) was primarily a swordsmith and worked in Nishijin, Yamashiro province. Although he was respected as a sword-

Figure 25   Figure 26   Figure 27

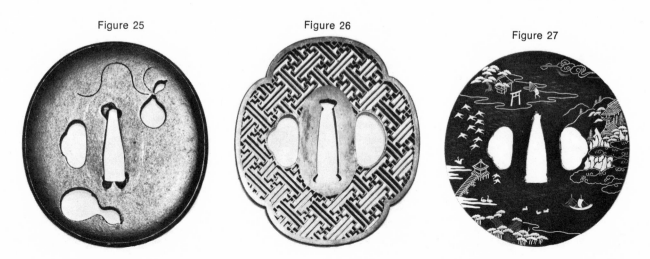

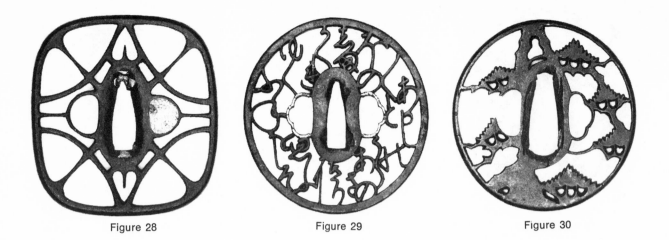

Figure 28   Figure 29   Figure 30

smith, his tsuba are far more sought after. He originated—and is most renowned for—the technique of flat inlay of *shakudo* on copper or brass tsuba. He was, however, also a master at working iron, *shakudo* and precious metals using not only his own inlay technique but relief carvings, open piercing and intaglio. He had numerous followers who sought faithfully to perpetuate his style, but, although technically their work will bear comparison with the master's, the cunning simplicity and delicacy that Myoju achieved was never truly captured by his pupils. Examples shown: No. 23, a very fine specimen by Umetada Mitsutada, late 16th century, with masterful inlays; No. 24, an unusual guard by Umetada Mioshin, the second master of the school, the iron plate carved with a European armillary sphere, signed and dated 1608.

ITO (Figs. 25 and 26)
A pupil of Umetada Myoju, Masatsugu founded a school in 1600 which bore his family name, Ito. The technique he inaugurated was quite distinctive and was achieved by drilling a minute hole in the iron plate, through which was then threaded a fine steel wire moistened with oil and coated with powdered garnets or silicose rock. By drawing this wire back and forth an extremely fine cut was pro-

duced. Examples shown: Both good quality, late 17th century; No. 25 shows the typical "thread-cutting" style. No. 26 is elaborately pierced in a close labyrinth design.

KAGA (Fig. 27)
Most renowned for their excellent *hira-zogan* (flat inlay), Kaga school artists are said to have migrated from Fushimi and settled in Kanazawa in the early seventeenth century. The delicacy of their designs and executions reflects the influence of the Goto artists. Generally, their basic material was iron and the inlayed designs silver, *sentoku* and copper. In the later periods of the school's work, *shakudo,* copper and *shibuichi* were used for the plate into which numerous varying shades of soft metals were imbedded. Example shown: 18th century, very fine gold and silver flat inlays.

SUKASHI (Figs. 28-31)
Sukashi-bori means "pierced carving," a style of tsuba-making practised in many parts of Japan (Kyoto, Akasaka, Heianjo, Owari, etc.) from the early seventeenth century onwards. The guard is iron and is decorated in positive or negative silhouette with geometric designs, naturalistic subjects (grasses, animals, insects, etc.) or stylised and

Figure 34   Figure 35

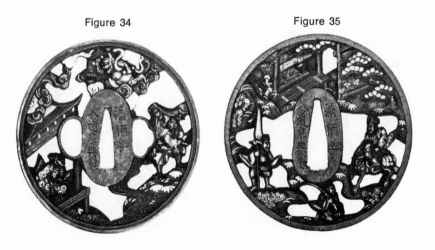

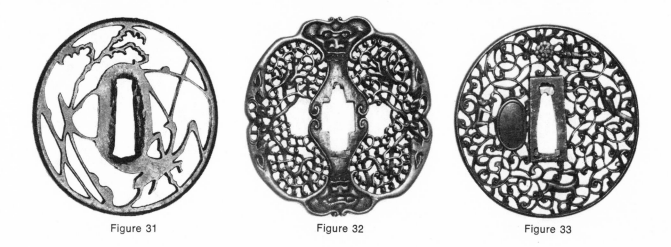

Figure 31   Figure 32   Figure 33

abstract patterns. These guards are highly prized in Japan but for a long time were ignored by Western collectors. Since about early 1972, however, interest in the West has much increased. The subject of Sukashi tsuba is a complex one. Examples shown: No. 28, Akasaka Sukashi work, probably by the fourth master; early 18th century. No. 29, Kyo Sukashi, iron plate pierced with a poem in Japanese characters; late 16th century. No. 30, Heianjo Sukashi, iron pierced with pine trees; late 16th century. No. 31, Owari Sukashi, iron pierced with a praying mantis amid grasses; early 17th century.

NAMBAN (Figs. 32 and 33)

The word *namban* literally means "southern barbarian," but when used in the context of tsuba it refers to the works produced in iron from a foreign source or using non-indigenous motifs as decoration. The iron could be imported from India, Java or Malaya. The subjects would be Chinese dragons and jewels, Dutch or Portugese ships or figures, and even Christian motifs. Tsuba made in the late eighteenth century in Hizen province by Mitsuhiro of Yagami are often classed with namban tsuba due to a certain similarity of technique and quality of iron. These generally represent the subject of "one hundred monkeys," but "one hundred horses," "one hundred rabbits" and centuries of other animals also occur. Examples shown: No. 32, carved from brass, shows the typically complex designs of dragons and foliage, 18th century; No. 33, iron pierced with insects and animals on a foliate ground, 18th century.

SOTEN (Figs. 34 and 35)

The influence of Chinese artists in the early seventeenth century is evident in the work of this school. Founded by Kitagawa Soten, who lived in Hikone in Goshu province, this school's work took both Chinese and Japanese historical and legendary events as its subjects and portrayed them in a technique known as *hikone-bori* (Hikone carving), after its place of origin. This technique involved carving in the round with details added in copper, gold, silver and other soft metals. The work of this school was continued into the late Edo period with little variation in style by numerous pupils and followers who maintained a high level of quality. However, in the nineteenth century, when tsuba of this nature were in great demand, mass-produced guards of comparatively poor quality were made in vast numbers at Aizu, and these should not be mistaken for authentic Soten. Examples shown: iron, both carved with scenes from Japanese legend, each signed "Soten of Hikone in Goshu Province".

Figure 36   Figure 37

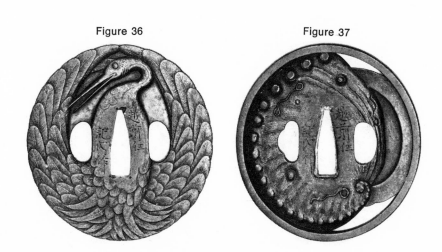

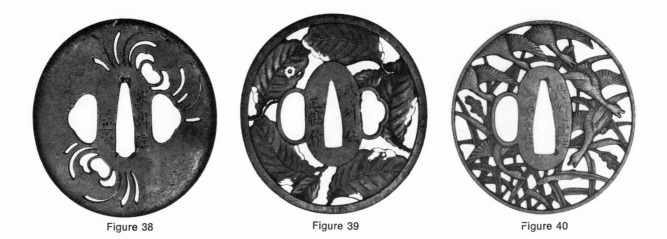

Figure 38   Figure 39   Figure 40

KINAI (Figs. 36 and 37)

The mid-seventeenth century saw the rise in Echizen Province of this famous school of artists who made guards of openwork iron in the form of flowers, birds, dragons, shells, insects, etc. The style is reputed to have been originated by Takahashi Kinai; successive generations all show a similarity in style and skill making distinction between the various masters extremely difficult. Examples shown: both very good and typical, both signed "made by Kinai of Echizen Province".

BUSHU and CHOSHU (Figs. 38-41)

These two provinces had many tsuba makers from the late seventeenth century onwards but never truly produced a style of their own. The artists of these areas were influenced by the works of other contemporary schools; a great variety of techniques is found in Bushu and Choshu work. Pierced guards, solid guards with low and high relief, inlay work, iron and soft metal alloys, are all present in Bushu and Choshu work, although iron is predominant, and soft metals are generally only found on guards made for presentation or by special order from a local lord. Because of this distillation of styles and techniques, neither school ever developed individuality, and even those techniques adopted from other schools were only rarely ex-

ecuted with more than mediocre competence. Because of the similarity between the two schools, we are forced frequently to rely upon the signature to ascertain its origin; this will usually state the artist's name followed by *Bushu ju* or *Choshu ju* "inhabitant of" Bushu or Choshu. Examples shown: No. 38, iron, pierced almost in Ito style (Figs 25 and 26) with stylised peonies, signed "Masakata of Bushu Province". No. 39, iron carved in oak leaves and gold *nunome* details, signed "Masachika of Bushu Province. No. 40, iron finely carved with a flight of geese, signed "Tomotomi of Hagi in Choshu Province"; 18th century. No. 41, iron, carved with a grape vine on a trellis; 18th century.

JAKUSHI (Figs. 42 and 43)

This style takes its name from Jakushi Kisaemon, a painter working in Nagasaki, who was greatly influenced by the people and objects he observed in that port, the only one where foreigners were allowed to call at this time (late seventeenth century). The works of Chinese artists in particular influenced Jakushi. He was fond of working in iron with landscapes in relief and gold *nunome,* and occasionally he used inlays of soft metal for detail work. He was succeeded by several generations of copyists who imitated him with greater or lesser success. Examples shown: No. 42, iron with gold

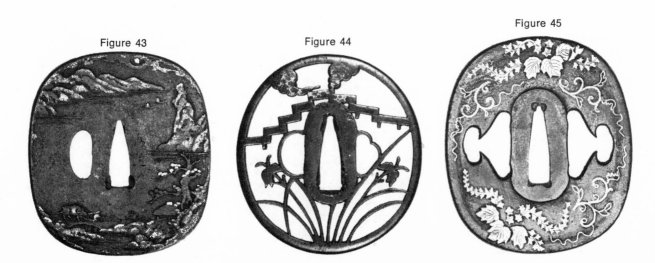

Figure 43   Figure 44   Figure 45

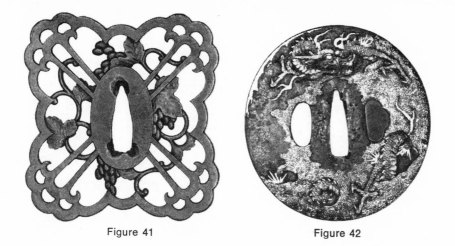

Figure 41   Figure 42

nunome details showing dragon amidst clouds, signed "Kisaemon Jakushi"; No. 43, another similarly worked, same signature.

HIGO (Figs. 44 and 45)
Hayashi Mataschichi came from a family of gunsmiths who moved to Higo Province from Owari in the early seventeenth century. Encouraged by the patronage of members of the ruling Hosokawa family, he produced very finely tempered iron guards, usually of circular or multi-lobed form decorated in elaborate openwork and with inlays rivalling those of the Umetada school, always finished in a glossy patina of delicate brownish-black tone. Examples shown: No. 44, a beautifully patinated iron guard pierced with a stylized bridge and irises, late 17th century; No. 45, iron, the metal finely forged and overlaid with an applied trailing plant in silver, 18th century.

MIOCHIN (Fig. 46)
The Miochin family were by tradition armourers, their line going back to Munesuke I (late 12th century), but are respected equally for their work on tsuba. These were of iron, the earlier ones being thin, plain plates, typical of the Katchusi style with occasional sparing use of applied soft metals. Example shown: roughly-hammered iron, signed "Miochin", late 16th century.

Figure 46

The foregoing is necessarily a very brief summation of basic facts about the major schools of tusba. Several schools have been omitted for reasons of space, but most students are unlikely to come across specimens of these in the normal run of things; moreover, these are not works of great importance artistically or historically.

A more substantial omission is mention of the works of the master artists Hirate Hikozo, Shimiju Jingo, Nara Toshinaga, Saguira Joi, Tsuchiya Yasuchika, Iwama Masayoshi, Omori Teruhide, Iwamoto Konkwan, Otsu Jimpo, Kano Natsuo and Goto Ichijo. Most genuine works by these artists are beautiful in the extreme, but owing to their popularity during their creators' lifetimes and after, many spuriously signed products are found, in part faithful copies of genuine works and in part just poor—and sometimes not so poor—imitations. This deliberate piracy of styles and techniques by artists bearing neither a family nor a master-pupil relationship to the perceptors causes considerable confusion and difficulty. The only means by which a true work can be distinguished from a good copy is by constant study of attested genuine pieces as well as of the copies and frauds. Only thus can the student develop an eye for subtle nuances, an invaluable capability and one quite impossible to impart through the written word.

It is hoped that this "Primer" will have proved interesting to readers who have little or no acquaintance with tsuba, and helpful to those contemplating the beginning of a collection.

The Winged Hussars of Poland

by ZDZISLAW ZYGULSKI, JR.

Dr. Zygulski, Curator of the National Museum in Cracow and Assistant Professor in the Cracow Fine Arts Academy, is one of Poland's foremost art historians, his sphere of special concentration being costume, arms and armor. Born in Boryslav in 1921, he earned his doctorates in Art History and English Literature at the University of Cracow immediately following World War II. He is the author of many articles and monographs published in periodicals and in book form in several languages; among the most important of these are A History of the Czartoryski Collection *and* On Rembrandt's "Polish Rider." *Dr. Zygulski travels widely for his studies. He is married and has a son studying art at the Cracow academy.*

Polish armoured units fighting at the side of the Allies in World War II wore as a badge a symbolic wing, almost vertical, slightly curved at the top. This emblem was taken over from an old Polish military tradition: huge wings made of wood and bird feathers were an emblem of the Polish Hussar Cavalry, established in the early 16th century, victorious on many battlefields (especially in the wars against Muscovy, Sweden, Tartary, and Turkey), and surviving until about the middle of the 18th century. The hussars were born anew in the national romantic legends of the 19th and the 20th centuries, gaining post-mortem a reputation of invincibility. As a matter of fact, like any other formation in any age and army, they encountered defeats along with victories, the former particularly when coming up against well-trained detachments of musketeers. These hussars should not be confused with the *hussards,* a light cavalry of purely Hungarian origin, popular in many armies all over the world (also in Poland) since the 18th century. The formation to which this article is devoted also derived from Hungary, but on Polish soil, and it was soon much altered, being a fortunate combination of Eastern and Western elements with a strong predominance of local traditions and inventions. In its developed form it was a half-heavy cavalry distinguished by a variety of arms and armour, very operative, ready to choose the tactics suitable for the immediate necessity. As a rule the hussars were formed into squadrons of 150-200 horsemen each, and attacked in two lines galloping knee to knee, their

long lances giving a tremendous shock to the enemy. In the mêlée they fought with side-arms and firearms. By daring charges they proved superior to the contemporary West-European cavalry, especially over cuirassiers and carabineers, who were conditioned to a much more static system according to which each rank in succession discharged its pistols and rode back to a place behind the squadron to reload. Hussars could also easily break troops of oriental cavalry because the oriental riders' armament was greatly inferior and devoid of firearms. Iconographical and written sources of the epoch, together with a choice of the best original arms, armour, and equipment preserved in museums, enable us now to present the Polish hussars accurately, particularly to students outside Poland.

Early Hussars

Almost till the end of the 15th century, Polish military forces and weaponry were of Western style, but the constant political and cultural contacts with the East changed the trend of development. The system of general levy of noblemen was replaced by the system of enlisting mercenary troops. Soldiers were recruited at home and abroad. In the wars against the Grand Duchy of Muscovy and against the Tartar Khanates, the kings of the Jagiellon dynasty, reigning in United Poland and Lithuania, had to reform their armies in order to get troops trained for campaigns in vast steppes intersected by marshy rivers. Heavy horsemen in medieval style, clad in armour from head to foot, handling thick lances, were practically

useless. In this situation, troops of light cavalry—hussars—formed chiefly in Serbia and Hungary in the time of Matthias Corvinus and proved excellent in wars against the Turks, were invited to Poland. In the rolls of the Polish and Lithuanian armies of the early 16th century, hussars are mentioned many times, being described as mounted soldiers equipped with thin lances, shields and sabres. The term *Racowie,* which means "Serbians", is generally used in these sources, but some Hungarian names are registered as well. *Hussar* or *gussar* originally meant "a robber" in Serbian. These horsemen served not only under the Polish and Lithuanian colours but also under those of the Holy Roman Emperor; images of hussars in Hungarian style may be easily found in the woodcuts illustrating the deeds of Maximilian I, particularly in the books of *Theuerdank* and *Weisskunig.* Far the best iconographic document of hussar formation in the early 16th century is to be found in an oil painting (Fig. 1) on wood measuring 162cm. x 232cm., datable about 1520, now in the National Museum in Warsaw, depicting the battle of Orsha.[1] In this battle, fought on September 8th, 1514, the allied forces of Poland and Lithuania won a telling victory over the army of Vassili III, Grand Duke of Muscovy. With some reservations, the picture is historically faithful, although the unknown artist was inclined towards exaggeration and multiplications of forms in his rendition of the arms and armour; he must have been well acquainted with the works of Albrecht Dürer and Lucas Cranach the Elder. The Polish-Lithuanian

Fig. 1—Hussars in the battle of Orsha, fought on September 8th, 1514, in a painting of about 1520. (National Museum, Warsaw)

Fig. 2—Hungarian hussar shield of about 1520. (State Collection of Art at Wawel Castle, Cracow)

army is shown as consisting of fully-armoured knights in the old style, of infantry and artillery of light mounted archers, and of the new hussars. The Muscovite side is formed entirely of the heavy-armoured boyar cavalry.

The Orsha hussars are shown precisely, from various angles: marching three or four horsemen in a rank, crossing the Dnieper river, charging, fighting, and in pursuit of the enemy. Lances are their basic weapon: rather thin, of the same width throughout their length, and bearing pennons with crosses. At the attack, the lances are held in the position of "halfway up the horse's ear," rested in the shield notch or free. The shields are typically Hungarian, made of wood, asymmetrical in a form sweeping upward to a sharp point at the top on one side, and painted in bright-coloured stripes (but there are also rondaches spiked in the middle). The sabres are also of Hungarian origin, unfortunately not much depicted in actual use, for the most part shown sheathed in large scabbards mounted with silvered or gilded metal. Some hussars, probably of officer rank, have *buzdygan* maces thrust back under their belts. Horses covered with cloths are led by bridles with heavy bits; saddles are not visible, but stirrups are shown as almost circular, each with a small ball underneath. Spurs

Fig. 3—Turkish *deli* horseman, after the drawing by Nicolas de Nicolay, about 1551.

Fig. 4—Polish hussar in an etching by Abraham de Bruyn, about 1587.

are very unusual, being fitted with large metal wings that cover the upper part of the rider's foot (we do not know any actual example of this kind of spur, but some analogies may be found in the painting and engravings of Albrecht Dürer). Head coverings are varied and numerous, one in the shape of a modern top hat apparently made of black felt being the most frequent; as a rule, it is decorated in the lower part and over the brim with a gilded circlet and a plume in a metal holder. There are also sugar-loaf caps with a similar plume, Hungarian flat caps with upright brims, caps with large flaps, and fashionable berets. No armour is worn by hussars, but short quilted *joupanes* seem to offer sufficient protection. There appears sporadically a short mantel with long sleeves, which may be identified with the national Hungarian article of costume known as a *mente*. Some hussar horses, perhaps those of officers, are decorated with horse-hair streamers called *buntchuks* tied to hang down under the neck.

Few real specimens of 16th century hussar arms and equipment have survived. Among such that have, we find a set of Hungarian shields in the Magyar Nemzeti Múzeum in Budapest and in the State Art Collection at Wawel Castle in Cracow (Fig. 2). Some of these have a painted emblem of an eagle's wing,

Fig. 5—Polish hussar in an etching by Stefano della Bella, about 1645.

93

Fig. 6—A squadron of Polish hussars in the "Stockholmer Roll" . . .

but from iconographical sources it is obvious that they were decorated originally with real eagles' wings, the custom deriving from Turkey. (Horsemen of Turkish crack troops, called *deli,* were distinguished by wings and wild animal skins. Such a *deli* is faithfully represented in an album of Turkish types drawn by Nicolas Nicolay [Fig. 3], who travelled to Istanbul in 1551, and then published his experiences.[2])

Hussars Adopt Armour, Wings and Wild-Animal Skins

In the first half of the 16th century some squadrons of hussars took on helmets and armour, probably to allow them to serve in lieu of the old heavy cavalry which was generally disappearing from the battlefields because it was outmoded. On military rolls and musters of the time (kept scrupulously because they were the basis for indemnities for casualties), the most important pieces of hussar armament were always registered: helmet, mail armour, shield and lance. Sabres, tucks, javelins, axes, bows and quivers, as well as various sorts of firearms, become frequent in the second half of the century. Just after 1550 the

skins of leopards, tigers, bears and wolves begin to be mentioned, but in the absence of these, hussars now wore special types of *kilims* or mantles thrown over the shoulders. Also from this time stem the first reports of huge wings made up of eagle, crane or ostrich feathers, the latter being dyed red, blue or green. In this the custom of the Turkish *deli* was surely imitated, but the form of Polish wings was quite original: feathers were inserted in a row into the appropriate holes drilled into a straight wooden batten which was painted or covered with crimson velvet and mounted in brass; by means of special metal rods riveted to the batten, the finished wing was fixed to the backplate of the man's armour, which was furnished with holders. Should a hussar be without armour or without backplate, he could fix the wing, or a pair of wings, in the holders of the cantle of his saddle; this could be done only after mounting. (Armourless hussars persisted for a long time in the 16th century, and even later [Fig. 4].) A Polish hussar without armour but with a single tall wing of ostrich feathers is perfectly represented in a fine

94

about 1605 or shortly after. (Livrustkammaren, Stockholm)

etching by Stefano della Bella, who observed Polish knights and soldiers in the company of Polish embassies to Rome 1633 and Paris 1645[3] (Fig. 5); both armoured and armourless hussars were used at that late date, but either way, wings were of the essence as the characteristic feature of the formation. Their function and meaning are still not thoroughly explained. It has been suggested that in battle the enemy's horses were frightened by the rustle of these wings—but surely the rustle of even a thousand must have been lost in the terrible cacophony of war. An attempt has been made to interpret the wings as protection against the lassos used by oriental horsemen, especially by the Tartars, but reflection and simple sense rule this thesis out, too. In fact, the function of the wings was surely and solely the creation of a powerful psychological impact. The winged knight clad in armour and wild animal skin must have had the appearance of a superhuman creature, arousing a maelstrom of emotions in the beholder—panic, respect, hate, admiration. But since in actual combat those long, clumsy objects rigidly fixed to the rider's

back could not have been very useful, we must conclude that hussars probably took the wings into battle only rarely if at all, reserving them rather for parade and ceremony.

Not long after the middle of the 16th century most of the hussars were changed into a heavy formation overloaded with equipment and ornaments. A further transformation was wrought by Stephen Batory, Duke of Transylvania, who was elected King of Poland in 1576. He was a man of outstanding military talent who waged a series of successful wars against Muscovy and planned a great expedition against the Turks, but died suddenly before this project could be realized. Batory established a new pattern for the hussar cavalry, making it much more mobile and meticulously disciplined. He discarded forever what remained of heavy helmets, wooden shields and large saddles in medieval style, introducing instead light *zischägge* helmets or special iron hats, light half-armour worn over mail shirts or only supplemented with mail sleeves, and practical hussar saddles and stirrups very much in oriental style, with spurs with protruding

95

Fig. 7—Polish hussar, early 17th century, in a painting in the National Museum in Poznan.

necks. Lances were shortened; the sabre remained the principal sidearm but an additional heavy sabre or pallash—often a long tuck—was tied to the saddle. Holsters in front of the saddle held two wheellock pistols or a short wheellock carbine. War-hammers and *buzdygan*-maces were favourite officers' weapons. The long pennons of the lances fluttering and flapping during the charge made a vivid and dreadful picture in the enemy's eyes.

The hussar style after Batory's reforms is fully displayed in the so-called *Stockholmer Roll* which has survived in the Livrustkammaren in Stockholm.[4] This is a painted frieze about 15 meters long and 50 centimeters high representing the ceremonial entrance of King Sigismund III Wasa and Queen Constance in Cracow in 1605. Besides other military groups, two squadrons of hussars in full gala dress and armament accompany the royal couple (Fig. 6). These hussars have light helmets and cuirasses with mail sleeves, single wings of black feathers, leopard skins or patterned *kilims* over the shoulders, lances with long pennons, sabres and pallashes. Their stirrups are of the Polish variety, deriving from the Tartar-Turkish type. From almost the same time stems a good portrait of a hussar officer in the National Museum in Poznan (Fig. 7), and a miniature of a pair of jousting hussars without wings in the Archives of the Cracow Cathedral (Fig. 8).

A small number of hussar objects dating from the late 16th and early 17th centuries may be found in Polish collections. A group of helmets, without doubt of local production, have been preserved in the Polish Army Museum in Warsaw, in the State Collection of Art at Wawel Castle in Cracow, and in the Castle Armoury at Malbork (Fig. 9). A typical helmet of this kind had the skull made of two pieces joined down the middle, not differing from the kettle helmet

Fig. 8—Hussars jousting: a miniature painting of the early 17th century. (The Archives of Cracow Cathedral)

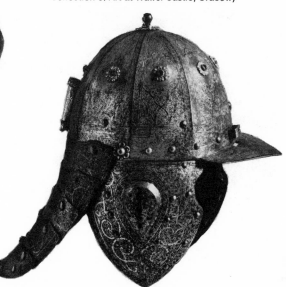

Fig. 9—Hussar iron hat
(*zischägge*), about 1600.
(State Collection of Art at
Wawel Castle, Cracow)

Fig. 10—Hussar officer's *zischägge*, probably
made in Nuremberg, about 1550. (State
Collection of Art at Wawel Castle, Cracow)

or the "iron hat" popular in the Middle Ages,[5] but
fitted with a flat brim and movable nose- ear- and
nape-guards. The ear-guards were pierced in a heart
shape. A whole wagon full of such hussar hats was
found in the bed of the Vistula near Warsaw just before World War 1. In spite of corrosion, the form of
these helmets is quite clear; they are very homoge-
neous, surely made in the same workshop for a hussar
squadron. The helmets of officers were usually much
more elaborate, in this period having been usually imported from abroad. It must be stressed that throughout the 16th century the hussar fashion was cultivated
also in Hungary and in Austria. Decorated *zischägge*
helmets were produced largely in South-Germany,
especially in Nuremberg. In the Armoury of the State
Collection of Art at Wawel Castle in Cracow we find
two such helmets, one of them sumptuously gilded
and set with semiprecious stones, ex-property of a
forefather of the Tyszkiewicz family (Fig. 10), datable about 1550, and the other of Hungarian-Turkish
fashion but with characteristic etchings of Renaissance motifs, dated 1561 and coming from the Rad-
ziwill family. A great number of hussar cuirasses
from the late 16th century are preserved in the old
Arsenal of Graz in Austria, but there are also good
examples in the museums of Warsaw, Cracow, and
Kórnik. Their form derives from the Italian half-
armour called *anima*, constructed entirely of horizontal lames, joined together underneath by a system of
rivets and leather straps and popular as early as 1530,
particularly in the naval service. A hussar cuirass of
the Hungarian-Austrian style consisted of breast and
backplates completed with a gorget worn beneath
them. The examples in Polish hands are sometimes
decorated (but perhaps were not originally) with
brass rosettes or small "vases" (Fig. 11). Mail shirts
or mail sleeves worn with these plate cuirasses were

Fig. 11—Hussar breastplate in Hungarian style, late 16th century.
(Museum of Kórnik)

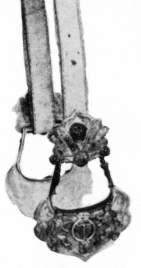

composed of riveted iron rings. (Since chainmail manufacturing techniques changed slowly, it is impossible to tell objects of the late 16th century from those made up to a hundred years later.)

Polish hussar saddles of oriental type but of local production are deep, to give a proper support to the rider's back, especially at the moment of a lance attack. Usually they are covered with embroidered leather or velvet, their bow being mounted in brass or silver while the stirrups, generally called the "Polish variety," are in fact strongly influenced by Tartar-Turkish styles. The best examples of these are now in the Livrustkammaren of Stockholm and in the Orusheynaya Palata of the Kremlin in Moscow (Fig. 12). In the Czartoryski Collection of the National Museum in Cracow we find several interesting hussar spurs of tinned iron with brass inlays, characteristic in their extremely long necks with stars. Poland has fairly rich collections of Hungarian-Polish sabres

Fig. 12—Polish hussar saddle, about 1600. (Livrustkammaren, Stockholm)

Fig. 13—Sabres of Hungarian-Polish style, about 1600. (National Museum, Cracow)

of the late 16th and early 17th centuries, used by the hussar cavalrymen as well as by the infantrymen (Fig. 13) (cavalry sabres always have longer blades, reaching about 80-85 cm.). The blades for these sabres were manufactured in Hungary and in Poland, though the best came from Styria and Italy, particularly from Genoa. They are rather large, and most have several fullers and outstanding yelmens; their hilts have long iron quillons, and the grips are covered with black leather (as are the scabbards, which are mounted with iron or brass furniture sometimes pierced with heart motifs, apparently a favourite among the hussars).

Highlights of Polish Hussar Cavalry

The Golden Age lasted from about 1630 until the middle of the 18th century.[6] In numerous battles of the 17th century hussars played a decisive role in the victory, as for instance at Vienna in 1683.

Fig. 15—Hussar winged armour from the late 17th century. (State Collection of Art at Wawel Castle, Cracow)

Fig. 14—Hussar armour and equipment of about 1640. (Polish Army Museum, Warsaw)

99

Fig. 16—Hussar breastplate, about 1640. (State Collection of Art at Wawel Castle, Cracow)

Fig. 17—Hussar *zischagge* of the early 18th century. (Polish Army Museum, Warsaw)

In the reign of the King Ladislav IV (1632-1648), whose military reforms were of the greatest importance, the national type of hussar armour was adopted. It was a splendid creation of Polish design and craftsmanship (Figs. 14, 15, 16). Uniform in shape and decoration, it consisted of a *zischägge,* breast- and backplates (or sometimes of a breastplate alone), a pair of pauldrons and a pair of arm-guards. Very rarely, long tassets made of lames were attached to the breastplate. The hemispherical skull of the *zischägge* had a beak fixed by rivets through which passed an adjustable nose-guard, leaf-shaped over the nose and secured by a butterfly nut; the ear-guards were movable, being riveted to leather suspensories, and often pierced in heart forms, while a lobster-tail neck-guard of several lames was riveted to the back. Skulls with a fairly high comb, styled after the Western morions or burgonets, were also frequent. In the late 17th century skulls of slightly conical form came into fashion, their surface embossed in large flutes, sometimes decorated in floral pattern and sometimes with brass rosettes, the ear-guards being no longer pierced but adorned with grotesque bronze masks (Fig. 17). In the first half of the 18th century a hussar helmet appeared usually made of blackened iron, with metal wings riveted on both sides of the skull (Fig. 18). The breastplate, the basic part of every armour, was made of bright steel, on the average 3-5mm. thick, and consisted of a large upper plate with a central ridge and of a lower part of three to five lames or splints riveted underneath to leather straps (Fig. 16). The backplate, constructed *en suite* and with the same number of splints, was joined to the breastplate by buckles and thongs. If there was a breastplate only, it was fixed by two crossed straps at the back with a round metal boss in the middle. The gorget was always of two plates pivoted on the left shoulder and secured on the right by a stud and key-slot—unlike its Hungarian counterpart, it was worn over the cuirass. Each pauldron was constructed of a single spherical plate covering the shoulder, having in the front one or several small "wings" protecting the armpit, and terminating in some lames of which the lowest was cut in S-shape to protect the elbow. Arm-guards were separate pieces, entirely in oriental style, similar to Turkish, Persian, or Indian armour ones: long, concave plates adapted to the shape of the forearm and a wristlet of two pieces secured with thongs and buckles. Tassets—used, as already noted, only sporadically—were made of several lames and conventionally styled like similar pieces of Western curassier armour.

This armour in its entirety was very effective and functional. Its weight rarely exceeded 15 kilograms (33 lbs.), the breastplates were bulletproof, all the portions were well adapted to the body (in fact, usually made to measure), and in fighting nothing hampered the wearer's movement. In comparison with corresponding armours from the world's main centers of production—Milan, Nuremberg, Augsburg and Greenwich—it was much simpler, not to say crude, but nevertheless of considerable decorative merit: a mixture of folklore and oriental motifs vigorously adapted and rendered by the makers, most of whom were probably country blacksmiths. Brass was the principal ornamental material, happily combined with brightly polished steel—a combination with a long medieval tradition. The borders of the plates were trimmed with brass, often embossed in small pearls; rivet heads were covered with brass cut in squares or rosettes. Most characteristic were the emblems of cast bronze or brass affixed to the breastplate, and sometimes to the gorget: as a rule it was the "knight's cross", symbol of nobility, i.e. a cross of four equal arms inscribed in a square or a circle; sometimes it was a medallion with the image of the Immaculate Virgin standing on a crescent, commemorating the first Polish Order under the patronage of the Virgin Mary (proposed by the King but rejected by the Seym [Diet]—the great majority of noblemen hated any distinction which could upset their equality. The Polish Order of the White Eagle was finally founded in 1705 by King Augustus the Strong, and its emblem cast in brass, a cross with the inscription *Pro Fide Lege et Rege,* appeared sometimes on hussar breastplates).

In the 18th century the armour style changed. Its forms became rounded, but the edges of the lames became simple and straight, no longer fretted or indented as before. Trimming with embossed brass went out of use, but large brass masks were applied on the pauldrons, and on the breastplates and gorgets the royal monograms or the knight's crest were displayed. Plumes on the helmets, wings and wild animal skins were still very popular, especially as 18th-century hussars became slowly but inexorably ever more a purely ceremonial formation. Some suits of armour with single or double wings, dating from the late 17th or early 18th century, have survived in Polish collections; their battens are straight with the top curved at a contiguous angle, only the armour at Wawel Castle having a pair of wings of S-form (Fig. 15). The wooden battens were by then covered with velvet and mounted in brass, being fixed by special rods into the holders of the backplates; some slight horizontal movement is possible. No original skins from the 17th or 18th century are extant but we know that they were lined, preferably with crimson silk, and were furnished with precious metal clasps.

The armour here described and shown served exclusively for the nobility that formed the elite of hussar squadrons. Each nobleman took with him a group of horsemen who were under his direct command and fought close to him in battle. They were mostly

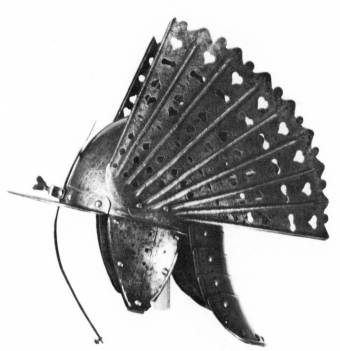

Fig. 18—Winged helmet of hussar style, early 18th century. (Polish Army Museum, Warsaw)

Fig. 19—Fragment of hussar lance, late 17th century. (State Collection of Art at Wawel Castle, Cracow)

young peasants, well trained for war, armoured in the hussar manner but in a much simpler way. These hussars of lower rank often used the helmets called "Dutch pots," being a Western version of the typical *zischägge,* and their armour, without ornaments or knightly emblems, was usually blackened to prevent rust.

The lance remained the most outstanding weapon of the hussars (Fig. 19). Some examples of them dating from the late 17th and 18th centuries are preserved in Polish museums. Their average length runs to 5 meters (just over 16 feet); they are made of two halves of fir wood hollowed out and glued together, only the wooden ball at the mid-point protecting the hand. They are painted in motifs of golden feathers against a red background. Their iron points are fairly small, about 10cm., ridge-shaped and furnished with long metal battens for fixing to the shaft. Nine original hussar pennons made of silk have survived in the Polish Army Museum in Warsaw. Two of them, triangular and dating from the late 17th century, 390cm. long (about 12½ feet) and 71cm. wide at the shaft, (about 28 in.) are of two fields, one crimson and one white, with a knight's cross incrusted; the other seven are slightly longer, of a single crimson field with a knight's cross set between two crossed sabres and two vipers. From iconographical sources we know that other colours were also used: green-red, blue-green, black-white, yellow-white, and sometimes chequered or zigzag motifs. On account of their partial hollow-

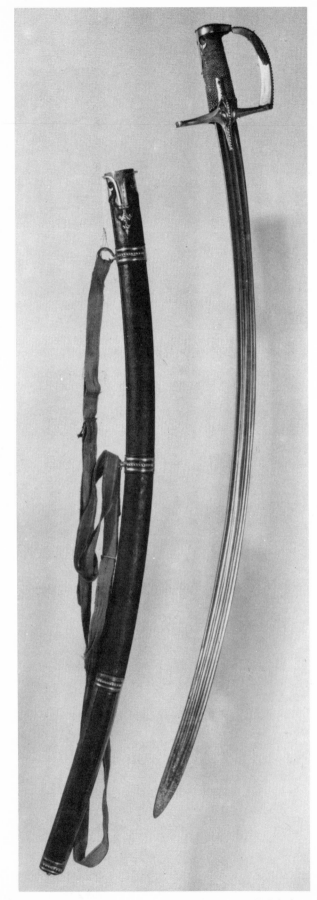

Fig. 20—Hussar sabre of the early 18th century. (Polish Army Museum, Warsaw)

Fig. 21—Hussar sabre hilt, late 17th century; note thumb ring. (National Museum, Cracow)

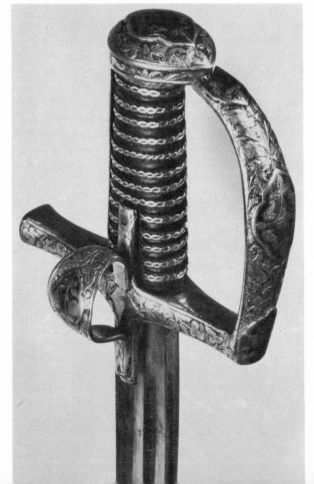

102

ness, the lances rarely exceeded 3 kilograms (about 6 lbs. 9 oz.) in weight and were easily manageable, especially as the "tail" was placed into a special leather tube tied on a thong to the saddle. When charging at a gallop a hussar could pierce an armoured enemy, but the lance usually splintered. In the next stage of fighting hussars used tucks, pallashes or sabres.

A special type of Polish hussar sabre was constructed in the second half of the 17th century (Figs. 20 and 21), eliminating the Hungarian-Polish sabre which dominated up to that time[7]. The hussar sabre was indeed versatile, designed for direct, swinging, and arc-like cuts, executed from the shoulder and elbow. The blade, between 82 and 87cm. long and of the same width almost for its whole length, was double-edged towards the point. Most blades were of Polish manufacture. But the true merit of the hussar sabre lay in the hilt, which had the quillons prolonged in a knuckle-guard and a thumb-ring riveted to the inner languet, while the grip of wood was covered with shark skin or leather and bound with iron or silver wire; the pommel was almond-shaped. The most important feature of this hilt was the thumb-ring: the pressure exerted by the thumb ensured a quick and efficacious cut. Hussar sabres were sometimes called "black sabres" because of the grips and scabbards clad in black leather. Heavy pallashes or tucks with long blades were strapped, as usual, to the saddles. Hussars always held firearms in readiness. At various times, though briefly, their lances were replaced by carbines, but this rendered them essentially equals of mounted arquebusiers in the Western style, and was not continued. Their officers went into battle without helmets to show courage and to be recognizable all the time to their subordinates. Their favourite weapon, besides the sabre or the tuck, was the *buzdygan*-mace, sometimes with a dart, and the warhammer. Along with the saddles and trappings of local make, numerous imported or trophy saddles of oriental manufacture were used by the hussars; Turkish, Persian, Tartar, and Circassian styles were appreciated. These articles were also made in Poland, chiefly by the Armenians imitating successfully Eastern patterns. Goldsmiths' work, embroidery, costly sorts of leather and textiles were lavishly adopted. Horses in parade attire were covered with sumptuous caparisons, while *buntchuk*-tails adorned their necks.

In the long periods of peace in the 18th century Poland, the hussar cavalry came more and more to serve as attendants of such ceremonies as royal entrances, enthronements, weddings or funerals. They always aroused enthusiasm and admiration echoed also by J. Kitowicz, an eminent writer of that period: "It was something to watch when a hussar squadron passed in parade! No monarch in the world had anything like this."

In recent times, hussar legend, tradition and history has been rediscovered by Polish painters and novelists. In the awareness of the national heritage, the hussars still live on.

REFERENCES

1. S. Herbst, M. Walicki—*Obraz bitwy pod Orsza. Dokument historii sztuki i wojskowosci XVI w./The "Battle of Orsha" Painting: A Document of Art History and Military History of the 16 Century/;* in Rozprawy Komisji Historii Kultury i Sztuki. Towarzystwo Naukowe Warszawskie, Vol. 1, 1949, p. 33-67.
   J. Bialostocki—*Zagadke "Bitwy pod Orsza"/"The Battle of Orsha" Enigma/;* in Biuletyn Historii Sztuki, Vol. 17, 1955, no. 1, p. 80-98.
2. Nicolas de Nicolay—*Quatre premiers livres des navigations et peregrinations orientales,* Lyon 1567.
3. Z. Zygulski Jr.—*Rembrandt's "Lisowczyk": " A Study of Costume and Weapons;* in Bulletin du Musée National de Varsovie, VI, 1965, no. 2-3, p. 43-67.
4. K. E. Steneberg—*Polonica.* Kungl.Livrustkammaren, Stockholm, 1943.
5. Claude Blair—*European Armour,* London 1958, p. 31-32.
6. B. Gembarzewski—*Husarze, ubiór, oporzadzenie i uzbrojenie 1500-1775/Hussars' Dress, Equipment, and Armament 1500-1775/;* in Broń i Barwa, Vol. V, Warszawa 1938, p. 207-254, Vol. VI, 1939, p. 51-70.
   Z. Bocheński—*Ze studiów nad polska zbroja husarska/Studies on the Polish Hussar Armour/ ;* in Rozprawy i Sprawozdania Muzeum Narodowego w Krakowie, Vol. VI, Krakow 1960.
   Z. Bocheński—*Próba okreslenia genezy polskiej zbroi husarskiej/Essay on the Origin of the Polish Hussar Armour/;* in Muzealnictwo Wojskowe, Vol. 2, Warszawa 1964, p. 141-166.
7. W. Zablocki—*Funkcjonalno-konstrukcyjna charakterystyka rekojesci dwóch typów polskich szabel bojowych z wieku XVII/Construction and Function of Two Polish War Sabre Hilts of the 17th Century/;* in Studia do dziejów dawnego uzbrojenia i ubioru wojskowego, V, Krakow 1971, p. 57-95.

French Royal Armour as Reflected in the Designs of Etienne Delaune

by BRUNO THOMAS

*Dr. Thomas is the Director of the most important repository of arms and armor
in the world: the* Waffensammlung, *i.e. the Arms Collection of the Hapsburg
Imperial Court, now a division of the Museum of Art History (Kunsthistorisches
Museum) in Vienna. He studied art history, history and languages (he speaks,
in addition to his native German, fluent English, French, Italian and Russian).
He began his career at the* Waffensammlung *in 1934; his principal aims—for the
realization of which he has done research all over the world—have been the
correlation of arms and armor history with generic art history, the development
of refined methods of historical research, the installation at the Kunsthistorische
Museum of effective and scientific restoration laboratories, and the reorganization
and display of the entire Hapsburg collection in correct chronological order.
He is the author of about two hundred publications in monograph and book form.
Since 1969 he has been president of the International Association of Museums
of Arms and Military History.*

European armour, whether gothic, renaissance, manneristic or even baroque, was not just a rough, simple object for military use, a defensive arm with no other aim than the primary one of safeguarding the wearer's life and limb. Rather, though wrought and riveted instead of scissored and sewn, it represented in all its periods of brilliant presence in our civilisation a species of iron integument created in accordance with those same laws and currents that governed the styles and evolutions of textile clothing—in a word, fashion. Moreover, weapons and their accessories, too—swords, daggers and firearms in their inexhaustible varieties over the centuries—were often chiselled, enamelled, bejewelled, chased, carved, inlaid and otherwise more or less resplendently elaborated constituents of the male costume. But armour was much more than just glitter and vogue: it forms nothing less than a vital chapter in the history of European sculpture, a very special type of three-dimensional art—sculpture in hard iron—which the onlooker must experience and enjoy literally from all directions. A mobile and stylised layer conceived and constructed almost like an outward extension of the human body it covered, armour was first of all required to adapt itself to, and to obey with elegance and precision, its wearer's every movement, idealizing his shapes and measures, transforming his appearance according to the dictates of art and ingenuity; it was a work of art often as astonishingly refined and rich in its solution of spatial and dynamic problems as in its realization of ornament.

Smooth armour is pure shape. Its surface could be left in the white or be decorated in many different ways: by gilding, bluing or blackening, by etching, engraving or by gold and silver damascening, and—most exalted of all techniques—by embossing and chasing into bas-reliefs ranging in complexity from sparse ornamental motifs, sometimes enriched by single figures, to vast tableaux depicting complete, often agitated and amply populated scenes within rich borders; drawings and paintings by celebrated contemporary masters were not infrequently used as sources. Embossed relief was sometimes left plain and at other times enhanced by overetching or by engraving, or by gilding and silvering, or by overpainting with oil paint to imitate lacquer or enamel. The final results were the parade armours reserved for emperors, kings and princes, and for their regents and marshals and dignitaries of rank and riches. There were several centers of production throughout Europe. In Italy, Milan ranked highest, not only on a peninsular but on a continental scale; Brescia was second. In Germany and Austria, Augsburg remained ever unsurpassed, followed by Innsbruck, Nuremberg, Landshut and Brunswick. In the Low Countries

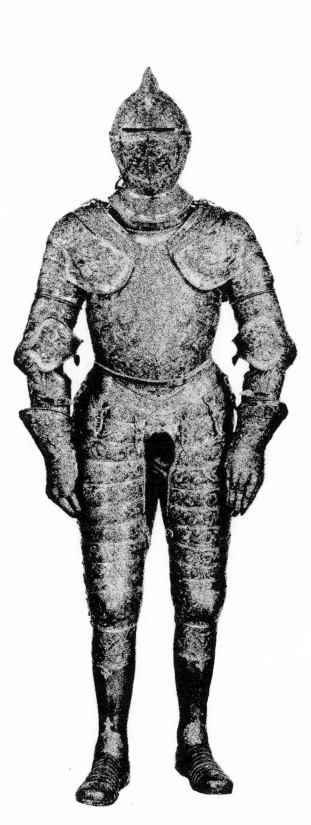

it was Antwerp and Brussels, in England, Greenwich. In France, too, a national school was active between about 1540 and 1630; but, whereas other schools have been explored and presented in works like *Die deutsche Plattnerkunst* (B. Thomas), *L'Arte dell'Armatura in Italia* (G. L. Boccia/E. Coelho), *L'Arte Milanese dell'Armatura* and *Die Innsbrucker Plattnerkunst* (B. Thomas/O. Gamber), *Greenwich Armour* and *Armour in Spain* (B. Thomas) and others, French armour, with its exquisite masterpieces conceived in very special taste, has never received the benefit of presentation in a comprehensive and representative volume. Only about a dozen publications exist, mostly monographs on single specimens and partly essays studying certain aspects. Moreover, owing to the total lack of pertinent documents in the archives and of positive identification of masters' marks and signatures, it has proven thus far impossible, in spite of all efforts, to locate the workshops of French armourers.

Hence the present writer deems himself fortunate to have at least succeeded in establishing the part played by Etienne Delaune (1518/19-1583), medallist, designer, engraver and generally Chief Artist to the court of Henry II (r. 1547-59), as almost the sole designer of the decorations on King Henry's parade armours—although it must be pointed out that except for the one single case of a morion and buckler that belonged to Charles IX (r. 1560-74),

Fig. 1—Suit of armour engraved and gilded throughout in imitation of textile and embroidery, made for Charles IX in about 1570. (Paris, Musée de l'Armée, No. G120)

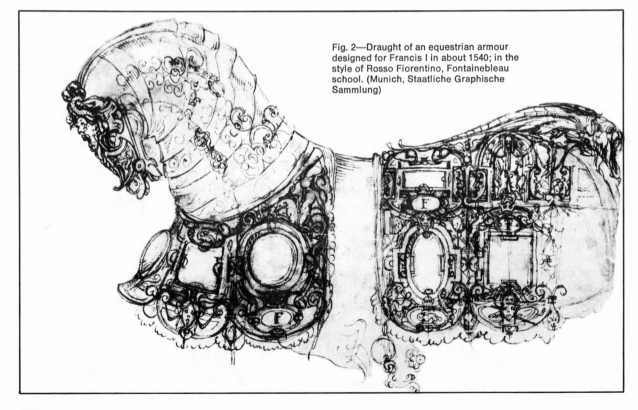

Fig. 2—Draught of an equestrian armour designed for Francis I in about 1540; in the style of Rosso Fiorentino, Fontainebleau school. (Munich, Staatliche Graphische Sammlung)

106

Fig. 3—Portrait by Jean or Francois Clouet, about 1540, of Francis I in an embossed armour which, like the equestrian complement, is of a true French style. (Florence, Uffizi Galleries)

now in the Louvre and executed after Delaune's drawings by the Parisian goldsmith Odilon Redon before 1572, no armourer's name has, in fact, been found for any other French arm or armour. If this seems astonishing, how much more so the fact that nowhere has there been preserved, not in France nor anywhere else, one single piece of armour of proved French origin made before the last years of the reign of Francis I, i.e. before about 1540-45, nor a single object of military use nor a single pageant piece (with but the one exception of the sad remains in the Chartre Museum of an armour of King Charles VI [r. 1380-92], Italian work or perhaps French, now reduced to fragments, dating from

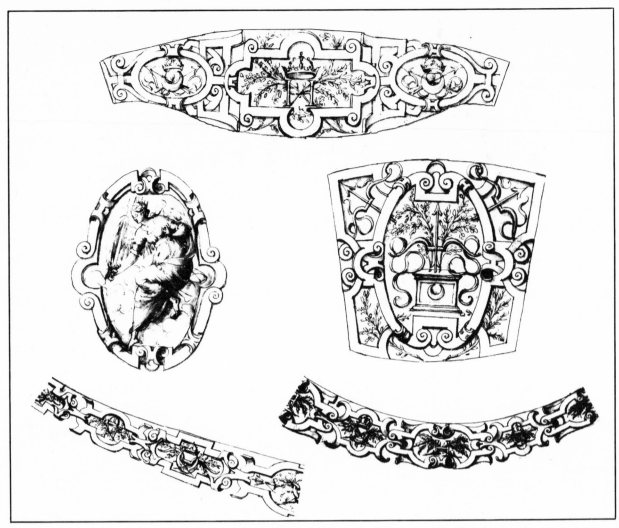

Fig. 4—Five drawings of components of a suit of man and horse armour, the ornamentation based on royal monograms and emblems, by Etienne Delaune, about 1555, in *First Variant* style. (Munich, Staatliche Graphische Sammlung)

about 1388-1400)! Therefore French armour before about 1540-45 can only be studied by means of contemporary iconographic sources depicting battles, tournaments, feasts and the like. In strange and dramatic contrast, the noble families of Italy, Austria and Germany carefully conserved personal arms and armour all through the centuries right down to our days. Why this should be so no one has ever really managed to explain, but it gives even greater urgency to the need for continuous researches so that perhaps one day we may come to know more about the character and development of the French armour proper.

But we do know that the inspiration—at least as far as the 16th century goes—derived from Italian models. In fact, all the 16th century French arts, major and minor, deriving from what is now called the *Fontainebleau* school, are strongly Italian-oriented, an all but indelible imprint that started when Francis I engaged Rosso Fiorentino (1494-1540) in 1530 (gallicised to le Roux, "the Redhead")

and Francesco Primaticcio (1504-1570) in 1532 *(le Primatice,* roughly "the Early One", although the Italian-French sense can't be really translated) for the express purpose of bringing and teaching the Italian arts to France. Just as Francis I collected masterpieces by Leonardo and Raphael, by Titian and Cellini, so he and his son Henry II demanded and wore the masterpieces of armour created in Milan. A dozen specimens of these have survived in different collections, particularly in the Musée de l'Armée in Paris—works by Giovanni Paolo Negroli and his more famous cousin Iacopo Filippo. Perhaps the Italian armour "alla romana" (a style created by the Milanese armourers in the image of Roman antiquity to vest contemporary regents in the aura of Roman emperors) worn by Francis on the tapestry *L'Unité de État* in Fontainebleau really existed and was not just a symbolistic invention of the painter. His *Lion Armour* with its silver cross can be seen in the Musée de l'Armée. The casque with the Medusa, believed to have been his (now in

Fig. 5—Two plaques from a horse armour made for Henry II after drawings by Etienne Delaune, 1556-59, in *First Variant* style. (New York, Co.O. Von Kienbusch Collection)

the Metropolitan Museum of Art, New York), bears the date 1543 and the signature of Filippo Negroli. The Musée de l'Armée possesses an exquisite armour of Henry II when dauphin, damascened in silver on blackened ground; the present writer attributes this, too, to Filippo Negroli. An Italian armour with scrolled foliage and the emblems of Henry II was illustrated by Filippo Orsi of Mantua in his book of drawings of 1554. An engraving by Nicolò della Casa dated 1547 represents the young king wearing an armour "alla romana."

In addition to favoring the Italian school, however, both Francis I and his son encouraged and promoted the development of a truly French one, too—Henry far more even than his father. In 1549, two years after the Nicolò della Casa engraving, Jean Goujon drew Henry and his horse in armours decorated with repeated scrollwork which is no longer pure Italian but emergent French. As the century progressed, French collaborators and pupils of the Italian masters at Fontainbleau and in Paris

—including the armourers—freed themselves, little by little but surely, from the powerful foreign domination; by about 1550-60 the body of the French armourers were working in a markedly French idiom —and a very fine one at that, destined to breed true, to flower and to influence the North and East of Europe via Antwerp and Augsburg, manifesting itself even in Sweden, in Saxony and in Poland. At first this new manner still hewed to Italian antecedents, but soon there appeared borderlines cut out to form semi-circles (or convex scallops), and an ornamentation consisting of interlaced bands characteristic of French mannerism; the technique of execution was *acqua forte* etching and gilding over the entire surface. One of Henry II's armours of about 1550, formerly in the Wartburg in Thuringia but missing since 1945, was covered with an etched copy of a drawing by Jacques I. DuCerceau, representing arabesques and figurative scenes enclosed by such interlaced bands; but DuCerceau still leaned heavily on the Fontainebleau school, and particularly

Fig. 6—Design for the backplate of the *Julius-Caesar-and-Pompey Armour* by Etienne Delaune, about 1556-59 in *Second Variant* style. (H.M. Armouries in the Tower of London)

Figs. 7 & 7a—Overall and closeup views (one with the pauldrons removed) of the backplate made from the Delaune design in Fig. 6. (Paris, Louvre)

110

on Rosso Fiorentino, for his inspiration in ornamental motifs. Three armours, also entirely gilded, belonging to Henry's three sons and successors (Francis II, r. 1559-60; Charles IX, r. 1560-74; and Henry III, r. 1547-89) and now in the Musée de l'Armée, are French works rendered very characteristic by their etched-iron imitations of painted paper, tapestry and embroidered textiles (Fig. 1). In short, French armour had its origins in italianate Fontainebleau, perceiving and transforming *à la française* the impulses and conceptions *all'italiana* imported from the South.

An extremely influential series of drawings in the manner of Rosso Fiorentino were found among the preparatory sketches for the wainscoting and a fireplace in Fontainebleau; they are part of an incomparable collection of 170 sheets in the Staatliche Graphische Sammlung (National Graphics Collection) in Munich, showing life-sized armour designs, all the parts of the armours being shown as entirely covered with the ornamentation that is to be transposed in bas-relief.* Most of these 170 works, but not all, are by the hand of Etienne Delaune and, in fact, to understand them in proper perspective one must first consider the ornamental devices found on those among them done by Delaune's forerunners in Fontainebleau, such as the drawings for the wainscoting in the Gallery of Francis I executed between 1535 and 1540 by the Italian master Francesco da Carpi, or the drawing for the fireplace in the Queen's chamber done by Primaticcio himself. (Parenthetically, the present writer would like to seize the occasion to urge competent specialists in these spheres to help make a little order by analysing and attributing these drawings to the most probable authors, Italian as well as French.) Of the many superb armour designs (e.g., Fig. 2), a few were realised in armours that are still extent or known to have existed until recently (e.g., a fine chaffron, until 1945 in the Musée de l'Armée, is now lost). A project for a burgonet by an unknown master, in the present writer's view a Frenchman, is outstanding for its new assertion of independence from the impassioned, muscular, almost acrobatic Italian themes; similarly conspicuous is a drawing for a missal binding and for a dagger sheath. But the decisive step from italicism to true gallicism appears on two modest sheets of draughts for two gorget lames of the very armour worn by Francis I in a portrait painted by Jean or Francois Clouet shortly after 1540 (Fig. 3).

_____

*For a complete episode treatment of the Munich drawings, see B. Thomas, *Die Münchner Harnischvorzeichnungen,* in the Jahrbuch der Kunsthistorischen Sammlungen in Wien, Vol. 55 (1959), Vol. 56 (1960), Vol. 58 (1962) and Vol. 61 (1965). Up to the moment of this writing, i.e. October 1973, these Yearbooks have been published only in German.

Fig. 8—Overall view of the entire armour shown in Figs. 7 and 7a.

This armour, now lost without a trace, was the first example of a French parade armour; although still owning debts to Italian embossed antecedents, it was nevertheless a French creation with a strong and sure French personality. The kings from Henry II to Henry IV were to pride and preen themselves in the subsequent flowerings of this seedling, and Etienne Delaune was to be its nurturing husbandman.

111

Fig. 9—Buckler probably for Henry II made after a design by Etienne Delaune in *Second Variant* style. (Turin, Armeria Reale)

All the remaining sheets consist of preparatory black-crayon *bozzetti,* pen-and-watercolour elaborations, and red-chalk copies of the latter, simply rendered, for execution in iron by the armourer-goldsmiths. Comparison with many undisputedly authentic drawings and engravings by Delaune confirms the attribution of about 146 of these 170 works to him. It is the impression of the present writer that this collection was, in fact, a part of Delaune's estate. Evidently he collected not only all the drawings of his Italian predecessors in Fontainebleau he could lay his hands on but of their French colleagues as well, adding also his own works. He and his son Jean seem to have lent a good many of these sheets to others, and finally to have bequeathed them all (also perhaps some now lost) to a pupil or companion in Antwerp or Augsburg: there would be no other way of explaining the fact that the goldsmith Eliseus Libaerts of Antwerp used and copied Delaune drawings when making embossed armours for King Eric XIV of Sweden between about 1560 and 1565, or that on the backs of five drawings by Delaune we find contemporary inscriptions in southern German, or that Delaune engravings were copied by an Augsburg artist in about 1575-80.

In short, careful studies of the Munich drawings inexorably reveal Etienne Delaune as the creator of truly French armour and pageant bucklers in the third quarter of the 16th century. Moreover, he arrived at three styles for embossed bas-relief that became recognisable "signatures":

First Variant (Figs. 4 & 5): The framing dominates—

it consists of renaissance interlacements formed of broad bands, masks and festoons, and central cartouches inhabited at most by one or two isolated figures.

Second Variant (Figs. 6, 7 & 7a): The framing is inhabited by more and more figures of symbolic and compositional importance, the border around the cartouche has become narrower, thinner; the cartouche shows whole scenes of battles, of ancient and modern history or of mythology; sometimes the cartouche is left without any enclosure.

Third Variant (Figs. 10 & 11): Elegant scrollwork covers the entire surface; it contains a wealth of fabulous beasts and grotesques, creatures springing from a rich but still Italian-influenced fantasy.

When was all this made? No doubt during the short reign of Henry II, i.e. between 1547 and 1559, while Delaune held, among other honours, the post of engraver to the royal mint, producing engravings for medals in 1556 for the commemoration of significant events in Henry's reign. No doubt it was he who was at the same time called upon to create sumptuous, spectacular pageant bucklers and parade armours to spread the renown of his master throughout the French and other realms. He also left many life-size drawings for five armours for man and horse ordered by Henry. The first set of six drawings is based on motifs of royal emblems: crown, fleur-de-lis, monogram H, crescent, and bow and arrows of Diana (Fig. 4), all very close in style to the fireplace ornamentations by Philibert Delorme executed between 1550 and 1556 for the ballroom at Fontainebleau; nothing has survived of the armour itself. These drawings are executed in the *First Variant* style. The second set, consisting of 71 drawings based on serpent motifs and also executed in *First Variant* style, is divided into twenty-five of man armour and forty-six of horse. The chaffron done from these existed until 1945 but is now lost, but three crupper plates survive in the Cluny Museum, Paris, and in the Kienbusch Collection, New York. Third comes a set based on the story of Julius Caesar and Pompey (Figs. 6, 7, 7a & 8), in *Second Variant* style, in which Henry II is identified with Caesar (his father had ordered himself to be represented as Vercingetorix!). The man's armour of this suite is preserved in the Louvre, the chaffron and saddle in Lyon. A fourth set is based on cornucopias (Figs. 10 & 11) and consists of twenty-one drawings in brown pen-and-watercolour done in *Third Variant* style, while a fifth set, also in *Third Variant* style, is based on a figure of a Roman emperor and consists of nineteen black-pen and gray-watercolour drawings; combinations of elements from these fourth and fifth sets were executed on Henry II's armour now in the Metropolitan Museum of Art, New York, i.e. the Roman-emperors theme for the breast- and backplate, the cornucopia for all the other parts. Three designs for the *Labours-of-Hercules Armour* now in the Arms Collection of the Kunsthistorische Museum in Vienna have also been preserved. There are five Delaune drawings with scrollwork for the non-extant armour of an adolescent, probably the young Charles; its decoration is very similar to the *Mars-and-Victory Armour*, c. 1565-70, now in the Musée de l'Armée. Another drawing for a backplate can be identified by a portrait sketched in black crayon by François Clouet in about 1570, in which Henry III is wearing his *Lion Armour,* the casque of which is in the Musée de l'Armée while one of its detached gorget plates rests in a private collection in the United States. Though no specific drawings have come to light, the spirit of Delaune was clearly the creative force behind several other armours of Henry III, now in Vienna and Dresden.

Let us briefly survey the embossed bucklers made after Delaune designs present in the Munich collection. Six bear the monogram and emblems of Henry II and illustrate events of his reign in embossed relief; most likely Henry had planned to hang these in the armoury projected for the Pavillon d'Armes at Fontainebleau; replicas without monograms exist, but it is not known for whom they were made. Delaune-designed bucklers executed in France (and also in Augsburg and Antwerp) are now present in collections all over the world, from New York to Skokloster (Sweden), from Leningrad to Turin, from Windsor Castle to Madrid. There are three shapes of Delaune bucklers: round, oval or pointed-oval, and fantasy shields with cut-out contours. There exists also a series of bucklers with purely ornamental scrollwork.

Eienne Delaune's genuis and taste reigned over the creations of royal parade armour in France until the death of Henry IV in 1610. His style was widely imitated in the North and the East of Europe; in France it underwent a revival in the 17th century through the designs of Jean Bérain and his son, and again very forcefully in the 19th century through the imitations, the variations, the rhapsodies of embossed pseudo-Delaune work produced by the Lorraine master Antoine Vechté (1799-1868). The problems of Delaune's influence, in his own time and long after, continue to offer absorbing challenges to the researcher.

Fig. 10—Armour made after Delaune designs mixing motifs of cornucopias and Roman emperors, probably made for Henry II, c.1555. *Second Variant* style, Lombard-French execution. (New York, Metropolitan Museum of Art, *ex* ducal collections of Weimar)

Fig. 11—Design for the left pauldron (shoulder piece), with cornucopias, of the armour shown in Fig. 10. (Munich, Staatliche Graphische Sammlung)

The World's Oldest Known Flintlock Pistol?

by W. KEITH NEAL

William Keith Neal, one of the world's foremost collectors of arms and armor and doubtless the *foremost of firearms, is the author of* Spanish Guns & Pistols *(London, G. Bell & Sons, 1955), and co-author, with D.H.L. Back, of* Forsyth & Company: Patent Gunmakers *(G. Bell & Sons, London, 1969) and* The Mantons: Gunmakers *(London, Herbert Jenkins, 1966). He resides in Wiltshire, England, but travels far and often for his unending researches into arms history.*

The flintlock pistol which is the subject of the present notes is a new and hitherto unpublished discovery which may, I think, be fairly described as sensational: for if it is not the actual pilot model for the world's very first military fintlock handgun, as it may well be, it is in any event an example of an archetypal flintlock weapon unknown in arms studies until now.

To begin with, it is a true fintlock, as defined by Torsten Lenk, in his classic work *Flintlaset,* (Stockholm, 1939): a mechanism in which a flake of flint, held in the jaws of a forward-snapping cock, is made to strike against, and excite sparks out of, the flat, vertical limb of an L-shaped piece of steel whose horizontal foot, pivoted at the toe, forms the flashpan cover, while internally a vertical-working scear engages notches in a vertically-working tumbler and holds the cock in the half- and full-cock positions. It is, in short, essentially—though prototypal and unrefined—the flintlock all collectors know, usually in its later forms; it remained in use in Europe and America into the 1830's (by the military into the 1840's), and elsewhere into the present century. Its antecedents in the sixteenth century were the Portuguese and Spanish miquelet locks, the Dutch-Scottish snaphaunce, the Italian snaphaunce and perhaps the Swedish snap lock.

It is this mechanism that constitutes the most important part of the pistol under consideration. Its approximate chronological and typal parallels are to be found on two long arms made by the Le Bourgeoys family of Lisieux between 1600 and 1620 for

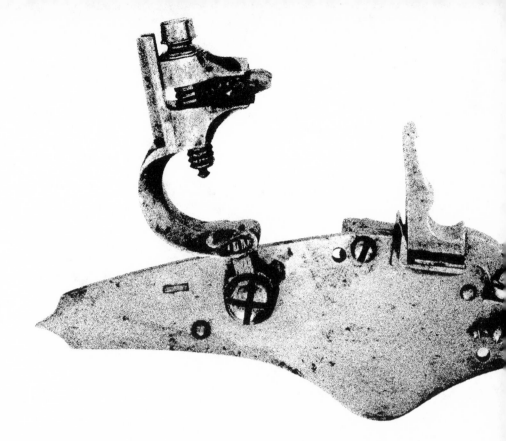

the French court (for full illustrations and descriptions, see *Flintlaset,* sup.cit.). Both of these are considered to be the earliest known true flintlocks, made by the inventors; both were once part of the *Cabinet d'Armes* of Louis XIII (born 1601, reigned 1610-43), of which a very complete inventory has come down to us. Both are luxury weapons, their stocks superbly carved and inlaid, the barrels richly ornamented—but the locks comparatively plain, though well-made and elegant. The earlier of these pieces, now in the Hermitage in Leningrad, may have been made for Henry IV (father of Louis XIII, born 1553, assured of the crown 1594, assassinated 1610). The other, until 1972 in the collection of the late William Goodwin Renwick of Tucson, Arizona, and now in the Metropolitan Museum of Art, New York, may be dated about 1615; it bears the cypher "L" of Louis XIII surmounted by a crown amidst sprays of leaves inlaid in silver on the stock, and is exactly described in the *Cabinet d'Armes* inventory as Item No. 134. (See sales catalog, Sotheby & Co., 35 New Bond Street, London W.1, *Sale of the W.G. Renwick Collection, Part II,* November 21, 1972, with additional notes in photocopy on the Le Bourgeoys gun by John F. Hayward.)*

A comparison of the lock of the present pistol with that of the ex-Renwick Le Bourgeoys gun shows common characteristics as well as significant differences. Internally, both arrangements of mainsprings,

Since this was written, Mr. Hayward's notes have been published in expanded form in *Livrustkammaren,* Vol. 13, 1973 (Stockholm)—Ed.

tumblers and scears are very similar, but the pistol lock plate is more full-bellied along its bottom edge, much as in contemporary French wheellocks, and the hole for the foremost of the transverse screws that hold the lock to the stock is placed almost below the screw that holds the mainspring in place (in the Le Bourgeoys gun the corresponding hole is in the normal position). The pistol cock is of a much more archaic form than its counterpart on the gun: its C-curve makes it a close relative still of wheellock dog-heads, its base is small and octagonal (no larger than the head of the retaining screw), and the main C-shaped mid section, terminating in the jaws, is supported by a square pillar between octagonal base and C-curve. Then, the fall of the Le Bourgeoys gun cocks is arrested by a buffer, that of the pistol cock by a stepped shoulder that strikes the top edge of the lock plate. An extraordinary feature of the pistol lock is the tail of the pan-cover: it has four projections, the first acted upon by the feather spring to present the frizzen in firing position with the pan closed, the second holding the pan-cover in the normal open position, and the third allowing it to rotate still farther forward, much like the rotation of the frizzen arm of a snaphaunce. The shape of the pistol frizzen follows very closely that of the frizzens on the Le Bourgeoys guns: the peascod front, the rolled top and the short, squat shape are sufficiently alike to speak persuasively of a connection between this pistol and the Le Bourgeoys pieces. If, however, the Le Bourgeoys and the pistol locks are examined side by side with both cocks set

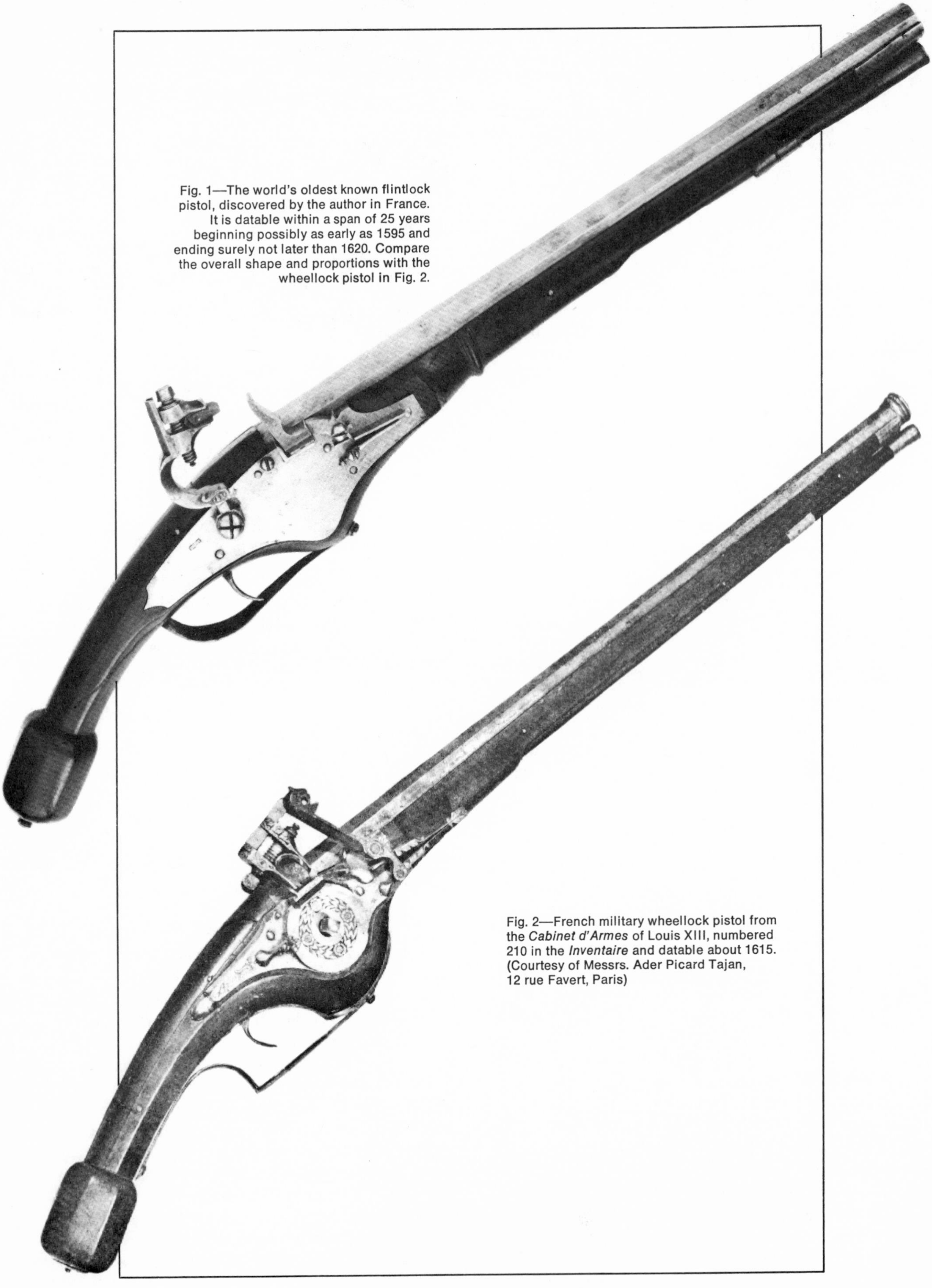

Fig. 1—The world's oldest known flintlock pistol, discovered by the author in France. It is datable within a span of 25 years beginning possibly as early as 1595 and ending surely not later than 1620. Compare the overall shape and proportions with the wheellock pistol in Fig. 2.

Fig. 2—French military wheellock pistol from the *Cabinet d'Armes* of Louis XIII, numbered 210 in the *Inventaire* and datable about 1615. (Courtesy of Messrs. Ader Picard Tajan, 12 rue Favert, Paris)

Figs. 3 & 4—Outside and inside views of one of the two Le Bourgeoys locks, considered the oldest extant examples of the true flintlock. Lock shown comes from the ex-Renwick Collection fowling piece, now in the Metropolitan Museum of Art, New York; it is datable about 1615. It is clearly two or three evolutionary steps beyond the lock of the pistol under discussion.

at half-cock, it becomes apparent that the pistol cock stands much higher against the face of the frizzen than does the gun cock—a position reminiscent of the sweeping or scraping action of the Scandinavian snaplocks. These small differences—the "paunchy" lock plate, the position of the transverse screw hole, the C-curved cock and its high position, the three-way frizzen rotation—would tend to suggest that the pistol lock represents an evolutionary step preceding the more sophisticated, far less uncertain and experimental Le Bourgeoys devices.

As to the general shape, style and outline of the pistol, comparison with the wheellock pistol numbered 210 in the Louis XIII *Cabinet d'Armes* inventory is profitable. Both butts, typically French for the period 1600-1620, are octagonal, faintly ovoid

cylinders with chamfered edges top and bottom, that of the flintlock terminating in a small iron pommel surrounded by four iron fleur-de-lis inlays. The shape of the flintlock pistol lockplate clearly shows its close family ties to the wheellock (whereas the Le Bourgeoys locks are already more elongated, more shaped to their own new needs rather than to lingering tradition). The rear transverse lock retaining screws of both pistols pass through the breech plug flats, retaining thus also the barrels in the stocks. The forward screw is placed, as already noted, to pass below the long mainspring, whose pin, in fact, takes up the usual position of the forward screw. Careful study of the inletting of the lock recess leaves no doubt whatever that the flintlock is the original, first and only lock made for

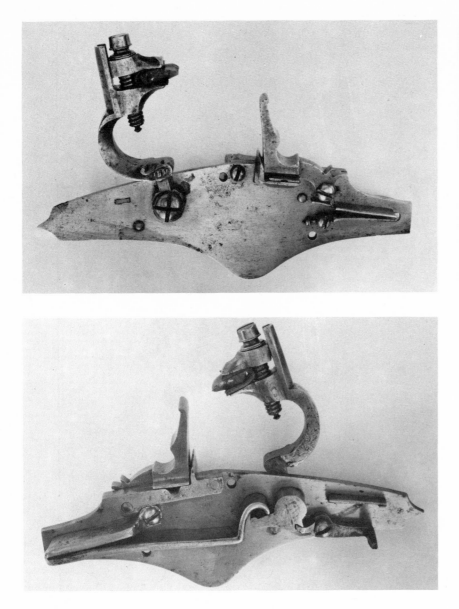

Figs. 5, 6 & 7—Outside, inside and top views of the pistol lock. Note its affinity to wheellock shape and proportions, the odd transverse screw holes, the obvious archaicness when compared to the Le Bourgeoys lock.

this weapon. Another point of interest is our pistol's trigger: it is hung vertically as in a wheellock, but has a rearward horizontal extension which, when the trigger is pulled, moves upward in order to lift the tail of the vertically-acting scear. This is another indication that the pistol represents a transitional step still harking back to wheellock conventions.

It was the present writer's good fortune to have found this challenging piece in France not long ago. At the time of its "discovery" it had the look of an arm that has long lain untouched. Lock, stock and barrel were all coated with that characteristic yellow film one often finds on old weapons which have been stored away for many years in arsenals or in very old collections—it seems to consist of animal oil with perhaps some shellac to harden it. At all

events, it was a wonderful preservative, as no trace of wood worm had infested the stock, nor had any rust formed on the barrel or the lock. The piece's overall length is 23 in. (58.4 cm.). The octagonal barrel is 14½ in. (36.8 cm.) long, and of .500 calibre (12.7 mm.). The wood is pear, much favoured by the French for quality service arms. The lockplate itself measures 6¼ in. (16.5 cm.).

Now, for the proper framing of the pistol's origins in terms of time and purpose, one must bear in mind one not-widely-known but extremely important historical fact, viz., that in 16th-century France it was illegal to possess or use pistols fired without conventional wheellocks, there being cases on record even from the end of the century of the death penalty threatened upon offenders. It is hence unlikely

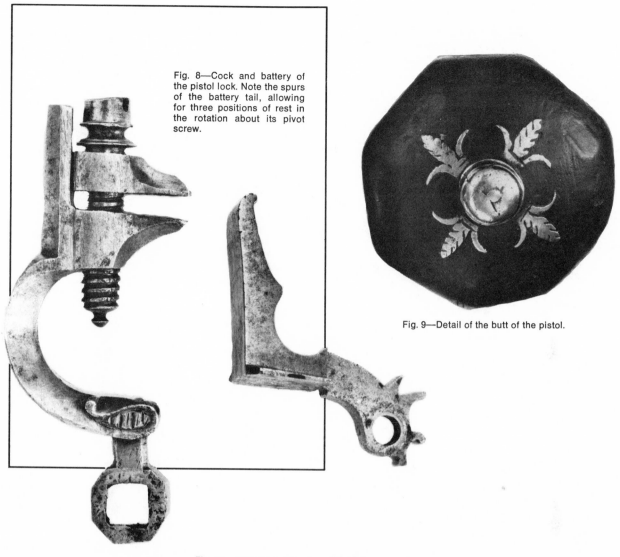

Fig. 8—Cock and battery of the pistol lock. Note the spurs of the battery tail, allowing for three positions of rest in the rotation about its pivot screw.

Fig. 9—Detail of the butt of the pistol.

Fig. 10—Unusual positioning of the transverse screws.

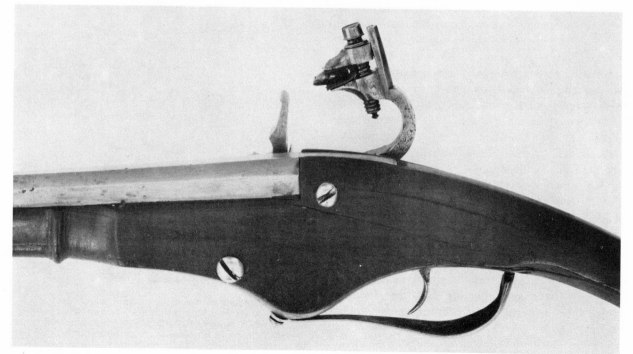

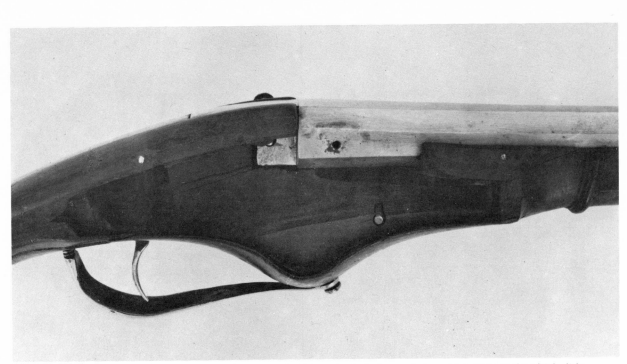

Fig. 11—Interior of the lock recess. The flintlock is the first and only lock ever to have been fitted to the pistol—it is not a substitution for an earlier wheellock or other snapping mechanism.

that any gunmaker would construct a flintlock pistol at the very beginning of the 17th century unless either for, or by the order of, a personage secure of his immunity from such dangers: and this personage, in the case at hand, could very plausibly have been the king, for both Henry IV and Louis XIII—especially the latter—were impassioned devotees of firearms and their development. Louis received his first gun at the age of four in 1605, and six years later had seven; throughout his life he collected firearms from all over the world, and it was largely due to him that France became the world's fountainhead of the gunmaking arts and sciences. He personally supervised the gunmakers working on pieces made to his order; he did not limit his interest to princely sporting weapons but was equally fascinated—as the inventory shows—by plain service and experimental arms.

Is it not quite tenable, then, that this remarkable pistol was designed as a prototype of a radically new service pattern, based on the then barely-invented true flintlock, made either by Louis's order or for presentation to him by an enterprising gunsmith?—and that by a trick of fate it has remained hidden away these past 350-odd years? The author of these lines thinks it not only tenable but likely. In any event, the piece surely stands in relation to military hand guns as the Le Bourgeoys long arms stand in relation to sporting weapons: in each case, the very first specimen known with true flintlock ignition. Until contradictory evidence comes to light, the pistol under discussion must stand as the oldest surviving true flintlock pistol.

Fig. 12—A flintlock cock from the pattern book of Philippe Daubigny, 1635. By the 1630's, flintlock cocks had developed into their essentially permanent, basically S-shaped form, already far removed from the Le Bourgeoys cock and even farther from that of the pistol under discussion.

A Cautious Announcement Concerning a Possible Reappraisal of the Accepted Theories on the Miquelet Lock's Time and Place of Origin

by ROBERT HELD

Our next contributor, as some readers may have observed, is ARMS AND ARMOR ANNUAL's *editor. Since he did not wish to appear an exploiter of his position for the promulgation of his discovery, he sent in the typescript of the present piece with the by-line "The Editors;" but we in the Northfield administrative offices decided to lift the mask and let his true and bearded face emerge, for if his conjectures and conclusions are as valid as indeed many authorities by now seem to think they are, they will prove of such importance to firearms history that he should, we think, get credit for them.*

—The Publishers

 In Spring, 1973, the little pistol shown in the accompanying photographs was sold at antique arms auction in Rome under the following catalogue description:

> *Importante e rara pistola con batteria alla micheletta. Montature e decorazioni in acciaio.— Spagna, sec. XVIII.* (Important and rare pistol with a miquelet lock. Mounts and decorations in steel.—Spain, 18th century.)

The purchaser—who desires to remain anonymous but who has kindly consented to examination of the piece by qualified students and to its publication in this volume—recognized at once not only the error of this identification but the possibly inestimable significance of the weapon. From the fact that the final price was the equivalent of well over $1000—an absurd figure for an 18th-century Spanish miquelet pistol of mediocre quality and in extremely bad condition—and that the bidding above $300 was a tenacious duel between the final purchaser and an unknown opponent, it would appear that at least one other person had arrived at the same conclusion about what was at stake. (Should these pages come to his eyes: the purchaser and The Editors salute him for his knowledge and judgment!)

And what was at stake? Before embarking on an exposition of the case, even in the most cautious of terms, we pause to underline in boldest red that all we say is a *provisional* viewpoint, an evaluation based on brief and perhaps insufficient comparisons with other specimens in various public and private collec-

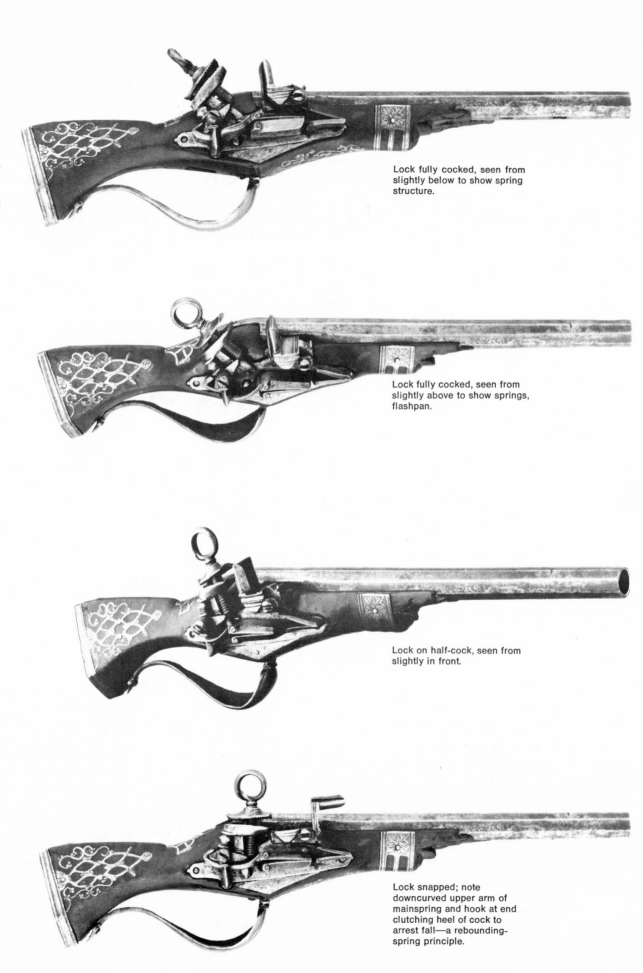

Lock fully cocked, seen from slightly below to show spring structure.

Lock fully cocked, seen from slightly above to show springs, flashpan.

Lock on half-cock, seen from slightly in front.

Lock snapped; note downcurved upper arm of mainspring and hook at end clutching heel of cock to arrest fall—a rebounding-spring principle.

tions throughout Europe and America, an attribution to a time and place for which hardly any hard-core research has ever been done, a dish served up with more spice and broth than meat and potatoes—in short, a pioneering sort of venture, not without its purely intuitive constituent but, on the other hand, not without claims to respectability and credibility: for in the corner of the arms and armor field here under discussion, no one anywhere has done more source research and specimen examination over the last twenty years or so than the several people who

chipped out of the left side of the stock near the barrel breech and tang, and the general wear, tear and surface corrosion would only qualify for "fair" on any scale of collectors' jargon. There are no markings of any kind anywhere. The furniture—trigger guard, curlecue inlays—are not "steel" but iron. Stock appears to be walnut, but this must be confirmed by laboratory analysis. The octagonal barrel is parallel, without any taper.

How the Rome auction cataloguer managed to arrive in 18th-century Spain is not easy to divine. There

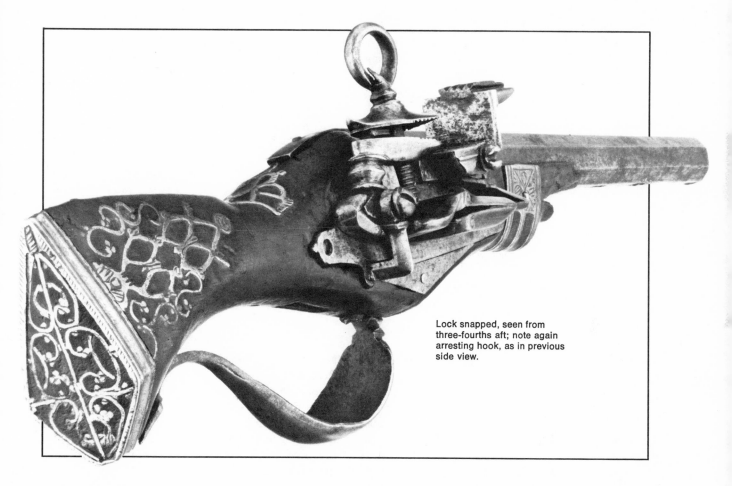

Lock snapped, seen from three-fourths aft; note again arresting hook, as in previous side view.

concur, essentially, in the *provisional* conclusion here presented. Time will prove it right or wrong, or a little of both. In the next issue of ARMS AND ARMOR ANNUAL we shall present the documentation and the concurring testimonies of scholars required to sustain the thesis—we say "we *shall*," not "we *may*," for we are convinced that the thesis *will* bear up and that the pistol will become a new structural element in the architecture of arms and armor history.

Let us describe the piece briefly. The overall length is 12⅞ in. = 32.5 cm,; the barrel is 7⅞ in. = 20 cm., and the bore is 7/16 in. = 1.1 cm. Condition is terrible: the front half of the forestock is broken off and missing, the trigger is gone, a large sliver has been

is nothing remotely 18th-century about the ornamentation, the mechanics, the shape or the general "feel" or "flavor" of the workmanship and materials. As to Spain, only confusion between the shape at hand and distantly related Spanish gun-butt pistols—not at all similar—and between the rough inlay ornamentation at hand and distantly related Ripoll work could have misled the author of that attribution.

What comes to mind at once, of course, upon first glance, is Italy, and specifically Brescia, about 1570-1600. It is not yet time in this Cautious Announcement to present documentation, but the prevalence of this very style of stock in Brescia in that period—the gun butt of that seemingly simple but elusive, very-difficult-to-draw geometry of curves, its section a sort of drop-shaped lozenge, and the lozenge- or rhomboid-shaped lock with the corresponding down-point in the stock—is too well established to require explication here and now. Every qualified student to whom the pistol has been shown *without removal of the lock,* or who has examined photographs of only the exterior, *lock in place,* from all possible angles, has reacted almost immediately "Brescian, late sixteenth century, maybe very early seventeenth but probably not, converted from wheellock to an odd sort of miquelet." No other conclusion would seem admissible; and if the weapon were in fact no more than an ex-wheellock now sporting *a miquelet lock of a kind not, to our knowledge, ever recorded anywhere, any-time, in arms literature,* the piece would merit bringing to the attention of arms students the world over.

fanciful to those not very familiar with Italian fire-arms of this period, but it is in fact very solid and simple: hundreds of stocks were prepared weekly in the Brescian stock-makers' shops, all, regardless of size or type, roughed out with the down-point below the middle of the lock space to accommodate the invariably rhomboid locks, for no other lock shape was used in the normal run of production (the one-in-five-hundred exceptions do exist). The lock-maker quite properly fastened the essentials of his new, probably all but untried, very experimental mechanism to an essential, minimal lockplate, and reached for the next available stock blank supplied by the stock-maker to mount a pistol on it. But the blank had the inevitable, the invariable point, for the taste of the time and place demanded that lock and butt, curves and angles, should complement each other

Left side; note wear marks left by a now-lost belt hook around rear screw.

But it is not a conversion. Examination of the lock recess—superficial, profound, under high magnification, under lights of highest intensity, any way, every way—leaves no doubt that the pistol was originally made ("born," in collectors' talk) with the miquelet lock now in place. In the next issue of ARMS AND ARMOR ANNUAL we shall publish, with the rest of the documentation, more detailed close-up views of the recess. Moreover, the lock's bottom edge is straight, not lozenge-shaped; the down-point of the apparent lozenge is completed by a small, long triangular plate below and separate from the lockplate—but this arrangement does *not* fill a rhomboid recess left by a previous rhomboid wheellock; the lock recess is cut straight on the bottom to accommodate the present miquelet lock, and the little triangular plate, about one-third the thickness of the lockplate, is a mere ornamental adjunct to fill up the wood remaining below the straight edge of the miquelet.

Critics will ask at once: if the pistol was born with the present lock, why was excess wood left below the plate, why was the stock not cut to fit the mechanism it was to bear? And the answer may seem a bit

according to inviolable canons of convention. The stock-maker very likely had already applied the decorative pierced-iron inlay on the underside on the forward slope of the point—elimination of the point would have meant elimination of that ornament, too; thus the gunmaker was doubly compelled to fit the little steel triangle beneath the lock, not only to obey the convention in shape demanded by his client's taste but to save the embellishments as well. Such functionless addition of rhomboid down-points to Italian locks and stocks long after the end of the time of rhomboid locks is not at all rare—throughout the period 1640-1750 one encounters specimens of straight-bottomed locks with fillers below similar to the one at hand, as well as locks that should have been straight-bottomed but were needlessly given rhomboid down-points just for the sake of tradition.

As to the lock, it is, so far as we have been able to establish, the only one of its kind. That it is also among the first of its kind, a prototype, a dawn specimen, a thinking-out-in-steel of an as yet unjelled but ingenious notion, is clear to any competent arms student with sympathetic understanding of mechani-

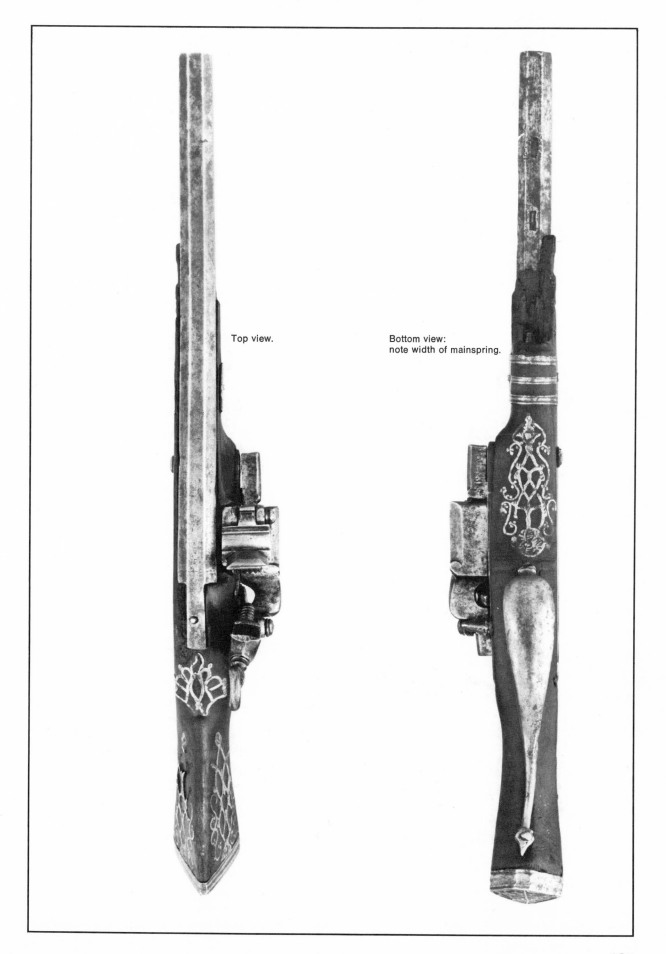

Top view.

Bottom view:
note width of mainspring.

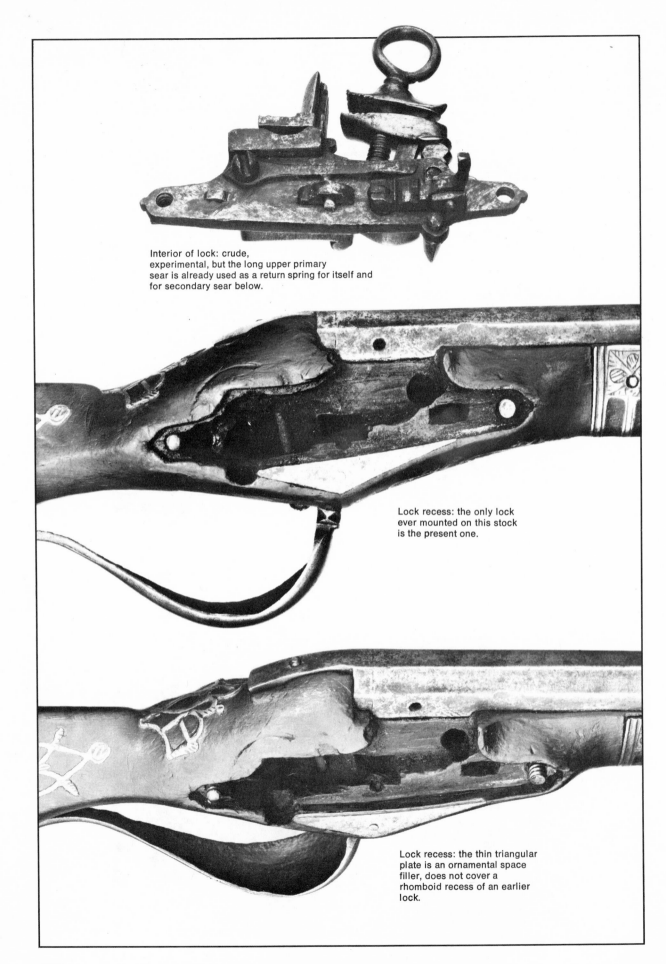

Interior of lock: crude,
experimental, but the long upper primary
sear is already used as a return spring for itself and
for secondary sear below.

Lock recess: the only lock
ever mounted on this stock
is the present one.

Lock recess: the thin triangular
plate is an ornamental space
filler, does not cover a
rhomboid recess of an earlier
lock.

cal evolution. In terms of later miquelet locks—say, 1650 and after, essentially fully developed or approaching full development—the efficiency of the present specimen seems wretched. The stroke of the cock, the angle of flint impact, the placement of components in relation to each other, the ineffectual bridle designed in hopes of anchoring the cock pivot screw—everything cries "experimental, archaic" to the experienced observer. It also cries "Brescian:" the filing of the springs, the cock jaws in debt to Brescian wheellock jaws, the style of finish. The upper mainspring arm, curving down around the toe and heel of the cock and coming up aft to embrace the heel by way of arrest of the snap, is unique in our experience with antique guns, though we should be more than pleased to hear from readers who know of similar devices. The grooved steel battery face is detachable from the upright limb of the flash pan cover, being held in place in vertical guides that embrace it right and left.

We submit, in conclusion, that the weapon under discussion may prove a proof, so to speak: proof that the variety of snapping lock now called the miquelet originated in or around Brescia sometime in the last quarter of the sixteenth centry and not, as hitherto

Flat butt end, with iron-wire inlays and ornamental border.

supposed, in Spain in the second quarter of the seventeenth. Next Progress Report in the second issue of the ANNUAL.

A Primer of Ripoll Gunlocks

by *EUDALDO GRAELLS*

Señor Eudaldo Graells y Puig was born in Ripoll 72 years ago. He is the Director of the Archivo-Museo Folklorico de Ripoll and President of the Council of Works of the Monastery of Santa Maria of Ripoll. He is an untiring, dedicated student and conservator of all Catalan arts and crafts, with emphasis on Ripoll weapons. Through his many articles and monographs he has done more than any other scholar—with the exception of Dr. James D. Lavin—to awaken the sensibilities of collectors to the validity and appeal of the artistry inherent in Ripoll products—never delicate or refined, but always tense with play of volumes and lines in strange evolutions and supremely assertive of their unmistakable identity.

The city of Ripoll is situated at the confluence of the rivers Ter and Freser, nearly two thousand feet above sea level in the pre-Pyrenees mountains about fifty miles to the north of Barcelona. In A.D. 850 Wifredo the Hirsuite expelled the Moors and founded the Benedictine monastery of Santa Maria, the ruins of which are an outstanding example of Spanish romanesque art and architecture. An abundance of coal and iron ore, together with the ample water supply of the two rivers, engendered a metal-working industry in the early Middle Ages, and the smelting techniques now known as the *Catalan forge* and *Catalan process* were initially employed in the manufacture of nails and pole-arms heads, and later, toward the middle of the sixteenth century, of crossbows. During the latter part of the sixteenth century and during all of the seventeenth, eighteenth and the first third of the nineteenth, Ripoll enjoyed a reputation throughout Europe for the production of firearms, especially of pistols, of a very individual, forceful character. But owing to foreign invasions and internal civil wars, the ravaging of archives, the repeated partial and then final utter destruction of the entire city by mining and blasting on May 27, 1839, not much is known of Ripoll and its industry to this very day.

Up to the First World War, most specimens of Ripoll arms in public and private collections were incorrectly catalogued; frequently they were ascribed to Oriental and North African provenances because of certain superficial characteristics shared by Ripoll,

Ottoman and North African weapons—the error lay in having based judgment on ornamentation rather than on lock mechanics, stock and barrel styles, and comparative study of marked *versus* unmarked examples. In Ripoll, lock-making had always been the prime specialty, and during the period of Ripoll's heyday the greater number of artisans were engaged in this part of production rather than in barrel- or stock-making. During the 1750-1800 period, when pistol production was at its quantitative but not qualitative height, there were no fewer than seventy-five master lockmakers with, fairly guessed, over three hundred apprentices and journeymen. Since the span covered by Ripoll gun production extends from the mid-1500's through a long ascent to about 1625, a Golden Age c. 1660-1740, and then a gradual but exponential decline to total extinction in 1839 (probably the end would have come commercially by 1850 even if it had not been for the physical destruction), the lock mechanisms were at first wheellocks, then miquelet locks and some flintlocks of the *a la moda* or "Madrid" style, and finally a variety of percussion systems from loose detonating powders to copper caps. No matchlock is known that can be attributed without doubt to Ripoll, but the probability of their manufacture verges on certainty—a community engaged in the manufacture of every species of weapons throughout the matchlock era could not possibly *not* have made matchlocks; moreover, a matchlock gun in the ex-Estruch/Pauilhac Collection is signed "Colom," a very Catalan name.

Ripoll Wheellocks

Ripoll wheellock manufacture spanned but three or four decades: from the 1580's into the 1620's, give or take a few early- or late-comers. Hence they are among the very rarest of wheellocks. They possess peculiar characteristics that strike the observer at once; these were first described correctly in considerable detail by Georges Pauilhac and Charles Buttin in their 1914 study of Ripoll arms—interrupted by the war—when the vast Pauilhac Collection, including the ex-Estruch Collection of Barcelona and the ex-Casa Torres Collection of Madrid, had already been housed in its splendid specially-constructed building on the then-Avenue Malakof (now rue Poincaré) in Toulouse. [The Pauilhac Collection was acquired by the French State in 1961 and is now partially housed and exhibited in the Musée de l'Armée in Paris.—*Ed*.]

The lockplates of these devices, at least in their earlier forms, (say, 1580's-1600's), are long, triangular and unlike any other wheellocks elsewhere; the rear tapers to a long point, the bottom apex, though very pronounced, is rounded (sometimes slightly, sometimes quite fully "bellied"), and the lower forward border sweeps elegantly upward through a double curve to conclude the front point around the elbow of the dog spring. The wheel, small in comparison with other European locks, not only is placed high up but is not centered in the optical triangle of the "belly" or lower apex. It is covered by a circular housing forged integrally with the lock-

129

Fig. 1—Engraving of a soldier with a Ripoll matchlock musket, 1641. (Museo de la Historia de la Ciudad, Barcelona)

plate. The plate edges are chamfered in a 45° bevel all around, except in spots where the mechanics demand flat edges. Almost without exception, the locks and their components are profusely ornamented with engraved and sometimes chiseled and etched arabesques, vines and foliage, at times inhabited by figures and urns. There is no inletted bed for the lockplate on the wood—only the protruding internal components find recesses for their accommodation, while the inner surface of the plate fits flat against the flat side of the lock area, where it is held by three transverse screws passing, conventionally, from the left side. The German-style loop-and-hook safety to

the rear of the wheel appeared after about 1610 (there are no fixed dates in Ripoll arms history, nor even very close approximations), but seems never to have been very frequent. The curved pancover does not slide horizontally as in nearly all other wheel-locks, but rotates, or pivots, concentrically with the curve of the top of the pan itself; its snap-release button, instead of protruding horizontally from the side of the plate, protrudes vertically from its top edge between pan and dog, and is pushed downward to release. The flashpan has a half-moon-shaped lower extension, curve up, straight edge down, which covers half of the wheel cover and is affixed to it by

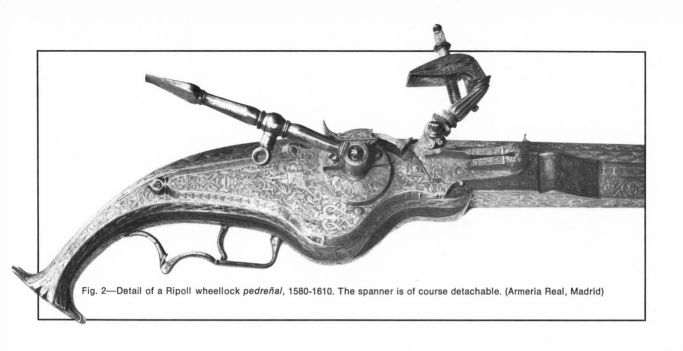

Fig. 2—Detail of a Ripoll wheellock *pedreñal*, 1580-1610. The spanner is of course detachable. (Armeria Real, Madrid)

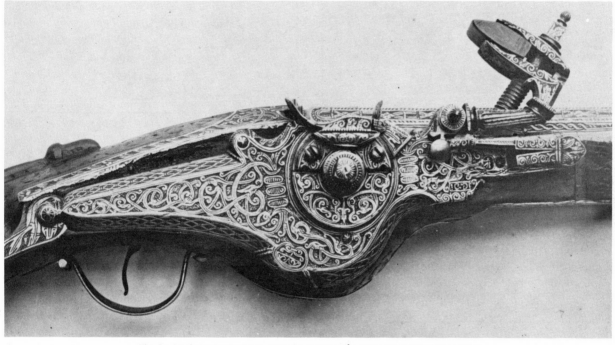

Fig. 3—Lock of an arquebus. (Musée, de l'Armée, Paris; Paulihac Collection)

two small screws. The inner surfaces of the dog's jaws were not roughened, as elsewhere, by washboard corrugations, simple cross-hatching or little teeth extruded by tiny chisel blows, but rather by engraving with one of about a dozen apparently fairly standardized geometric designs, repeated without much variation. This was to remain a common but by no means indispensable Ripoll feature throughout the stone-in-jaws era.

Early Ripoll wheellock pistols were very long, some alarmingly so—one of over 33 in. (84 cm.) survives and there may be longer ones, while the shortest known example, that in the Victoria and Albert Museum, is 22 in. (56 cm.). Their stocks are remarkable: the very thin, sharply arched grips terminate in a very small fishtail. Later, in the 1620's it would seem, these exaggerated lengths were reduced to more manageable proportions, and the cannon-ring muzzle, which was to remain a Ripoll characteristic (but not an invariable one) began to appear. At the same time, the extravagant fishtail grip yielded to ovoid and ball butts of a more nearly conventional—though still unmistakably Ripoll—nature. The earlier ornamentally engraved iron sheathing, which at times had covered so much of the stock that only a few small patches of wood

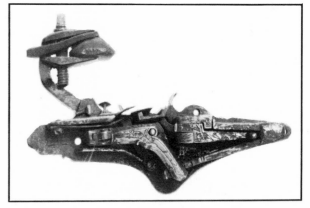

Figs.4, 4a & 4b—Short, later-style wheellock pistol. Figures 4a and 4b show the lock removed and the internal mechanism. (Museo de Ripoll)

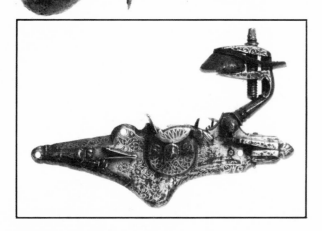

showed through, gave place to much more open iron scrollwork, usually not inhabited by figures, that covered only half or less of the wood surface.

The local Catalan name for these weapons was *pedrenyal* (pl.: *pedrenyales*), from Latin *petrinula,* = a little stone; the Castilian version was *pedreñal* (pl.: *pedreñales*). But since gun parlance ever since the end of Ripoll's wheellock phase, right down to modern students' usage, has tended to reserve this term for the weapons to be described in the section immediately following, it would probably be best to

speak of "Ripoll wheellock pistols" or at least of "wheellock *pedreñales*." Because of their very great rarity, a list of a few of the best-known examples will be found at the end of this article.

The *Agujeta* or Snaplock *Pedreñal*

Ripoll gunmakers, unlike their German and other North-Central European colleagues, did not overlap their production of wheel- and snaplocks for more than the briefest of transition periods (in Germany, especially in Bavaria and in Austria, wheellock man-

Fig. 5—Shorter, later-style wheellock of a silver-sheathed pistol datable in the 1610-20 span. (Museo Arqueologico, Madrid)

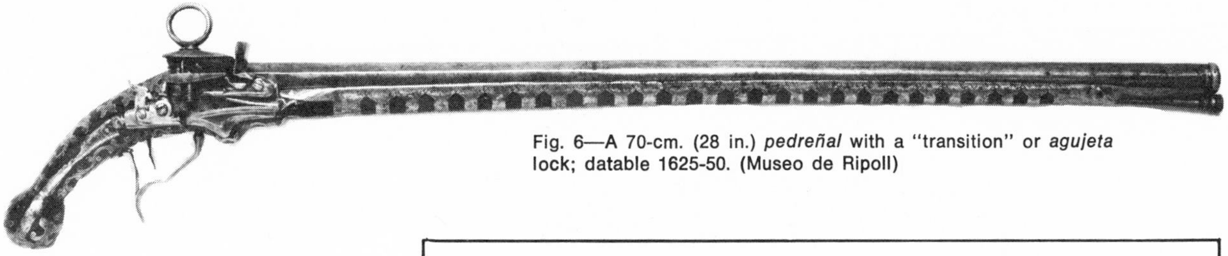

Fig. 6—A 70-cm. (28 in.) *pedreñal* with a "transition" or *agujeta* lock; datable 1625-50. (Museo de Ripoll)

Fig. 7—A "transitional" or *agujeta* lock, 1625-50, marked *DEOP*. (Museo de Montjuic, Barcelona)

ufacture continued, as is well known to all, into the 1740's and in isolated cases even beyond). It is not within the scope of the present observations to venture theses on the geographic and chronological provenances of the many different snapping, flint-against-steel devices known at various times and places ever since, say 1530. Whatever the origins of that particular type of snaplock in which the external mainspring acts downward on the toe of the cock, and in which the flashpan cover is a single L-shaped piece integral with the battery or steel, it was man-

ufactured in Ripoll in the second third of the seventeenth century. In due time—say, in the course of the first half of the eighteenth century—it was to reach its highest form of development in Central Italy and is now known by the misleading and probably nineteenth-century scholars' term *alla romana*, "in the Roman style;" in Spain, this fully-evolved version became known as *la llave de invención*, literally "the invention lock" but perhaps better rendered as "the fancy-free" and perhaps even "mighty strange" lock. In its earliest Ripoll version

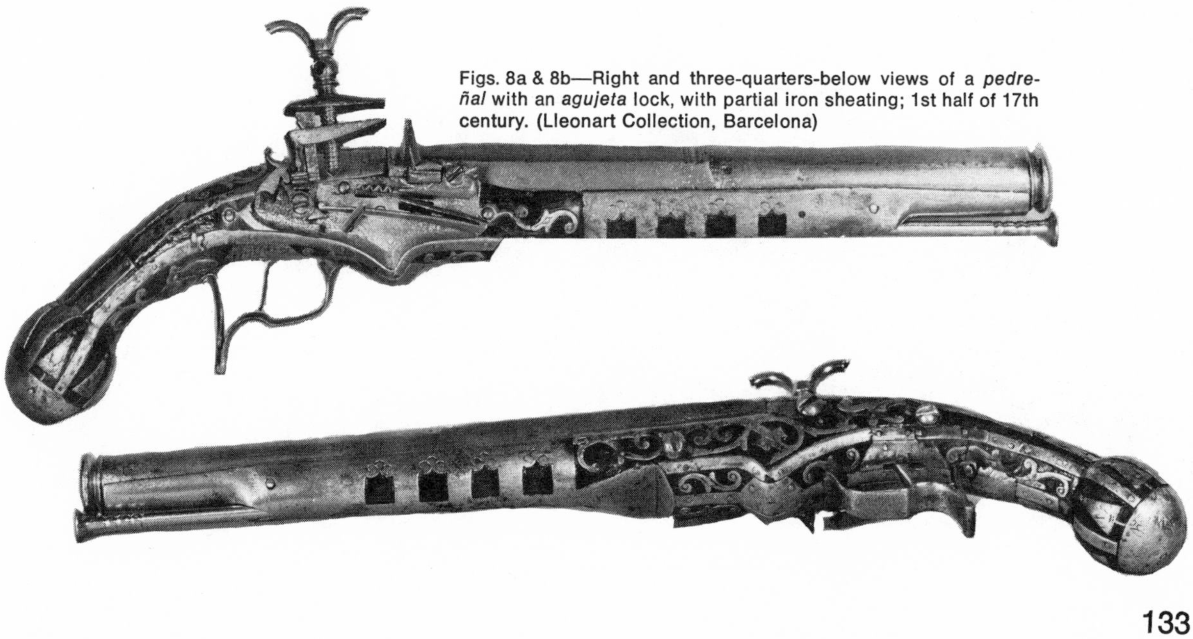

Figs. 8a & 8b—Right and three-quarters-below views of a *pedreñal* with an *agujeta* lock, with partial iron sheating; 1st half of 17th century. (Lleonart Collection, Barcelona)

133

Fig. 9—Designs engraved on the inner surfaces of many Ripoll wheellock and snaplock jaws has roughening for better purchase of the leather or lead that holds the pyrites or flint.

Fig. 10—A very typical, standard, medium-quality commercial Ripoll *patilla* lock, datable anywhere between 1660 and 1750, and even later. (Museo de Ripoll)

it was the *agujeta*, or, in modern terms, *la llave de transición*. Examples are among the very rarest of European firearms.

Stock- and butt-forms of these weapons are in all respects the same as those of the wheellock pistols of both the early, long, fully-sheathed and the later, shorter, openwork-sheathed kinds. The lockplate retains about half of the basic triangular shape of the wheellock, but its front end terminates abruptly in a vertical face, from which extends a more or less elaborated curlecue pierced by a round hole threaded for the foremost of three transverse lock-holding screws. The beveled edge of the wheellock plate was carried over, as was the absence of an inletted bed for the plate (and since only the sears were internal, the amount of wood removed from this, the weakest, part of the stock was minimal). The full-cock sear is engaged by the heel of the cock, not—as found in successive evolutions of Spanish miquelet locks— by a quadrant of the toe. Instead of by a half-cock sear, safety is provided by a spring-loaded hook at the rear of the cock, so arranged that it engages a notch on the cock's heel under continuous spring pressure when the weapon is at rest, while the act of cocking to firing position automatically causes the hook to disengage and, again under spring pressure, to remain disengaged until once again moved forward by the shooter. The steel or battery face is deeply grooved and fitted with a little projection or "ear" on its upper right side (seen from the striking surface, i.e. from behind) as an aid to opening and closing for priming. The steel or pancover spring is straight.

Owing to the vast volume of commerce between Spain and North Africa, and in particular between the Ripoll manufacturers and the North African arms market, the *agujeta* or "transition" lock became established early and very solidly in Arab, Berber and Bedouin lands. Its production there lasted into

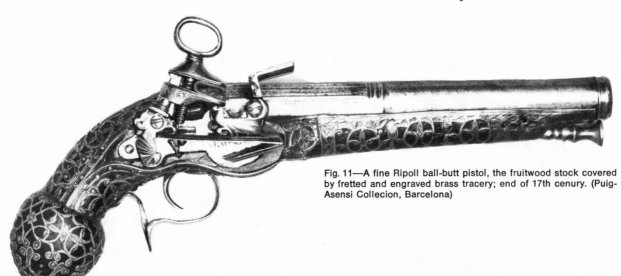

Fig. 11—A fine Ripoll ball-butt pistol, the fruitwood stock covered by fretted and engraved brass tracery; end of 17th cenury. (Puig-Asensi Collecion, Barcelona)

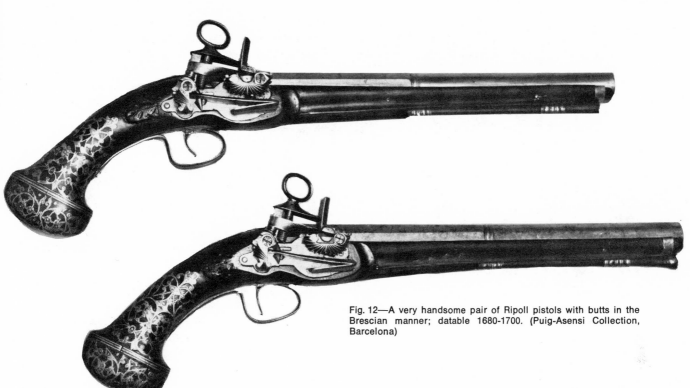

Fig. 12—A very handsome pair of Ripoll pistols with butts in the Brescian manner; datable 1680-1700. (Puig-Asensi Collection, Barcelona)

the 1880's, and its employment for and against Turkish and British forces in World War One, and against French Foreign Legion posts into the 1920's, often with telling results, is too well known to require elaboration here.

Pedreñales with *agujeta* locks being much rarer still than those with wheellocks, a listing of a few well-known extant specimens of these, too, will be found at the end of this article.

The Perfected Ripoll *Patilla* Lock

As the result of experiments and improvements in the transitional lock, and of the adoption of many features of the Castilian *patilla* lock, there appeared in Ripoll toward the middle of the seventeenth cen-

tury the device we must call "the Ripoll *patilla*," in Spain also known as the "Catalan lock," a term that will cause confusion for non-Spanish students. Simple, strong, very well worked out in all details and evidently perfectly responsive to the demands made of it by users and devotees, it was destined not only to remain unchanged in all ways for 170 or 180 years—right down to the very last afterglow of flint-and-steel in the 1830's—but to be exported with signal success to all Spanish colonies and to the Kingdoms of Naples and of the Two Sicilies. Only a minor stylistic modification to the cock- and flash-pan bridles distinguishes a Ripoll *patilla* lock of 1660 from one of 1830.

Characterized by its oddly-shaped lockplate—

Fig. 13—Another similar to those in Fig. 10, but of better quality; the italianate flavor is even more marked here; datable 1680-1700. (Puig-Asensi Collection, Barcelona)

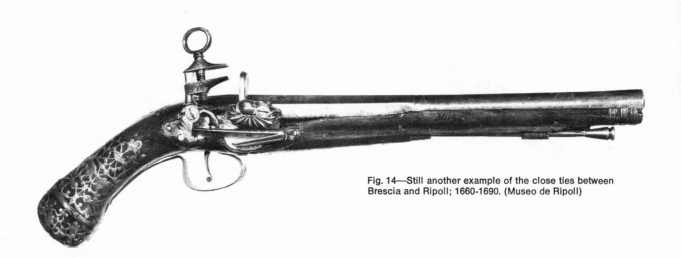

Fig. 14—Still another example of the close ties between Brescia and Ripoll; 1660-1690. (Museo de Ripoll)

variously pointed, wide, narrow and bellied according to the shape of the components fitted to it, with no surrounding plate to waste or spare—the *patilla* differed from the *agujeta* in many other ways. The mainspring acted upward on the heel of the cock, not downward on the toe, and the half- and full-cock sears protruded through the lockplate in front of the cock, where they engaged successively a blade-like quadrant integrally formed with, or as, the toe of the cock. The *agujeta* safety hook had disappeared, the very deeply notched half-cock sear rendering it unnecessary. The lockplate was no longer fastened against flat wood without inletting: it was now recessed into its own contoured space in the wood, and held with two, not three, transverse screws. The feather- or battery- or pancover spring, a V opening toward the muzzle, was set beneath the pan and above the upper arms of the mainspring, behind a shield that served simultaneously as screw bridle

and kept the spring completely concealed. Both this shield-bridle and the vertical bridle anchoring the cock pivot screw were invariably decorated with deeply-filed grooves of triangular cross-section arranged in fans or sunbursts, usually four or five radiating upward and to the rear from the cock bridle, and as many as twenty downward and outward from the flashpan in a 180° spread. It was the eventual modification of this ornamentation that constituted the only real difference between the 1660 and the 1830 locks: after the middle of the eighteenth century, the fans often appear at first in simpler, broader slashes, then in engraved form and finally vanish altogether, being replaced by flat bridles more or less fretted in curlecue outlines and engraved with usually crude but sometimes quite fine rococo scroll motifs.

Like the Castilian and other similar locks, the Ripoll *patilla* had a jaw-fastening screw headed by

Fig. 15—A splendid Ripoll carbine signed *ROVIRA* and dated 1694. (W. Keith Neal Collection, England)

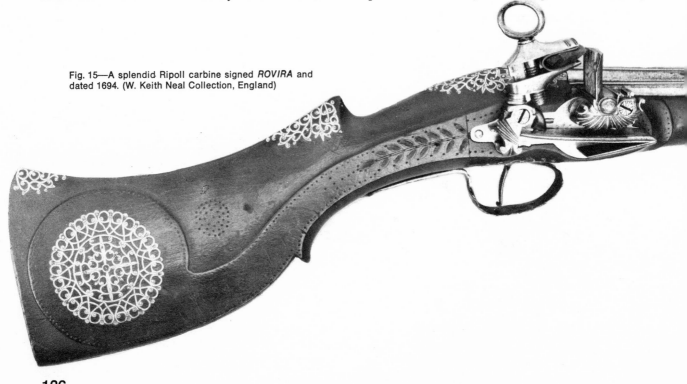

Fig. 16—This type of exuberant metal overlay, often in silver, is very typical of the better-quality Ripoll products, as is the "gunbutt" pistol grip. The motif of the she-pelican biting herself to feed her young with her own blood, well-known to students of Kentucky rifles and of Central-Italian pistols, found its way to Ripoll, too. (Xavier Sala Collection, Olot, Spain)

a large ring, rather than by a slotted bulb. Battery- or steel faces are always striated in vertical grooves that grew less and less deep with time, until by 1750-80 they were not much more than gouge marks; no doubt these gave a better purchase to the flint's edge and hence were more readily abraded into abundant sparks, but on the other hand were consumed quickly and sometimes gave such purchase that the flint became stuck and the pancover failed to open. An ingenious solution may be found among older examples, generally pre-1700: the very deeply grooved steel face is separate from the vertical limb of the pancover, to which it is attached by a protruding screw held by a wing nut on the back (i.e., on the muzzle side) of the vertical limb, and secured from rotary motion by guides or rails at the extreme left and right edges of the accepting blank limb face, between which the insert fits snugly. This permitted not only easy replacement of a worn face, but the

employment of a relatively soft-tempered pancover —unlikely to break under the impact of the cock— together with a very hard battery for maximum sparking efficiency.

Although Ripoll *patillas* will be found on firearms of every description, they are most closely identified with pistols, and among these most closely with those endearingly clumsy, short-gripped, ball-butted ones known to every apprentice collector as "Ripoll pistols" (as though there were no others!). It is usually impossible to distinguish true Ripollese from Neapolitan examples, since many Ripoll gunmakers settled in Naples in the second half of the eighteenth century and for fifty years and more produced their wonted weapons without variations of any sort; only in a very few cases of clearly signed specimens, or those with unmistakably Neapolitan references in the ornamentation—and, sometimes but very rarely, and only in pistols made after 1800, in a couple of me-

Figs. 17 & 18—Two Ripoll *patillas* of the second half of the 18th century: the fanned striations have yielded to flat bridles engraved with rococo motifs. Left: signed *IOSEPH DEOP RIPOLL* (W. Keith Neal Collection, England); right: signed *LLORENS DEOP* (Museo de Ripoll)

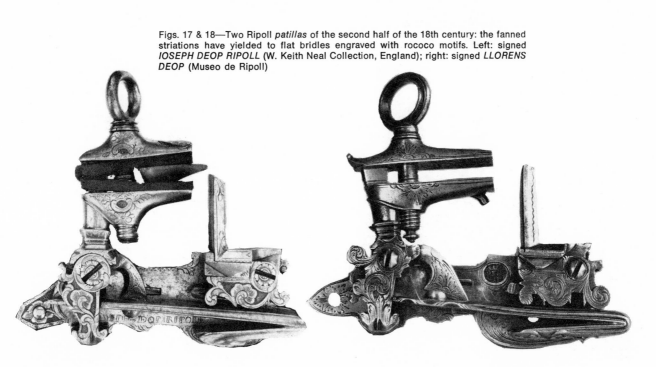

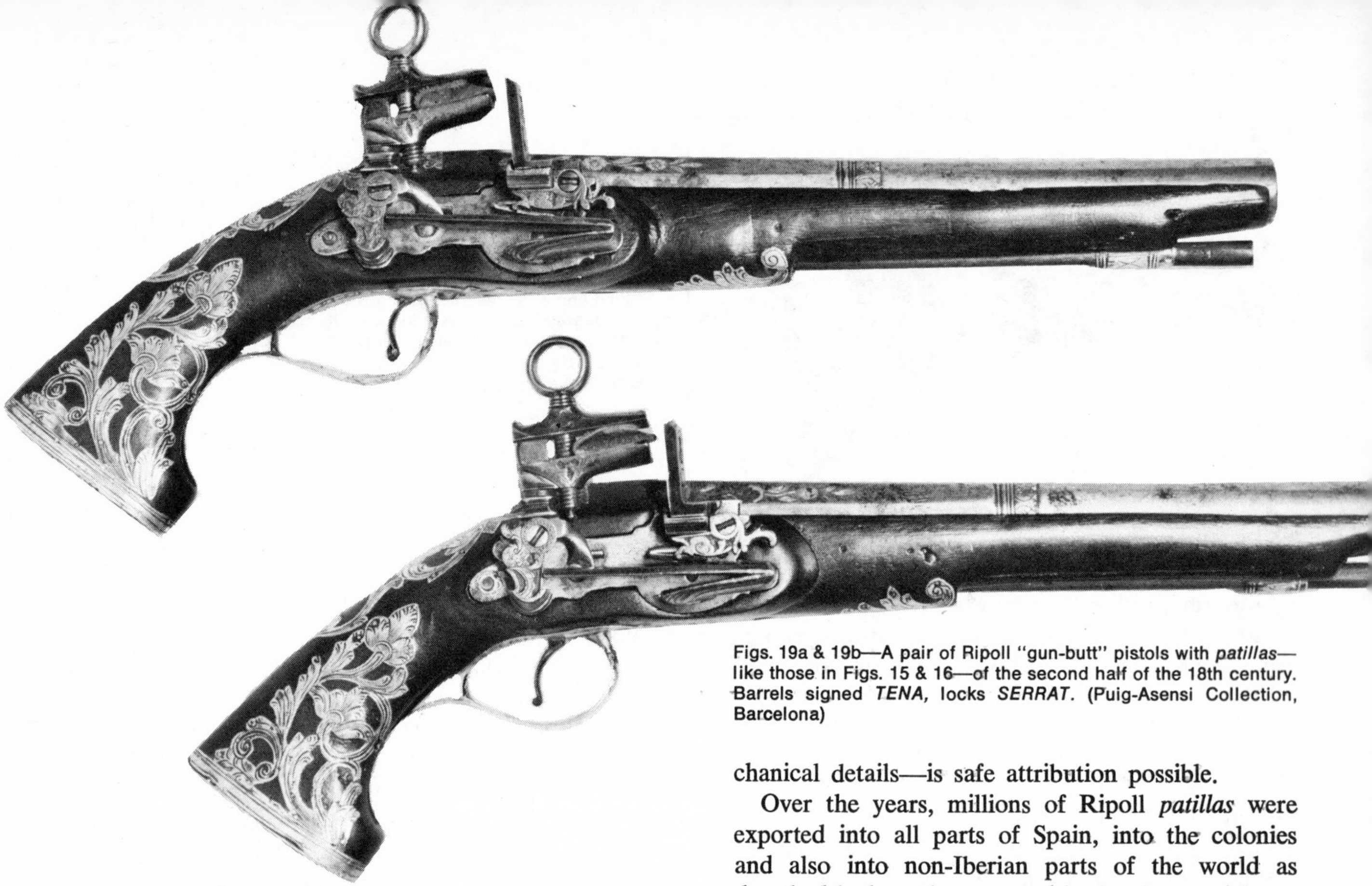

Figs. 19a & 19b—A pair of Ripoll "gun-butt" pistols with *patillas*—like those in Figs. 15 & 16—of the second half of the 18th century. Barrels signed *TENA*, locks *SERRAT*. (Puig-Asensi Collection, Barcelona)

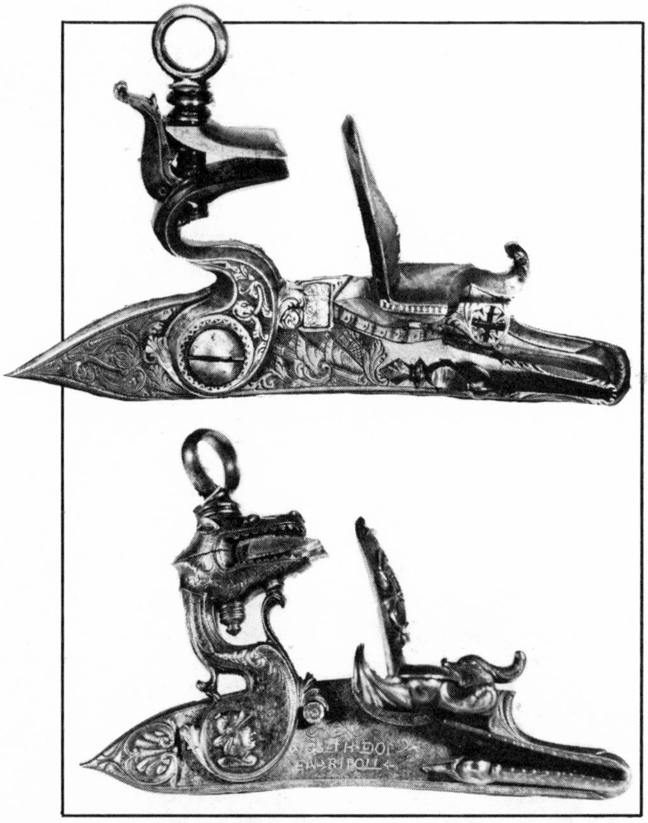

Figs. 20 & 21—Two Ripoll *a la moda* or "Madrid" locks, mid-18th century or after; the upper one is signed *DEOP*, the lower *IOSEPH DEOP*. The cock chiseled in the form of a monster and the other chiseled details of the Joseph Deop lock are very attractive, while the upper lock has very handsome, squared-off jaws, good engraving and well-filed feather spring, and is earlier by 20 years. (Upper: Aldecoa Collection, Barcelona; lower: Musée de l'Armée, Paris)

chanical details—is safe attribution possible.

Over the years, millions of Ripoll *patillas* were exported into all parts of Spain, into the colonies and also into non-Iberian parts of the world as detached locks to be mounted by local gunsmiths on their own products. Now and then one comes across incongruities like an undisputably Central-German pistol with a fine original *patilla* (recently offered in London and disdained by all but one wise man as a clumsy fake!), and a Czech rifle of the cheek-stock variety, about 1730, with an original *patilla* engraved with Austro-Bohemian rocailles and signed *Hoepfer in Prag*. No doubt more separate export locks than finished arms were made in Ripoll in the course of its history.

A La Moda ("Madrid") and Percussion Locks

Inevitably, French influence penetrated first Madrid and Barcelona, then Ripoll gunmaking. Unwilling to abandon the principle of sears protruding horizontally through the lockplate, some Spanish gunsmiths of 1690-1720 wrought a compromise between the by-then-universal Parisian fashion of the evolved true flintlock and the *llave nacional*: a more or less French flintlock with sears protruding fore and aft of the cock, engaged by corresponding curlecues projecting from the cock. Now often called the "Madrid lock," its name in eighteenth-century Spain was *la llave a la moda*, "the new-fashioned lock." Its highest development was reached in Madrid (some of the finest firearms in the world have *a la moda* locks of Madrid manufacture), but Ripoll artisans also sought to cash in on the "new-fashioned" market and created a considerable number of these devices, usually not finely wrought and finished but sometimes possessed of that same inventive,

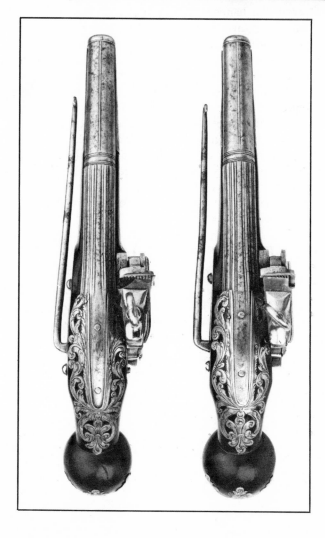

Figs. 22, 23 & 24—A good pair of ball-butt pistols probably of Ripoll but possibly Neapolitan manufacture—if Neapolitan, then by Ripoll emigre lock- and gunsmiths. Locks signed *PA.FEO.;* engraved brass sheating at muzzle end, engraved and pierced overlay on wrists around tangs and on ball butts; datable 1760-80. The C-shape of the cock stem tends to suggest Naples, but this is a slim basis for attribution, since everything else—and not excluding the C-stem!—is of exemplary Ripollese style. (Palasciano Collection, Bari, Italy)

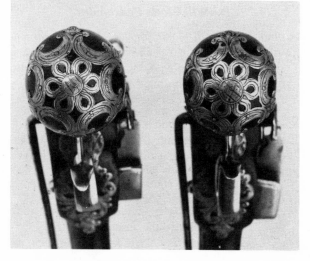

Fig. 25—A Ripoll percussion lock, born as such, not a transformation from flint. (Museo de Ripoll)

folksy vigor and artistic urge that invests Tosco-Emilian and Anghiari pistols.

As to percussion locks, by the time the percussion period dawned toward 1815-20, Ripoll had been invaded by Napoleonic troops four times: in 1794, 1809, 1812 and 1813, and on the last of these occasions the arms industry was all but wiped out, the shops destroyed, the tools scattered, many workmen slaughtered. Somehow the survivors, embers in the ashes, managed to resume a slow and desultory production, dedicated at first to the traditional flintlocks but gradually adopting detonating powder, side-tube and finally nipple-and-cap. But at the end of the Carlist Wars, Ripoll was utterly leveled to the ground on May 27, 1839, the mines leaving hardly one brick on top of any other. Hence Ripoll percussion locks are undistinguished. At first their mechanics followed those of the *patilla*, substituting a percussion hammer for the flint cock (but with the same sear arrangement), and fitting a percussion bolster with nipple onto the barrel so that it would project in place of the flashpan. Later, some more sophisticated, wholly-internal-sears locks were made, but they are of no significance in arms history and represent a mournful swansong for Ripoll.

The subject of gun types, shapes and sizes—all the pistols, shotguns, carbines and blunderbusses of Ripoll origins—lies beyond the present thoughts on locks and basic stock styles. The author hopes nevertheless to have presented a summary that will prove helpful to some readers not hitherto familiar with the subject.

LIST OF SOME WELL-KNOWN EXAMPLES OF RIPOLL LOCKS

A. Wheellock *Pedreñales*

Aromory of the National Palace, Madrid. An unusually long (97 cm. = 38 in.!) specimen with a small fishtail grip; Inv.No.K.42. Lock, stock and barrel are richly decorated with arabesques. (Fig. 2).

W. Keith Neal Collection, Wiltshire, England. Shorter than the preceding, but of the same general characteristics; lock, stock and barrel engraved with primroses.

Museo Civico Correr, Venice. An example in general characteristics very similar to the preceding two. The stock bears the inscription *P.L.S. ERCOLE TASCHA DI VENECIA*, but the spellings betray the non-Italian, Spanish author. See article on this piece by Thomas T. Hoopes in *Zeitschrift für Historische Waffen- und Kostümkunde,* Year 1934, reprinted as separate monograph.

Victoria & Albert Museum, London. The shortest of the surviving specimens: 56 cm. = 22 in. Richly chiseled with arabesques and dated 1614.

Royal Scottish Museum, Edinburgh. A good specimen.

Museo Arqueologico, Madrid. A pair with ball butts; stocks completely overlaid with silver scrollwork sheathing, barrels and locks richly engraved with arabesques. Both signed *SOLER* (Fig. 5).

Musée de l'Armée, Paris. Pauilhac Collection. A pistol 43 cm. = 17 in. long, decorated only with engraved iron stock sheathing; ovoid butt. Also: two detached locks of 15 cm. each, and one of the extraordinary length of 32 cm. = 12.6 in., this last richly decorated with engraved arabesques etc. Also: a fine arquebus (Fig. 3).

Museo Episcopal, Vic, Spain. A very fine, profusely decorated example by Soler, 37 cm. = 15.1 in., with a ball butt.

Museo de Ripoll. Apparently the mate to the preceding one, not in a good state of conservation (Figs. 4, 4a & 4b).

B. Snaplock *Pedreñales*

Museo de Montjuic, Barcelona. Unusually fine specimen 70 cm. = 28 in. long, with ovoid butt, the stock completely covered with engraved iron sheathing; signed *DEOP*, the name of a numerous and long-lived clan in Ripoll lockmakers, probably the leading gunmaking family in Ripoll history. (They first appear in the records in the fourteenth century— three brothers: Pedro, Rafael and Arnal Deop—and end in the nineteenth, producing in the interim forty-one master lockmakers.) (Fig. 7).

Museo de Ripoll. An example very similar to the preceding, but without marks (Fig. 6).

Tøjhusmuseum, Copenhagen. Two examples very similar, also in length, to the two preceding ones. One has a barrel signed *VALLS*, while the other bears an engraved rooster (the principal figure in the Ripoll coat-of-arms).

Musée de l'Armée, Paris. Pauilhac Collection. Another 70-cm. specimen, with unusually fine engraving covering lock, stock and barrel. Still another similar with an ovoid butt, marked *COMA* on the barrel. Another of 57 cm. = 23 in., marked *JOAN B.T.* on the lock. Another of 40 cm. = 16 in. with a carved stock and signed *RIBES* on the back of the battery. Also an unmarked lock chiseled with floral motifs.

BIBLIOGRAPHY

The most important work ever published on Spanish firearms is the splendid *A History of Spanish Firearms,* by James D. Lavin, Ph.D., published by Herbert Jenkins Ltd., London, 1965. Another work (indeed, the only other one on this subject readily available) is *Spanish Guns and Pistols,* by W. Keith Neal, published by G. Bell & Sons, London, 1955; both are indispensable to the student of Iberian weapons.

English Swords 1600-1650

by JOHN F. HAYWARD

Mr. Hayward requires no introduction. An art historian of international repute, he has greatly advanced the serious study of arms and armor throughout his twenty years with the Victoria & Albert Museum and, since 1965, as an Associate Director of Sotheby & Co. His articles and monographs are by far too numerous to list here; they have been published in most major languages in the world. His most celebrated single work (already a classic, a scant ten years after its first publication) is The Art of the Gunmaker, *a two-volume, profusely illustrated study of firearms ornamentation 1500-1830. Mr. Hayward's wife Helena is a well-known authority and lecturer on English furniture and decorative arts. The Haywards are life-long residents of London, save for Mr. Hayward's postwar duty as a British Monuments and Fine Arts Officer in Austria.*

This account of English swords of the reigns of Elizabeth I (r. 1558-1603), James I (r. 1603-1625) and Charles I (r. 1625-49) starts at the very end of the Elizabethan period, as it is not possible to identify earlier specimens with any certainty. There is no lack of evidence showing the various hilt fashions favoured by English noblemen during the 16th century, for a great many portraits survive depicting them with their hands proudly resting on their sword hilts. Many of these swords must also survive somewhere, but unfortunately they do not differ in any essential detail from those in contemporary Continental portraits and therefore cannot be identified as English.

There are, it is true, a few Holbein designs for sword hilts that were made either for Henry VIII or the young Prince Edward, later Edward VI, but these were intended to be executed in gold and are of exceptional elaboration and costliness.[1] They do not, therefore, bear much relevance to the typical English sword hilt of the mid-century—that is, if an English type did exist at all at that period. We must therefore begin at the end of the Elizabethan period, though the types described may have been known a decade or so earlier. No dated hilts are recorded, but by about 1600 no fewer than four different hilt types existed, all of which can be seen in contemporary English portraits and may be recognised with some degree of confidence as English. This does not necessarily mean that all swords fitted with one or another of these hilt types must be English. Many of them are now to be

seen in Continental museums and collections; some may have been purchased in England at the time, some may have been presented to foreign visitors either at the time or subsequently, and others again may have been wrought abroad by special order in the English manner.

While the hilts are not dated, some of the blades do bear a date etched or engraved on them, including those illustrated here in Figs. 5 and 8. The presence of a date on a blade cannot be accepted as conclusive evidence of the date of the hilt it accompanies. A new hilt may have been fitted to an old blade or vice-versa in the 16th or 17th centuries; alternatively, the blade may have been changed by a collector in the course of the last hundred and fifty years—that is, in the period in which old swords have been collector items.

FOUR BASIC TYPES

The types of swords here to be considered are: (1) backswords, (2) broadswords, (3) riding swords and rapiers, and (4) hangers or hunting swords. While it is possible to trace the development within each type, one cannot say which if any, had priority.

Backswords

The Elizabethan backsword has a hilt of simple construction (Figs. 1a and b), with straight, usually counter-curved quillons, knuckle-bow and ring-guard on one or on both sides of the cross. This simple construction persisted for a long time and is still found on a backsword with a Hounslow blade in the Burrell

Collection, Glasgow (Fig. 2). A more evolved type of hilt is shown in Fig. 3. This has the heavy globular or octagonal pommel which is one of the characteristic features of late 16th or early 17th century swords made in England. The quillons are counter-curved, and the hilt has fully developed arms, knuckle-bow and a loop guard reaching from halfway along the bow down to join the rear arm. This particular construction was not confined to backswords but will be found on rapiers and riding swords as well.

Broadswords

The typical broadsword had a basket hilt, but a somewhat earlier example is shown in Fig. 4. In this case the blade must once have been of considerable weight but repeated grinding has reduced it to a shadow of its former self. The shell, which is divided into two halves, one on either side of the cross, is another feature that will frequently be noticed on English swords. The English basket hilt, which is, of course, the ancestor of the Scottish basket-hilted sword of the 17th and 18th centuries, was, if the dates on portraits showing it can be believed, already in existence before the last quarter of the 16th century. A portrait of Sir Edward Lyttleton at Hagley in Worcestershire dated 1568 shows him with one of these basket-hilted swords with long counter-curved quillons. The earlier examples can be recognised by the presence of the long quillions, while the later ones have only a rear quillon and have developed the two loops at the base of the basket in front (Fig. 5), char-

143

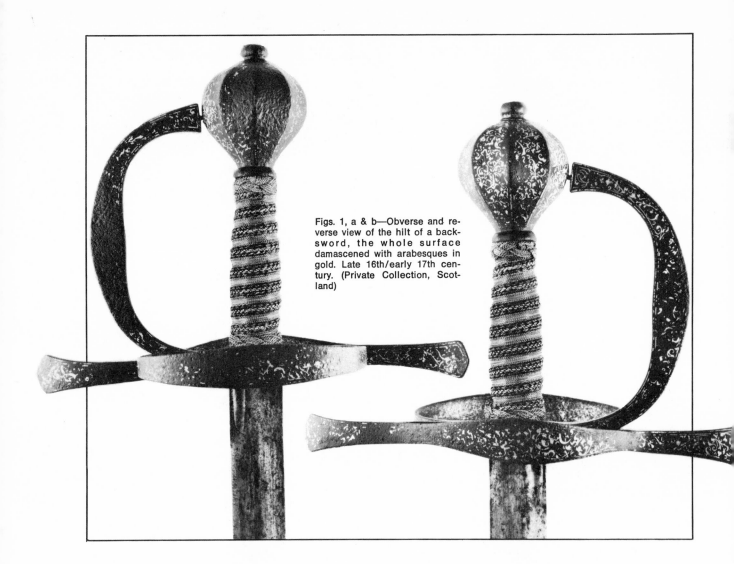

Figs. 1, a & b—Obverse and reverse view of the hilt of a backsword, the whole surface damascened with arabesques in gold. Late 16th/early 17th century. (Private Collection, Scotland)

acteristic of the later Scottish versions of this hilt. The two hilts illustrated both have the large globular pommel but of rather flatter form than that found on the backsword or rapier hilts. That in Fig. 6 can be dated approximately, as it belonged to Sir William Twysden of Roydon Hall, Kent, who was created a knight by James I in 1603 and a Baronet in 1611. The blade of the sword in Fig. 5 is dated 1611 and is one of a number by Clemens Horn of Solingen bearing the same date.

A second type of broadsword had a simple cross hilt; many samples of this particular type survive, a high proportion of them in Continental collections. Thus there are examples in the Hermitage, Leningrad, in the Tøjhusmuseum, Copenhagen, the Swedish Royal Armoury, Stockholm and the Swiss Landesmuseum, Zurich. There are two versions of these cross-hilts, differing in decoration rather than in form. In the one type the ornament is of silver or gold and silver encrustation in the iron of the hilt, while in the other thin medallions of silver, embossed or stamped with figure subjects, are inset in the hilt

and the surrounding areas are either damascened with gold or encrusted with silver. The finest of all these swords is that illustrated in Fig. 7: this was made for Henry Frederick, Prince of Wales, the eldest son of James I. The blade is decorated with the Prince of Wales's feathers and the sword can, therefore, be dated between 1610, when Henry was created Prince of Wales, and his death in 1612. The blade is further damascened in gold with the monogram *PH* of the Prince and signed "CLEMENS HORN ME FECIT SOLINGEN." The Prince of Wales's sword appears to have lost its original grip; this was probably of iron damascened en suite with the rest of the hilt. The sword at Leningrad, which has a hilt of comparable richness to the Prince's sword, retains the original grip (Fig. 8). In this case the silver encrustation differs in many details from the established English patterns and its origin is not certainly English, though like so many of the fine English swords, it also has a Clemens Horn blade, dated, as is that of the basket-hilted broadsword in Fig. 5, 1611. Horn must have received an important order for blades from an Eng-

144

Fig. 2—Backsword, the hilt incised and damascened with silver, pierced pommel, the blade signed "ME FECIT HOWNSLO"; about 1630-40. (Burrell Collection, Scotland)

Fig. 3—Backsword, the hilt incrusted with silver floral scrolls; first quarter of 17th century. (Victoria and Albert Museum, London)

Fig. 4—Broadsword, the hilt chiselled with profile heads in relief, incised and damascened with gold; about 1600. (Royal Scottish Museum, Edinburgh)

lish sword-cutler, for, in addition to the three mentioned above, there is the blade in the Victoria and Albert Museum, which is etched and gilt with the Royal Stuart arms, and two swords in the English Royal Armoury at Windsor Castle, which are believed to have belonged to James I and Prince Charles (later King Charles I) respectively. A less richly decorated version of this cross-hilted type is illustrated in Fig. 9.

The finest of the second type of cross-hilt is that in the Swiss Landesmuseum (Fig. 11). The hilt is set on each side with four shaped silver plaques embossed in low relief with scenes from the Passion of Christ while the surrounding areas are damascened with gold. The blade is exceptional in that it is of Persian origin. Of somewhat earlier date than the hilt, it was re-mounted when the hilt was made. Three other hilts, preserved in Copenhagen and Stockholm respectively, are of closely similar design: the silver inserts, all circular in form, are embossed in low relief with a group of St. George killing the dragon. Similar swords are to be seen in portraits of Knights of the Order of the Garter, and in view of the very similar

145

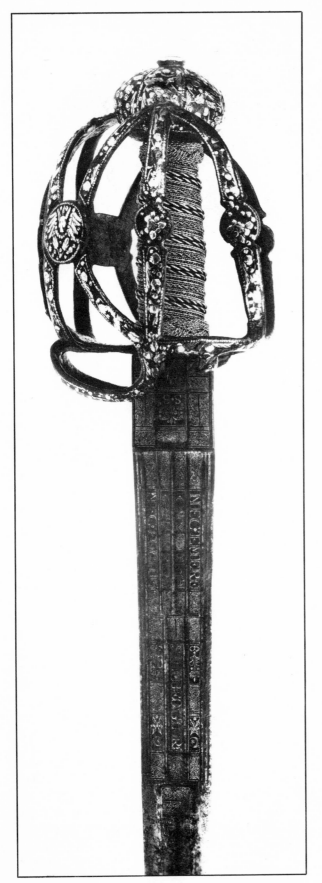

Fig. 5—Broadsword, the basket hilt encrusted with silver, the blade etched and gilt, signed and dated "CLEMENS HORN ME FECIT SOLINGEN ANNO 1611." (Private Collection, London)

design of these three hilts, together with the presence of the badge of the Order, it seems possible that they also were intended to accompany the regalia of the Garter which were sent to the Kings of Denmark and Sweden by James I and Charles I respectively.[2] (Figs. 10 and 12)

One further cross-hilted sword remains to be mentioned; this is the sword of state of the City of Canterbury (Fig. 13). It is an enlarged version of the second type, the pommel and cross being set on each side with four silver plaques, now much damaged, one of which appears to represent Judith with the head of Holophernes. As in the case of the swords described above, the remaining area is damascened with silver lines enclosing areas of gold arabesques. The blade is damascened on one side with the arms of the city and on the other with the Stuart royal arms and further inscribed "THIS SOVRDE WAS GRAUNTED BY OUR GRATIOUS SOVERAIGNE LORD KING IEAMES TO THIS CITTY OF CANTERBURY" and on the other with an extract from the law of Moses. The sword was acquired in 1607 and its cost is recorded in the accounts of the city for that year as 41/-. The silver grip engraved with the royal arms and that of the city together with roses and thistles is a later substitution and dates from the reign of Charles I or II.

Riding Swords

The next two types, namely riding swords and rapiers, can be dealt with together as their hilts do not differ, the distinction lying in the weight of the blades. The earlier type of hilt has either straight or counter-curved quillons, knuckle-bow, and arms with a single loop reaching from the knuckle bow to the rear arm while a short guard projects at right angles from the front arm. There are two or three counter-guards behind. Examples are shown in Figs. 14 and 15. These two hilts are richly damascened with silver lines enclosing panels of gold arabesques, but plainer versions (Fig. 16), some even undecorated, are known. During the second quarter of the century a distinctive type of cup-hilted rapier makes its appearance. In this the large globular pommel is abandoned in favour of an ovoid (Fig. 18) or a lobate one (Fig. 17). The cup was either composed of two up-turned shells (Fig. 18) or it was a true cup pierced with a simple repeating pattern (Fig. 19).

Hunting Swords or Hangers

The last hilt type to be mentioned is that of the hunting sword or hanger; a great many of these have survived, all conforming closely to the pattern of the two illustrated in Figs. 20 and 21.

GOLD AND SILVER EMBELLISHMENTS

A feature of some of the English swords discussed

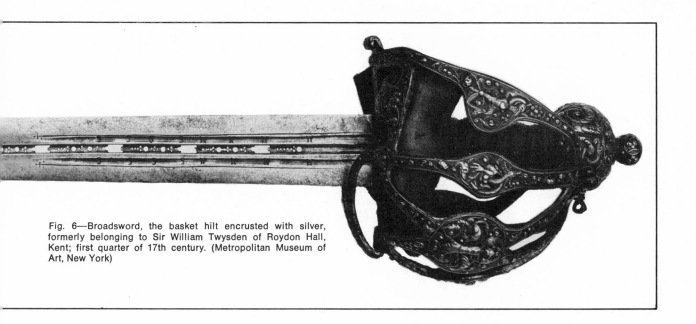

Fig. 6—Broadsword, the basket hilt encrusted with silver, formerly belonging to Sir William Twysden of Roydon Hall, Kent; first quarter of 17th century. (Metropolitan Museum of Art, New York)

above is the excellence of the encrusting and damascening in gold and silver. The quality does, however, vary considerably, ranging from the cross-hilted sword of Henry, Prince of Wales (Fig. 7) down to the backsword in Fig. 2. This difference has, of course, been noted by earlier writers on the subject and they have tended to ascribe only the coarser pieces to English masters, while giving the finer ones to Italian craftsmen. Thus Laking in his *Catalogue of the Windsor Armoury* describes two of the finest of them (nos. 60 and 61) as 'of English fashion, but probably of Italian workmanship'. When discussing these same pieces in his *Record of European Armour and Arms,* he relented so far as to call them "probably of English workmanship." They are, in fact, both quite typically English hilts, and the decoration was doubtless carried out in England, though whether by a native or an immigrant master there is no means of determining. Even as recently as 1962, in the second edition of the Wallace Collection Catalogue, three of these English swords, including that here illustrated in Fig. 15, are described as German, but for the insufficient reason that the blades are of German or, in one case, of Italian origin. Until the establishment of the Hounslow factory, the vast majority of English swords had imported blades and would, according to this system of classification, not rank as English. The presence of several of these finely decorated hilts in foreign collections, including two riding swords in the Dresden Historisches Museum and the three cross-hilted ones in Copenhagen and Stockholm respectively, has led to their being regarded by some writers as Continental; but the few examples recorded abroad are greatly outnumbered by those in old, established English collections, such as that at Warwick Castle. One is shown in Grose's *Treatise on Antient Armour*

which was published as long ago as 1786.[3] While English swords can be identified with some certainty by reference to their hilt construction, their ornament is a less reliable indication. Damascening in gold and encrustation with silver were forms of decoration that were applied in most western European countries, and the details—cherub's heads, floral scrolls, trophies of arms, etc.—were also in general use. While some of the very simply decorated silver-encrusted hilts can be recognized as English by reference to the silver-work, the more richly decorated the hilts the more difficult it is to establish their origin. Some of the craftsmen who executed the damascening in England may themselves have been immigrants and followed there the style and technique they had learned elsewhere. The cross-hilt shown in Fig. 9 could be of English or Continental origin.

The most striking feature of the decoration on the Prince of Wales's sword (Fig. 7) and on that in the Hermitage (Fig. 8) is the high relief and fine chasing of the silver, in particular the profile heads copied from classical medals. Next in quality to these two cross-hilted swords comes the broadsword of Sir William Twysden and the two hangers illustrated in Figs. 6, 20 and 21. On these the decoration is less crowded but at the same time executed in somewhat lower relief. Another type of decoration on English hilts combines panels of minute gold damascening with silver encrustation. This is found on a good many English swords, though the damascening is rarely in such good condition as is that of the fine rapier illustrated in Fig. 15. Some earlier swords, including the backsword in Fig. 1 were decorated exclusively with fine gold damascene which once covered the whole surface. The most pleasing of these hilts, which combine silver encrustation with gold damascene, is a sword

147

Fig. 7—Cross-hilted sword of Henry Frederick, Prince of Wales, the hilt encrusted with silver including profile heads of Roman Emperors, the blade damascened in gold and signed "CLEMENS HORN ME FECIT SOLINGEN"; about 1610. (Wallace Collection, London)

formerly in the Spitzer and now in a Danish collection.[4] The English origin of this sword, which was not recognised when it was in the Spitzer collection, is beyond doubt, and it is one of the finest surviving examples of the Elizabethan sword-cutler's art. It has a cup hilt upon which the ornament is arranged in alternate panels of silver and gold which run spirally.

An offence committed by a member of the Cutlers' Company, which is referred to in a minute dated November 26, 1607, gives an insight into other methods of decorating sword-hilts. A certain William Oldrenshawe was accused of selling for sixteen shillings at Sturbridge Fair a rapier and dagger described as 'plain silvered'. As, however, he received no earnest money and another customer then appeared, he sold the same goods to him "with warranty it was hatched" for twenty six shillings and eight pence. It was proved to the Court that the silver was not applied to the hilt by the process of hatching, —which called for a greater expense of silver as well as of labour—and the offender was accordingly fined. In 1632 a silvered sword was taken from another member of the Company, who promised not to repeat the offence. He had presumably tried to pass off a plated hilt as a solid silver one. A more common offence was the use of brass and copper for sword hilts instead of iron. In November 1635 the Court of the Cutlers' Company agreed to use their best endeavours "to suppresse and vtterly abandon the worcking and Tryming vp of swords, Rapiers and Skyrnes with Brasse and Copper Hilts and Pummels wch are Cast in moulds or any such deceiptfull way." Further, in September 1639, "Certeyne hilts handles and Pummels of Cast Brasse" which had been offered for sale "for sufficient worck made of Iron" were defaced by order of the Court.

Pierced Pommels and Guards

The various hilt types described above were exclusively English; another type which was fashionable in early 17th century England cannot be claimed as a purely English phenomenon. Its main feature is the fact that the pommel is pierced. The most important of these swords from our present point of view is one in the Windsor Castle Armoury, which, according to a reasonably convincing tradition, belonged to James I.[5] Laking gives the following description of it:

> The hilt might belong to the closing years of the sixteenth century, but the very fine blade associated with it, a blade made by Clemens Horn of Solingen, bears the date 1617. The pommel of the King James I sword is of inverted pear-shape, and is hollow, and constructed of five spiral scrolls à jour. The knuckle guard is flat, swelling in the centre where it is pierced with a

Fig. 8—Cross-hilted sword, the hilt profusely encrusted with silver, the blade signed "CLEMENS HORN ME FECIT SOLINGEN A° 1611." (The Hermitage Museum, Leningrad)

149

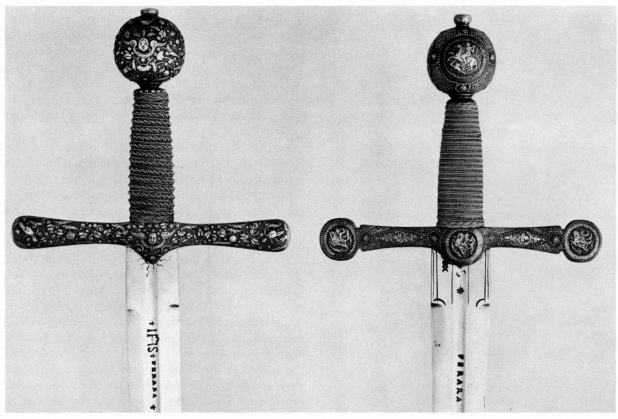

Fig. 9—Cross-hilted sword, the hilt encrusted with silver, the blade signed "FERARA"; first third of 17th century. (English?) (Tøjhusmuseum, Copenhagen)

Fig. 10—Cross-hilted sword, the hilt set with silver panels chased with St. George and the Dragon, the remainder of the hilt damascened with gold scrollwork enclosing panels of silver encrustation; first third of 17th century. (Tøjhusmuseum, Copenhagen)

diamond shaped aperture. The quillons are short and flat, with ribbon pattern ends; from ill-treatment they are now possibly more incurved than as originally made. The single bar is constructed on the same principle, and the shell is framed in similar ribbon pattern bands. The decoration of the hilt consists of trophies of arms, festoons and bouquets of flowers and fruit, boldly engraved and gilt upon a russeted groundwork. The whole of this ornamentation is bordered by a beading incrusted in silver. The underside of the bars is entirely gilt and punched with small circles.

The broad blade is elaborately etched and gilt with inscriptions but, unlike some of the other Clemens Horn blades made for England, it bears no device connected with the English royal house. The traditional association with James I must therefore be taken on trust, but the date 1617 on the blade shows that it could have belonged to him. Another sword with pierced pommel is that from the Burrell Collection illustrated in Fig. 2. This hilt is a simpler version of the Windsor sword. It has similar perforations in the hilt and the guards are also of ribbon-like construction, but there are no arms (pas d'âne) to the guard, nor a shell guard. The English association is quite convincing, for it has a Hounslow blade, and it

is doubtful whether Hounslow blades ever found a market abroad, where they had to compete with the products of Solingen, Passau and Toledo. It is tempting to attribute a third sword with pierced pommel and guards (Fig. 22) to the same workshop as the other two. The resemblance of this rapier to the two English swords is noticed in the Wallace Collection Catalogue (No. A595), but its attribution there to Germany is based upon the source of the blade. In fact it has not only the same shape of pommel but the guards are incised with similar motifs, i.e. trophies of arms, festoons, fruit and masks. The technique of applying the decoration is, however, different: whereas the other English swords discussed here have encrusted or damascened ornament, in this case the ornament is chiselled in the metal of the hilt and then overlaid with gold. Similar ornament is found on French hilts and the English origin of this superb rapier must remain less certain. Further evidence for the use of sword-hilts with pierced pommels in England can be found in contemporary portraits. A pommel of this type can be seen on the rapier carried by Francis Manners, 6th Duke of Rutland K.G., in a portrait dated 1614 at Woburn.

Changes After 1625

During the second quarter of the 17th century, that

is in the reign of Charles I, a number of changes in hilt forms took place. These affected backswords, broadswords and rapiers. A new type of backsword hilt was introduced which was to become the standard horseman's hilt of the Civil Wars. This was a half-basket hilt which offered a great deal of protection to the hand. The example illustrated in Fig. 23, which comes from the Copenhagen Tøjhusmuseum, is typical in form and construction but still shows the silver-incrusted ornament, which by this date was somewhat old-fashioned, chiselled and pierced work being preferred. This hilt was usually roughly chiselled with masks amidst scrolls and the fancied resemblance of these masks to Charles I gave rise in the 19th century to the name Mortuary sword, the idea being that the masks commemorated the Martyr King. In fact the style was introduced long before the execution of Charles I in 1649. It is, however, true that some of the finer hilts of this type were chiselled with bust portraits of Charles I and finished with close-plated silver. The portraits were, of course, patriotic and royalist in intent. These backswords survive in great numbers and of varying quality. The less pretentious

Fig. 12—Cross-hilted broadsword, the hilt set with silver panels embossed with St. George and the Dragon, the remainder of the hilt damescened with silver; first third of 17th century. (Tøjhusmuseum, Copenhagen)

Fig. 11—Cross-hilted sword, the cross and pommel set with silver plaques stamped with scenes from the Passion of Christ, the intervening panels damascened with gold scrollwork. Earlier Persian blade. Perhaps made in England for export; first quarter of 17th century. (Schweizerisches Landesmuseum, Zürich)

examples were finished black or simply painted black with a few of the details of the ornament picked out in gold paint. This was a very perishable type of decoration, but a few examples in good condition have survived. Besides the hilts which appear to show royalist sympathy, others are merely chiselled with figures of warriors, either mounted or on foot or trophies of arms which have no political significance. The finest of all these backswords, now in the C. O. von Kienbusch collection[6], is supposed to have belonged to Oliver Cromwell and the blade is inscribed "FOR THE COMMONWEALTH OF ENGLAND" with the date 1650, a fact which proves that these hilts were in general use. Of the known Hounslow blades a high proportion are found in this type of hilt, which, when intended for common troopers, was finished with a roughly chiselled feather pattern. Many of these were doubtless made in London, but as the capital was closed to the royalists during the Civil War, the latter must have obtained their supplies elsewhere. Some of the Hounslow blade-makers followed the king to Oxford and it is probable that some of the hilt-makers went with the royalist armies as well. On the other hand, the production of sword hilts does not call for specialist equipment, and it is probable that blacksmiths all over the country turned their hand to making them.

151

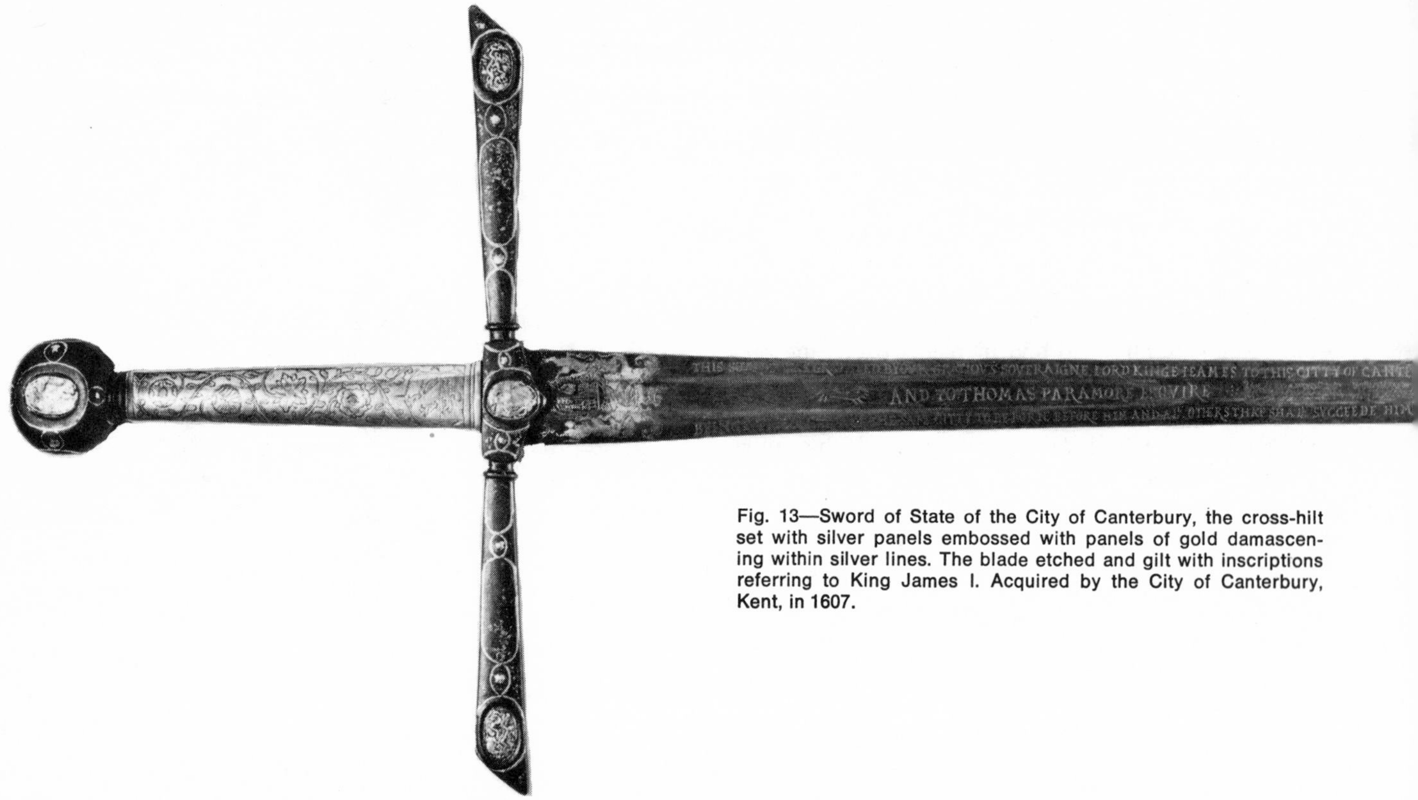

Fig. 13—Sword of State of the City of Canterbury, the cross-hilt set with silver panels embossed with panels of gold damascening within silver lines. The blade etched and gilt with inscriptions referring to King James I. Acquired by the City of Canterbury, Kent, in 1607.

The new type of broadsword is well represented by the two examples in Figs. 24 and 25, each with blade by Johannes Kinndt. One has the earlier ornamentation consisting of silver incrustation, while the latter has the hilt chiselled with masks and scrollwork and finished with silvering. The head is protected by a shell on each side turned upwards towards the pommel and a single knuckle-bow.

Rapier hilts of the second quarter of the century are usually based on the cup, either pierced in petal-form or in panels running around the cup. The pommel was fluted and of exaggerated elongation (Figs. 26 and 27). An alternative form with flattened pommel and chiselled hilt is shown in Fig. 28. In this case the cup is chiselled with a portrait bust on each side, representing Charles I crowned and his Queen Henrietta Maria. The chiselling is of exceptional quality by English standards of the time but there is no trace of the silvering that was the usual finish of such hilts.

Little is known of the makers of the many superbly decorated hilts of this period. There are a few references to such sword hilts in the records of the London Company of Cutlers. From this source we know that in 1626 the price of a sword with damasked hilt was between forty and fifty shillings. An undecorated hilt was much cheaper. In 1614 the Cutlers' Company supplied 'a very good turky blade and good open hilt' for six shillings.[7]

BLADE MANUFACTURE

The making and decorating of a sword hilt called for different techniques from the making of blades. Whereas the blade was of steel, the hilt was of softer iron; it was composed of various bars and other members which were hammered to shape by the blacksmith, forged together and then damascened with silver or gold. A noticeable feature of English hilts is the softness of their metal. The quillons have often been bent out of position and the loops fractured. One of the reasons for the softness of the metal used is the fact that the surface had to be sufficiently soft to permit the process of damascening which involved cutting V-shaped channels into which the precious metal could be hammered. If the iron were too hard the sword-furbisher would have difficulty in cutting his grooves and, when the silver or gold was hammered on, the iron would not give way and gain a purchase on the softer precious metal. For the same reason the silver which was used to decorate Elizabethan and Jacobean hilts had to be soft and hence very pure. This meant, however, that the silver decoration did not stand up to wear and it is rare to find such silver-encrusted hilts preserved in pristine condition. Swords and daggers were supplied by the same cutlers who made table cutlery. While no English sword blades, other than the later Hounslow blades discussed below, are known, English table knives were struck with the maker's marks, most of which are recorded in the mark book of the London Cutlers' Company. Moreover, under the Ordinance which followed the grant of James I's Charter to the Company in 1606, the use of the dagger mark was also made compulsory, not only for members of the Company but also for foreigners working in London. These were not literally foreigners but cutlers who were not freemen of the City of London. This regulation is recorded in the Cutlers' Company records of June 25, 1606, when at a Court of the Company were "summoned most parte of the forreyne workinge cutlers in and about the Citie and suburbs of London . . . and they were generallie charged . . . to strick a proper marke by the allowance of this howse whereon is on a part thereof to be strock the dagger being the Armes of the Citie." Most of the surviving knife blades of the first half of the 17th century do, in fact, bear the dagger mark together with the personal mark of the cutler and can therefore be readily identified. There was much less space available on a knife handle than on a sword hilt or a dagger handle for damascened decoration, but the shoulders of good-quality London-made knives were decorated in the same way as sword or dagger hilts, with gold damascening or silver incrustation, or with a combination of these two techniques. There can be little doubt that the decoration was carried out by the same craftsmen.

According to Stow's Survey of London, the most influential cutler during the reign of Queen Elizabeth was Richard Mathew, who worked at Fleetbridge. The same source informs us that he was granted a privilege by the Queen for manufacturing knives by a special process, but this was subsequently withdrawn after protests had been made by the other members of the craft. Presumably he was also a maker of sword hilts, but unfortunately neither knives nor swords by him have hitherto been recognised.

Spurious Foreign Marks

A good deal more is known about the manufacture of blades than of sword hilts in England. As long as blades were imported from the Continent—that is until the 1630's—the only names that were recognised as a warranty of quality were Spanish, Italian or German: Clemens Horn, Andrea Ferara, Picinino, Juan Martinez and so on. It was not until the foundation of the Hounslow sword factory in 1629 that the Solingen smiths who worked there introduced the practice of signing blades with their own name. The English bladesmiths, so far from putting their own names or marks on their productions, evidently followed the custom of their Solingen contemporaries and struck whatever mark or name seemed to offer the greatest inducement to the potential purchaser. Benjamin Stone, a London entrepreneur who had set up a blademaking factory at Hounslow, wrote in or after the year 1638 to the Office of Ordnance requesting that he be granted the power to hinder the striking of Spanish and other marks upon blades made by the workmen of the London cutlers.[8] It follows that some of the blades with transparently false Spanish or

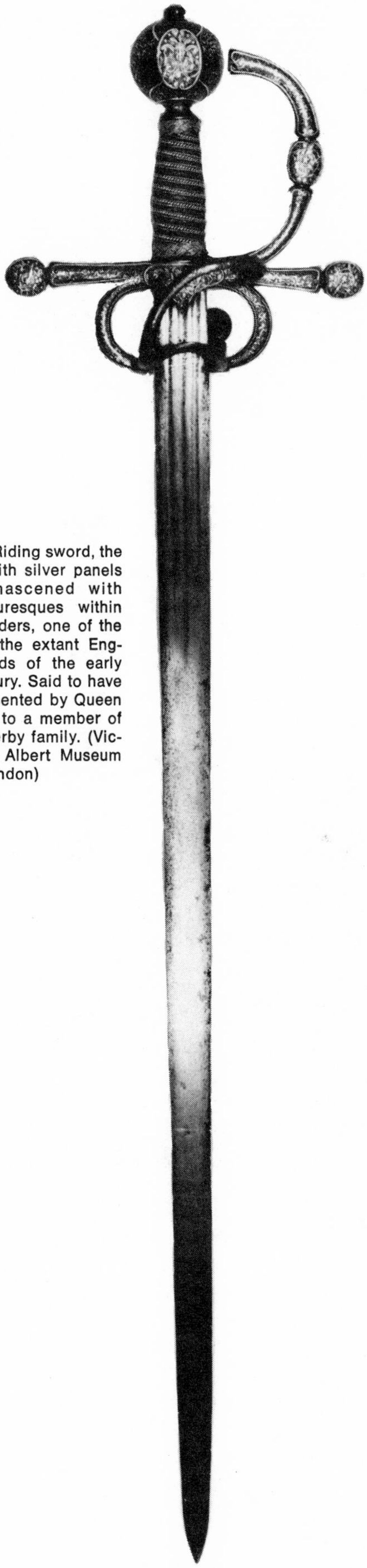

Fig. 14—Riding sword, the hilt set with silver panels and damascened with gold mauresques within silver borders, one of the finest of the extant English swords of the early 17th century. Said to have been presented by Queen Elizabeth to a member of the Wetherby family. (Victoria and Albert Museum [loan] London)

153

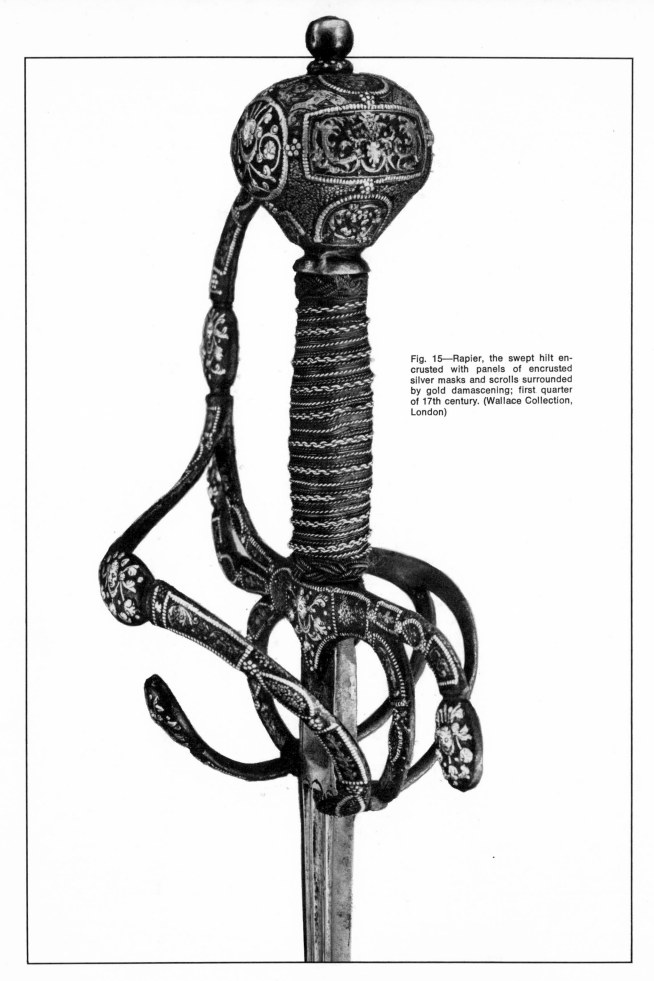

Fig. 15—Rapier, the swept hilt encrusted with panels of encrusted silver masks and scrolls surrounded by gold damascening; first quarter of 17th century. (Wallace Collection, London)

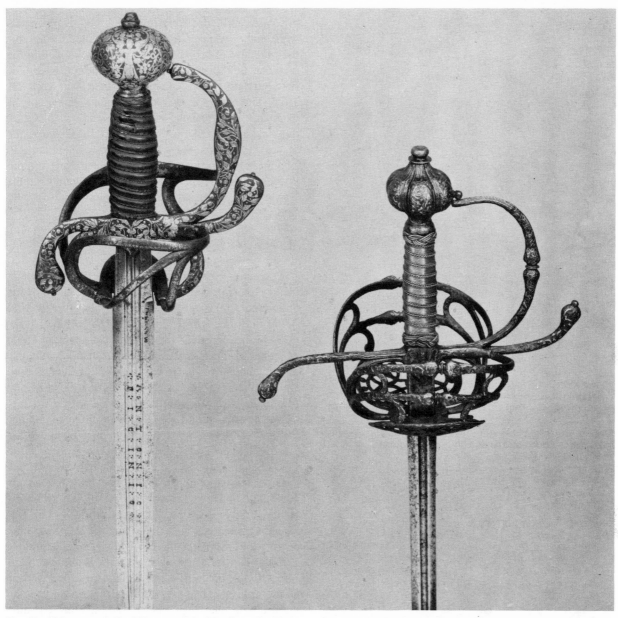

Fig. 16—Riding sword, the hilt encrusted with silver, the blade with the probably spurious signature "ANTONIO PICINIO"; first quarter of 17th century. (Victoria and Albert Museum, London)

Fig. 17—Cup-hilted rapier, the hilt with double-shell cup encrusted with silver, the blade signed "TOMAS AIALA IN TOLEDO 1610"; second quarter of the 17th century. (Victoria and Albert Museum, London)

Italian marks may be English, and not, as is commonly assumed, of Solingen make. The earliest reference to the manufacture of sword-blades in the records of the Cutlers' Company dates from July 1608 when it was agreed "that suit be made to the Lord Mayor and Council for the provision of such swords and other things appertaining to the Company for the service of the Realm as from time to time hereafter shall be provided for." This does not, however, mean that the manufacture of blades should be undertaken. We have fairly decisive evidence that their production had not begun in 1621. One of the beneficiaries under James I's scheme of granting patents and monopolies to certain favourite courtiers was Thomas Murrey, described as "Secretary to the Princes Highness." He

received a patient for the sole making of sword and rapier blades. In July 1621 he made the Company the first offer of this patent, but the latter rejected it "by reason of the large expences . . . wch this worck as they thinck will require before it come to perfection . . . and many other difficulties depending therevpon." It is unlikely that the offer of this monoply would have been turned down so definitely if the manufacture of sword blades were already a practical possibility. In 1624 the London Cutlers' Company undertook to provide monthly for His Majesty's service 5000 swords with hangers and girdles, the service for which they were required being "when the Earle of Southampton and other honourable persons . . . ymployed beyond the seas." It is quite clear that in

Fig. 18—Cup-hilted rapier, the hilt constructed of two shells and concentric rings; second quarter of 17th century. (Victoria and Albert Museum, London)

Fig. 19—Cup-hilted rapier, the hilt encrusted with silver, now much worn; second quarter of 17th century. (Victoria and Albert Museum, London)

this case the blades were imported, for arrangements were made by the Company to advance money for the purchase of foreign blades which were sold to the members at a fixed price some eight months later. The first purchase was of 48 dozen blades on April 29, 1624. These were then sold to sixteen members of the Company in parcels of two dozen costing £5. Other purchases followed during the next three years, the blades being obtained wholesale from merchants in London and Birmingham. Having been made up into swords by the cutlers, they were delivered to the Tower of London where the accounts were finally settled.

Robert South

The leading London cutler during the first half of the seventeenth century was Robert South, who was appointed Cutler to James I and subsequently held the same office under Charles I. His name first appears in the records of the Cutlers' Company in 1603, when he was described as a member of the Yeomanry of the Company, i.e. he was free but not yet clothed with the Livery. He was Renter Warden in 1628 and Master in 1629. He supplied James I with a number of fine swords and knives and when, three years after the latter's death, he at last obtained payment for "wares delivered to the Office of the Robes in the time of the late King," the amount involved was the considerable sum of £158-15. The only hilt so far attributed to Robert South is that of the sword of Henry, Prince of Wales, illustrated in Fig. 7. This follows the usual fashion of the early decades of the 17th century but is of distinctly higher quality. Another hilt that can be attributed to South is the sword of James I with blade by Clemens Horn in the Windsor Castle armoury. It is not unlikely that South was the importer of the Horn blades and that all the hilts originally furnished with such blades can be attributed to him. Not much is known about him. His name appears again in the records in 1631. On April 22, 1631 his name, together with that of William Cave, is on a petition from the Cutler's Company, addressed to the committee for the Company of Armourers and Gunmakers, which was set up to consider the rates due to these craftsmen and also to establish a list of persons entitled to make or repair arms for the public service. The petitioners requested that they might be joined in the Commission for the supply of swords. Though the request was granted, no action seems to have been taken upon it. Robert South may well have been a promoter of the mill referred to in a Cutlers' Company Minute of June 13, 1631: "At this Court order was given to the Mr. John Porter that he with Mr. Thos. Chesshier and others shold see and vewe a certyne Mill erected for the making of swords blades and to give their judgements and opinions therein at the

Figs. 20 & 21—Two hunting swords, both decorated with silver encrustation in the same workshop; first half of 17th century. (Messrs. Sotheby's, London)

Fig. 22—Rapier, the hilt with pierced pommel, chiselled with trophies of arms and masks, and gilded. Perhaps English, early 17th century. (Wallace Collection, London)

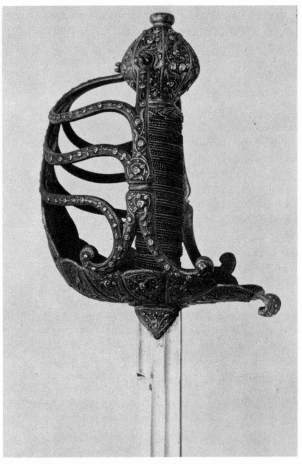

Fig. 23—Basket-hilted backsword, the hilt encrusted with silver; second quarter of 17th century. (Tøjhusmuseum, Copenhagen)

next Court."[9] In the following years South again appears in the Company records, when he had £100 "lent to him for one whole yeare gratis out of the stock of this Howse towards the makeing of Sword and Rapier blades for the good of this Companie and Kingdom." On August 7, 1632, he was granted by the Company the mark of "a Murrian Head to be strouck upon sword blades." He evidently succeeded in setting up his blade factory, for a petition addressed by him in 1639 to the Council of War states that he had supplied 4000 swords for the service of His Majesty's late Northern Expedition to the Office of Ordnance. He goes on to offer the same or a greater number.

THE HOUNSLOW FACTORY

It is now necessary to go back a few years to follow the history of the Hounslow factory, from which so many signed blades survive. The date of its establishment is clearly given by the terms of a petition addressed to King Charles II in 1672. The petitioners, two German smiths named Henry Hoppie and Peter English, stated that they were brought over from Germany (actually Solingen) by Sir William Heydon and King Charles I in 1629. The next date in the history of the factory is July 1, 1636, when a petition to

the King was made by Benjamin Stone, blademaker on Hounslow Heath. In this, the first of a series of similar petitions, he stated that he had been at great charge in perfecting the manufacture of sword blades and entreated the King to take into his store 2000 blades which were then in readiness. He further asked that the Lord Treasurer be instructed to advance money for these blades and thereby to encourage the said manufacture, which had never been brought to such perfection before. The petition concluded with the dramatic statement that, as a result of the great expenses he had incurred in the manufacture, he was indebted to various persons in London and dared not walk about as they threatened to arrest him. A note on this petition by the Attorney-General explains that Stone was making sword, rapier, skein (dagger) and other blades for his Majesty's store and for the service of his subjects, which had up to that time been made in foreign parts. This petition was followed by another of the same year. In this, Stone, who must have been a man of means, stated that at his charge, namely £6000, he had perfected the art of blademaking, so that he made "as good as any that are made in the Christian world." As a result of great complaints made by the Lord Deputy of Ireland and others of the unserviceableness of the swords brought into the Office of the Ordnance by the cutlers, his Majesty had ordered that the Office of the Ordnance should be supplied with blades made by the petitioner, who was thereupon made a member of the Office and undertook to make 500 blades a week. He went on to complain that the London Cutlers' Company had received orders to supply 4000 swords "which were for the most part old and decayed" although he had great quantities lying on his hands and was ready to deliver in short time any proportion his Majesty should have occasion to use. The petition concluded with the request that no further blades should be admitted to the Office of Ordnance that had been made abroad. This attack on the Cutlers was rejected by the Company; in their reply they alleged "that the swords which he petitioneth to be received into the store and pretends to be blades of his own making, are all bromedgham (i.e. Birmingham) blades, they are no way serviceable or fit for his Majesty's store."

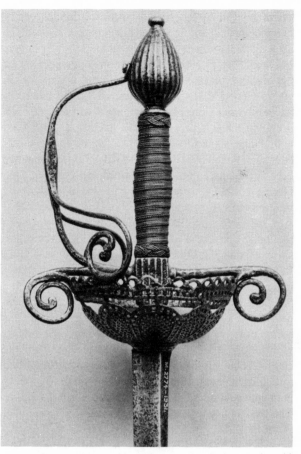

Fig. 26—Rapier with cup hilt composed of radiating petals; mid 17th century. (Victoria and Albert Museum, London)

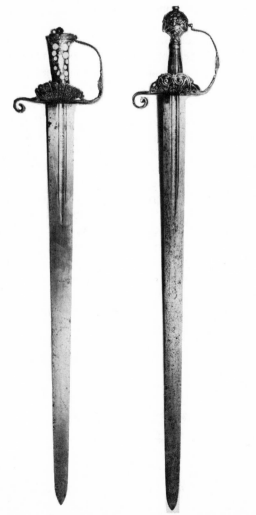

Figs. 24 & 25—Two broadswords, the hilt of No. 24 encrusted with silver, that of No. 25 close-plated with silver. Both blades signed by Johannes Kinndt of Hounslow, and dated 1634. (Victoria and Albert Museum, London)

This last claim is of particular interest as it shows that the manufacture of sword blades in Birmingham had already started and that the London trade did not place much store upon them, though this may have been due to commercial rivalry. In a final petition, also dated 1638, Stone describes himself as Cutler for the Office of the Ordnance' and states that he has spent £8000 (all his estate) in the manufacture of blades and is able to deliver 1000 per month.

German Workmen

Whether Benjamin Stone was in control of all the German immigrant bladesmiths then working at Hounslow is not clear. In view of the quantity of blades he was able to supply, this seems likely. Production had certainly begun long before Stone's petitions, for signed blades of earlier date are known. Thus Johannes Kinndt, who sometimes anglicised his name as John Kennet, is represented by five blades bearing his signature together with the location Hounslow and the dates 1634 or 1635. Three are in the London Museum,[10] the other two are in the Victoria and Albert Museum. Johannes Hoppie, perhaps the father of the Henry Hoppie who signed the 1672 petition, is also represented by signed blades dating from before 1636. It seems that Hoppie did not go directly to Hounslow when he came from Solingen, but was first established at what would seem to be the obvious place for a German, namely Greenwich, where Henry VIII's Almain armourers had been settled and where the royal armouries still existed. His presence there is proved by the existence of a sword with blade signed "IOHANNES HOPPE 1634 ME FECIT GRENEWICH IN ANGLIA." The postscript "IN ANGLIA" can be explained by the fact that Hoppe wished to establish that he was now working in England. A daughter of John Hoppie was christened at Greenwich Parish Church in 1632, so we can reckon with a sojourn there of some years. In addition to the blade signed Greenwich there are others by John Hoppie signed London; these also probably date from his Greenwich period. It is possible that the Solingen bladesmiths working at Hounslow may have begun by signing their wares LONDON, but this seems unlikely. Although Hounslow is now a suburb of London, it is some twelve miles distant from the city and could in the 17th century hardly be regarded as belonging to the purlieus of London. Another German smith who signed LONDON was Kaspar Fleisch. The blade of the sword illustrated in Fig. 27 is signed "CASPER CARNIS ME FECIT LONDON"; Carnis is, of course, the Latinised version of the German word *Fleisch*.

Judging by the number of extant signed blades, one of the most important of the German smiths at Hounslow was Peter Munsten, who came from a well-known Solingen family. His name does not, however, appear in the various documentary references to the Hounslow factory and it has been suggested that he may have changed his name to Peter English. He may have chosen another name because Munsten does not readily lend itself to anglicisation. The last of the German smiths who is believed to have worked at Hounslow is Clamas Meigen, whose name appears on a number of rather rough broadsword blades.

Besides the Germans, a number of English-born smiths worked at Hounslow, and blades signed by them survive. These include Richard Hopkins, represented by a sword in the London Museum[11] with blade signed "RECARDUS HOPKINS FECIT HOUNSLOE," and Joseph Jencks, represented by a sword in an English private collection signed "JOSEPH JENCKES ME FECIT HOUNSLO." Jencks is the only working Hounslow smith who is known to have been a member of the London Cutlers' Company. His mark, a thistle with a dagger, is found on a number of finely finished table-knives. The majority of the Hounslow blades are not signed with the smith's name, and it is probable that the practice was given up. It seems that the earlier blades are signed while the later ones, which are often more roughly finished, bear only the name "HOUNSLOE" or "ME FECIT HOUNSLO."

Slow Decline and Cessation

The Hounslow factory is shown on the map published by Moses Glover in 1635, as is "Mr. Stones' house."[12] Stone's name does not appear on any of the blades, although he was a member of the Cutlers' Company and actually had a mark allotted to him. It is clear from the statements in his petitions that he became a merchant and was more concerned with the financing and organisation of blade manufacture in England. As Hounslow was outside the jurisdiction of the London Company, the German smiths did not need to secure admission to the Company, which would in any case probably have been refused. During their early days in England, when they seem to have worked in London, they probably enjoyed royal protection against interference by the Company. When the Civil Wars began, the Hounslow bladesmiths seem to have split into two camps according to their political sympathies. We know from the 1672 petition that Hoppie and English followed Charles I to Oxford and that Cromwell confiscated their mills and turned them

Fig. 27—Cup-hilted rapier, the blade signed "CASPER CARNIS ME FECIT LONDON," mid-17th century. (London Museum)

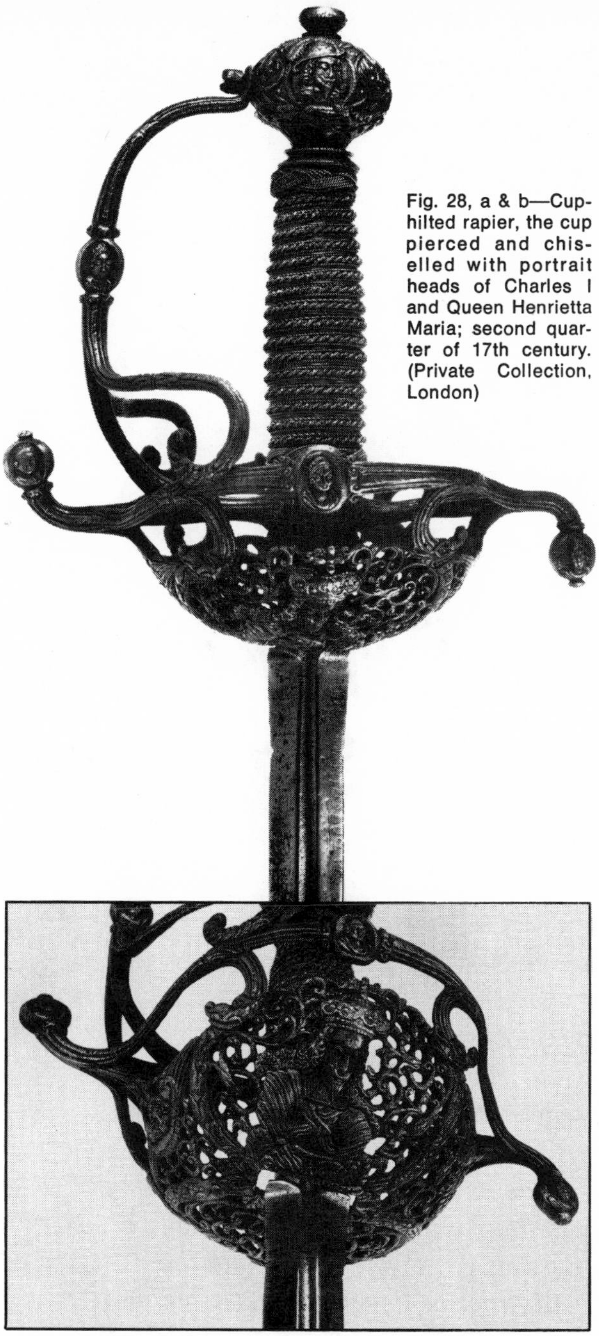

Fig. 28, a & b—Cup-hilted rapier, the cup pierced and chis-elled with portrait heads of Charles I and Queen Henrietta Maria; second quar-ter of 17th century. (Private Collection, London)

into powder mills.[13] On the other hand Johann Kinndt (Kennet) remained at Hounslow; a letter from Sir William Waller, dated April 1643, to Parliament requests the supply of "200 Horsemen's swords of Kennet's making of Hounslow." The bladesmiths who remained at Hounslow were not without their difficulties for in 1649 their tools and stock in trade were distrained upon by the Commissioners of Taxes for non-payment of taxes due. The bladesmiths petitioned the Council of State with satisfactory results, for the latter sent a stiff minute to the Tax authorities requiring them to return the tools, which should not have been distrained upon as long as any other appropriate surety could be found. Further, the Commissioners were instructed to examine the bladesmiths' petition and to "take order that in future assessments they may not be oppressed with payments beyond their proportions, and that their working tools be made good to them and the manufacture may have all encouragement."

The latest dated Hounslow Blade is of the year 1637 but there are many references to the blade factory of later date. In 1650 an order was made to deliver ten trees from Windsor Forest to Paul and Everard Ernious, "strangers," for the repair of the sword mills. Various petitions dating from between 1650 and 1660 from John Cook, Gentleman, refer to "the encouragement of his manufactory of sword and rapier blades at Hounslo." In spite of the critical comments of the London Cutlers' Company, the Hounslow blades were quite serviceable; according to the account of Benjamin Stone in the Dictionary of National Biography, some of his blades were shown to Robert South, the royal cutler, described as of Toledo make and accepted by him as such. William Cavendish, first Duke of Newcastle (1592-1676), refers to the high quality of Hounslow blades in two of his plays.

NOTES

1. Ill. H.A. Schmidt, *Hans Holbein de Jüngere,* Basel, 1945, fig. 139.
2. Christian IV of Denmark (1588-1648) was appointed Knight of the Garter in 1605 and Gustavus Adolphus of Sweden in 1628.
3. F. Grose, *Treatise on Antient Armour,* Vol. II, pl. 33.
4. See E.A. Christensens *Vaabensamling, Vaabenhistoriske Aarbøger,* Copenhagen, 1935, pl. C5.
5. Ill. Laking, *The Armoury of Windsor Castle,* pl. 9, cat. no. 62.
6. Ill. *Kretschmar von Kienbusch Collection,* Princeton, 1963, pl. CIV, cat. no. 356.
7. This and the following extracts from the records of the Worshipful Company of Cutlers of London are taken from Charles Welch, *History of the Cutlers' Company,* London, 1922.

8. This and the following extracts concerning the petitions addressed by Benjamin Stone to the Office of Ordnance are taken from the Calendars of State Papers for the appropriate years. For further information concerning Benjamin Stone see Meredith Colket, "The Jenks Family of England," *The New England Historical and Genealogical Register,* Vol. CX, nos. 437-440, 1956.
9. Thomas Cheshire was probably an associate of Robert South; his name appears as well as that of South as a supplier of richly decorated swords to the Royal Wardrobe.
10. Ill. M.R. Holmes, *Arms and Armour in Tudor and Stuart London,* London, 1957, pls. xii and xiii.
11. Ill. *ibid.* pl. xviii.
12. Ill. M. Colket, *op. cit.* pls. 3 and 6.
13. *S.P. Dom. Car. II,* 295.41.

The Significance of "Inventor" in Felix Werder's Signature

by ARNE HOFF

Dr. Hoff, born in Denmark in 1907, is director of the Royal Danish Arsenal Museum in Copenhagen, familiarly known as the Tøjhusmuseum. His many articles and monographs are known to arms students everywhere; his outstanding works in book form are his doctorial dissertation Aeldere Dansk Bøssemageri *(Danish Gunmakers of the Past),* Rassmussens Revolvergewehr, *and the internationally acclaimed two-volume history of firearms* Feuerwaffen *(Klinkhardt & Biermann, Braunschweig, 1969). He is a Knight of the Royal Danish Order of Dannebrog. The inordinate thoroughness with which Dr. Hoff approaches his inquiries into arms history, whether prolonged major projects or brief, particularized* ad hoc *investigations like the one here reported, is exemplified by the metalurgical analyses with comparative control specimens undertaken to satisfy his curiosity in the case at hand.*

On the barrel of a light flintlock carbine in the arms collection of the Kunsthistorisches Museum in Vienna (No. A-1454) the following inscription is to be found: "Felix Werder Tiguri Inventor 1652" (Figs. 1 and 2). *Tigurus* is Latin for Zürich, and *Tiguri* the locative form "in (or from) Zürich". But what does the word *Inventor* mean in this context?

Normally, the term used in connection with a firearm would mean the person who had literally invented or thought up the essential working principles of the arm in question, in contrast to the person who actually, physically, constructed it. An example would be a snaplock magazine gun in the Bargello in Florence (No. 70) whose lock bears the legend "Sigmund Klett infentiert mich, Hans Paul Klett macht mich"—"Sigmund Klett invents me, Hans Paul Klett constructs me." Similarly, a Danish breechloading rifle in the Tøjhusmuseum in Copenhagen (No. B-1114) is signed on the barrel "Johan Seckfort Invent[or]" while the lock is signed by the well-known Danish court gunmaker Heinrich Kappel, who actually made the piece. In other cases, the same person claims to be both designer and executor: for example, a flintlock repeating rifle of the so-called Lorenzoni system in the Livrustkammar, Stockholm (No. 49/50-51), is signed "Fecit et invenit Wetschgi Augustae," while another flintlock repeating rifle in the Musée de l'Armée in Paris (No. M-665) has the signature "Fait et inventé par Jean Bouilliet à St.Etienne." (In neither of these last two cases would the claim of originality

hold up in court, but that is quite another story.)

Sometimes, however, the term "inventor" does not apply to the construction but to the decoration. Many of the well-known designers of pattern books for gunmakers used the term "Inv." or "Invenit" with their signatures, meaning "designed," in contrast to the "sculpsit", i.e. "engraved it," or "fecit," i.e. "executed it," which qualified the signature of the actual engraver. But in the case of the Werder carbine in Vienna, the point of departure for our present considerations, the rather commonplace engraving of foliage in the style of Michel le Blond could hardly justify the term "inventor"; we shall therefore have to take the term as referring to some aspect of the weapon's construction.

As early as 1898, Wendelin Boeheim suggested that Felix Werder might have been the inventor of the true flintlock, although he felt that the form of the cock of the Werder flintlocks was not archtypal but in fact represented an already somewhat advanced evolutionary step.[1] The question was taken up again by E.A. Gessler in 1922.[2] Gessler connected a brace of pistols in the Landesmuseum in Zürich (No. K.Z. 5316/17) with a note in the city archives dated March 10th, 1652, which records that the city fathers had received from the goldsmith Felix Werder a carbine and a brace of pistols "as a rarity" to be kept "in memory of the inventor." These pistols were no doubt those now in the Landesmuseum. They are not signed, but according to the old inventories they were made by Felix Werder in 1652; moreover, on the inside of their lockplates Gessler found a very tiny master's mark, a pentagram in a shield, which proved to be one of the figures in the coat-of-arms of the Werder family. But the carbine in question had disappeared—though quite likely it was the one now in Vienna signed "Inventor". Still Gessler thought that "inventor" referred to the lock (a follower of Moritz Thierbach, he believed that the true flintlock had developed step by step from the snaphaunce, but he conjectured that

cracking. When asked about his process, he explained airily that he added "something" to the orichalcum which made it fusible and tough, but declined to say what. He was not unprepared to sell his secret for 200 doubloons, or for half this price if he would be permitted to teach his process to others. No one but his daughter, who had assisted him but had recently died, had ever been initiated into the mystery, which could not be taught by correspondence but only by the mas-

Fig. 1—Flintlock carbine signed on the barrel "Felix Werder Tiguri Inventor 1652." (Arms collection of the Kunsthistorisches Museum, Vienna, No. A1454)

perhaps "inventor" here was only intended to denote Werder's claim of having been the first to use true flintlocks on pistols). Alternatively, Gessler toyed with the possibility that "inventor" could refer to the thin walls of the barrel, but almost at once rejected this theory as improbable.

But when Lenk in his study of the origins of the flintlock made it quite clear in 1939 that the true flintlock was generally known by 1615-25, another solution had to be found. It was then suggested by Hans Schedelmann that the term "invention" applied to the particular alloy used in the brass barrels.[3] An indirect support of this thesis could be found in a military handbook by Hans Conrad Lavater, himself a citizen of Zürich, written in 1644 and printed in 1667; in it, pistols with gilt brass barrels are listed among the most important military products of the city, referring no doubt to Werder's production, which consisted mostly of pistols.[4] This special-alloy thesis became even more probable when in 1966 the present writer discovered that Felix Werder had approached the Royal Society in London in 1662 in order to sell the secret of "a way of his own invention to make handguns and pistols of a metal called orichalcum."[5] He said that he could make that brittle metal so tough that it would be a great deal freer from the danger of bursting than iron. Besides, the pistols and guns made of it were promised to be so thin and light that they would weigh scarcely half the weight of iron ones and would bear a double charge without ever bursting or

ter in person by performing it on the spot. As to the final tube-smithing method. Werder said that the barrels of his pistols and guns were all cast and then scoured, lapped and polished within and without.

In order to establish whether indeed Werder barrels were "inventions" by virtue of a special alloy, the Tøjhusmuseum arranged to have one of his products submitted to various tests in the metallographic laboratory of the Nordisk Kabel- og Tradfabrik in Copenhagen. The barrel was taken from a brace of flintlock pistols (No. B-678/9) which have the previously-mentioned pentagram mark on the inside of the lockplates and are therefore without doubt the work of Felix Werder (Fig. 3). By way of control and comparison, another brass pistol barrel underwent similar tests; this one was taken from a brace in the Tøjhusmuseum (No. B-1248/9) signed on the lockplate by the Belgian gunsmith Philipe Selier and struck three times on the barrel with his mark (the initials "PS" under an open crown—Støckel 1021), a typical Liège product of the early 18th century. The two barrels were of almost the same length and width, the Werder being 14.4 mm calibre and the Selier 15.5 mm. The thicknesses of the walls, however, measured at the muzzle, were very different: 0.60 mm for the Werder and 2.00 mm for the Selier. The conclusions of the analyses were a surprise. Both samples were made of a brass containing a small quantity of lead; there was a difference in the percentage of copper in the alloy, but it was hardly this which constituted the secret of "orichalcum". Both brasses were of alpha type, and the lead component had no doubt been added to increase the machinability. The brass of the Werder barrel had a little more tin, iron and nickel than the Selier, but it was impossible to say whether this had been added intentionally or by oversight and accident. Thus the main difference was not to be found in the composition but rather—surprisingly—in the production method: the Werder barrel was cast as a tube and

frequent that approximately a third of all 14th- and 15th-century barrels seem to have been made this way. Among these was, for example, the Loshult gun (Statens Historiska Museum, Stockholm, No. 23136), probably the oldest handgun in existence. It is difficult to establish exactly how many surviving specimens are of true bronze (copper and tin) and how many of brass (about 80% copper, 20% zinc)— only a metallurgical analysis could show that; but a

Fig. 2—Detail of the signature of the carbine in Fig. 1.

then given a very extensive cold hammering, probably over a mandril. The Selier barrel, on the other hand, was cast as an oblong plate, then bent over a mandril and tin-soldered to form a tube, the soldering seam being reinforced by inletting a number of brass squares across it.

This unexpected result invited a control test, and most kindly my colleagues of the Royal Army Museum, Stockholm, having recently acquired a brace of Werder wheellock pistols (No. 63/205), offered to send one of the barrels for testing by the Swedish State Institute for Testing Materials. The analysis of the alloy showed only very small and probably unintentional differences from the Copenhagen barrel, and the production method was the same, i.e. tube-cast and cold-hammered. It should be noted that there is a considerable difference in manufacturing dates between the two braces involved, the Stockholm wheellocks stemming from the early 1640's while the Copenhagen flintlocks date from about 1660.

Now, at this point we must digress from our main theme for a few moments and examine some considerations of brass barrels in general. These have never been the objects of a special study, and what is said in the following three brief paragraphs constitutes only some preliminary observations perhaps some day to be elaborated. Every arms student knows that brass barrels occurred on handguns in fair numbers from the earliest times almost up to the present. In the dawn days of firearms, cast copper alloys were so

superficial estimate based on surface colour points to an overwhelming majority of bronze. Then, in the 16th century, when brass production was increasing, the opposite seems to have become the case, and in the following centuries bronze barrels on handguns diminished almost to extinction.

There seem to have been three different production methods: oblong plates soldered into tubes, cast tubes and drilled-out solid cast rods. Of the five 16th-century brass barrels in the Tøjhusmuseum, two (Nos. B-100 and B-152), both datable about 1580, are cast as tubes. A close examination of the surface shows a number of small dots of iron: remnants of small iron pins fixing a central core in the casting mold; after the casting was finished, the core was removed and the ends of the pins filed off, leaving only these small marks, and finally the inner surface of the barrel was ground and polished. The other three Tøjhus brass barrels, two of which are datable about 1570 (Nos. B-47 and B-71) and one about 1550 (No. B-278), were made by bending brass plates over a mandril and soldering the seam. The thicknesses of their walls run from 3.5 to 5.0 mm.

In the 17th century there were certain species of firearms closely associated with brass barrels. One was the Scottish cast brass snaphaunce pistol often made with heavily moulded cast brass barrels, perhaps bored-out solid rods—a muzzle-on view will often show a bore that is not quite concentric. Another group is exemplified by at least a dozen snap-

Fig. 3—A pair of flintlock pistols, ca. 1655-60, bearing the mark of Felix Werder on the inside of the locks. (Tøjhus-Museum, Copenhagen, Nos. B-678/9)

Fig. 4—Wheellock pistol signed on the inside of the lock "Felix Werder Fecit in Zürich Ao 1630," by tradition from the collection of King Charles I. (Metropolitan Museum of Art, New York, Acc. 10.42 [Rogers Fund])

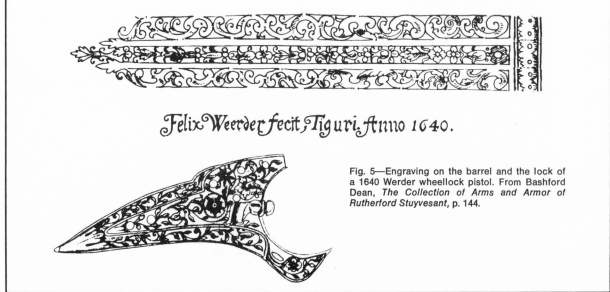

Felix Weerder fecit Tiguri, Anno 1640.

Fig. 5—Engraving on the barrel and the lock of a 1640 Werder wheellock pistol. From Bashford Dean, *The Collection of Arms and Armor of Rutherford Stuyvesant*, p. 144.

haunce rifles with locks of the Baltic type and stocks with long, straight butts[6]; their barrels, too, were no doubt cast—very likely as solid rods, since they have a bore of only 6.7 mm, less than the thickness of the walls. From the beginning of the 18th century we find (aside from some odd cases) a group consisting mainly of pistols that seem to have originated in Liège and in the Low Countries; their vogue extended over the first third of the century. Some of these are soldered—like the previously mentioned Selier pair—

while others are cast as tubes. Later in the century, brass barrels grew more frequent, especially in Britain; as a rule they were cast tubes. All cast barrels have much thicker walls than the soldered ones—*except* (and here we return to our main theme) *barrels by Felix Werder, whose wall thickness is only about one tenth of the average!* This remarkable feature places them in a class quite by themselves.

Back now to Felix Werder Inventor.

Although Hans Conrad Lavater in his previously

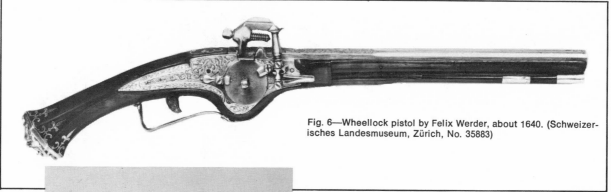

Fig. 6—Wheellock pistol by Felix Werder, about 1640. (Schweizerisches Landesmuseum, Zürich, No. 35883)

Fig. 7—Grotesque mask butt-cap of the pistol in Fig. 6.

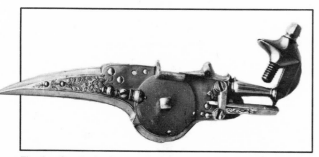

Fig. 8.—One lock of a pair of Felix Werder wheellock pistols of the 1640's. (Swedish Army Museum, Stockholm, No. 63/205:1-2)

mentioned military handbook tells us that beautiful, gilt brass-barrelled firearms were used as presents for foreign princes, only very few such pieces are known. In all, however, about thirty weapons of Werder's production have survived and are catalogued, a few of them signed. The oldest is a wheellock pistol in the Metropolitan Museum, New York (Rogers Fund No. 10.42) (Fig. 4). It is signed on the inside of the lockplate "Felix Werder Fecit in Zürich Ao 1630." Most interestingly, this pistol has an ordinary iron barrel, with a sort of decorative brass sleeve over the breech end. The lockplate and furniture are likewise of gilt brass. The clumsy, rather straight stock of walnut is inlaid with silver floral scrolls. On the buttplate is a figure of a contemporary officer, armed with a sword of Scottish broad-sword type, a feature that could perhaps support the tradition that the pistol once belonged to King Charles I.[7] The next dated piece is a wheellock in the Rutherford Stuyvesant Collection (No. 193), signed on the barrel "Felix Werder fecit Tiguri Anno 1640" (Fig. 5). Here we meet for the first time the thin-walled, gilded and engraved brass barrels that were from then on to be his specialty. One feature repeated on almost all Werder pistols after 1640 is a cast brass butt-plate forcefully modelled in a grotesque mask. An interesting detail on the 1640 Stuyvesant pistol is the form of the lockplate: contrary to normal wheellock plates with a rounded lower edge, the lowest point is not directly below the wheel axis but somewhat to the rear of it. The stock of ebonized fruit wood has now a more curved butt,

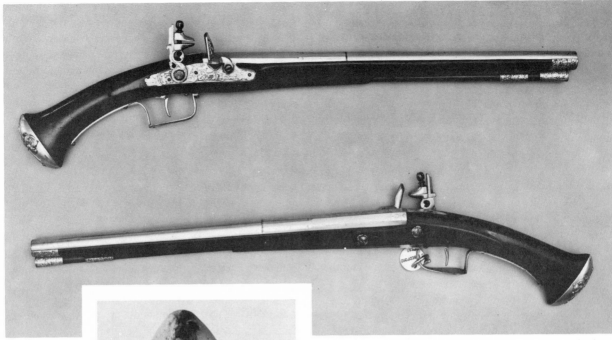

Fig. 9—A pair of flintlock pistols by Felix Werder; on the butt-cap, in high relief, the Austrian *Binnenshild*. (Clay P. Bedford Collection, Scottsville, Arizona, No. 797)

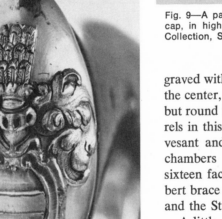

Fig. 10—Detail of butt-cap of one of the pistols in Fig. 9.

graved with a floral pattern and secured by a screw in the center, while the barrel is octagonal at the breech but round for the foremost two-thirds (the other barrels in this group are either all-octagonal—e.g. Stuyvesant and Aitkens—or more often with octagonal chambers and the foremost two-thirds bevelled in sixteen facets). This would place the Victoria & Albert brace between that of the Metropolitan Museum and the Stuyvesant, or between 1630 and 1640.

A little different is a type where the lower edge of the lockplate follows the curve of the wheel. This is the case with a brace of pistols in the Windsor Castle Armoury (Nos. 361 & 363), a single pistol in the Livrustkammar, Stockholm (No. 1741), and a pair in the Swedish Army Museum (Nos. 63/205:1-2) (Fig. 8).

A brace of wheellock pistols in the arms collection of the House of Braunschweig-Lüneburg at Marienburg Castle (Nos. 9-10) have the Werder mark on the inside of the lockplate, but their original barrels have been replaced by ordinary iron barrels bearing a mark of a hunting horn (almost Støckel 5226-27).

In the Musée de l'Armée, Paris, a Werder-type pair of pistols from the former Pauilhac Collection (No. P.O. 847) has a most unpleasant signature "G.W." on the lockplate—otherwise they look fairly inviting and authentic; perhaps the signature is only a recent addition to otherwise genuine pieces.

Among Werder *flintlock* arms, the starting point is the garniture of two pistols and a carbine presented to the city authorities of Zürich in 1652. The pistols, as already noted, are now in the Schweizerisches Landesmuseum (No. K.Z. 5316/17), while the carbine

octagonal in section, very slim and elegant and ending in the Werder-style grotesque mask. Very close to the Stuyvesant pistol is a brace in the Russel Aitkens Collection, New York, another brace in the Livrustkammar, Stockholm (No. 42/52 a-b), a single pistol recently bought for the Schweizerisches Landesmuseum, Zürich (No. L.M. 35883) (Figs. 6 and 7), and a brace and a single pistol in the W. Keith Neal Collection, Warminster, England (the last-mentioned comes from the armoury of Louis XIII). A brace of pistols in the Victoria & Albert Museum, London (No. M.2798-1931), also belongs to this group; it differs, however, in the form of the butt, which is round in section with an oval convex butt-cap en-

rests in the Kunsthistorisches Museum in Vienna (No. A-1454). The pistols bear only the Werder mark on the lockplates—while the carbine, as we have seen, has the full signature "Felix Werder Tiguri Inventor 1652". In both cases the locks are of the type with rather simple cocks and with the spring of the steel placed on the inside of the lockplate. (This is also the case with a most interesting brace in the Clay P. Bedford Collection, U.S.A., No. 797, in which, however, the cock is of a more developed type with a ringshaped neck. See Figs. 9 and 10). The back-end of the lockplate is chiselled as a monster's head, a feature also found on French and Dutch flintlocks of a little earlier date. The butt-caps are cast and gilt in high relief showing the Austrian *Binnenschild*. One should like to date these pistols between 1655 and 1660.

Still another brace of flintlock pistols, probably contemporary with the garniture of 1652, are two double-barrelled (side-by-side) pistols in the Armoury of Schloss Dyck (No. 545); they have almost wheellock-shaped lockplates (as is the case with a single pistol in the Wrangel Armoury at Skokloster, Sweden [No. 31], which in most details is very close to the Dyck pistols except for the single barrel; see Fig. 11).

Finally we have the pistols of the Tøjhusmuseum, Copenhagen, where the spring of the steel is placed on the outside of the lockplate, but the stocks have the same fleur-de-lys decoration as that found on the wheellock pistols in Zürich and Windsor.

In short, Felix Werder discovered a very simple secret (most ingenious discoveries are at heart simple) —namely that cast brass acquires a great tensile strength by being cold-hammered hard and for long. He knew also, of course, that cast barrels were inherently safer than lap-welded ones because they were seamless—but conventional cast barrels had to be thick and heavy. Thus the combination of very thin cast barrels with his cold-hammering process produced barrels that had the virtues of lightness, thinness, elegance and safety!

According to several different sources[8], Felix Wer-

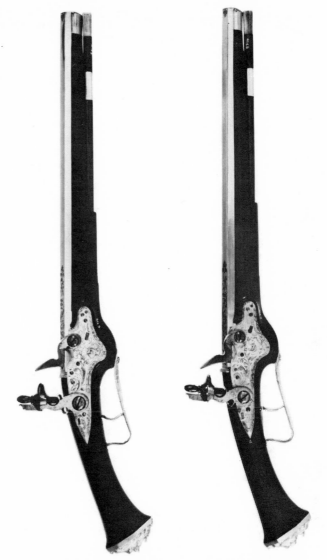

Fig. 11—Pair of flintlock pistols by Felix Werder with wheellock-shaped lockplates; about 1650 (Skokloster, Sweden, No. W-31)

der died in 1673, the last of his line. One of the texts named him "an artistic founder of pistol barrels of brass,"—a *Kunstgiesser* of highest skill. And that single line contains, and has always contained, the solution to the riddle of the "Inventor."

NOTES

1. Zeitschrift für historische Waffenkunde, I, p. 180 ff.
2. E.A. Gessler, "Der Gold- und Büchsenschmied Felix Werder," in *Anzeiger für schweizerische Altertumskunde,* N.F. XXIV, p. 113 ff.
3. Alte und Neue Kunst, No. 13, Zürich, 1953, p. 8 ff.
4. "Dahin gehöret auch / Dass man Pistolen macht / (Die kleine Büchsenform) / Ein schöner Kriegspracht / Von Möss / Im Feur vergult: Daher man sie verwendet / In fürstliche Present / Von hieraus weggesendet".
5. Th. Birch, *A History of the Royal Society,* I, p. 115 ff. The intention of using the term "orichalcum" must

have been to impress the members of the Society, although most of them were probably familiar with it since it was used not only in contemporary metallurgy but also by Cicero and Pliny.
6. A. Hoff, *Feuerwaffen,* I, p. 196.
7. According to Bashford Dean, *Notes on Arms & Armor,* 1916, p. 43 ff., the pistol was said to have been acquired in about 1790 "of a Scotch nobleman in whose family it had been handed down as having been in the celebrated collection of King Charles the First."
8. Gessler, *op. cit.,* p. 115.

169

Gunners' Daggers

*Marcello Terenzi, born in Rome in 1923, is one of Italy's foremost arms and armor
historians. He is Conservator of the Armory in the Castel Sant'Angelo in Rome,
Italian delegate to the Congresses of the International Association of Museums of
Arms and Military History, and the President-Ordinator of many Exhibitions of
historical arms held under Italian State aegis, on and off the Peninsula (the most
important of these for its profound scholarly innovations and implications was the
International Exhibition of Firearms of the Tosco-Emilian Apennines held in
Anghiari, Tuscany, in 1968). His articles and monographs are too numerous to list
here; his most widely esteemed works in book length are* L'Arte di Michele Battista,
Armaiolo Napoletano *(Rome, Edizioni Marte, 1966), and* Gli Armaioli Anghiaresi
nei Secoli XVIII e XIX *(ib., 1971). He divides his time—when not traveling abroad
for arms studies—between his residence in Rome and his medieval* casa-torre *(tower
house), restored with consummate taste, in the Umbrian walled city of Spoleto.*

There is a species of 17th- and 18th-century daggers with certain characteristics that has fascinated arms and armour scholars for generations, and is still the subject of lively and conflicting polemics. They are generally known as "gunner's" or "bombardeer's daggers" or, in the language of their native Italy, *fusetti* and (more correctly) *stiletti da bombardiere*. They may be distinguished at a glance from other basically similar *pugnali* by a numbered scale and corresponding gradation lines engraved on one of the facets of the long, slender awl-like triangular blades (almost always isosceles in cross-section), the numbers always to be read with the arm held point-up.

The most common variety is that fitted with a grip made of spirally twisted or carved horn, often with little bone or ivory discs inlaid on the spiral ridge, and with twisted or braided copper wire bedded in the groove from pommel to quillons; the pommel and the knobs at the ends of the quillons, all roughly pine-cone-shaped, repeat the spiral motif in iron. But many other styles, some quite elaborately chiselled in iron, are found beyond this basic one in the better European and American collections both public and private. As a genre, bombardeer's daggers are not extreme rarities, but never-the-less the procurement of well-made and authentic ones is growing ever more difficult.

Comparison of many specimens has raised ample discussion and widely disparate opinions on their origins and use. The present observations make no pretense of definitiveness, but do seek to bring to the attention of students certain elements which may help establsh the true function and origins of these objects.

Fusetti seem to have been weapons and tools at the same time, carried by cannoneers in the late 17th and early 18th centuries. It would be scholastically very risky to maintain, as has at times been done by various writers, that their use was limited to the forces of the Venetian Republic—a thesis only acceptable in the very broad sense of "artillery in the Venetian tradition," Venice's "fire mouths" of that time having been the best organized and equipped on the peninsula and among the very best anywhere in the world. (Oddly, there are only six examples of gunners' daggers in Venetian museums: one in the Doge's Palace, the other five in the Museo Correr.) Comparison shows that the scales are often quite different from specimen to specimen, which would indicate that they stem from various periods and places and hence are rooted in different units of measure and different types of artillery pieces—but more on this score in a moment. The tool function was born of the incorporation in one unit of several different implements long used by cannonneers for the exercise of their craft; the

Fig. 1—*Fusetto*, grip of carved horn, quillons and pommel of iron. Overall length 38 cm., blade length 27 cm. The scale conforms to Cattaneo's calibres of 1571. (Courtesy Harding Museum, Chicago)

Fig. 3—Another, similar to Figs. 1 & 2. Cattaneo's calibre scale. Overall length 32 cm., blade length 22.2. (Courtesy Harding Museum, Chicago)

Fig. 2—*Fusetto* similar to Fig. 1. Overall length 45.5 cm., blade length 32 cm. (Courtesy Harding Museum, Chicago)

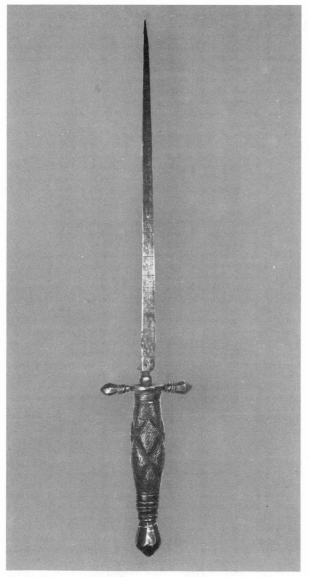

Fig. 4—*Fusetto* with iron furniture, wire-bound grip. Scale is Cattaneo's, with the variant of two numbers 30. Overall length 36 cm., blade length 24.5 cm. (Courtesy Dr. G. Bini, Rome)

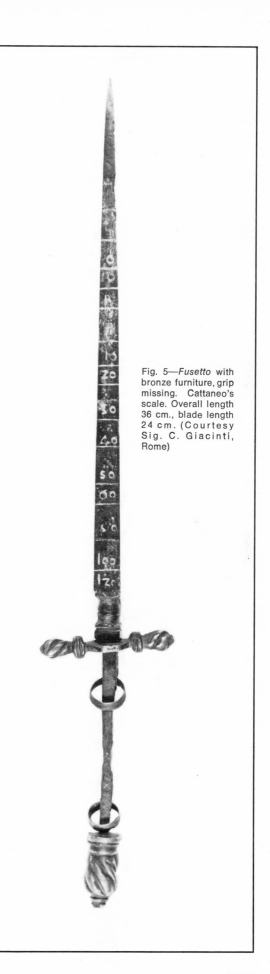

Fig. 5—*Fusetto* with bronze furniture, grip missing. Cattaneo's scale. Overall length 36 cm., blade length 24 cm. (Courtesy Sig. C. Giacinti, Rome)

weapon function, besides the obvious one of providing a useful defense in case of hand-to-hand engagement, might well have derived from a badge of corps or specialization, and perhaps also of rank, since it was the Chief Cannoneer to whom the most important operations were entrusted. But since ordinary citizens were not, as a rule, allowed to carry *stiletti* or other "insidious weapons," one can never be absolutely sure that an apparent bombardeer's dagger was not in fact an assassin's *pugnale* disguised by more or less nonsensical numbers on the blade to exploit the law's concession to artillerymen (the bearer presumably palming himself off as a *bombardiere* from some distant unit), especially in the Venetian Republic after 1661.

In every work on artillery of the era in question we find mention of certain tools that are united, as it

Fig. 6—*Fusetto* with iron furniture filed in facets, horn grip. (Formerly in the National Museum in the Castel Sant'Angelo, Rome)

were, in a *fusetto*. Let us see what a *fusetto* could be used for:

—measuring the diameter of the bore at the muzzle;

—choice of correct-calibre ball;

—ripping open the cloth or paper powder container prior to its being rammed down the barrel;

—opening the powder container through the touchhole;

—cleaning out the touchhole;

—spiking a piece;

—stoppering the touchhole during loading.

Muzzle calibre could be measured by laying the blade across the hole. The tips of short blades, Value Zero on the scale, were placed against a point on the inside rim of the muzzle, and the calibre read at the point judged by eye and by rotation to be 180° opposite. Blades of unwieldy length bore a zero notch at some point up from the tip (or down from the tip, as it were, the scale increasing toward the hilt with the hilt held down), the measure beginning from there and the 180° diameter being established as though with a yardstick and hence with somewhat greater difficulty than with a "hinged" tip striking against the inside rim. Most long blades still have the blank zero notch, and the present writer feels that in the case of those not bearing it today, the loss may be attributed to repeated breaks and resharpenings of the tips.

Balls were chosen by marking off the bore diameter of a given piece crosswise on a wooden board and sticking two *fusetti* at the extremities, vertically and parallel; this formed a gauge through which a ball would or would not roll.

The powder charge, when not taken as loose powder from the barrel and loaded with the "long spoon", was kept in waterproofed paper or canvas cylinders of calibre diameter in the required quantity for one shot—a system still in use for big-bore naval guns. This *cartoccio* (whence "cartridge") was rammed down the piece integrally, but had first to be pierced at various points at the breech end so that some powder would spill and take fire more readily—an operation for which the needle-like fusetto was obviously ideal. Moreover, it was good practise to pierce the paper or canvas also through the touchhole after the charge had been rammed home, and again the long needle-like blades served perfectly.

Repeated primings and atmospheric effects tended to clog and corrode the touchhole. Nothing would have been more adapted for cleaning than a thin, triangular dagger.

Whenever the fortunes of war required the abandoning of cannons, it was necessary to "spike" these in order to render them useless to the enemy. The *fusetto* was inserted into the touchhole and hammered inward as far as possible, both the touchhole and the blade being deformed until the entire canal was totally plugged up, at which point a sharp sideways blow broke off the protruding part, the remaining bit of protrusion (if any) being driven down flush with the top of the barrel—and the piece was out of commission until the capturing enemy could drill the touchhole out afresh.

For obvious reasons, touchholes had to be closed during loading. In the case of mortars, loaded in almost vertical position, it was important that the coarse propellent powder should not enter the touchhole canal, which was reserved for finely-grained priming powder. For both these purposes the insertion of the *fusetto* was, though not ideal owing to the triangular shape, sufficient, and probably constituted another function of the arm.

Fusetti were specifically prescribed elements of cannoneers' equipment. In their native place and time—Northern Italy, mid- or late 17th century—the popularity of multiple-purpose weapons had already been well-established for two centuries and more (e.g., dagger-crossbows, axe-pistols, halberd-pistols, dagger-pistols, and so on through a chimerical panoply well known to collectors and scholars). Hence our *fusetti* fit well into their *zeitgenössliche* concept of five-in-one weaponry. It would be well to banish from this and all future discussions the absurd notion that the numbered scale served to prove to the client of a pro assassin the depth of penetration into the victim's body by the tell-tale blood mark; or, as hypothesized by Seyssel in the first cata-catalogue of the Royal Armoury of Turin in 1840, that its function was the calculation of the angle of elevation of the piece. Even Maj. Angelo Angelucci, illustrious and devoted scholar of arms history *(Catalogo dell'Armeria Reale,* Turin, 1890), at first denied that *fusetti* had been official and hence legitimate; later he accepted the thesis that they had been, yes, issued to Venetian cannoneers, but only as badges of corps, without any function as tools or weapons. He dismissed the scales as "applied without order or meaning *(cervelloticamente poste)."*

But in fact, the scales bear not only a logical relationship to one another, but even great similarity over a wide sampling. They were not, of course, precise, but precision was not an essential nor even a desirable parameter for machinery—cannons—whose original dimensions were only approximate when new owing to manufacturing methods of the day thereafter were rapidly altered by use (widening of bores owing to friction and corrosion), and whose complementary gear—cannonballs—were even more subject to vagaries of cast-metal contraction and physical attrition by any number of agencies. Balls were never of bore diameter—they would have been

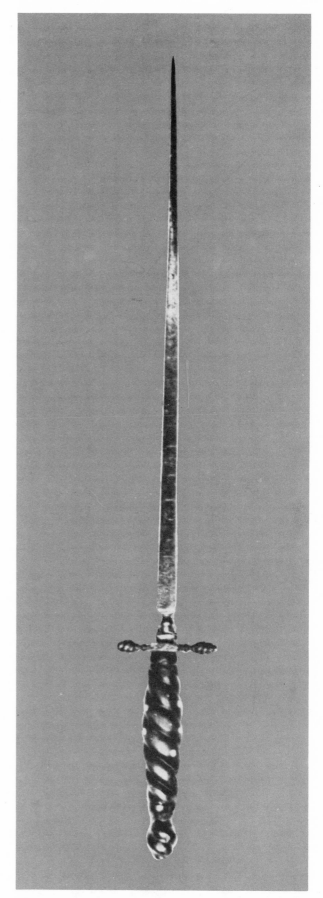

Fig. 7—*Fusetto* with iron furniture and horn grip. Overall length 51.7 cm., blade length 38 cm. (Author's collection)

Fig. 8—*Fusetto* with broken and re-sharpened blade, bronze furniture, horn grip. Cattaneo's scale. (Author's collection)

unrammable—but quite a bit smaller, though by how much was not a critical factor, the difference being made up by wooden, leather, or other waddings. Therefore the scale markings could be, and were, rather crudely applied by the gunners themselves on daggers of various lengths and strengths, though always triangular. For the most part, only two primitive dies were used: a short straight dash and a small semi-circle, out of which all the arabic numerals and the graduation lines could be composed. Most scales were probably copied from colleagues' daggers. The many widely varying differences encountered may be easily attributed to the fact that the given specimen was intended for a specific type of piece measured by terms and units different from the next, and that many standards existed from time to time and place to place in the vast extension of North-Central Italy over better than a hundred years. Nevertheless, it is the similarity that is far more outstanding than the diversity, and one thing is absolutely certain, viz., that all the scales (barring of course the spurious ones applied recently or in the last century) conform, within the limits of requirements, to the calibre scales published in the many contemporary works on artillery. Calibres were thus expressed in a few basic volumes: in Cattaneo's *Trattato degli Esamini di Bombardiere,* Venice, 1571, calibres of 1, 3, 6, 9, 12, 14, 16, 20, 30, 40, 50, 60, 90, 100, and 120; in Giacomo Marzari's *Scelti Documenti in Dialogo a Scolari Bombardieri,* Vicenza, 1596, calibres for colubrines of 14, 20, 30, 50, 60 and 100, and for cannons of 12, 20, 30, 50, 60, and 100; in Eugenio Gentilini's *Il Perfetto Bombardiere,* Venice, 1626, calibres of 1, 2, 4, 6, 8, 14, 16, 20, 30, 40, 50, 60, 90, and 100; and so on. Not all these measurements—nor, hence, those found on daggers—referred to iron balls; there were special scales for lead and stone.

The fact than on many specimens the numbers are barely legible and even almost totally obliterated would indicate frequent scourings and polishings, necessitated by the corrosive contact with gunpowder and by the need for very sharp points and edges. In Venice, *fusetti* were so well known that they were popularly called *un centoventi,* i.e. "a hundred-and-twenty", from the highest number usually found on the blades; a character in a Goldoni comedy avails himself of this term.

It is likely that the heyday of numbered *fusetti* falls between about 1660 and the middle of the 18th century, since 1661 was the year in which the Council of the Ten in Venice granted the right to wear them freely to certain persons—presumably all *bona fide* artillerymen—specified in the edict, while in 1728 this privelege was bestowed (with reference to the 1661 decision) on a certain Antonio Spadon, a functionary of rank in the Venetian artillery. After

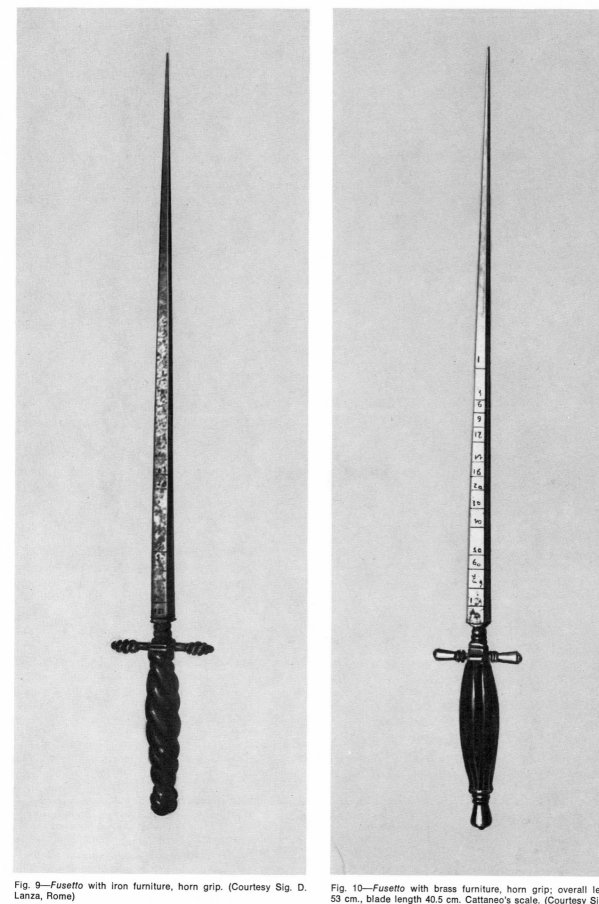

Fig. 9—*Fusetto* with iron furniture, horn grip. (Courtesy Sig. D. Lanza, Rome)

Fig. 10—*Fusetto* with brass furniture, horn grip; overall length 53 cm., blade length 40.5 cm. Cattaneo's scale. (Courtesy Sig. D. Lanza, Rome)

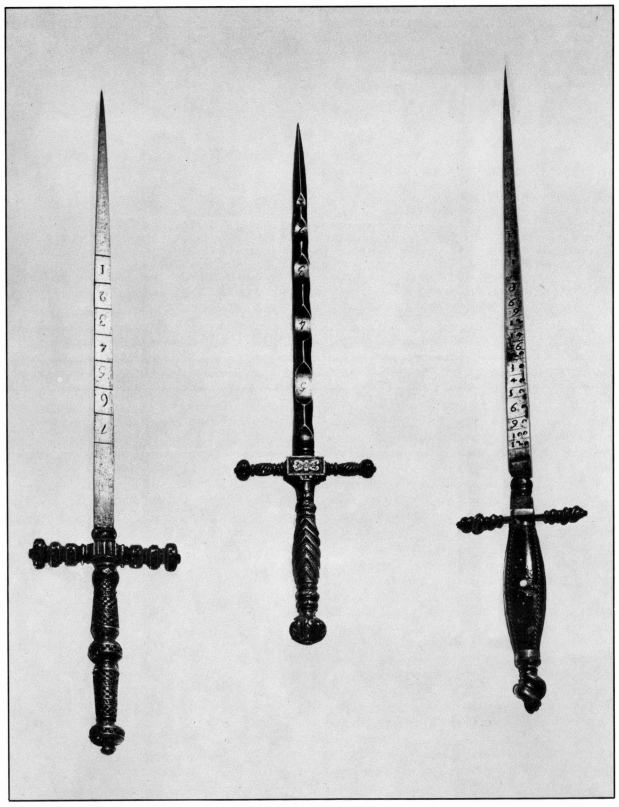

Fig. 11—Dagger (*pugnale*) of the 17th century. Blade length 26.5 cm. Nineteenth-century fake gunner's marks on an arbitrary scale from 1 to 7, legible with point downward. (Odescalchi gallery, Rome)

Fig. 12—Dagger (*pugnale*) of the 17th century. Blade length 19.5 cm. Nineteenth-century fake gunner's marks on an arbitrary scale from 1 to 5, legible with point downward; ornamentation also 19th c., at least partially. (Odescalchi Gallery, Rome)

Fig. 13—*Fusetto* with bronze furniture, horn grip. Although the numbers are those of Cattaneo's scale, the distances between them do not correspond to actual bore or calibre sizes. (Odescalchi Gallery, Rome)

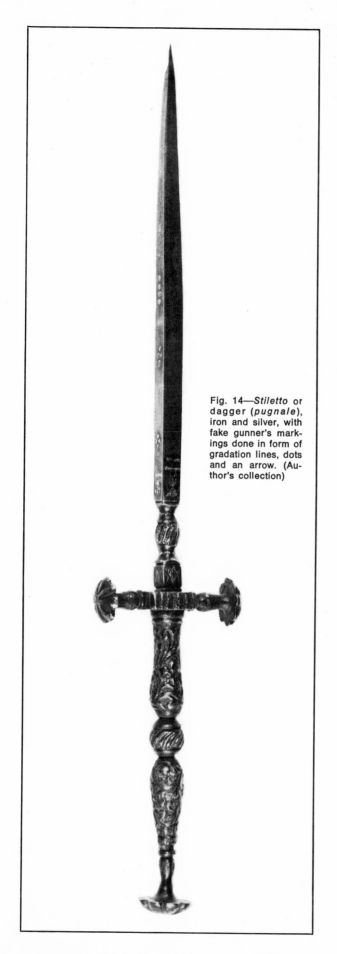

Fig. 14—*Stiletto* or dagger (*pugnale*), iron and silver, with fake gunner's markings done in form of gradation lines, dots and an arrow. (Author's collection)

the latter date the numbered *fusetto* seems to pass quite swiftly from the scene, but no real date for its demise can be given. Perhaps the numbered scale ought to be considered a personal adjunct applied by individual gunners to implements which today, in modern arms students' terms are sufficiently interesting for their other attributes even without the intriguing markings.

BIBLIOGRAPHY

Sardi, P.—*L'Artiglieria,* Venice 1621, Bologna 1659.

Martena, G.B.—*Flagello Militare,* Naples 1676.

Sorra, A.—*Esercizio del Cannone,* Venice 1703.

Le Blond-Zener—*L'Artiglieria per Principi e Raziocinio,* Venice 1772.

de Petersdorf, J. Ravichio—*Traité de Pyrotechnie Militaire,* Paris 1824.

Seyssel d'Aix, V.—*Armeria Antica e Moderna di S.M. Carlo Alberto,* Torino 1840.

de Gheltof, D. Urbani—*Difesa di un Vecchio Pugnale Veneziano, Venice* 1876.

Angelucci, Maj. Angelo—*Catalogo dell'Armeria Reale, Torino* 1890.

Mann, Sir James G.—*The Gunner's Stiletto,* in The Antiquaries Journal, Vol. XI No. 1, London 1931.

The Master of the Animal-Head Scroll

by HANS SCHEDELMANN

Professor Schedelmann, who will celebrate his 80th birthday in 1974, German by birth but Austrian by choice and citzenship, is in all probability the authority ultra quem nemo *on firearms of the German baroque and rococo—though his competence, broad and deep, encompasses all aspects of European arms and armor, with particular emphasis on the weaponry of the Holy Roman Imperial Court at Vienna. In 1944 he published* Die Wiener Büchsenmacher und Büchsenschäfter *(Gunmakers and Gunstockers of Vienna), the result of some thirty-odd years of research and observation. In 1963 his collaboration with Dr. Bruno Thomas and Dr. Ortwin Gamber of the Vienna Waffensammlung bore fruit in the publication of the beautiful volume* Die Schönsten Waffen und Rüstungen *(The Most Beautiful Weapons and Armors). His crowning achievement, published in 1972, is* Die Grossen Büchsenmacher, 1500-1900: Leben, Werke und Marken *(The Great Gunmakers, 1500-1900: Their Lives, Works and Marks), an indispensable volume for serious arms study. Professor Schedelmann lives in Salzburg. His contribution to the present volume, patiently assembled photographically and archivally over many years, allows the emergence of the* Gestalt *of a very gifted if anonymous artist in the service of armscraft.*

 Scattered far and wide in public and private collections in Europe and America there exist more than fifty finely-carved gunstocks —mostly for German-Austrian wheellock long arms, but also for a few wheellock pistols and for at least one flintlock long arm—distinguished by an extensive surface coverage in low bas-relief of vegetoid scrolls (in German: *Ranke*) terminating at intervals in various sorts of animal heads (*Tierkopf*), all but one executed after 1625 and most before 1650 (a few perhaps a bit later). Their author's identity is unknown; he has passed into the annals of art and arms history as *Der Meister der Tierkopfranke*—the Master of the Animal-Head Scroll.

The many surviving specimens of highest-level Austro-German stock work have led to the identification of a respectable number of masters by name, recorded in guild rosters, in the accounts and ledgers of princely courts, and by their own signatures. Others can be synthesized from monograms, from the gunmakers' signatures on the locks and barrels which their stocks accommodate, and by critical comparisons of styles and techniques (this last means sometimes allows the attribution of certain several works to one and the same creative hand: for example, the magnificent works by Peter Opel of Regensburg or by many members of the wood-carver family Maucher are positively identified both by signature and by old documents, but the unsigned flintlock pistols of Johann Michael Maucher can be ascribed to this master only by analysis of technique and of ornamentation.

Perhaps some day patient research will lift the veil of anonymity from The Master of the Animal-Head Scroll and reveal his identity. Recent studies and comparisons of stocks by the Master "N.H." lead to the conclusion that he is not The Master of the Animal-Head Scroll, as the present writer had hitherto believed. Rather, our *Meister* is surely to be sought among the artisans of the Imperial Court at Vienna; quite likely he was "officially favoured" *(hofbefreit)* and supplied stocks to the court-appointed gunmakers; but since court accounts were settled directly with these latter, only *their* names, not his, would appear in the ledgers. True, his work is not of the very finest quality, not on a par with that of Peter Opel or the Maucher family, but it is just one or two levels below that olympian one; his activity seems to have been limited to gunstock carving, since no furniture, boxes, frames or other generically-related subjects carved by him have come to light. He is particularly well-represented in the Court Gun Chamber *(Hofgewehrkammer)* in the Vienna Arms Collection *(Waffensammlung),* and no doubt many of his other works now scattered throughout the world were originally commissioned directly by the Court or executed for firearms destined for it.

The following is a list of his known works; more will doubtless surface as ever more hitherto neglected and sometimes even forgotten collections find their way into the auction rooms. The list is preceded by a table showing the geographic distribution. The first twenty-five specimens on the list are shown in the

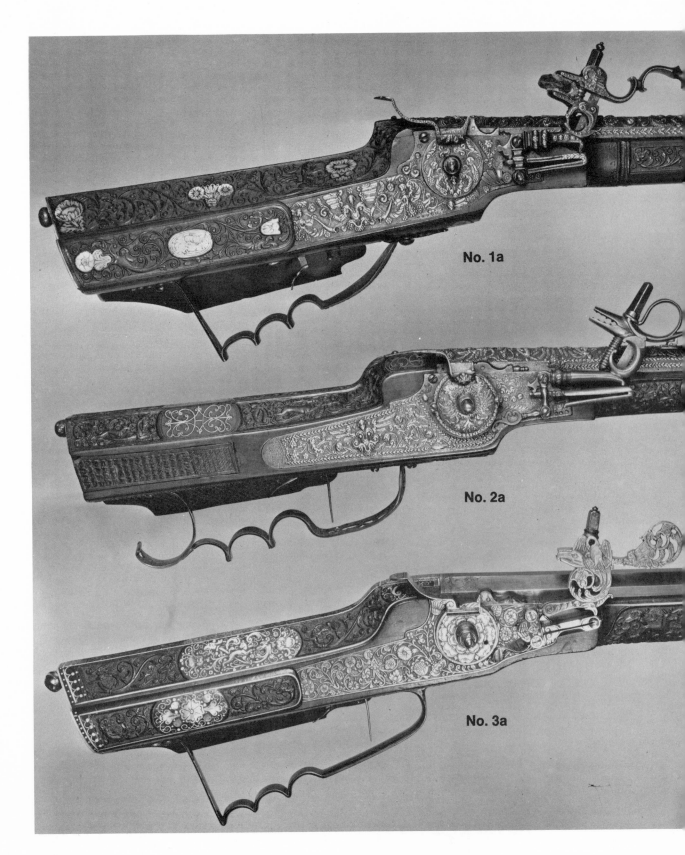

No. 1a

No. 2a

No. 3a

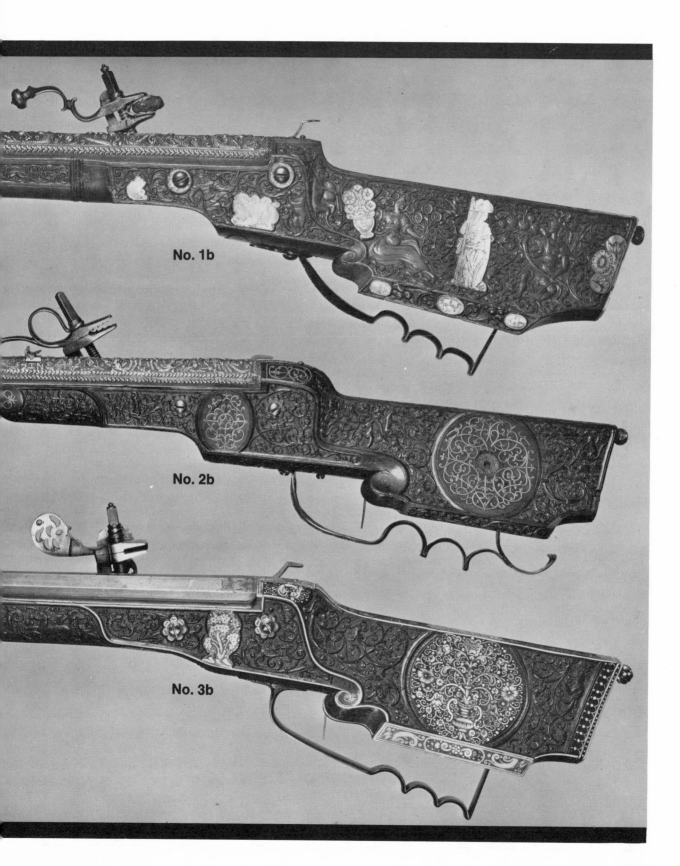

No. 1b

No. 2b

No. 3b

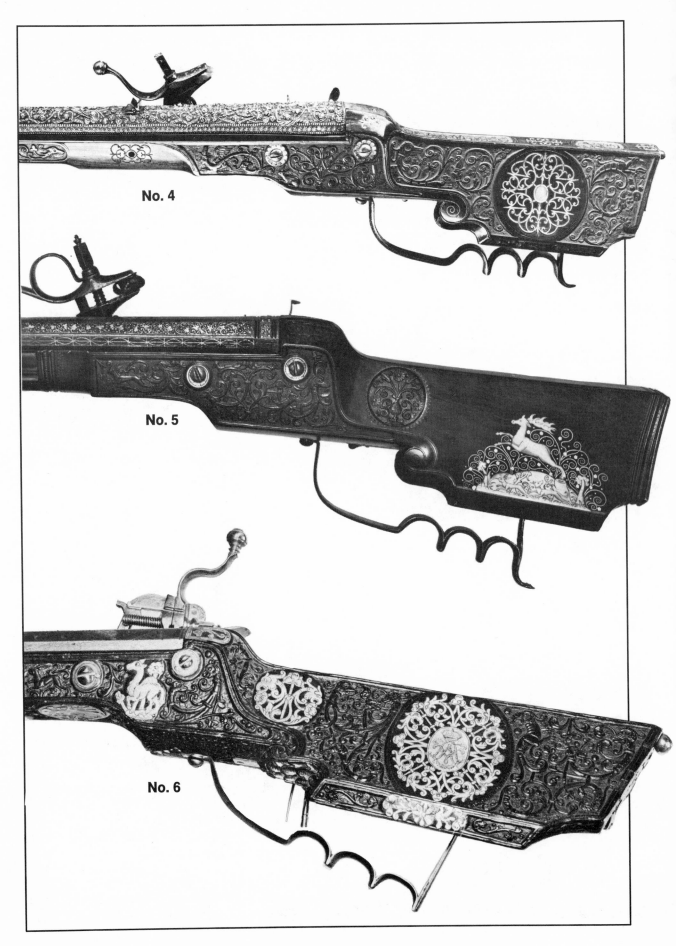

No. 4

No. 5

No. 6

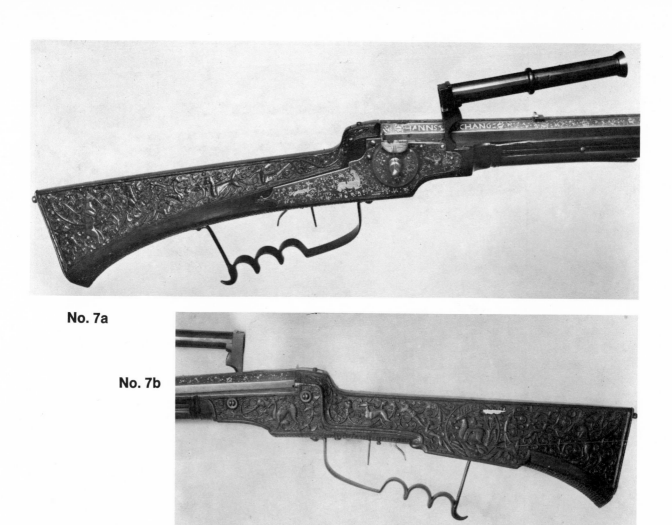

No. 7a

No. 7b

accompanying illustrations. Parenthetic references to other published works are:

Ra. [*plus number*] —Item number in "Firearms Carved by the Master N.H.", by Richard H. Randall, Jr., in *The Walters Art Gallery Journal,* Vol. XII, 1949.

DGB [*plus page or fig. no.*] —Hans Schedelmann, *Die Grossen Büchsenmacher,* Kinkhart & Biermann, Braunschweig, 1972.

DWBB [*plus page or fig. no.*] —Hans Schedelmann, "Die Wiener Büchsenmacher und Büchsenschäfter," in *Zeitschrift für Waffen- und Kostümkunde,* Supplement, Berlin, 1944.

GEOGRAPHIC DISTRIBUTION OF KNOWN WORKS

AUSTRIA

Vienna, *Waffensammlung,* Kunsthistorisches Museum: Illustrations 5, 7, 9, 10, 17, 20, 21. In addition, not illustrated here, Nos. 46 and 47.

Salzburg, author's collection: Illustration 18.

BELGIUM

Brussels, Royal Hunting Collection: Illustration 8.

CANADA

Toronto, Royal Ontario Museum: Not illustrated here, No. 51.

CZECHOSLOVAKIA

Konopiste, State Art Collections: Not illustrated here, Nos. 36 and 40.

DENMARK

Copenhagen, Tøjhusmuseum: Not illustrated here, Nos. 26 and 27.

FRANCE

Paris, Musée de l'Armée: Not illustrated here, Nos. 33, 42 and 43.

GERMANY

Karlsruhe, Landesmuseum: Not illustrated here, No. 30.

Kassel, City Art Galleries: Illustration 25.

Munich, Deutsches Jagdmuseum: Not illustrated here, No. 50.

———, Bayerisches Nationalmuseum: Illustration 13.

Rhineland, near Dusseldorf, Schloss Dyck: Not illustrated here, Nos. 32, 34 and 35.

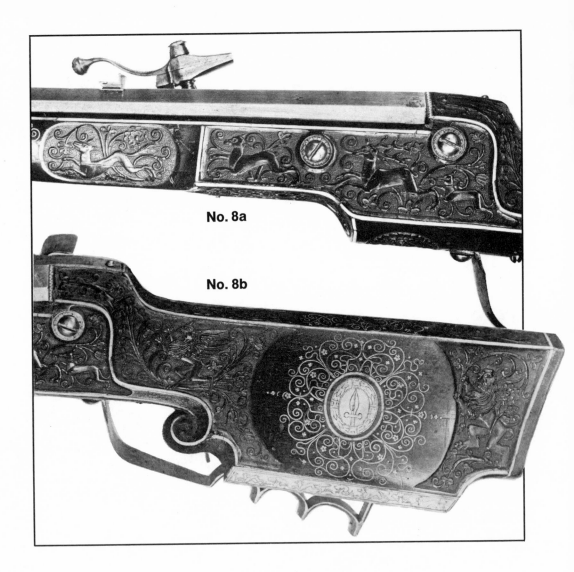

No. 8a

No. 8b

GREAT BRITAIN
   London, Tower: Illustration 15.
   ———, Wallace Collection: Not illustrated here,
     No. 28.
ITALY
   Florence, Museum Stibbert: Not illustrated here,
     No. 37.
   Rome, Odescalchi Collection: Illustration 4, In
     addition, not illustrated here, No. 29.
   Turin, Armeria Reale: Not illustrated here, No. 41.
LIECHTENSTEIN
   Vaduz, The Reigning Prince's Collection: Illustra-
     tion 24. In addition, not illustrated here, Nos.
     38 and 39.
UNITED STATES
   Baltimore, Walters Art Gallery: Illustration 22.
   New York, C.O. von Kienbusch Collection: Illus-
     trations 6 and 12.
   ———, Metropolitan Museum of Art: Illustration
     23. In addition, not illustrated here, No. 48.
   York, Pa., Collection of the late Joe Kindig, Jr.:
     Illustrations 1 and 2. In addition, not illustrated
     here, No. 49.

U.S.S.R.
   Leningrad, Hermitage: Illustration 11.
ANONYMOUS AND PRESENT
LOCATION UNKNOWN
   Illustrations 3, 14, and 19. In addition, not illus-
     trated here, Nos. 31, 44 and 45.

LIST OF ALL KNOWN WORKS
Nos. 1-25 incl. are illustrated in this article.
No. 1—Wheellock rifle, the barrel and lock richly
   encrusted with bas-relief silver ornaments, the
   stock with engraved mother-of-pearl inlays. Joe
   Kindig, Jr., Collection, York, Pa., U.S.A. (Ra.2)
No. 2—Another similar, signed and dated on the barrel "H.W.—1628". Joe Kindig, Jr., Collection,
   York, Pa., U.S.A. (Ra.1)
No. 3—Wheellock rifle, the barrel signed "K.Z." with
   a squirrel mark, the lock chiseled with floral scrolls
   in the style of the Eger masters, the butt inlaid with
   bone tendrils. Ex Collection Prince Thun, Teschen,
   ex Collection William Randolph Hearst, now private collection, U.S.A. (Ra. 21)
No. 4—The oldest known dated specimen of the

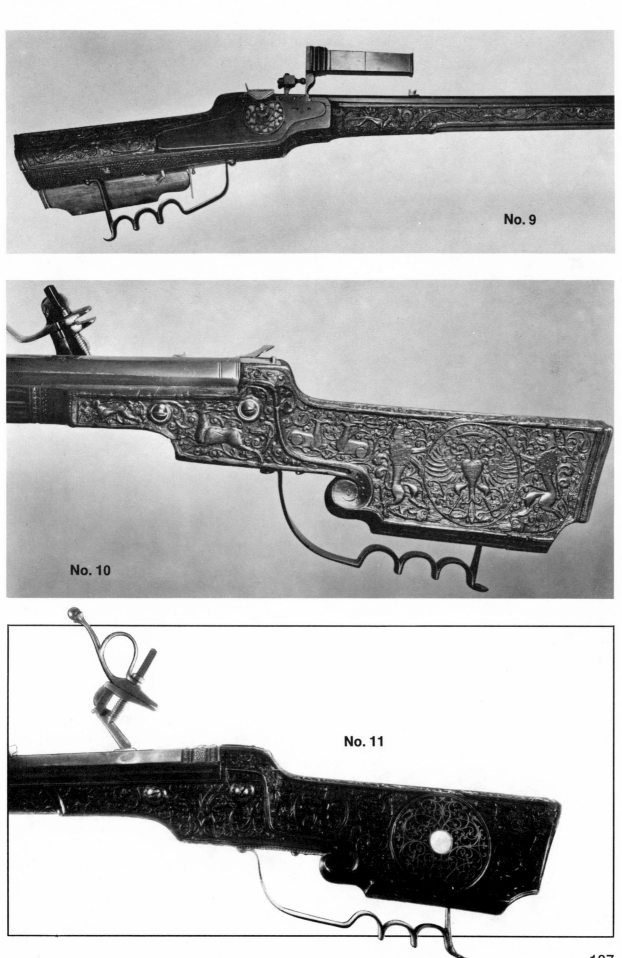

No. 9

No. 10

No. 11

187

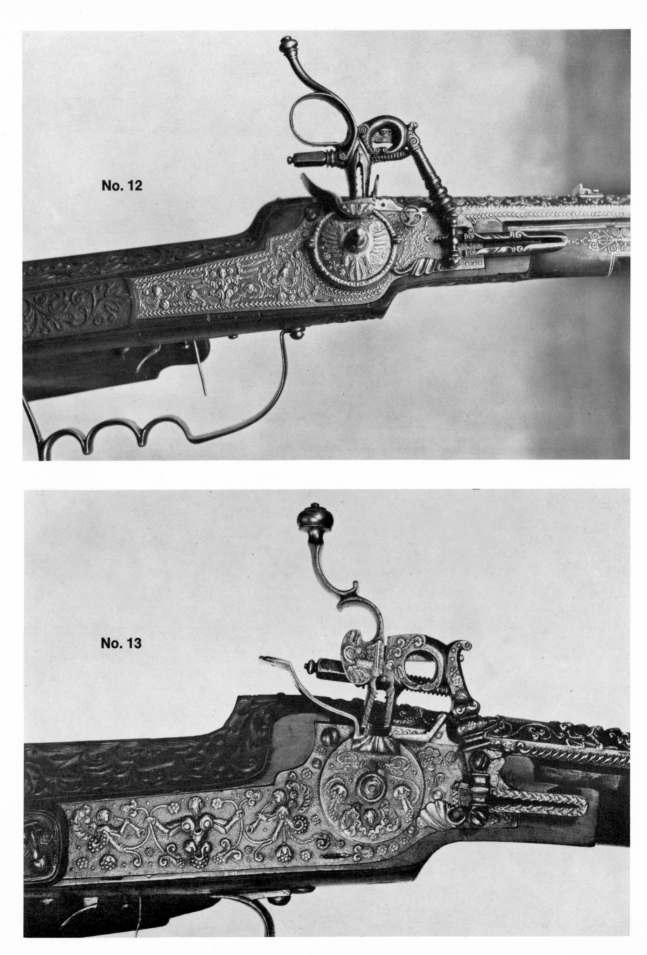

No. 12

No. 13

No. 14

Meister's work: a wheellock rifle, the lock and barrel very richly inlaid with bas-relief silver ornaments, the barrel signed "H.W.—1624" (cf. No. 2). Sold in Cologne, Germany, at auction of the Museum Hammer in 1892 (Herberle, Cat. No. 996), sold in Berlin at auction of Zschille Collection in 1900 (Lepke, Cat. No. 192), now Odescalchi Collection, Rome, No. 1526. (Ra.1)

No. 5—Wheellock rifle, dated 1631, the silver-damascened barrel signed "G.F.," on the cheekpiece a deer and scrolls in bone tendrils and plaques. Vienna, *Waffensammlung,* No. A2282. (Ra.23, DGB Fig. 168)

No. 6—Wheellock rifle, datable between 1631 and 1637 by the royal crowned monogram "F.M.A." engraved on the silver-filligree cheekpiece rosette: Ferdinand Maria Anna, i.e. Ferdinand III of Bohemia, married in 1631 Maria Anna of Spain who died in 1637. Ex Fink Collection, Vienna, ex William Randolph Hearst Collection, now C.O. von Kienbusch Collection, New York, No. 647. (DWBB Fig. 106)

No. 7—Wheellock rifle (obverse and reverse), the barrel signed "Hans Faschang, 1637" and ornamented with silver damascened leaves, the lock fitted with a priming smoke chimney and ornamented with silver deer, dog, flowers. Vienna, *Waffensammlung,* No. D101 (Ra.7, DGB Fig. 166, DWBB Fig. 59)

No. 8—Wheellock rifle (two views), one of a pair, the barrels signed "M.S.H.—1631". Ex Austrian private collection, now Collection of H.M. King Leopold of Belgium. (Ra. 5 and 6, DWBB Fig. 108)

No. 9—Wheellock rifle, the barrel signed "H.F." (Hans Faschang) and dated 1638, the lock fitted with priming smoke chimney. Vienna, *Waffensammlung,* No. 103. (Ra.8, DGB Fig. 167, DWBB Fig. 110)

No. 10—Wheellock rifle, the barrel signed "H.F." (Hans Faschang). Vienna, *Waffensammlung,* No. D 347. (Ra.19, DGB Fig. 170)

No. 11—Wheellock rifle, Arms Collection, The Hermitage, Leningrad, No.3.0.5811. (Cf. *Journal of the Arms and Armour Society,* London, 1959, Vol. III, No. 1, Plate X, D)

No. 12—Wheellock rifle, the barrel and lock with bas-relief silver inlays, on cheekpiece a rosette of

No. 15

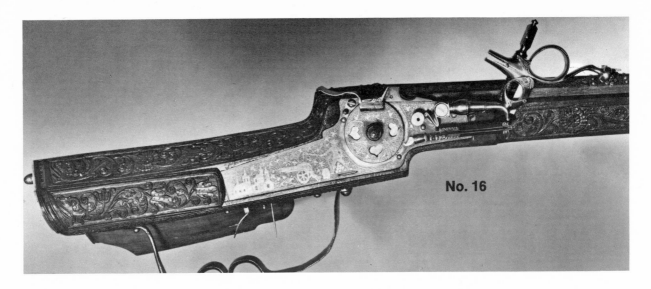

No. 16

brass wire. Ex Collection of Prince Starhemberg, now C.O. von Kienbusch Collection, New York, No. 648.

No. 13—Wheellock rifle, the barrel and lock with bas-relief silver inlays, the butt with engraved brass plaques and brass wire inlays. Bayerisches National-museum, Munich, No. W826 (Ra.14)

No. 14—Wheellock carbine, the stock inlaid with engraved brass plaques, on the butt an engraved lion medallion. Sold at Parke-Bernet, New York auction of Litchfield Collection, December 1951, Cat. No. 253, now in a private collection in Berlin. (RA.28)

No. 15—Wheellock rifle, the barrel signed "G.F.—1639", the stock with engraved mother-of-pearl plaques and wire inlays. Ex William Randolph Hearst Collection, now in the Tower of London.

No. 16—Wheellock rifle, the barrel with inlaid silver ornamentation in bas-relief and signed "H.F." (Hans Faschang), the lock dated 1647, on the butt a depiction in engraved bone plaques of a hunter killing a bear. Vienna, *Waffensammlung,* No. D111.

(Ra.16, DGB Fig. 165 and Plate XV)

No. 17—Wheellock rifle, on the richly engraved bar-rel the imperial two-headed eagle, on the butt en-graved bone plaque inlays, dated 1648. Vienna, *Waffensammlung,* No. D98. (Ra. 17)

No. 18—Wheellock rifle, on cheekpiece and side-plate a depiction of the Virgin and the unicorn, the barrel and lock richly ornamented, on the barrel the mark "MF" (cf. Støckel, II, a3910). Author's collection, Salzburg.

No. 19—Wheellock rifle, smooth barrel and lock, the lock signed "MS". Private collection, Germany.

No. 20—Wheellock rifle, barrel with silver dam-ascening on hatched ground, on cheekpiece the initial "E" with crown and laurel wreath (Empress Eleonore, third wife of Emperor Ferdinand III, died 1652). Vienna, *Waffensammlung,* No.D112. (Ra.9, DGB Fig. 169)

No. 21—Wheellock rifle, the barrel signed "PSK" (Paul and Sigmund Klett, Salzburg/Ebenau). Vi-enna, *Waffensammlung,* No. D99. (Ra.18, DGB Fig. 164)

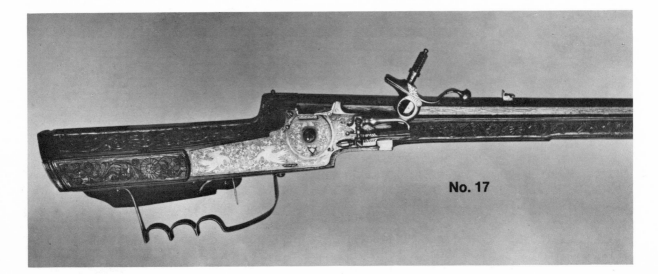

No. 17

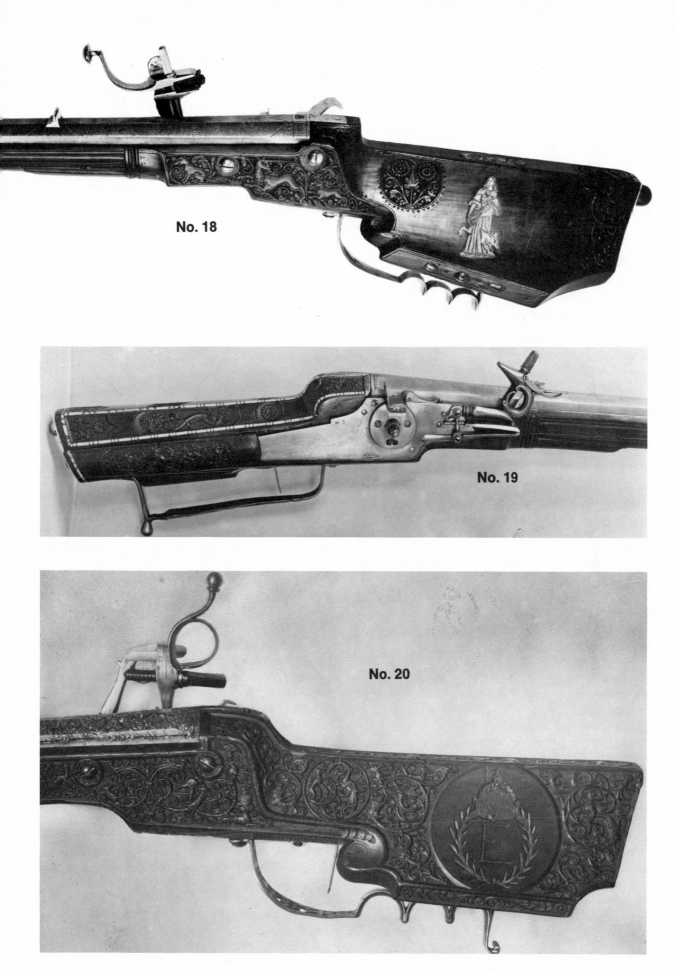

No. 18

No. 19

No. 20

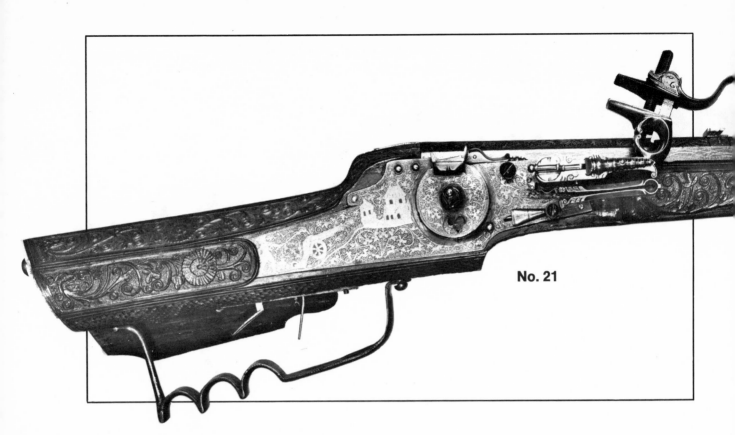

No. 21

No. 22—Pair of wheellock pistols, the barrels and locks with silver bas-relief ornaments. Baltimore, The Walters Art Gallery. (Ra.24-25)

No. 23—Wheellock pistol. New York, Metropolitan Museum of Art. (Ra.11)

No. 24—Wheellock rifle, barrel and lock silver damascened, the cheekpiece with brass inlay rosette. Vaduz, Liechtenstein, Collection of the Reigning Prince.

No. 25—Wheellock rifle, c. 1630-40. Kassel, Germany, City Art Collection.

The remaining twenty-six weapons are not illustrated in this article:

No. 26—Wheellock rifle, signed "H.F." (Hans Faschang) and dated 1632, the cheekpiece with a brass inlaid rosette. Copenhagen, Tøjhusmuseum, No. B312. (Ra.34)

No. 27—Wheellock rifle, similar to the preceding. Copenhagen, Tøjhusmuseum, No. B311. See Otto Smith, *Det Kongelige Particulaere Rustkammer,* Copenhagen, 1938. (Ra.25)

No. 28—Wheellock rifle, one of a pair with No. 6. London, Wallace Collection, No. A1100. (Ra.3)

No. 29—Wheellock rifle, the barrel and lock with bas-relief silver encrustations, the cheekpiece with brass wire spirals. Rome, Odescalchi Collection, No. 1527.

No. 30—Wheellock rifle. Karlsruhe, Germany, Landesmuseum.

No. 31—Wheellock carbine, one of a pair with No. 14. Sold at auction, Christie's, London, 17 July 1961, No. 156; now private collection, Great Britain.

No. 32—Wheellock rifle, the barrel signed "S.M.". Schloss Dyck, near Dusseldorf, Germany, No. 166.

No. 33—Wheellock rifle, the barrel signed "PSK" (Paul and Sigmund Klett, Salzburg-Ebenau), on the cheekpiece two-headed eagle. Paris, Musée de l'Armée, No. M159. (Ra.12)

No. 34—A pair of wheellock rifles, similar to No. 33. Schloss Dyck, near Dusseldorf, Germany, Nos. 169-70.

No. 35—Wheellock rifle, similar to Nos. 33 and 34. Schloss Dyck, near Dusseldorf, Germany, No. 171.

No. 36—Wheellock rifle, barrel and lock with traces of silver damascening. Ex Collection Archduke Franz Ferdinand d'Este, Konopiste, Czechoslovakia, now State Arts Collection.

No. 37—Wheellock rifle. Florence, Museo Stibbert, No. 3985.

No. 38—Wheellock rifle, barrel and lock silver damascened, the barrel signed "G.F.—1641", on lock silver damascener's monogram "HH", on the carved cheekpiece a depiction of St. George. Vaduz, Liechtenstein, Collection of the Reigning Prince, No. 157.

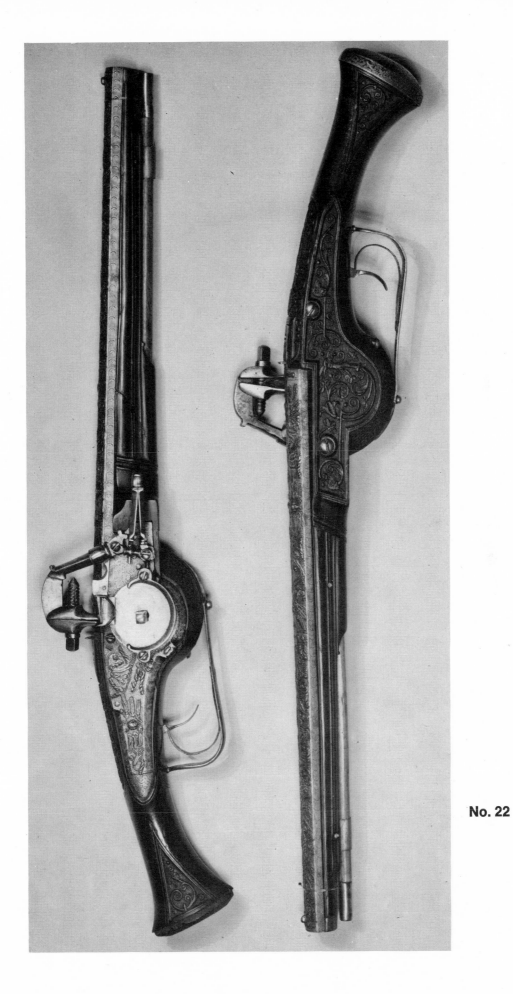

No. 22

No. 23

No. 39—Wheellock pistol, the barrel and lock silver encrusted in bas-relief, the partially carved stock with engraved metal inlays. Vaduz, Liechtenstein, Collection of the Reigning Prince, No. 3621.

No. 40—Wheellock rifle, the smooth barrel dated 1646. Ex Collection of Archduke Franz Ferdinand d'Este, Konopiste, Czechoslovakia, now State Arts Collection.

No. 41—Wheellock rifle, the barrel and lock with silver inlays in bas-relief. Turin, Armeria Reale, No. M17.

No. 42—Wheellock rifle, the barrel and lock silver damascened. Paris, Musée de l'Armée, ex Pauilhac Collection, No. 776.

No. 43—Wheellock rifle, smooth barrel and lock, on the cheekpiece a two-headed eagle. Paris,

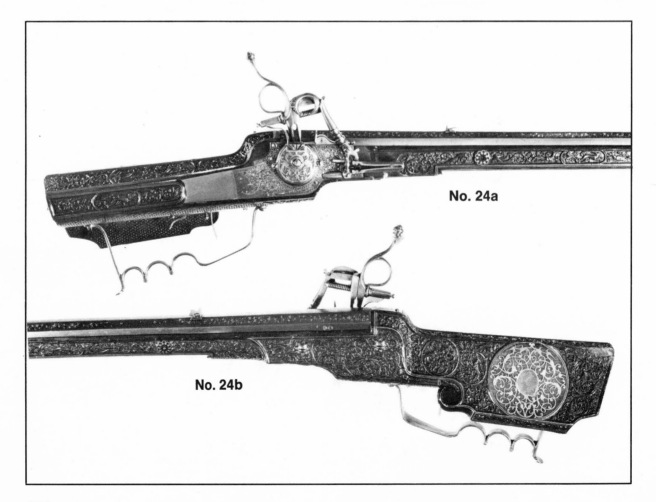

No. 24a

No. 24b

No. 25

Musée de l'Armée, ex Collection Pauilhac, No. 788.

No. 44—Wheellock carbine. Sold at auction, Cologne, Germany, Leiden Collection, 1934, No. 713, illustrated in catalogue Plate 37-38. (Ra.10)

No. 45—Wheellock rifle, barrel and lock smooth, stock inlaid with engraved bone plaques. Sold at auction, Vienna, Kende Collection, 1933, No. 388, illustrated in catalogue.

No. 46—Wheellock carbine, the barrel signed "M.S. —1632". Vienna, *Waffensammlung,* D284. (DGB page 98)

No. 47—Wheellock rifle. Vienna, *Waffensammlung,* No. D311. (DGB page 98)

No. 48—Wheellock rifle, the barrel (two-calibre, re-movable smallbore inner barrel) signed "Cornelius Klett, 1653". New York, Metropolitan Museum of Art, No. 28.27.

No. 49—Pair of wheellock pistols. Sold at auction, New York, Parke-Bernet. Wigington Collection, 1951, No. 221, illustrated in catalogue, now Joe Kindig, Jr., Collection, York, Pa. (Ra.30)

No. 50—Wheellock rifle, the lock signed "MS", on the richly carved stock the coat of arms of Herberstorff. Munich, Deutsches Jadgmuseum, No. 2449.

No. 51—Flintlock repeating gun, the barrel signed "Cornelius Klett". Ex Schloss Sieghartstein, now Toronto, Royal Ontario Museum.

English Provincial Gunmaking, 1680-1720, as Exemplified by Some Works of Henry Ellis of Doncaster

by ANTHONY D. DARLING

Anthony D. Darling is a Fellow of the Company of Military Historians and Associate Editor of The Canadian Journal of Arms Collecting, *working from his home in New Haven, Conn.*

He has specialized in the history, organization and arms of the British Army and is the author of numerous magazine articles on small arms and edged weapons. His book Red Coat and Brown Bess *(Museum Restoration Service, 1971) is recognized as the outstanding treatise on the subject.*

The period from about 1680 to just after 1725 was an age of elegance for English gunmaking. As works of ornamental art and excellent armscraft, the firearms of this area are unchallenged by any made in England before (or, many students feel, after). Their style reflects the blending of pleasing design, tasteful appointments and high technical efficiency.[1]

Prior to 1680, English gunmakers tended to emulate the work of their contemporaries in Holland to such a degree that the origins of unsigned arms of the third quarter of the seventeenth century are difficult to determine. English pistols of the 1660-80 period usually had straight-grained stocks with little carving except around the barrel tang and round-surfaced locks ending in a pronounced point at the tail. The flat lock, often attached by three screws and usually with a back- (or "dog") catch was standard on English firearms until c. 1650 when the round-surfaced lock began to make its appearance.[2] In the 1660-80 period, the lower edge of the plate was relatively straight. The sideplate had become standard but for the most part it was nothing more than a curved, tailed strap connecting the two lock screws—only occasionally was it pierced or engraved. The trigger guard was usually a nailed-on piece of sheet metal. The butt-cap, rounded in form by c. 1670, had long spurs running up either side of the grip.[3] During this period, the profile or angle of the butt began to drop somewhat, and in fact, it is interesting to compare the butt angle of pistols made after 1650 with those dating from about 1580-1650: the latter are usually very flat, at times downright straight. Ornamentation was usually restricted to the engraving of serpents and minor floral work on the metal parts. These characteristics are in contrast to most English pistols made prior to 1660 which, as a rule, have flat locks of snaphaunce form and nearly straight grips with oval pommels.[4] Usually these pre-Restoration handguns have no sideplates and often were made without trigger guards. The lower ramrod guide becomes prevalent c. 1670, as does the emanation of the barrel screw from the tang on arms of quality.[5]

During the last quarter of the seventeenth century, the English makers turned their attention to the style that had established itself in France in the 1670's, designated as the "Classical Louis XIV Style" by Lenk. Two factors were responsible for this. First, in 1685, Louis XIV revoked the Edict of Nantes, which, issued on April 15th, 1598, had hitherto secured equal political rights for Protestants; thus he precipitated an exodus of over 50,000 families which included not only military leaders and men of letters but also a large part of the skilled artisans of France. The loss of these craftsmen, many of whom had emigrated to other European countries prior to 1685, was a blow to the nation's industry. Some of the Hugenot exiles settled in England, particularly after they had been granted denization[6] without cost by Charles II in 1681. Twenty Hugenot gunsmiths took up residence in Soho and others established themselves throughout London. The most famous was Pierre Monlong, late of Paris, who emigrated in 1684 and received an appointment as gunmaker to William III in 1699. Others included Landreville and Pierre Gruché, the latter having previously made firearms for Louis XIV.

The second factor that contributed to the universal assimilation of the Classical Louis XIV Style throughout England was the publication of the pattern book *Plusièurs Pieces et Ornements d' Arquebuzerie* by the engraver Claude Simonin in 1685 at Paris (a second edition, by Claude and Jacques Simonin, was published in 1693). These designs, based on the work of Laurent le Languedoc, an "arquebusier du roi," epitomized the basic form and ornamentation of French firearms at that time. Copies of this book soon found their way to England. None of the earlier French pattern books seems to have been used by English gunmakers, or at least no evidence has been unearthed to show that any did.[7]

Continental masters emigrated to London from countries other than France during this period; these included Andrew Dolep, who first applied for admission to the Gunmaker's Company in 1681, James Ermedinger, given membership in 1682, and Jacques

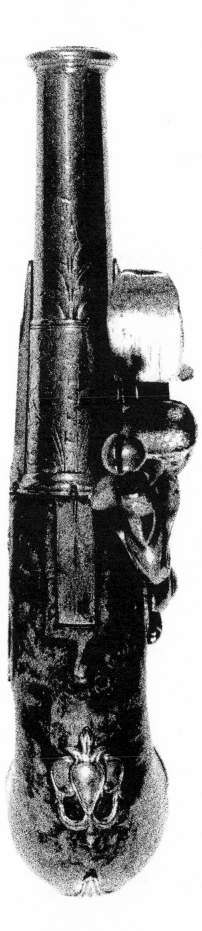

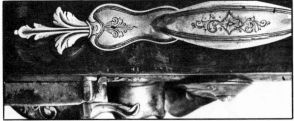

Figs. 1, a to d—A pair of silver-mounted holster pistols, c. 1690-1700, signed "Henry Ellis in Doncaster" on the barrels and "H. Ellis" on the lockplates. Barrels in two round stages, the rear section chiseled with scrollwork and a cartouche; engraved and chased silver furniture (sideplates, lion-mask butt caps, trigger guards, escutcheons bearing crest of Bagshaw family of London, Derby and Essex); burl walnut stocks. Much in these weapons reflects the "Classical Louis XIV Style" and the patterns in Claude Simonin's 1685/93 book, but the character is already quite English in the widely-flaring butts, the leaf-tailed *Lindwurm* sideplate and the robustness of the stock around the tang and escutcheon. Quality is very good but not Ellis' best (compare Fig. 2), about on a par with any competent master gunmaker's output in England or on the Continent; design is pleasing but conventional. Overall length 18.75 in., barrels 12 in., calibre .60. (Clay P. Bedford Collection)

Gorgo, a Swiss refugee working in Soho in 1689. All three utilized the new French style. Dolep and Gorgo are known for their multi-shot revolvers and superimposed-load guns. The French presence soon affected the work of the native-born London makers. John Dafte and Edward Nicholson, previously utilizing the post-Restoration style, quickly adopted the new mode of design, as did masters Green, Gregory, Matthias, Nutt, Turvey, Warren and Wornall. After 1700, the names of Barbar—probably a French emigré—and Harvey must be added.

What, then, was the Classical Louis XIV Style, and how was it applied to English-made firearms? For one thing, all elements of a gun, i.e., lock, stock, barrel and furniture, were in harmony in respect to design and execution. The gunmaker did not sacrifice one component for the benefit of the others; each bears a relationship to the other. A skillful hand is apparent in the workmanship, and no single element

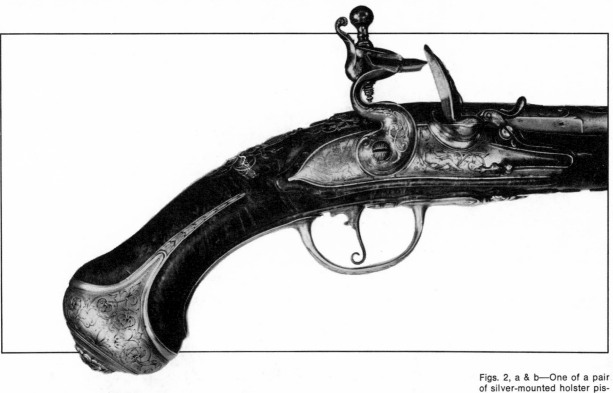

was overdone at the expense of the gun in its entirety. The graceful swan-or goose-neck cock was standard and contributed to an elegant profile; it is rounded in section, and thicker than those seen on earlier arms, thus allowing for chiseled design in relief. The lockplate, too, is rounded in section and terminates at the rear in a long teat or point; its lower edge curves slightly upward under the cock and slightly downward under the pan, a graceful undulation and a characteristic absolutely essential to any arm that seeks to be defined as being a true Louis XIV flintlock; at the rear the plate dips again, though not nearly as much as in the so-called "banana"-shape locks of about the same time (see Fig. 5b). An internal bridle over the tumbler is present on high quality arms; the external bridle connecting the pan and frizzen hinge screw is occasionally seen but need not be considered a standard or even frequent feature. The metal parts are pro-

fusely engraved, often with representations of human figures. Additional chiseling is sometimes encountered on the back of the steel and on the barrel breech. The barrel is usually round but in two or three stages, each delineated by a baluster turn or girdle. Burl-walnut is used for the stock (although on lesser-quality arms, field maple was often substituted) or straight grained wood, stained by spot-charring to give the appearance of natural striping or figuring. A raised molding was usually carved around the lock, and molding also appears along the fore-end, often in the form of undulating scrolls or grooves. The angle of the grip is more downward, while the pommel flares out to provide not only a cushion for the heel of the palm, but also a setting for the grotesque mask or lion's face on the underside. Its spurs nearly reach the lock and sideplate on either side. On long arms, the buttplate is no longer nailed-on sheet metal but cast brass or silver,

199

Figs. 3, a & b—Pair of pocket pistols signed "Ellis" on the barrels, 1685-1700. Although apparently turn-off or screw-barrel pistols, they are in fact muzzle-loaders. No guards protect the button triggers, but in addition to the usual half-cock notch in the tumbler there is a "dog"-like spring-loaded safety catch at the lower rear of each cock that prevents an undesired snap. Iron furniture is conventionally engraved and lightly chiseled. Character is very strongly English and owes no great debts to France or Italy. (Glasgow Art Gallery & Museum, Scotland)

or wrought iron, with a pronounced heel and a long finial. Like the lock, the furniture has rounded surfaces and is of steel, usually engraved or chiseled, although silver was often substituted in the last decade of the century, while arms of lesser quality have brass mounts, sometimes gilded. The trigger-guard is strong but yet of graceful and slender proportions; it is inletted into the stock and held by cross-pins passing through pierced tangs projecting into the stock, rather than by nails or screws; the finial terminates on a stylized leaf pattern. The trigger has an exaggerated backward curl. The side-plate is extremely ornate, usually in an openwork pattern of one or more serpents with so-called "dolphin" heads and scaly bodies, or intertwined foliage; ramrod guides have transverse moldings, and the more expensive arms were profusely inlaid with silver wire.

Strangely enough, the French makers abandoned

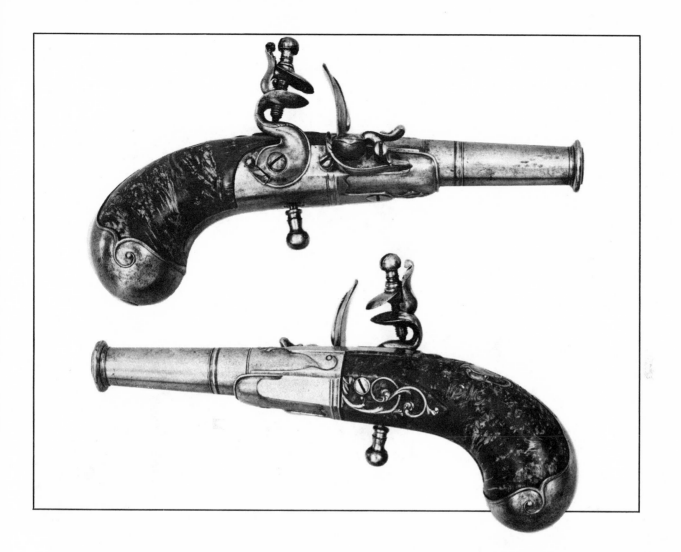

Fig. 4—Although unsigned, this little pistol is so similar to those in Fig. 3 that it may cautiously be attributed to Henry Ellis. But it has a turn-off, not muzzle-loading barrel, rifled with six grooves, .36 calibre (overall length 6⅞ in., barrel 3⅝ in.). Attribution to Ellis rests on a fairly high measure of probability, but this style of pocket weapon was also produced in London and in other provincial centers; nevertheless, Ellis' personal touch does appear to be incorporated in the overall design and in most of the details of ornament (sparse in this case) and execution (very good). (Clay P. Bedford Collection)

the classical Louis XIV Style early in the eighteenth century in preference to a less elegant if somewhat more practical design. The master Bertrand Piraube, working in the 1690's, was probably responsible for the return of the flat lock, a straight grain stock, a sideplate no longer pierced and, on long arms, a shortened buttplate tail.

Certain changes occurring on many English-made arms within the first twenty years of the 18th century heralded the gradual degeneration of the Classical Louis XIV Style on that side of the channel, too. The use of burl wood for gun stocks was superseded by dark-coloured, straight-grain walnut, contrasting with the bright silver mounts which had in effect replaced steel on arms of quality. The practice of steel chiseling was gradually abandoned. Other changes, although subtle, began to appear; these included a "covered vase" finial on the trigger guard and a sharply-defined three-leaf finial on the feather

spring. The comb of the cock was given a straight profile at the rear.

Other modifications were to assert themselves in the period 1720-25 and after. The lower edge of the lock began to lose its curve so that by the 1730's it was just about straight. The ornate carving on the stock was abandoned, except for some shell-design at the barrel tang and a narrow border of molding around the lock. The barrel was often completely round in an unbroken line, although a few were made octagonal at the breech. Except on the finest arms, there was little if any engraving on the lock; a thin raised border was chiseled around its edge, but in a short time this diminished to no more than an engraved line. The bow of the trigger guard was wider at the points of attachment to the tang and finial, a necessity on account of the use of fragile metals like silver and brass; inside the bow, at the rear, a reverse curl began to make its appearance.

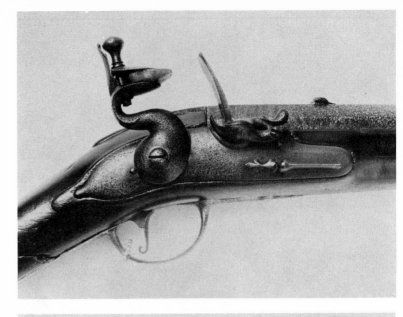

Figs. 5, a to e—Massive wildfowling gun, 83⅝ in. overall, barrel (in three stages) 66¼ in., weight 17 lbs. Barrel London-proofed and fitted with front and rear sights. 7⅝-in. lock is of marked "banana" shape and signed "H. Ellis". Straight-grain walnut stock, no ornamental carving save simple ferrules / borders around tang, lockplate, along both sides of ramrod channel. Iron furniture, incl. serpent sideplate, "covered vase" trigger guard finial, long (5½ in.) buttplate tang and four baluster ramrod pipes. Piece is datable 1710-20, shows early 18th-century cock profile and feather-spring and trigger guard finials. In spite of strictly utilitarian character, quality of execution is high.

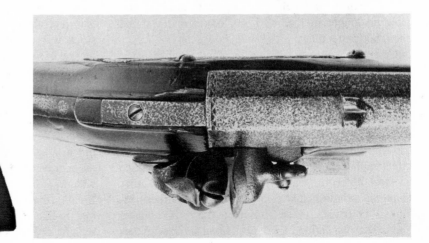

Fig. 6—Plate 6 of *Plusièurs Pieces et Ornements d'Arquebuzerie* of Claude Simonin, Paris, 1685.

The most striking change was in the sideplate, which became stylized into a few set patterns of trophies of arms or foliate scrollwork, not bad in themselves but reduced to banality by constant repetition. Gradually the manufacture of silver mounts passed into the hands of the silversmiths[8], and the London gunmakers turned more and more to Birmingham for the supply of locks and barrels. Even the brass furniture was obtained already cast. In effect, the London makers for the most part became highly skilled assemblers of firearms components. After 1750 in England the emphasis was placed on technological improvement rather than on ornamentation. To be sure, highly engraved and inlaid firearms continued to be made, but for the most part these are inferior to those of the late seventeenth and eighteenth centuries.

The popularity in England of turn-off pistols, most of which have no wooden fore-end and a lock forged integrally with the frame, may have contributed indirectly to the decline of the Classical Louis XIV Style.[9]

But the gun trade was not limited to London. Some of the finest work was produced by provincial makers: Nicolas Paris of Warwick, Nicholes of Oxford, Ellis of Doncaster and others. Henry Ellis of Doncaster has been selected to represent the English gunmakers who worked in the Classical Louis XIV

Style for several reasons. He was unquestionably one of the most skillful and imaginative in this period of tasteful elegance, from its flowering in the last decade of the seventeenth century to the nuances of its decline some twenty years later. Enough examples of Ellis's work, which was not limited to holster pistols, are available to mark him as a master gunsmith familiar with the pattern book of Simonin. There is the enigma of why so versatile and talented a craftsman would have chosen to work in so remote a provincial community as Doncaster, far removed from the center of the gunmaking industry in London. But little is known of Henry Ellis. Several families with that surname were residing in London in the seventeenth century, and there exists the possibility that Ellis, if born and raised there, might have been apprenticed to one of the London makers and then moved north. His production appears to date no earlier than around 1690 and at least as late as 1712, for the following entry, dated 18 April 1712, appears in Volume I of the Calendar to the Records of the Borough of Doncaster:

> Indenture of lease of William Justice of York, gentleman to Henry Ellis of Doncaster, gunsmith, for seven years from May 1st next, of a messuage with orchard and garden thereto belonging in Frenchgate Street, Doncaster at a year rent of 8 Lbs 1 s.

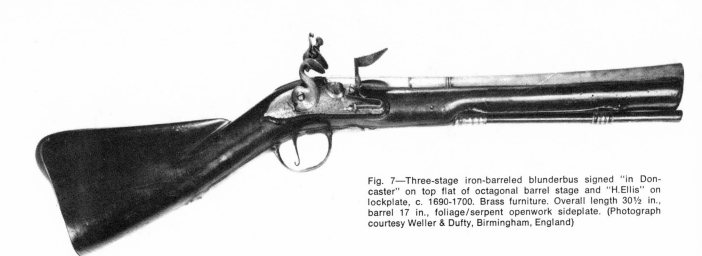

Fig. 7—Three-stage iron-barreled blunderbus signed "in Doncaster" on top flat of octagonal barrel stage and "H.Ellis" on lockplate, c. 1690-1700. Brass furniture. Overall length 30½ in., barrel 17 in., foliage/serpent openwork sideplate. (Photograph courtesy Weller & Dufty, Birmingham, England)

Another volume of the Calendar makes reference to the existence of a Henry Ellis, "Capital Burgess," who presented a seal to the Corporation. A Capital Burgess was in fact a life member of the town council and indeed an eminent figure in municipal life at the time. It is not known whether the two Henry Ellises, gunmaker and burgess, are the same man.

Doncaster, now a city of over 86,000 inhabitants in the West Riding of Yorkshire and nearly 150 miles north of London, lies astride a ridge dividing the watershed of the rivers Don and Trent. Originally a Roman *danum,* or way station, its first charter of incorporation was granted by Richard I in 1194. Today, heavy in agriculture with many markets, Doncaster is the center of a large coal mining area. At the beginning of the eighteenth century it was a typical rural township with a population of probably less than 4,000 and the center of an agricultural community. Around 1722 the town began to expand when the Don was developed to allow the passage of larger vessels.

Five specimens of Henry Ellis's work are represented in this article. These include two pairs of holster pistols, a pair of pocket pistols, a blunderbuss, and a wildfowler of exceedingly large proportions. A turn-off pistol is illustrated which, although unsigned, is believed to have been made by Ellis.

The work of Henry Ellis represents the period of greatest refinement and elegance in the art of English gunmaking. It is in this context that Ellis and his contemporaries must be ranked; their achievements are among the most beautiful in the history of English firearms manufacture, and in some respects perhaps unsurpassed.

NOTES

1. Few books are available which deal authoritatively with the artistic aspects of firearms. The two best works in this field are: Hayward, J. F.: *The Art of the Gunmaker, 1500-1830,* 2 Vols., London, 1962, 1963; and Lenk, Torsten: *The Flintlock,* Urquhart, G.A., (Trans.) and Hayward, J. F., (Ed.), London, 1965. The former deals with gun design and ornamentation in Europe and to some degree in America while the latter is concerned primarily with French arms (first published in 1939 in Swedish).

2. Strangely, military muskets and pistols often retained features that had long been dispensed with on private arms. Flat, three-screw locks, occasionally with back-catches, were often utilized for military muskets as late as the early 1720's. The 'banana' profile on military locks was common until the 1750's, several years after the advent of the straight, uncurved lock on civilian arms.

3. Some butt caps are deeply fluted or pierced; see Claude Blair, *Pistols of the World,* New York, 1968, ills. 236, 239. Rudimentary spurs began to develop c. 1650-60.

4. Three major snaphaunce types were in use in England. The first, often called the Anglo-Dutch snaphaunce, developed in the last quarter of the sixteenth century; it has a horizontally operating sear and a separate steel and pan cover. The second, referred to as the early form of the English or Jacobean lock, has a combined steel and pan cover (cf. R. Held, *The Age of Firearms,* rev. ed., 1970, Fig. 169). These two ignition forms have a sear which passes through the lock to engage the tail of the cock, and, usually, a buffer or stop screwed to the center of the lock to arrest the fall of the cock upon firing. A dog safety catch behind the cock is often seen on the English lock, thus giving rise to the comparatively modern term "dog lock". Still another snaphaunce—an advanced form of the English lock—developed c. 1640;

in this, the sear is enclosed within the lock and the external buffer is dispensed with; a shoulder, or step built up on the back of the cock arrests the fall of the cock. This ignition type usually has a throat-hole or reinforced cock and the dog safety catch was generally retained.

5. English handguns dating from the end of the sixteenth century to c. 1640 are illustrated in: Ian Eaves, *Some Notes on the Pistol in Early 17th-Century England,* in the Journal of the Arms and Armour Society, Vol. VI, No. 11, London, 1970. Three typical pistols of the English Civil War period are shown in: Howard L. Blackmore, *British Military Firearms,* London, 1961, p.34. Other pre-Restoration pistols are illustrated in: Clay P. Bedford and Stephen V. Grancsay, *Early Firearms of Great Britain and Ireland,* New York, 1971.

6. The admission of an alien to residence and certain rights of citizenship, but without confering citizenship upon him.

7. J. F. Hayward, *op. cit.* (fn. 1).

8. Until the Plate Offences Act of 1738, silver gun mounts were rarely submitted for assay at the Goldsmith's Hall in London; hence hall marks on silver furniture are not often encountered on arms made prior to that date. Probably many of the earlier gunmakers chose to cast their own mounts or submitted specific patterns to the silversmiths.

9. A turn-off pistol was one having a barrel that unscrewed just ahead of the powder chamber in the fixed breech and had a ball chamber just slightly wider than the rest of the bore up to the muzzle, so that a slightly over-sized ball could be loaded from the breech end and allowed to roll forward until it came to rest on the stricture of the narrower bore. This caused, upon the piece being fired, an increase of compression and hence a more forceful shot. Many of these pistols were also rifled. The system developed just prior to c. 1640 and was used for all types of pistols until the end of the seventeenth century, when it was restricted to belt and pocket pistols. The earliest turn-off pistols were often made with wooden fore-ends. A collectors' term, "box lock" refers to those turn-offs made after c. 1750 which have the cock, steel, pan and feather spring mounted atop the breech instead of on the side.

A Brief History of Powder Testers

by H. G. MULLER

*H. G. Muller, Ph.D., M.Sc., was born
in Germany but has long lived in
England, where he is a Lecturer in
Food Sciences at the University of Leeds.
He collects antique firearms as a hobby
and is particularly interested in
English flintlock and percussion pistols.
He has published various articles and
given many lectures in this field.
His main publications, including textbooks,
are in the realm of nutrition sciences.*

For almost 600 years, from about 1250 to 1850, gunpowder was the only explosive and propellant known. It consists of a mixture of carbon, sulphur and saltpetre. On ignition, more stable products of combustion, largely gaseous, are formed, and a considerable amount of heat is produced. The sudden increase in volume results in a loud noise and the heat produced causes a flame: this is an explosion.

The composition of gunpowder, i.e. the ration of the three ingredients, varied widely through the centuries. J.R. Partington, in his *A History of Greek Fire and Gunpowder* (Heffer, 1960), gives 38 different compositions which were used between 1260 and 1827, and an even greater number for various uses after that date, as for instance in small arms, cannon, sporting and blasting powders. In 1792 the great French chemist Berthollet[1] concluded from theoretical considerations that the best ratio was 75 parts of saltpetre, 12 parts of sulphur and 13 parts of charcoal. In 1888 Nobel and Able[2] established that 1 gram of powder gave 271.3 mililiters of gas at 760 mm pressure and 0°C. Since the heat liberated in the explosion amounted to 700.7 calories, the gasses would be hot and the volume larger still.

Early Powder Tests

Early tests on gunpowder depended on an inspection of the powder, an observation of its burning in the open and finally, on an inspection of the residue.[3,4,5] Fig. 1, taken from a 15th-century Viennese

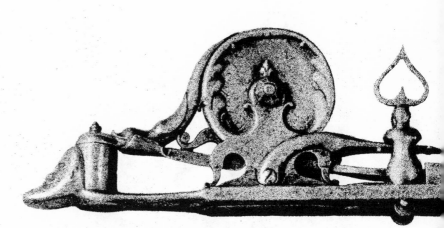

manuscript, shows such a test. Several pictures of this type can be found in old manuscripts, and Guttmann[6] noted that some of the experimenters shown invariably cover their eyes. The reason is not hard to guess—there exists at least one tombstone of a master gunner wearing an eye patch.

Certainly not the earliest, but perhaps the most concise account of this type of testing is given in Chapter 14 of the book *The Art of Gunnery* published in London in 1647 by Nathanael Nye, mathematician and master gunner of the city of Worcester:

How you may by taste, feeling, colour and burning, know good and ill powder, and how amongst many sorts of Gunpowder you may know the best sort.

1. By how much gunpowder is the harder in feeling, by so much the better it is.

2. Gunpowder of a fair Azure or French Russet colour, is very good, and it may be judged to have all its receipts well wrought, and sufficient of the Peter well refined.

3. Lay two or three corns of Gunpowder upon a white piece of paper, the one three fingers distant from the other, and put fire to one of them, if the powder be good and strong, you shall see them all on fire at once, and that there will remain no grossness of Brimstone or of Saltpeter, no not any thing but a white smoky colour in the place where they were burned, neither will the paper be touched.

4. If good Gunpowder be laid upon the palm of your hand, and set on fire, you will not be burned.

5. Gunpowder that hath a very sharp taste, hath abundance of the Peter not well refined, and will moisten again.

6. If white knots, or knots of a French russet colour, shall remain after powder is fired, it is a sign that the Saltpeter was not well refined, but left full of salt, and grease, especially when the same knots shall in burning be dankish, and leave moisture in the place where the Gunpowder was burned.

7. If hard, dry and white knots, or pearls, shall remain after the Gunpowder is set on fire, it is a sign that the Gunpowder is not well wrought, and it becometh every gunner to beware of such powder, because if it doth lie long in a Piece it will wax so fine, that if you unload not the Piece, it will in his discharge indanger the Piece of breaking.

8. If small black knots (which will burn downwards in the place where proof is made) remain after firing, they do show that the Gunpowder hath not enough of the Peter, and this it is of little force or strength, and slow in firing.

9. If a little heap of Gunpowder set a fire, doth make a noise, rise up with great speed, and yield little smoke, it is a sign of very good powder.

10. If the flame of fired Gunpowder shall rise

207

Fig. 1—Testing gunpowder by flashing it on a table. From a Viennese manuscript, 1437.

the touchhole, and then the powder will blowe vp the couer or lid, and then the teeth or notches being well filed or trimmed of purpose, will holde vp the lid at the highest, and yet not staying in the blowing of it vpwards, for that the teeth standeth so, to stay it that it shal not come downwards, and then trying or prouing diuers sorts of powder, you shall knowe which is the best or strongest powder, or weaker powder, by the blowing vp of the lid or couer, you putting in the powder by weight. &c. And this is the forme of the engine or instrument.

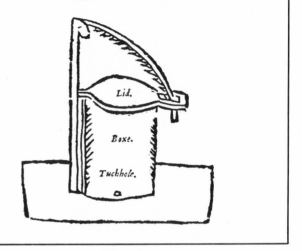

Fig. 2—Bourne's powder tester of 1587.

up slowly, continue long, make little noise, and yield smoke in great abundance, it is a sign that the powder hath much Cole and Brimstone and too little Peter.

11. If Gunpowder burned upon a board shall black the same, it is a sign that there is overmuch Cole in that powder.

12. When Gunpowder is moist, or full of the earth of Saltpeter, it is naught to be shot out of great Ordnance, for it shameth the Gunner which useth it.

13. If Gunpowder be very black, it is either a sign that there is too much Cole, or that it is moist, and when you rub it upon white paper, it will black it more than other good Gunpowder will do.

14. Amongst many sorts of powder to know the best, make a little heap of every sort, and then setting those heaps one from another mark well when you put fire unto them, which of the heaps did soonest take fire, for that powder which will soonest be on fire, smoke least, and leave least sign behind it, is the best sort of Gunpowder.

Early Powder Testers

It seems that the first powder tester was described by William Bourne in 1587 in a book printed in London entitled *Rare Inventions and Strange Devises Very Necessary for all Generalles and Captaines.* The 54th "devise" describes a powder tester but it is not known if Bourne invented the instrument himself or merely recorded it. His book is now exceedingly rare and for this reason the section will be given verbatim (cf. Fig. 2):

And as touching this, how for to make an Instrument or Engine for to knowe the goodnesse or the badnesse of powder (that is to say) to know the strength or weaknesse therof, they may doo it in this manner: first make in mettall or yron a round boxe of an ynch and a halfe in breadth more or lesse at your discretion and of two ynches deepe more or lesse, at your discretion, and then let that be placed so, that it may stand vpright, and haue a little tuch-hole at the lower part thereof, and then let the vppermost part at the mouth thereof, haue in mettall or yron a lid or couer that may goe with a ioynt vpon the one side thereof, and the couer or lid to be of a reasonable weight, and the other side of the couer or lid right against the ioynt to haue a square hole fitted of pupose, and then vppon that side that the ioynt of the couer or lid is of, there must bee raised a thing that must haue of yron or other mettall a part of a circle, and the other ende to goe through the square hole in the lid couer, and the other ende to goe with a pinne or ioynt right ouer the ioynt of the couer or lid, and the sayd crooked thing or part of a circle, to haue teeth or notches like vunto a Sawe, and the teeth to stand vpwards, and then it is finished, and then whensoeuer that you lift to prooue the strength of powder, and you hauing of diuers sortes of powder then wey some small quantitie of the powder and then put that into the Boxe, and then let downe the couer or lidde, and then giue fire vnto it at the touchhole, and then the powder will blowe vp the couer or lid, and then the teeth or notches being well filed or trimmed of purpose, will holde vp the lid at the highest, and yet not staying in the blowing of it vpwards, for that the teeth standeth to, to stay it that it shall not come downwards, and then trying or prouing diuers sorts of powder, you shall knowe which is the best or strongest powder, or weaker powder, by the blowing vp of the lid of couer, you putting in the powder by weight &c. And this is the forme of the engine or instrument.

It is apparent from the drawing (Fig. 2) that the tester had a very large volume. Either the powder was extremely weak or else we have an explanation of the fact that none of Bourne's "wretched little engines" has survived. A third explanation is that since the lid yielded at the slightest pressure, there was a flash rather than a detonation, and hence little pressure was produced.

Furttenbach's Tester

Johann Furttenbach described his tester in 1627 in his *Halinitro-Pyrobolia,* printed in Ulm, Germany, and states that he invented it himself. After discussing the disadvantages of the visual and auditory tests he states:

It is almost impossible to know precisely which, and how much, advantage one powder has before the other, from which arises a great error because by guess the worse is taken for the better in consideration; where no certain end point exists, there no infallible decision can be. Which error I have considered for many years, [and] whether a means could not be invented to ascertain closely how one powder compares with the other, and allow recognition of a forceful rise of an inch higher or less high. Finally, and not long ago in particular, I invented an instrument which in my opinion serves the purpose . . .

I do not wish to inflict upon the reader the full

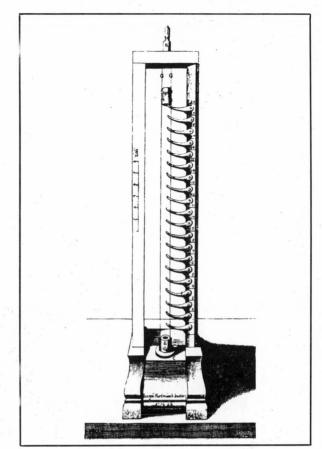

Fig. 3—Furttenbach's powder tester of 1627.

description of his instrument—it is shown in Fig. 3. The powder is placed into the barrel E and the weight F is shot upwards guided by two wires. Furttenbach recorded that cannon powder (*Carthaunen Pulver*) lifted the weight 4 inches, Mezan Powder, 5 inches, sporting powder (*Bürch Pulver*) 9 inches, and an "extraordinarily fine powder prepared with particular diligenzia", 12 inches. With Furttenbach, powder testing had become a science.

It is perhaps amusing to record that the copy of Furttenbach's book in the library of the British Museum shows his autograph in his own handwriting, together with the comment "I have signed this, so that my character may be diagnosed."

It should be pointed out that in the Kunsthistorische Museum in Vienna there is, according to Guttmann,[7] a 19th-century replica of the Furttenbach tester. This was recently mistaken for an original.

The Work of Nye

The work of Nye was, as already observed, published in 1647. In it, he describes in detail a vertical tester, virtually identical with that of Furttenbach except that the former had 20 ratchets and the latter only 9. There can be little doubt, if we compare the two drawings, that Nye copied Furttenbach, al-

209

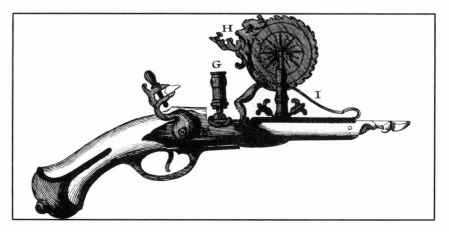

Fig. 4—A pistol eprouvette from St. Remy's *Memoires d'Artillerie*, 1697.

Fig. 5—A French flintlock tester signed *J.B. Muit* (an unlisted maker), mid-18th century. (Paul J. Wolf collection)

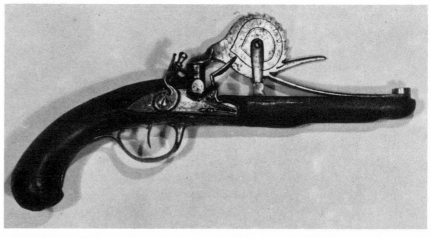

Fig. 6—A match-type tester from St. Remy (see Fig. 4), 1697.

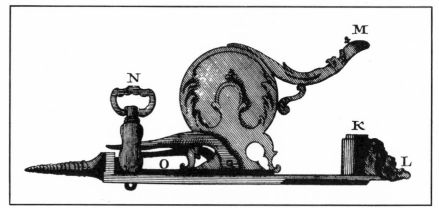

Fig. 7—An Italian (Brescian) match-type tester, 17th century. (In the Walters Art Gallery, Baltimore, Md.)

though he does not acknowledge him. There is also no mention of Bourne's tester but, like him, Nye calls his own an "engine".

Nye introduced two other quantitative tests: discharging a pistol against a bank of clay, and, more important, testing by *mortar eprouvette*. The latter was adopted by Louis XIV of France (b. 1638, reigned 1643-1715) officially on September 8th, 1686, and was used by most European countries until well into the 19th century.

Figure 11 shows an English *mortar eprouvette* which was used as late as 1895 for the testing of gunpowder. Guttmann gives a full description of the gun and its use. (The French word *eprouvette* for powder tester appeared in English about the middle of the 18th century and disappears from British encyclopedias about 1900.)

Again it is worth while to quote Nye *verbatim:*

How to try the strength of powder some other ways than is before rehearsed.

If you charge a pistol, and discharge it against a bank of clay, do this with a little powder, always observing to take the like quantity to a grain of one sort of powder, as you do another sort: then by measuring how far the bullet pierced in the clay, you may have some guess at the strength: also if you can make Rockets, such as fly into the air, and are made of powder dust, and charcole dust, by the strength or weakness of these you may know the like of powder.

If you can get a little Morter Piece (what a Morter Piece is you may read anon) cast at the iron furnace where the iron is made, to get one made in such a place is no difficult thing: Let it be made about three inches Diam: at the mouth, and let the Chamber of the said Piece be three quarters of an inch Diam: and two inches and one third part of an inch deep, load the Chamber with about half an ounce of powder, but put no wad in after it, the reason is, because one wad may be bigger than another, which will cause error, then put into your Morter a bullet of lead or iron that will just fit the bore: now if it be of Iron, it will weigh three pound and ten ounces, if of Lead, almost five pounds: This Morter-piece being erected at a certain and unvariable elevation, and then being discarged, shall (by its several ranges) tell the exact difference of powder above any other instrument that can be invented, for by noting how many paces a shot rangeth, you shall find the true difference and be able to set down the true and infallible proportion betwixt all sorts of powder whatsoever.

Because you may fail in procuring one made at the Furnace where iron is made, I will show

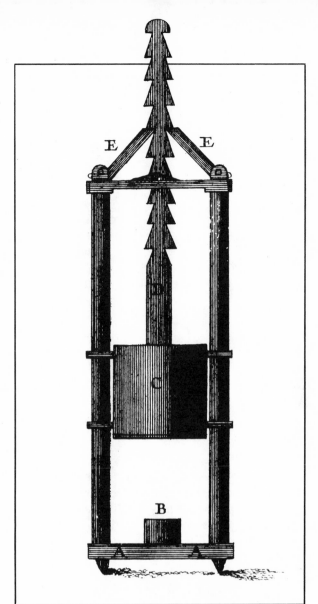

Fig. 8—A vertical ratchet tester from St. Remy (see Fig. 4), 1697, similar to Fig. 3.

you in the following Treatise how you may make such a one which may serve your turn.

Thus having in the foregoing Treatise set down by whom, at what time, of what strength and violence Gunpowder was and when invented, also how to make any sort of gunpowder, & lastly to try its strength: I shall hencefollowing set down such Rules, that an ingenious man may learn to be a perfect Gunner, for I have omitted nothing that is necessary in that art.

The Work of St. Remy

Surirey de Saint Remy published his book *Memoires d'Artillerie* in Paris in 1697 and in it described three testers. One is the pistol eprouvette shown in Figure 4. A surviving model is at present in the collection of P. J. Wolf and shown in Figure 5. Figure 6 shows a match-type tester and Figure 7 a similar one in a style of chiselled metal most clearly identified with Brescian (Italian) work of the second

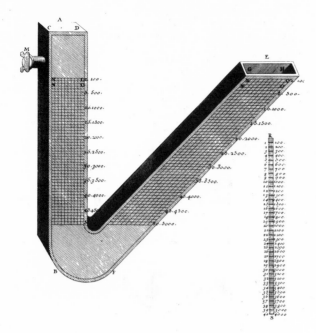

Fig. 9—The tester of du Mé, 1702. The powder was ignited at M and displacement of water by the gases of combustion was measured.

half of the 17th century. Hence, while St. Remy's vertical ratchet tester (Fig. 8) is of German origin (Fig. 3), his match type may be of Italian origin. He is, however, generally regarded as the inventor of the pistol eprouvette (Fig. 4). Diderot stated in 1777 that the pistol eprouvette of St. Remy was the most common type in France.[8]

The Tester of du Mé

The tester described in 1702 by du Mé[9] and shown in Figure 9 operated on a principle different from any tester previously developed, and it proved to be of great significance in elucidating the mechanism of the explosion. The tube was filled to the mark with water, and one cubic inch of powder ignited in sidearm M. The water displaced by the gas produced was determined, and found to be 4000 cubic inches.

The Work of Robins and Hutton

Principles of Gunnery (London, 1742), the authoritative work by Benjamin Robins, the noted mathematician, authority on fortifications and Engineer General to the East India Company, was of great significance and was translated into both German and French. He noted that de la Hire supposed the force of gunpowder to be due to the increased elasticity of the air contained in and between the grains and resulting from the heat of the explosion. Robins, however, using du Mé's principle, discovered that gunpowder fired in a vacuum or in air produced 244 times its volume of elastic fluid (today we would call it a gas). Hence he argued that at

explosion the elasticity of the "fluid" produced by the powder and contained in its original space was about 1,000 times greater than the elasticity of the air (the atmospheric pressure).

He also introduced what is now known as the ballistic pendulum (Fig. 10). He fired a ball of 0.25″ diameter against the plate GKHI and measured the swing from the tape M. In this way he calculated the ball's velocity as 2,400 ft. per second. The method also allowed a fairly accurate evaluation of several different powders and as a result of his work the performance of English powder was greatly improved.

Robins concludes by stating that "the ascertaining of the force of powder and thence the velocity of bullets by its explosion, and the assigning of a method of truly determining their actual velocities from experiments, are points from which every necessary principle in the formation and management of artillery may be easily deduced. Considering, further, the infinite importance of a well-ordered artillery to every state, the author flatters himself that whatever judgment may be formed of his success in these enquiries, he will not be denied the merit of having employed his industry on a subject which,

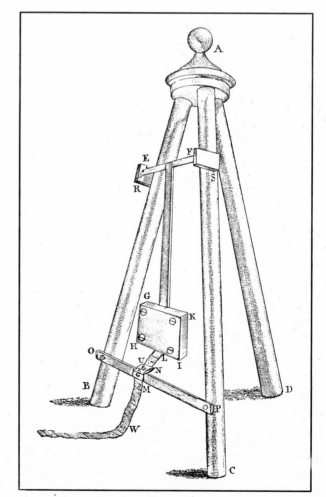

Fig. 10—The Ballistic Pendulum of 1742 invented by Robins.

though of a most scientific nature, and of the greatest consequence to the public, has been hitherto almost totally neglected".

Charles Hutton,[10] Professor of Mathematics at the Military Academy, Woolwich, continued these studies. He revised and edited Robin's *Principles of Gunnery* in 1805. Hutton experimented with a modified form of the ballistic pendulum and stated that the maximum pressure of gunpowder was about twice that given by Robins (2000 atm. or 13 tons per sq. in.). He also concluded that "it would be a great improvement in artillery to make use of shot of long form, for thus the momentum of a shot, when fired with the same weight of powder, would be increased in the ratio of the square root of the weight of the shot".

Hutton also used a recoil gauge with which the recoil of a gun or cannon barrel could be measured. This type was in general use in England from about 1811[11,12] to after 1857[13]. Several modifications are on record: In 1812 Durs Egg took out a patent covering his invention where the recoil was measured against a spring or weight. As late as 1906 the *Harmsworth Encyclopedia* mentions under the entry

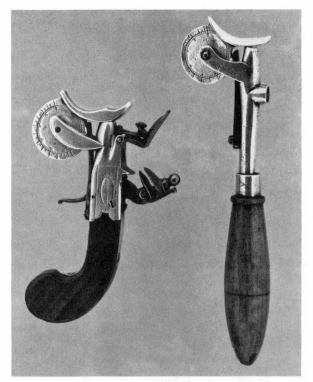

Fig. 12—Two powder testers: "Commonly sold at the shops" in the early 19th century. (Author's Collection)

Fig. 11—An English Mortar eprouvette.

"Eprouvette" a half-pounder gun where a tracer marked the extent of recoil over a waxed drum.

Count Rumford's Experiments

In 1797 the classical experiments of Count Rumford were communicated to the Royal Society.[14] He was previously known as Sir Benjamin Thompson, but on being created a *Graf* (count) in 1792 by the Elector Karl Theodor of Bavaria for his services rendered as a Bavarian General, he took his title from the name of his native town in America. He published several books and, although his experiments were made in Munich in 1792, they were communicated to the Royal Society. In prosecuting his remarkable experiments Rumford had two objects in view: (a) to ascertain the force exerted by explosive powder when it completely filled the space

in which it was exploded; and (b) to determine the relation between the density of the gases and the tension.

The apparatus used by Rumford consisted of a small wrought iron vessel 0.25 inch (6.3 mm) in diameter, and containing a volume of 0.0897 cubic inch (1.47 cc). It was so arranged that the charge could be fired by the application of a red-hot ball: at the other end it was closed by a hemisphere upon which any required weight could be placed.

For carrying out an experiment, a given charge was placed in the vessel, and a weight considered equivalent to the resulting gaseous pressure was applied to the hemisphere. If, on the charge being fired, the weight was lifted, it was gradually increased until it was just sufficient to confine the product of explosion, and the gaseous pressure was calculated from the weight found necessary. The powder employed was sporting powder of very fine grain and, as it contained only 67 per cent of nitre, it differed considerably from ordinary powder. Its gravi-metric density was 1.08, but in his experiments Rumford appears to have arranged it so that the weight of a given volume of gunpowder was nearly exactly equal to that of the same volume of water. The charges with which Rumford experimented were very small: the largest, with one exception (which destroyed his vessel) was 18 grains (1.17 grams). The total quantity of powder required to fill the vessel was about 28 grains (1.81 grams). Rumford calculated that the tension of exploded gunpowder such as that employed by him, when filling completely the space in which it is confined, is 101,021 atmospheres (663 tons/sq. in.). He accounted for this enormous pressure by ascribing it to the elasticity of the steam contained in the gunpowder, the tension of which he estimated as being doubled for every addition of temperature equal to 30°F. He further considered the combustion of powder in artillery and small arms to be comparatively slow, and hence he assumed that the initial tension is, in their case, not attained.

Fig. 13—A tester of unknown origin. (Paul J. Wolf Collection, Missoula, Montana)

Some Other Eprouvettes

Contemporary with these scientific experiments, the pistol eprouvette of St. Remy was adapted in several European countries to existing pistols. Although all eprouvettes are extremely scarce, it is these which occasionally turn up in the antique trade. Figure 12 shows two such "powder-triers acting by a spring, commonly sold at the shops"[11]. Both are English and, judging by the almost identical wheel engraving, contemporary.

Figure 13 shows an interesting tester from the P.J. Wolf collection. This is possibly the Hoër recoil gauge described by Guttmann[7], who stated that "the unequal friction in the joints, the variation in the length of arms with varying temperatures, and the small charge, all go to make this instrument very untrustworthy."

The Regnier tester (Fig. 14) was used in France in about 1840 for the testing of sporting powder. "Powder for sporting usually marks 12 on this eprouvette and superfine powder 14. Each degree represents the effect of 1 kg. of powder placed so as to bring the two legs nearer together."[15] The tester of Devisme (Fig. 15) was depicted in the *Illustrated London News* of July 5th, 1851. Quite a number of these commercially sold, hand-held eprouvettes are still in existence.

Electrical Testers

The first idea of using electricity in ballistic experiments came from Prussia, where, in 1838, the Testing Commission of the artillery had such an instrument constructed to measure the muzzle velocity of a projectile. Progress in electricity gave rise to several such instruments in various European countries. In England, Sir Charles Wheatstone (the inventor of the Wheatstone bridge) experimented with his "electromagnetic chronoscope", but the error was too large: the velocity under identical conditions varied from 38.5 to 88.9 m/s). The instrument of the Belgian Capt. Navez,[16] built in 1847, was an improvement, and by the 1890's the chronograph of le Boulengé was widely used (Fig 16). Here the missile broke two wire screens (R and R_1) a given distance apart, and the time taken for it was measured in terms of the space traversed by a freely falling body in the same time.

Conclusion

The history of gunpowder tests and eprouvettes is too interesting to merit the neglect it has suffered in general arms literature. Quite a number of eprouvettes are still in existence, but if these are studied in the light of their contemporary literature, it becomes apparent that they generally are not the ones that

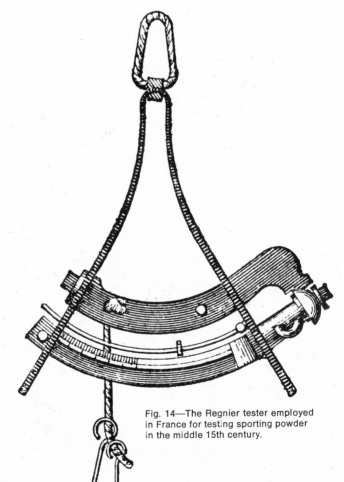

Fig. 14—The Regnier tester employed in France for testing sporting powder in the middle 15th century.

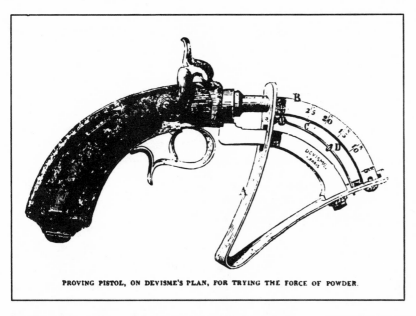

PROVING PISTOL, ON DEVISME'S PLAN, FOR TRYING THE FORCE OF POWDER.

Fig. 15—The Devisme tester, middle 19th century.

produced the great advance in scientific knowledge, but rather everyday household and gunshop devices.

Bourne's "wretched little engine," however feeble, was the first attempt at measurement. Furttenbach's invention was the next milestone and was to be used for over 200 years. Robins, Hutton and Rumford will be remembered for their great skill in applying analytical thought to the problem. Navez and le Boulengé pioneered electrical methods; and finally, with Capt. T.J. Rodman of the U.S. Army[17] and his pressure gauge, we have one of the last experiments on gunpowder. By then Schönbein had invented gun cotton and gunpowder had largely run its course. The era of the high explosive, for good or bad, had arrived.

ACKNOWLEDGEMENTS

I wish to thank most sincerely Mr. M. McLaren of the Explosives Research and Development Establishment, Waltham Abbey, for some fascinating early material, and Mr. P.J. Wolf, Missoula, Montana, for Figs. 5 and 13. Fig. 7 is reproduced by permission of the Walters Art Gallery, Baltimore, Md.

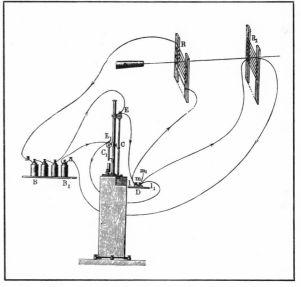

Fig. 16—The chronograph of leBoulengé, 1890s.

NOTES

1. Berthollet, M.: (Trans. Hake, C.N., and Macnab, W.): *Explosives and Their Power;* Murray, 1892.
2. Nobel, A., and Able, F.: 1880, *Phil. Trans.,* 170, 203.
3. *Codex German.,* 600, Munich Staats-Bibliothek, Paper 22, 11 folio, ca. 1350-1400.
4. *Feuerwerkbuch.* Vienna Nationalbibliothek, M.S. 3062, ca. 1437.
5. Biringuccio, V.: Della *Piortechnica,* 1540; Trans. Smith, C.S., and Gundi, M.T.: Amer. Inst. Mining and Metall. Engin., 1942.
6. Guttmann, O.: *Monumenta Pulveris Pyrii;* London. 1906.
7. Guttmann, O.: *The Manufacture of Explosives;* Whittaker, 1895.
8. Diderot: *Encyclopédie,* Paris 1751-88 (Entry *Eprouvette.*)
9. du Mé, M.: 1702, Machienes approuvee acad. roy. sci. Paris, 2, 29.
10. Hutton, C.: 1778, Trans. Roy. Soc. 114, 50.
11. *Encyclodaedia Londiniensis,* London, 1811.
12. Drayson, F.: *A Treatise on Gunpowder;* Waltham Abbey, 1830.
13. Baddeley, F.: *Manufacture of Gunpowder;* Waltham Abbey, 1857.
14. Rumford, B.: 1797, *Phil. Trans.* 87, 222.
15. *Saturday Magazine Suppl.* No. 422. Jan. 1839.
16. Capt. Navez: *L'Application de l'Electricité a la Mesure de la Vitesse des Projectiles;* Paris, 1857.
17. Rodman, T.J.: *Experiments on Metal for Cannon and Qualities of Cannon Powder;* Boston, Mass., 1861.

215

The Function of the Perfected Lorenzoni Repeating Flintlock System

by THOMAS T. HOOPES

Dr. Hoopes, Curator emeritus of Arms & Armor at the St. Louis City Art Museum, a Grand Master of American arms studies and author of many well-known tracts and articles, was a life-long friend of the late William Goodwin Renwick of Tucson, Arizona, one of America's ten foremost collectors. Dr. Hoopes and Mr. Renwick took the remarkable series of photographs here presented (for the first time—a World Premiere!) in about 1934. Current American (and British?) usage airily bandies about grandiloquent adjectives with nary a care, and arms publications proclaim as "magnificent," "splendid," "stupendous" and "fabulous" arms that usually are, objectively appraised, good upper-middle-quality commonplaces. But if ever that Ultimate List of History's Fifty Finest Firearms gets carved in marble and set on the slopes of Parnassus, the pistols subject of the next few pages will be among the topmost few.

On July 17th, 1972, a pair of flintlock pistols was sold for sixty thousand pounds—one hundred and forty-four thousand dollars, until then a world record for firearms—in the Sotheby sales rooms in London. Such a price would suggest that the objects in question possess some remarkable qualities of beauty and ingenuity—and indeed they do, as the following examination will attempt to show.

These weapons were formerly in the collection of William Goodwin Renwick of Tucson, Arizona, and before that in the Imperial Russian Collections in the Hermitage, Leningrad. They are engraved "Lorenzoni," "Cocchi" and "Firenze," i.e. the famous court gunmaker of Grand-Duke Cosimo III of Tuscany, Michele Lorenzoni of Florence (worked actively from about 1684, died 1733), while "Cocchi" is probably the signature of a member of a well-known family of silversmiths who seems to have provided the fine silver furniture. They are *superlative* examples (in the sense that nothing better of their kind has ever come to light, nor is likely to) of a type of repeating breech-loading flintlock firearm which was popular at the end of the seventeenth and through much of the eighteenth century. Many makers' names have been found on arms of this general type: Wetschgi, Acquafresca, Berselli, Parreaux, Cookson, Le Nivernois, Mortimer, Lamarre, Paris, Fombuena, Constantino, Wilson, del Po and others—but Michele Lorenzoni, though probably not the inventor of the system, not only made many specimens of it but brought it to its highest level of development in practicability and safety.

The principle of what collectors now call "the horizontal transverse cylinder repeating flintlock" (or, rightly or wrongly but in any case briefly, "the Lorenzoni system") is a simple one: the chamber in which the gunpowder is exploded is a cavity in a bronze cylinder which, lying horizontally across the long axis of a firearm, obturates the rear end of the barrel and can be rotated by an attached operating lever to transport priming, main charge and ball from various magazines into their proper loaded positions, and to activate, in a return rotation to the operating lever's repose position, the closing of the flashpan cover and the cocking of the hammer. An experienced user was surely capable of firing up to a dozen shots at a rate not much slower than that of the Volcanic arms or of the Winchester '66.

Let us now consider the operating cycle of one of these pistols, beginning just after it has been fired.

217

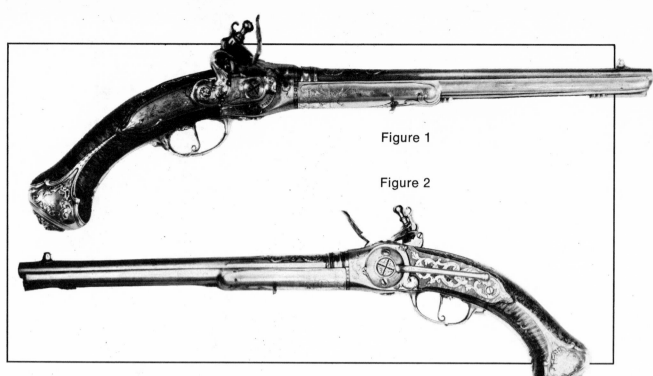

Figure 1

Figure 2

Figure 3

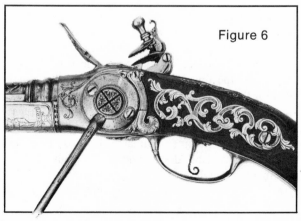

Figure 4

The hammer is down, the steel is turned toward the muzzle and the pan is uncovered (Fig. 3). A projection or cylinder stop screwed onto the edge of the cylinder (Figs. 22-26) impinges on the lower edge of the lockplate, preventing further rotation of the cylinder. The operating lever is pointed straight back (Fig. 4) and is held in this position by a spring catch (the

long curved steel strip ending in a volute curling to the right).

To reload the pistol, we first depress this catch, then start to rotate the lever clockwise. Fig. 5 shows the lever pointing downward; the cylinder stop is just passing counter-clockwise (as seen from the lock side) and upward behind the hinge of the steel. Fig. 6

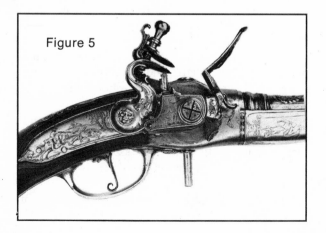

Figure 5

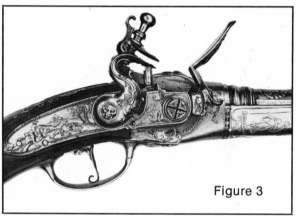

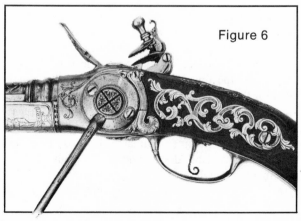

Figure 6

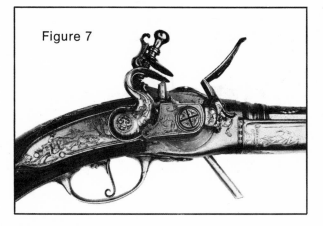

Figure 7

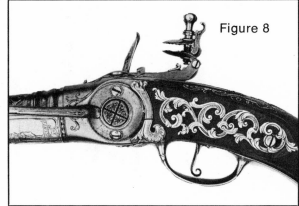

Figure 8

shows the operating lever turned just a little farther (it also shows the step or shoulder on the spring catch that holds the lever in repose or all-the-way-backward position, as in Fig. 4). In Fig. 7 the cylinder stop has disappeared behind the steel hinge and is about to

mer has pushed the hammer up into half-cock position. All this time the pistol has been held with the muzzle pointed up. In Figs. 10 and 11 the operating lever has been turned to the limit of its travel and the cylinder stop has brought the hammer to full-cock

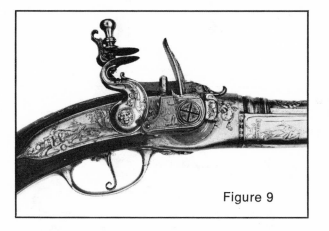

Figure 9

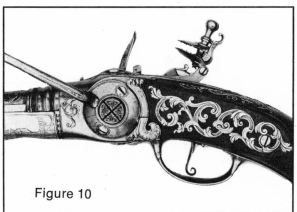

Figure 10

push the steel closed, having engaged the mating notch on it. Fig. 8 shows the lever moved parallel with the barrel; in this and in the lockside view (Fig. 9), we see that the cylinder stop has forced the steel toward the butt and has closed the pan cover, while the connecting rod between the cylinder and the ham-

via the connecting rod. The muzzle of the pistol is now pointed down, allowing gravity to work on the powder and ball in the stock so that they fall into their respective cavities in the cylinder. In Figs. 12 and 13 the operating lever has been returned to its initial position; the pistol is loaded and ready to be fired.

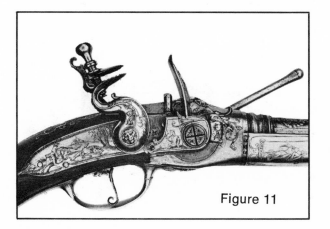

Figure 11

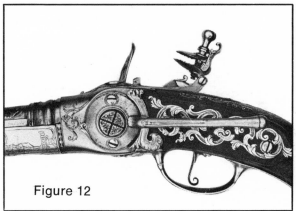

Figure 12

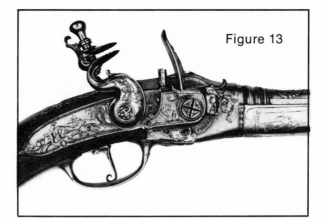

Figure 13

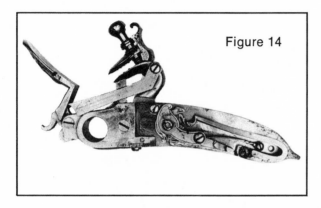

Figure 14

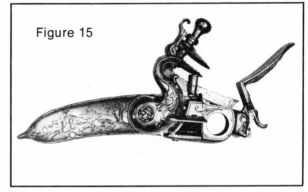

Figure 15

Now let us consider the workings of this mechanism. Fig. 14 shows the interior of the assembled lock but without the cylinder, Fig. 15 the exterior (note the open door of the priming powder magazine), Fig. 16 all the constituent parts disassembled, and Figs. 17 and 18 respectively the inside and outside of the stripped plate. Notice the large hole in the front of the lockplate: through it passes an extension of the bronze cylinder which contains the actual flashpan (cf. Figs. 22-25). Note also the connecting rod attached to the hammer by which the rotating cylinder cocks the

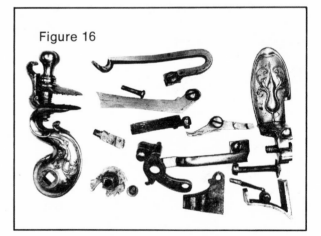

Figure 16

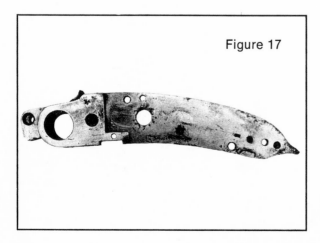

Figure 17

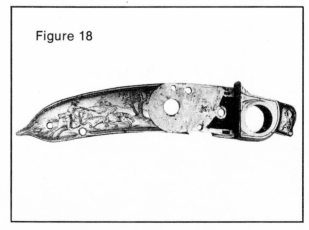

Figure 18

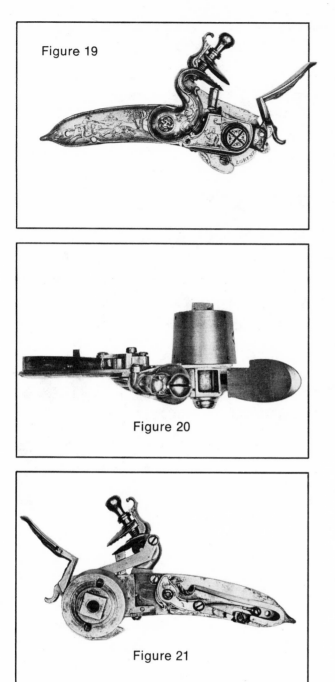

Figure 19

Figure 20

Figure 21

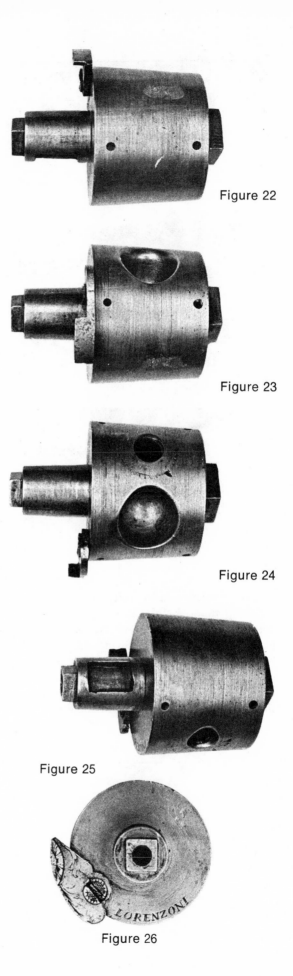

Figure 22

Figure 23

Figure 24

Figure 25

Figure 26

hammer. Fig. 19 shows the lock assembled, with the cylinder in place, Fig. 20 shows the same but from above, and Fig. 21 shows it from the inside; the steel is turned toward the muzzle, and the flashpan is exposed. The floor of the flashpan is the extension of the cylinder, clearly seen in Figs. 22-25, a four-view presentation of the cylinder seen as though it were rolling toward the reader—note the large hole in it for transporting the ball from magazine to breech chamber, the smaller hole which is the powder or firing chamber, the four (two and two) small grease holes for lubrification, and the cylinder stop projecting from the right. Fig. 26 is a side view of the cylinder, seen from the right or flashpan side.

Figure 27

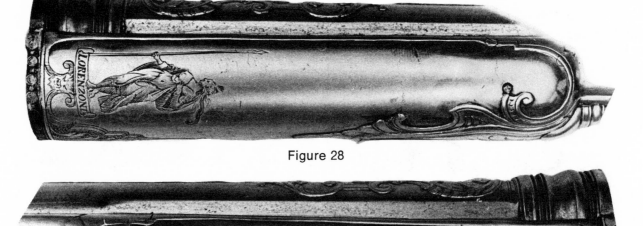

Figure 28

Figure 29

In the earlier—and in most of the contemporary—repeating flintlocks of this type, the magazines for both bullets and gunpowder were in the rear portion of the stock. This simplified the mechanism, but exposed the shooter to the danger of an accidental explosion directly in his hand. Lorenzoni avoided this danger by placing the powder magazine in an all-silver forestock shaped like a wooden one—or, to be exact, in the simulated ramrod of such a forestock. Fig. 27 shows the top view of the breech section of the barrel (note the inscription "Firenze", Italian for Florence); Figs. 28 and 29 show respectively the right and left sides of the same section (note signatures of Lorenzoni and Cocchi), and Fig. 30 shows the muzzle end, the simulated "ramrod" being in fact the powder magazine which may be closed by a small

Figure 30

222

spring-held iron plug. The barrel, together with the silver forestock and magazine, unscrews from what we may call, in modern terminology, the "receiver" or "action" of the weapon; Fig. 31-right shows the flat inner face of the barrel breech, the upper large hole being the bore enlarged and tapped to be screwed over the projecting male thread on the flat front face of the receiver shown in Fig. 31-left, and the small hole of the powder magazine in the forestock then lining up with the continuing powder duct in the receiver. Fig. 32 shows the underside of the receiver; the large hole just in front of the trigger guard is positioned to line up with the ball-transporting chamber in the cylinder when the pistol is loaded—i.e., when the operating lever is in repose position, as in Fig. 3 —so that the pistol may also be used as a single-shot breech-loading weapon when the ball magazine in the hollow butt is empty, the shooter inserting first a ball which is transported into the firing chamber by a short rotation of the cylinder, the powder charge being thereafter picked up in the regular fashion (which will be described in a moment). The ball magazine is simply a tube drilled through the grip or butt; it is filled through an opening in the butt cap (shown open and closed in Fig. 39-left and 39-right) and holds about ten or twelve balls (the lion-mask cover is held in place when closed by a spring catch).

Now we come to the amazingly ingenious solution which Lorenzoni applied to the problem of getting the gunpowder from its magazine in the forestock past the mechanism of the action and into the powder chamber in the cylinder. Fig. 33 shows the receiver with lock, stock and cylinder removed. At the left we see the breech opening of the barrel into which the ball is deposited by the cylinder, and with which the powder chamber in the cylinder lines up when the lever is back in repose position. Below this is the hole for hand-loading bullets which was observed in Fig. 32; at the right we see the two long tangs which grasp between them the wooden stock. On the upper side of the lower tang is attached a short closed tube; this is the powder measure which receives the gunpowder from the forestock magazine and later delivers it to the powder chamber in the cylinder. Just to the left of the powder measure can be seen the nose of the cut-off valve. This valve allows gunpowder to flow from the magazine in the forestock to the powder measure when the pistol is held muzzle-up. Its construction is concealed behind a cover plate which separates it from the powder measure, but when that plate is removed together with the powder measure, we see the valve exposed (Fig. 34). Since the powder measure, to which is attached the spring which normally holds the valve plate raised, has been removed, the plate has fallen down to the position it assumes to allow the powder measure to empty into the powder chamber in the cylinder. The parts of the cut-off

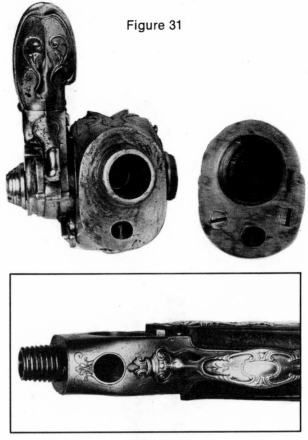

Figure 31

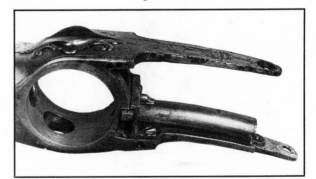

Figure 32

Figure 33

Figure 34

223

Figure 35

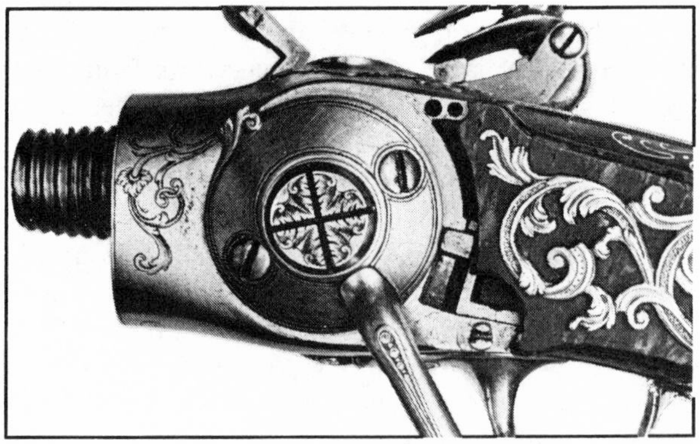

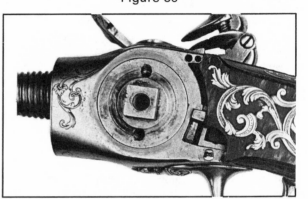

Figure 36

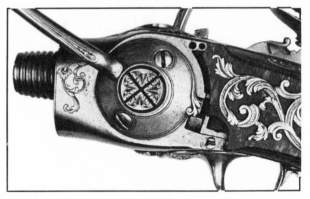

Figure 37

Figure 38

valve, including valve plate, cover plate and spring (attached to the powder measure) are shown in Fig. 35.

Now look at Fig. 36. The spring catch which holds the operating lever has been removed, and we see the nose of the cut-off valve protruding above the partially rotated lever. This is more clearly seen when we also remove the operating lever (Fig. 37). Replacing it and continuing to rotate it to the limit of its travel (Fig. 38), we observe a spur in the form of a nicely-sculptured curlecue on the central disc of the operating lever pressing down on the nose of the cut-off valve. As described above, this cuts off the flow of gunpowder from the magazine in the forestock to the powder-measure tube, and simultaneously opens a passage for the powder in the measure tube to pour

into the firing chamber in the cylinder, the pistol being now held muzzle-down. After the firing chamber has been filled, the return motion of the operating lever rotates the cylinder to bring the firing chamber in line with the barrel. At the same time, the ball-transporting cavity in the cylinder has picked up a ball from the magazine in the grip and, on the return rotation, deposited it into the barrel breech ahead of the powder charge.

As the cylinder performs its 210° rotation, the extension of it that passes through the lockplate also rotates, and the excavation in it that constitutes the flashpan, rotating in the priming powder magazine below the pan (extending from the lockplate just in front of the hammer—see Fig. 15), picks up a suitable quantity of priming powder.

Figure 39

But how does the main charge of gunpowder get from the magazine in the forestock into the powder measure tube on top of the lower tang? Look at Fig. 33 again: there doesn't appear to be any tube or channel through which the powder could flow; moreover, there is that big hole right in the middle of the floor of the receiver! Return now to Fig. 31-left: in the middle of the opening of the powder duct (small lower hole) we see a thin whitish line with a few reflected highlights; this is a dividing partition between two passages, both of which run from the oval duct-opening rearward, *within the thickness of the receiver's floor,* back to the powder measuring tube behind the valve, dividing first into left and right branches to pass left and right around the single-shot bullet-loading hole in the receiver floor, then curving down, around and back up to meet again only at the end of their courses just before the shut-off valve!

How did the ingenious Florentine bore those holes, each doubly curved in three dimensions? Was the receiver made in separate parts, then carefully fitted together? Or was some now-forgotten secret of lost-wax casting involved? Thus far, investigation has not provided an answer, but perhaps the weapons' new owner will initiate some further examinations and let the results be made known to arms students should anything interesting be established.

Notes of the Firearms of the Tosco-Emilian Apennines

by NOLFO DI CARPEGNA

Nolfo di Carpegna was born in Rome in 1913. Having earned his doctorate in Law and Letters, he joined the Italian National Fine Arts Commission in 1940, specializing in the protection and restoration of war-damaged art works. In his capacity of Conservator of the National Gallery in the Barberini Palace, Rome, he compiled the Catalogue of the arms collection of the Princes Odescalchi when this was bought by the Italian government in 1961. He has published important monographs and catalogues in Italy, Germany and England[20]; and is considered the leading authority on Central Italian firearms. Signor di Carpegna, who resides in Brussels and Rome, has brought together from all parts of the world a sort of Central Study Archive on Italian firearms—hundreds of photographs, rubbings, names, dates and places—for future publication, and would greatly appreciate any information, especially photo-documented, sent to him in care of the Editor.

THE GEOGRAPHY OF PRODUCTION

The Exhibition arranged in 1968 in the ancient Tuscan gun-making town of Anghiari by Marcello Terenzi[1] devoted to firearms produced there and, more generally, in Central Italy throughout the eighteenth century and in the early decades of the nineteenth, has made a great contribution to our knowledge of a subject that has attracted the attention of students only in the last ten years. The results of recent research have shown that the firearms produced in Tuscany and, in particular, in the Apennines between Florence and Bologna—hitherto summarily called "Brescian"—show highly individual characteristics and are on the average of good, at times of outstanding and in one case of superlative quality.

To summarize our knowledge of this subject, it might be useful first to examine the villages and hamlets found along the roads which join Tuscany to Emilia, in an area conventionally called the Tosco-Emilian Apennines, and to postpone the overall discussion to Section II. Let us begin with the home town of the most illustrious of all the Tosco-Emilian masters:

BARGI—This village harboured the celebrated Acquafresca family, makers of some of the most superb firearms in existence (e.g., a pair of pistols in the Musée de l'Armée, Paris[2], another in the Gwynn Collection, Epsom, England, and still another in the Bayerisches Nationalmuseum, Munich, dated 1683).

Their real name was Cecchi but, for reasons not entirely clear, they adopted the pseudonym *Acquafresca* ("Freshwater," "Coolwater") and preferred to be thus known. Lionello Giorgio Boccia has recently reconstructed from virgin documentary sources their complete genealogical tree and illustrates in detail two beautiful guns with repeating systems in the Museo della Storia delle Scienze (Museum of the History of the Sciences) in Florence.[3] These guns—two similar ones are known, one preserved in the Museum of Science and Industry in Birmingham, England, the other in the Keith Neal Collection in Warminster, Wiltshire, England—put their author, probably Matteo Acquafresca (1651-1738)[4], among the several 17th- and 18th-century makers who produced repeating guns in Central Italy, among them the celebrated Michele Lorenzoni of Florence and the no less important Giacomo and Francesco Berselli, Giacomo Filippo Bondioli and Antonio Constantini, all of Bologna.

Lionello Boccia is currently preparing for publication an exhaustive study of the Acquafresca family's products, dealing not only with the work of Matteo and of his father Sebastiano (1619-1692) but also with that of other members who were active up to the last quarter of the 18th century.[5] In fact, only few of the earlier works of the Acquafresca family are dated, and fewer still bear the Christian names of their authors. To those signed by Matteo already published we may add a gun in the Bayerisches Nationalmuseum, Munich, superbly decorated with chiselled sil-

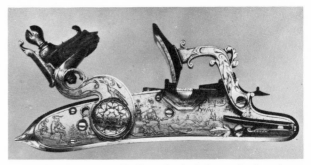

Fig. 1—Flintlock signed "Acqua Fresca", not by either of the great Acquafrescas, i.e. Matteo or Sebastiano, but by one of their many descendants and relatives (see note 3) working between 1720 and 1750. (Soligo Collection, Rome)

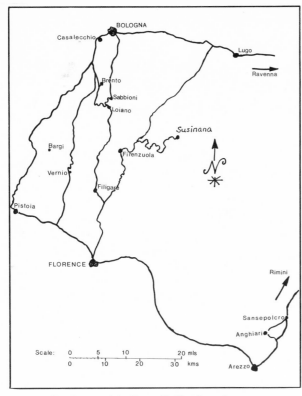

Sketch map of the Tosco-Emilian Apennine zone.

Fig. 2—Snaphaunce or *alla fiorentina* lock from a fowling piece. In regards to signature, same comments as those in caption Fig. 1 apply, but date may be later. The delightful little scene of the flute-player, the lady and the puppydog amidst a bucolic landscape is typical of Tuscan flat-lock engraving: the apparent naiveté and rusticity mask the skill and discipline required for the execution of this genre, often considered—very unjustly—unsuccessful provincial imitations of big-city patterns. (Museo Stibbert, Florence)

ver mounts and bearing a monogram which probably refers to Francesco Maria (1670-1711), brother of Granduke Cosimo III de'Medici. The lock is signed *Acqua Fresca* near the pan and *Matteo* under the cock. As for the other members of the family, great numbers of locks of medium to excellent quality (none, though, up to Matteo standards) bearing the signature *Acqua Fresca* were produced throughout the 18th century, but only in one case can an individual family member be identified: a lock mounted on a pistol in the Germanisches Nationalmuseum in Nuremberg (W. 381) which has the family name beneath the pan and the letters *G.F.* under the cock, probably the initials of Giovan Francesco Acquafresca (1691-1762). Among other little known works by Acquafresca is a small flintlock pocket pistol in the A.N. Kennard Collection, London, an exquisite piece of work on technical as well as artistic grounds, with the blade of a dagger concealed in the stock, the butt acting as a grip for it; its lock is dated 1690. Another fine Acquafresca pistol is in the C. Katsainos Collection, Washington, and a lock signed *Acqua Fresca* is mounted on a fowling piece, with a barrel by *Nicolas Bis,* in the W. Tonolini Collection, Brescia.

LOIANO—A group of firearms bears the name of this village, which is situated between Bologna and Florence on the road that crosses the Raticosa Pass. They often bear the name of a gunmaker as well, usually one of the Ghini family who lived in Loiano and who are recorded as owning property there.[6] None of these weapons is dated, but a beautiful pair of pistols (Fig. 3) signed by Claudio Ghini (with barrels signed by the well-known French gunsmith Le Lorain of Valence), plus the fact that Calindri does not list any Ghinis in 1781, leads to the conclusion that most probably they were active only in the first half of the 18th century.

Other known works from this town are signed *Alessandro Ghini, Loiano,* and include a detached flintlock with two superimposed flashpans (Fig. 4), a contrivance often used by Italian gunmakers both in Brescia and in Central Italy; a pistol in the Marzoli Museum, Brescia; a pair in the War Museum, Riga; another in the C. Canepari Collection, Milan; and a detached lock in a private collection, Rome. The pistols in Riga have barrels signed by Vincenzo Cominazzo, a member of the famous Brescian family —in fact, notwithstanding the presence of well-known

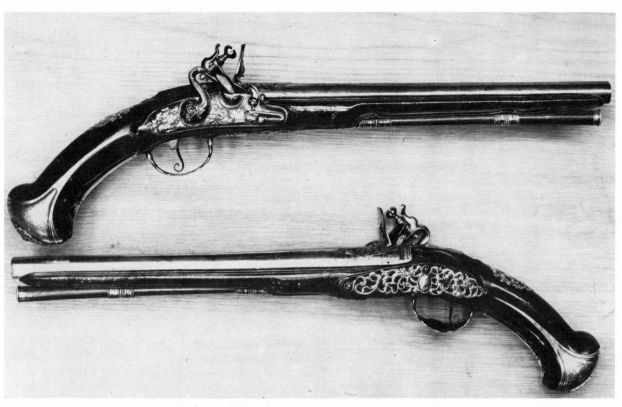

Fig. 3—A pair of flintlock pistols, late 17th-century, signed "Claudio Ghini Loiano" with French barrels signed "Le lorain a Valence en Dauphine". (Giacinti Collection, Rome)

barrel-makers in the neighbouring city of Pistoia, Brescian barrels are often fitted to firearms produced in this area. Two other pistols, with their locks signed *Loiano,* have barrels by Giovanni Beretta of Gardone.[7]

The general appearance of the pistols signed by Claudio Ghini points to strong French influence, but the decoration of the locks and that of other examples signed either by Alessandro or bearing simply the legend *Ghini, Loiano* show a rather personal style in the harsh chiseling of the foliage and sometimes a somewhat excessive accumulation of decorative details. Examples are to be found in Milan in the Museo del Castello Sforzesco and in Paris, where two other locks are in the Musée de l'Armée (Fig. 5). A rather different style, closer to the works produced in Emilia, was used by another gunmaker working in Loiano, a member of the Negroni family (see below) whose Christian names were Giovan Battista.[8]

BRENTO—This village, some ten kilometres north of Loiano, was entirely destroyed during the Second World War when the Germans established the Gothic Line across the Apennines and forced the Allies to halt during the Winter of 1944-45, before continuing the advance towards Bologna and Milan the following Spring. Local archives, like those of other towns in the area, have disappeared, and the only sources of information concerning the important family of gunmakers who lived there, the Negroni, are entries in the State Archives in Bologna[9], inscriptions and dates found on several firearms, and an observation in Calindri, *op. cit.* (see note 5), 1781, page 370: "Not far from Brento is a place known as Ca' de Mazza which is well known for its excellent gunmakers who produce works in iron and steel, both chiselled and engraved; their locks and mounts are greatly appreciated and widely sought after . . . as far away as Rome." The most representative member of this family, whose known dated works range from 1740 to 1767[10], called himself simply "Il Negroni" and gave no Christian name. A lock, however, in the Museum of Saint-Etienne (Fig. 7) showing the same stylistic features as the work of "Il Negroni" is signed *F.co Negroni Brento* and dated 1734. Thus we may infer that the Christian name of "Il Negroni" was Francesco, a man who is recorded in documents of this period.

Fig. 4—Another fine late 17th-century work by one of the Ghini family of Loiano: a flintlock with two superimposed flashpans, the lower opening automatically upon the second snap of the cock to fire either the lower of two barrels or the rearmost of two superimposed loads; signed "Ales.ro [Alessandro] Ghini a Loiano". (Barroero Collection, Genova)

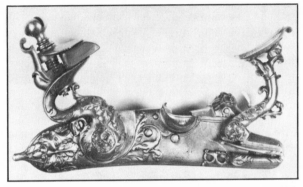

Fig. 5—One of a pair of *alla fiorentina* locks signed "Ghini, Loiano", well-chiselled in bas-relief of faces composed of leaves etc., animal-head scrolls, *putti*-faced screws. (Musée de l'Armée, Paris)

Other members of the Negroni family, all apparently working at the end of the 18th century, signed with their Christian names. Strangely enough, only one work is known for each of them at present. They were Pier Paolo (undated lock in the Aria Collection, Bologna), Angelo (undated gun, Stibbert Museum, Florence, No. 267), Carlo (a pair of pistols dated 1785, Bartolozzi Collection, Florence; Fig. 10), and Carlo Maria (a pair of pistols dated 1795

in the Stibbert Museum, Florence, No. 576/7; Figs. 12-14). As already observed, another family member, Giovan Battista Negroni, worked in Loiano, but his only known work is the lock mentioned in note 8. Modestly enough, another maker put the full name of his town, Brento, on his work, but added only his initials, P.F.N. We may infer that this stands for Pier Francesco Negroni; he was, in any case, the last of the artisans of Brento about whom anything is known: the two weapons signed by him are dated respectively 1815 and 1821 (Fig. 2). This leads to a cardinal observation about the firearms of Brento and, indeed, those of the Tosco-Emilian Apennines: the *alla fiorentina* or snaphaunce lock, which had become obsolete almost everywhere in Europe in the second half of the 17th century, was still employed in this area well into the 19th. This device, however, does not deserve the derision it usually receives from arms writers. Modern tests show that snaphaunces fired as rapidly and as reliably as flintlocks of comparable quality, and had the additional virtue of 100% positive safety if carried with the steel turned forward; they were, however, more fragile.

The name *Brento* on its own is found on many other firearms, but only a few of these are dated. Some, judging by their fine quality, might have come from pairs made by "Il Negroni" who, like many other gunmakers of the region, used to put his name on the lock of only one of a pair and the name *Brento* and the date on the other. Some examples seem to be the work of other members of the family or were made after "Il Negroni's" death. It seems that the form of the signatures cannot be of any help in attempting to classify them, as the comparison of some thirty examples shows considerable variety in the way of writing "Negroni" and "Brento" unrelated in either style or period to the single pieces. The suggestion that the use of a small letter "b" instead of the capital "B" indicated later production—both Carlo and Carlo Maria signed in this way—is not convincing.[11] One can only conclude that the task of signing the finished

Fig. 6—Typical upper-quality 18th-century Tuscan fowling piece, the snaphaunce lock chiseled in the conventional Apennine style shown in Fig. 7, the stock carved in scrolls inhabited by an angel-like trumpet-playing half-figure. Lock is signed and dated "Il Negroni, 1761"; barrel by C. Caltrani. (Collection of the late Joe Kindig, Jr., York, Pa.)

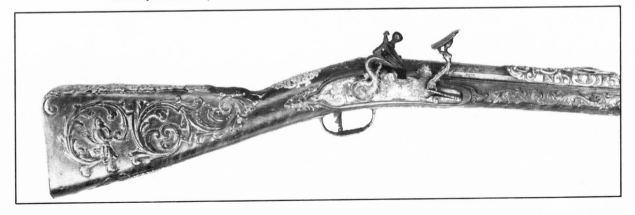

Fig. 7—Snaphaunce or *alla fiorentina* lock signed "F.co [Francesco] Negroni, Brento, 1734". Cfr. Fig. 9. (Musée d'Armes, St. Etienne)

work was left to an assistant or apprentice. This habit is quite different from that of the Acquafrescas, who signed the outside face of the lock-plate, always in script, sometimes very elegantly. It seems clear, anyhow, that Brento was the centre of all those villages of the Apennines which produced firearms.[12]

CASALECCHIO DI RENO—At the end of the 18th century at least two gunmakers lived in this town near Bologna, on the road to Florence. One is mentioned by Calindri as being "a pupil of those of Ca' de Mazza". In fact his name was Negroni and his work is identical to that of the best Brento products. Two of his locks are dated respectively 1794 and 1795 and bear the inscription *Il Negroni in Casalechio* (Fig. 25). A third piece, a gun dated 1792 (Tonolini Collection, Brescia) is signed *Brento in Casalecchio,* a puzzling oddity that can be explained by assuming that this craftsman, recently arrived in Casalecchio from Brento, for a time used the name of his home town to distinguish himself from his new fellow citizens; and indeed, in the archives of Casalecchio, Gen. Agostino Gaibi found documents concerning a certain Angelo Negroni, dead by October 1803: perhaps the Brentian *emigré* fashioner of the weapons in question.

The second Casalecchio gunmaker is known only by his initials, M.C.[13], which are inscribed on the lock of a pistol and followed by *Casalechio* and the date 1800. This furnishes another proof that in many cases the name of the place of manufacture—probably corresponding to some particular technicalities employed in the construction of its firearms—was more important to potential purchasers than that of the actual maker. There is anyway a considerable difference, both in quality and style, between the work of Negroni and that of the master M.C.

SABBIONE—Several places bear this name both in the Apennines and in the Po Valley, near Reggio Emilia, but most likely the one in which we are interested is that situated between Brento and Loiano. A gunmaker named Ottaviano Pozzi lived in Sabbione: several locks, either detached or still mounted in guns and pistols, bear his full name, but none of them is

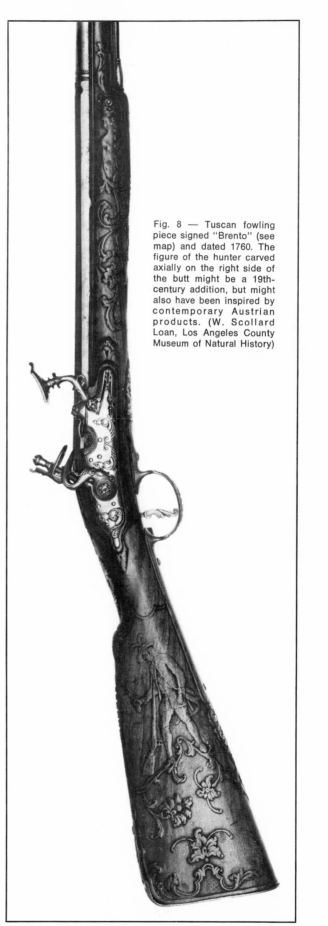

Fig. 8 — Tuscan fowling piece signed "Brento" (see map) and dated 1760. The figure of the hunter carved axially on the right side of the butt might be a 19th-century addition, but might also have been inspired by contemporary Austrian products. (W. Scollard Loan, Los Angeles County Museum of Natural History)

231

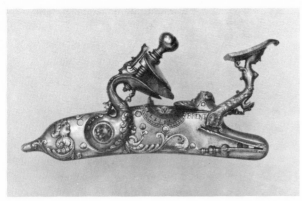

Fig. 9—Snaphaunce or *alla fiorentina* lock signed "Brento 1734". Cfr. Fig. 7. (Metropolitan Museum of Art, New York)

Fig. 10—Snaphaunce pistol lock, flat type, signed "Carlo Negroni in Brento 1785", not of the quality of those in Figs. 2 and 31, but amusing and imaginative. (Bartolozzi Collection, Florence)

Fig. 11—Detail of a lock signed "Brento". What is the curly object seemingly attached to the lady's chair? (Calvasina Collection, Milan)

dated. Their style is among the closest to that used by "Il Negroni", and Calindri does not mention this maker in 1781 we may infer that he lived and worked round about the middle of the century. His best work, a pistol in a private collection, Brussels, also shows in several details of the decoration, especially on the barrel and on the butt, the influence of the work of Acquafresca (Fig. 30).[14]

FILIGARE—This tiny village is on the road from Loiano to Florence. We know that some unnamed gunmakers lived there because the inscription *a Filigare* is found on at least two locks. One, converted to percussion, is now in the A. Bartocci Collection, Flor-

ence (see *Diana Armi,* December 1972, p. 31), and the other, *alla fiorentina,* is of the flat and engraved type (see below) mounted on a beautiful gun in the Joe Kindig Jr. Collection, York, Pa. The latter has a Pistoian barrel and its mounts and stock are decorated and carved in the typical Tosco-Emilian style. The butt plate is engraved *A.Z., Forli,* i.e., a man's initials and the name of a town not far from Ravenna, and the date 1791.

SUSINANA—A place not far from Firenzuola, in the center of the area under consideration. There is no evidence that gunmakers worked there, but the name Susinana is engraved on the inner side of the frizzen of a lock mounted on an unsigned pistol in the State Historical Museum, Moscow (No. 8993), showing all the typical features of the Tosco-Emilian production.

VERNIO—This village is not far from Filigare and is some 42 kilometres from Florence. The only evidence of gun production here is furnished by the signature *G. Albertacci Vernio* on the lock of a pistol in the Tonolini Collection in Brescia. It must be added, however, that, stylistically, this pistol does not belong to the group of firearms considered so far and shows strong Brescian influence. Its elongated form, a lock of true flintlock type and the presence of the signature on an external surface, all follow Brescian custom, together with the simply carved decoration of the stock.

GENERAL OBSERVATIONS

Before giving consideration to the main characteristics of Tosco-Emilian firearms, it would be well to emphasize that their makers produced principally locks (as already noted, almost exclusively snaphaunces), stocks and mounts; they did not usually make barrels but found it more expedient to import these from other sources. Barrels came from Brescia (Lazarino Cominazzo, Vincenzo Cominazzo, Domenico Bonomino, Pietro Moretta, Giovan Beretta, Bartolomeo Caltrani *et al.*). They were also obtained from France (Le Lorain) and Spain (Nicolas Bis, Pedro Esteva, Bustindui). The city of Pistoia, not far from Florence, which had been famous for its gun barrels since the first half of the 16th century, was also drawn upon.

Similar comments may be made on the stocks of these weapons. In the case of ordinary firearms, they were probably made by the lock- and mount-makers themselves, or else by local carpenters; but for better weapons, elaborate carving in typical patterns— scrolls, harpies, and acanthus leaves and mermaids on the fore-end—prove the presence of many very expert craftsmen. The existence of individual schools in particular centres is strongly indicated, but it appears ever more likely that stocks of the very best quality, espe-

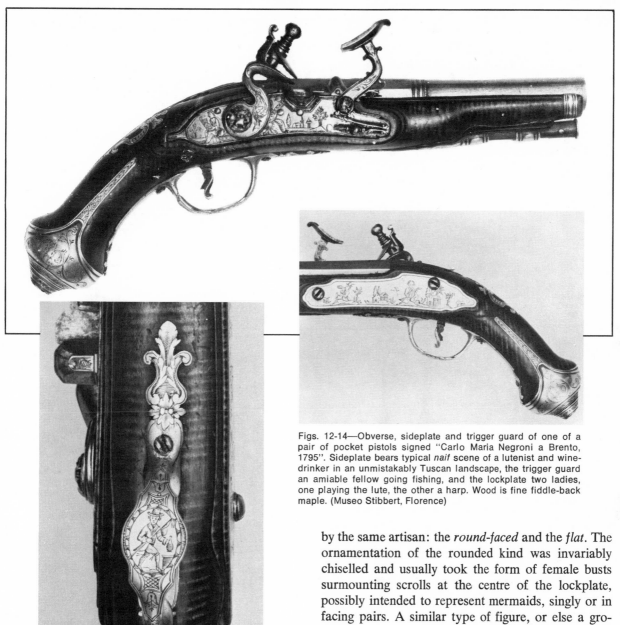

Figs. 12-14—Obverse, sideplate and trigger guard of one of a pair of pocket pistols signed "Carlo Maria Negroni a Brento, 1795". Sideplate bears typical *naif* scene of a lutenist and wine-drinker in an unmistakably Tuscan landscape, the trigger guard an amiable fellow going fishing, and the lockplate two ladies, one playing the lute, the other a harp. Wood is fine fiddle-back maple. (Museo Stibbert, Florence)

cially for long arms, were made mostly in Bologna. Research on the subject of Bolognese production has been carried out by Messrs. G. Cano and G. Simoni of Bologna but, as yet, their findings have not been published. A particular feature found on Tosco-Emilian stocks, but one which is not exclusive to them, consists of four thickenings on the borders of the lower part of the stock corresponding to the holes for the screws which hold lock- and side-plates together. This detail, originally perhaps functional, sometimes assumes a purely decorative aspect.[15]

Let us now look at the production of these gun-makers as a whole. There were two alternative types of *alla fiorentina* or snaphaunce locks, often produced by the same artisan: the *round-faced* and the *flat*. The ornamentation of the rounded kind was invariably chiselled and usually took the form of female busts surmounting scrolls at the centre of the lockplate, possibly intended to represent mermaids, singly or in facing pairs. A similar type of figure, or else a grotesque mask, can be found at the rear finial of the lock-plate (see various accompanying illustrations). The breast of the cock is chiselled to represent a bearded mask in profile, while the screw heads of both cock and battery are decorated with full frontal faces of *putti* or cherubs. The sliding flashpan cover is chiselled to represent a comic sphinx. The battery arms may be stylized flower stems, or harpies and grotesques intertwined. The most elaborate examples bear additional decoration in the form of chiselled masks, human heads or animal muzzles (e.g. Figs. 7, 25, etc.). Some observers of Italian firearms feel that the degree of changeover of the lockplate mask from purely abstract curlecews to realistic anthropomorphic faces may well be a chronological process, so that the very interesting pair of unsigned pistols in Figs. 15-20 could constitute examples of the Tosco-Emilian style at its earliest, free from Brescian domi-

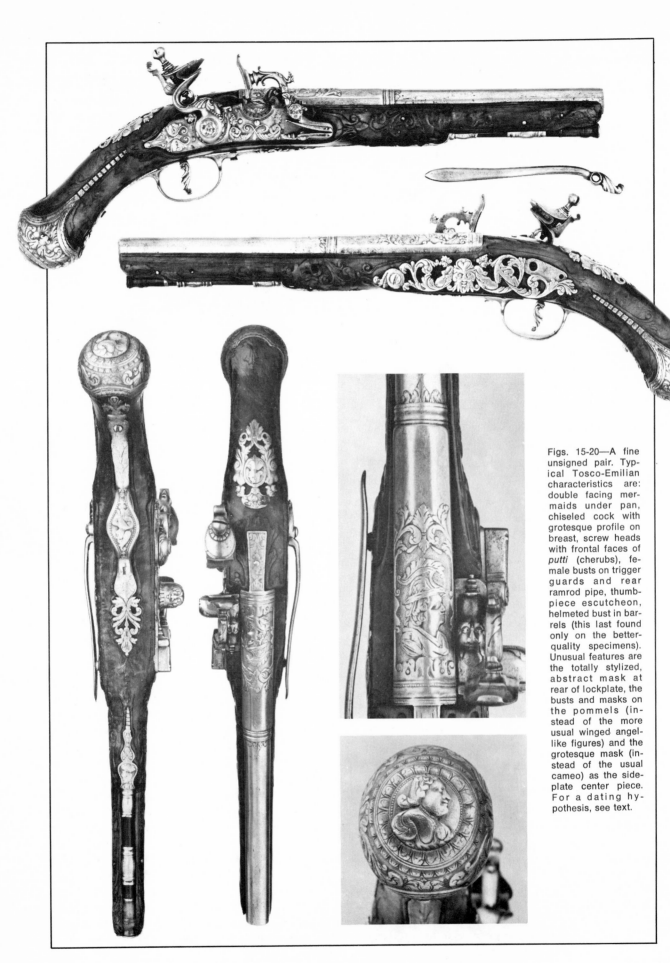

Figs. 15-20—A fine unsigned pair. Typical Tosco-Emilian characteristics are: double facing mermaids under pan, chiseled cock with grotesque profile on breast, screw heads with frontal faces of *putti* (cherubs), female busts on trigger guards and rear ramrod pipe, thumbpiece escutcheon, helmeted bust in barrels (this last found only on the better-quality specimens). Unusual features are the totally stylized, abstract mask at rear of lockplate, the busts and masks on the pommels (instead of the more usual winged angel-like figures) and the grotesque mask (instead of the usual cameo) as the sideplate center piece. For a dating hypothesis, see text.

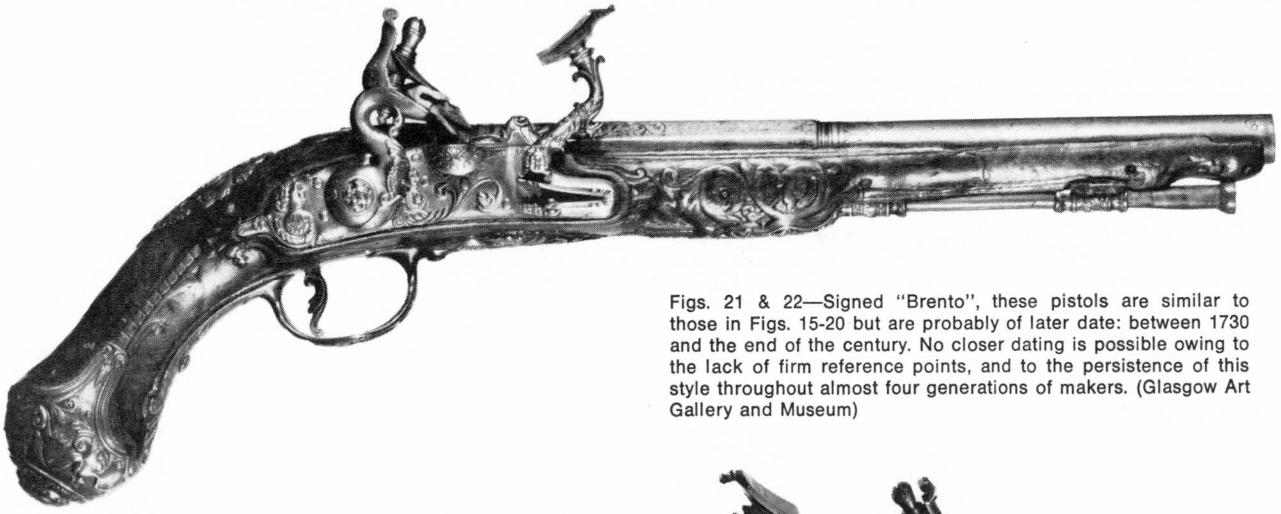

Figs. 21 & 22—Signed "Brento", these pistols are similar to those in Figs. 15-20 but are probably of later date: between 1730 and the end of the century. No closer dating is possible owing to the lack of firm reference points, and to the persistence of this style throughout almost four generations of makers. (Glasgow Art Gallery and Museum)

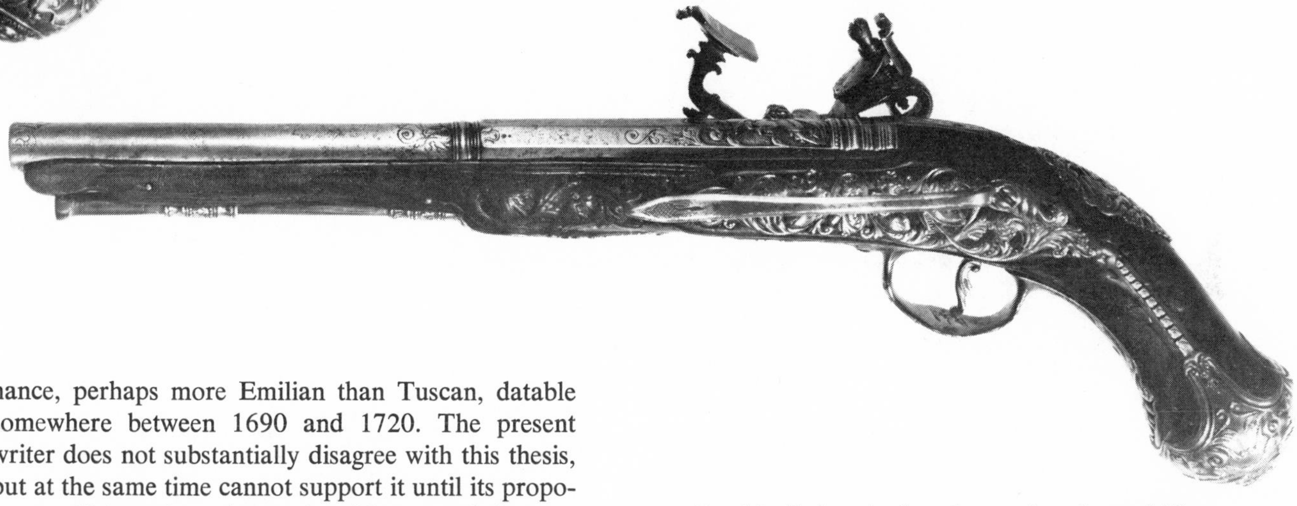

nance, perhaps more Emilian than Tuscan, datable somewhere between 1690 and 1720. The present writer does not substantially disagree with this thesis, but at the same time cannot support it until its proponents will have brought much evidence to their case.

Flat lock-plates, on the other hand, were always engraved. Only lock- and steel-screws are chiselled, always in *profile* busts (rather than the frontal cherub heads of the round-faced type locks.) The engraving of the lock-plate tends to favour scrolls, often ending in animal heads, but the most captivating work is the representation of figures, sometimes mythological or allegorical though in the majority of cases they are people dressed in contemporary costume busily playing musical instruments or indulging in the pursuit of everyday life against contemporary everyday backgrounds—little landscapes quite recognizably Tuscan with cypresses and old farm houses and, occasionally, interiors such as that of the tarot players on the Brento lock in Fig. 11.

There is no special style of mounts and side-plates that can be regularly associated with one or the other of the two different types of lock. Some side-plates are engraved and are *en suite* with the flat lock with which they are associated (Figs. 12-14), but generally they follow a design of their own, monotonously repeated, of open-work chiselled steel with scrolls ending in profile masks or animal heads and enclosing a grotesque mask or, sometimes, an oval medallion with profile bust, flanked by nude females (Fig. 28). The same busts are often found at the centre of the trigger-guard, though this may be engraved in accordance with the type of lock. Pistol pommels are

generally chiselled and often bear winged angel-like figures blowing upon trumpets, but on occasion they are engraved. Pierced escutcheons with profile portraits within a crowned cartouche are usually found on the backs of the grips of these firearms. The sear mechanism is often but not always the type known as a *box-sear* because of the rectangular box containing the tumbler (Fig. 31); it is a contrivance so far recorded only on Central Italian firearms and, in particular, on those made in the area under consideration.[16] In Italian it is a *scatto a cassetta*.

As for the sources of the various decorative patterns, they go back, in large part, to French seventeenth-century pattern-books. A local historian, G.B. Comelli, in the course of researches in Bargi at the end of last century, found the remains of two French pattern books, Johan Theodor de Bry's and Jean Berain's, in Acquafresca's home, which still exists.[17] One might add that the oldest known *dated* example of the chiselled round-faced lock is signed by Francesco Negroni and dated 1734, and is already a fully-developed example of its type. It seems to have been taken as a model by many other gunmakers and repeated, with trifling variations, until the end of the century. It is a type of decoration that includes, in a rich and harmonious whole, some motifs probably invented by Francesco Negroni and others taken from various earlier and contemporary sources, including Brescia. As for the engraved locks, their

235

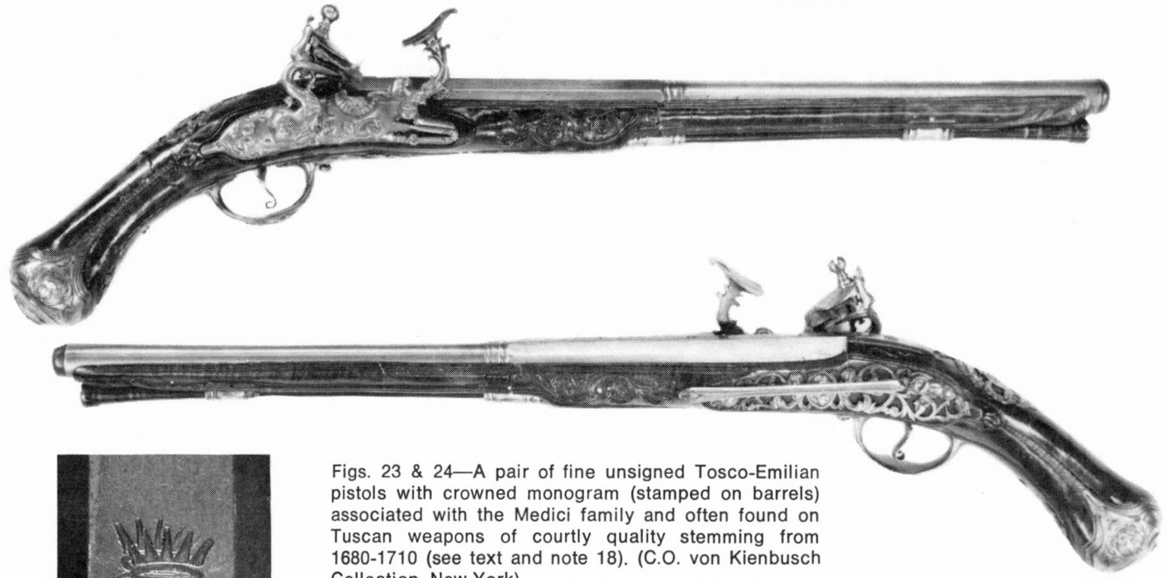

Figs. 23 & 24—A pair of fine unsigned Tosco-Emilian pistols with crowned monogram (stamped on barrels) associated with the Medici family and often found on Tuscan weapons of courtly quality stemming from 1680-1710 (see text and note 18). (C.O. von Kienbusch Collection, New York)

Fig. 25—Lock signed "Il Negroni in Casalechio 1795". The extreme elaborateness (note profile masks fore and aft on cock, on crest behind jaws, etc.) would seem to be a later characteristic. The intentionally humorous, satirical quality that marks almost all Tosco-Emilian production is here very plain, down to the long-nosed, mustachioed "sphinx" on the pan cover. (Armeria Reale, Turin)

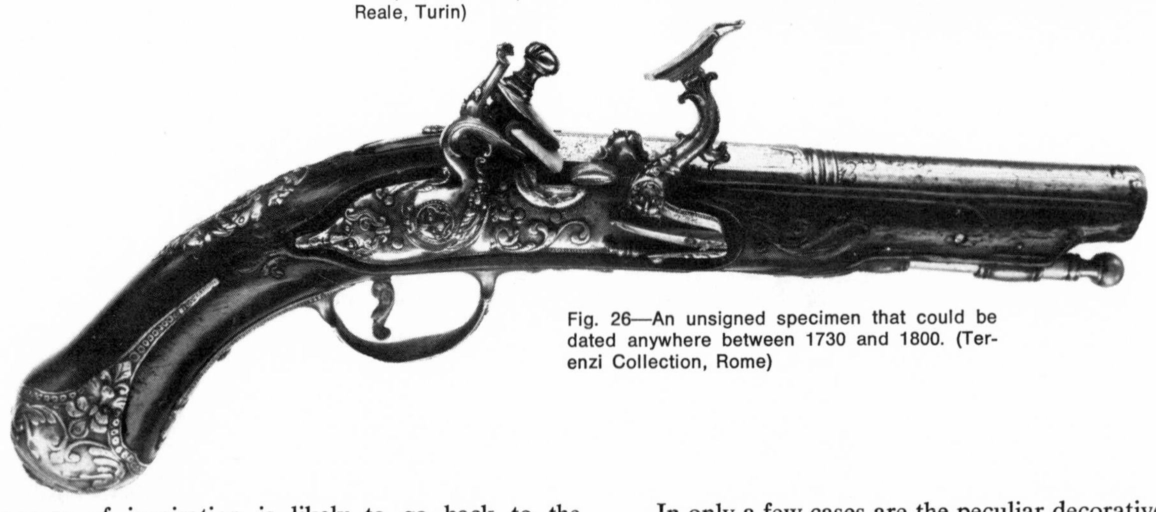

Fig. 26—An unsigned specimen that could be dated anywhere between 1730 and 1800. (Terenzi Collection, Rome)

source of inspiration is likely to go back to the French: quite manifest, especially in the best specimens, is the connection with the works of Thuraine and Piraube, and particularly with that of Simonin. Yet the Italian craftsmen lent a personal touch to their work, giving preference to contemporary subjects instead of classical and mythological ones, and investing these in a seemingly rustic but actually carefully studied *naiveté* which has great charm and often considerable artistic freshness, vitality and comicalness.

In only a few cases are the peculiar decorative features of the Tosco-Emilian style used on true flintlocks, as opposed to the standard *alla fiorentina* (snaphaunce) locks. One example is a pistol formerly in the Joe Kindig, Jr., Collection, York, Pa., the lock of which, signed *Brento,* has the typical engraved decoration of the flat locks mentioned above (Fig. 32); another, with a round-faced, chiseled lock-plate, bears the inscription *Il Sigre. Gio. Suz. F.F.,* that is, "Signor Giovanni Suz. [surely an abbreviation of the

Fig. 27—Fowling piece, the lock signed "Marco Antonio Corsini 1770". (Museo Stibbert, Florence)

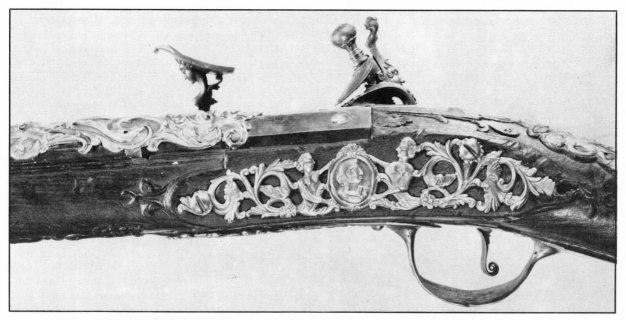

Fig. 28—Detail of a fowling piece, the lock signed "Brento", the barrel by Bustindui of Eibar, Spain.

Fig. 29 — Lock signed "P.F.N., 1821", engraved with one female figure apparently reading a newspaper, though in fact she is playing a harp, and another reclining amidst cannons, flags and drums —again in the typical satirical style. (S.V. Grancsay Collection, Brooklyn, New York)

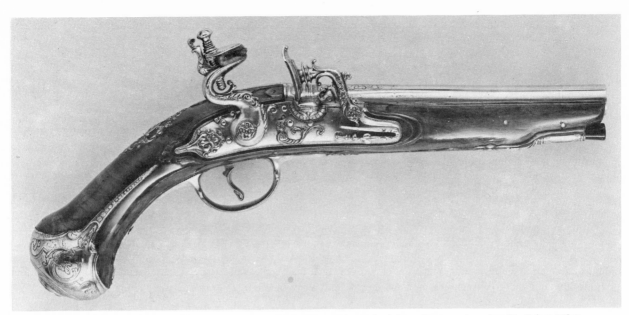

Fig. 30—Pistol by Ottaviano Pozzi of Sabbione shows influence of the work of Acquafresca on barrel and butt decoration. (Private collection, Brussels)

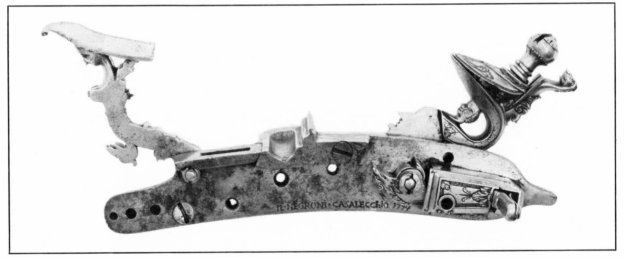

Fig. 31—Interior of a lock with a box sear, signed "Il Negroni, Casalechio 1794".

owner's surname] had this made for him (f[ece] f[are])" and the date 1805 (Fig. 33).

All the various features by now described allow us to attribute a considerable number of firearms to either the Tosco-Emilian area or to its close influence. These—some of them signed and others anonymous—are scattered in many private collections and Museums where, until recently, they were almost always labelled as Brescian and dated 17th century. Some of them are of excellent quality, and it is surprising that so very many have no signatures: for example, a pair of pistols—very elegant in both shape and decoration—in the C.O. von Kienbusch Collection, New York (Figs. 23-24), which only bear a crowned monogram on the barrels, probably referring to the Medici family[18], or the already-cited pair in Figs. 15-20.

In other cases, the presence of a signature provides evidence for the existence of craftsmen not otherwise known to us through documents or other references. Examples of these are Astolfi, Luigi Bani, Thomas Cursio, Il Ferretti, Il Giovani and Il Mazanti (e.g., Fig. 36). Others are known simply by their initials. Among the latter, a beautiful pair of pistols, illustrated in Jackson and Whitelaw, *European Hand Firearms* (London, 1923; Fig. 40), now in a private collection in Milan, bears the initials *G.G.*, which could stand for Giuseppe Guardiani of Anghiari, although the form differs from all the known signatures of this maker. In fact, exactly the same initials are to be found on other pistols (one in the F.E. Bivens Collection, Santa Monica, Calif., a pair in the W. Scollard Collection, Anaheim, Calif.), which, like those quoted above, show in the decoration a marked connection

238

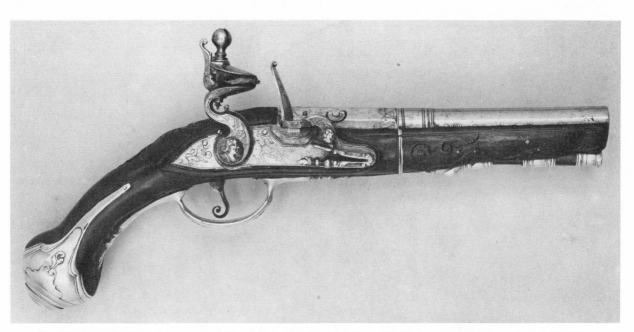

Fig. 32—A very handsome piece signed "Brento" showing French influence in the lock architecture, and unusually inter-esting. The figure engraved on the center of the lock plate is copied from Claude Simonin's pattern book, published in 1685, i.e. about a century earlier. The rifled barrel is of the turn-off type (unscrews with forward half of forestock), perhaps con-verted from normal muzzleloader. Datable 1760-1790. (Ex collection of the late Joe Kindig, Jr., York, Pa.)

Fig. 33—Lock signed "Il sig.re Gio. Suz. F.F. 1805" ("Signor Giorgio Suz. [abbrevi-ation of surname] F. [ece] F. [are]", i.e. "Mr. George Suz. ? ordered this made".) By this late date, the humor of the usual cartoon-like figures has grown a bit weary, and the quality of chiseling as well as the archaic construction leaves much to be desired; but the study value of this piece is high. (M.R. Forman Collection, Birming-ham, England)

with the works of Negroni, but bear also some fea-tures which are typical of the works produced by the members of the Zanotti family, active at the end of the 18th century in Lugo near Bologna, out of the area under consideration but very close to it. We might conclude that this unknown "Master G.G." can be reasonably listed among the Tosco-Emilian gun-makers.

On the other hand, there is no evidence that these gunmakers *originated* in the mountainous country which lies between Florence and Bologna. Indeed, the Tosco-Emilian styles of decoration and construc-tion were lavishly applied in one very important cen-ter outside this area: in Anghiari, not far from Arezzo.[19] Then, a gunmaker named *Marco Antonio Corsini,* who made what conforms to Tosco-Emilian criteria, lived in a place called Massa. There are at least a dozen places of this name scattered across Cen-tral and Southern Italy, but none in the area under consideration. Most likely the one in question is a village not far from Pistoia, where a Corsini family still lives today. Two weapons signed Marco Antonio Corsini are dated respectively 1770 and 1780 and are done in both main types of Tosco-Emilian decoration, the chiselled and the engraved (Figs. 27 and 35).

Returning to the gunmakers known to us only by their initials, it is interesting to note that some of their works are dated, as though their authors had given more importance to the chronological statement than to the specification of the authorship. Two pistols once in the Pyron Collection (Sale Catalogue, Nos. 648 and 744) have snaphaunce locks signed respec-tively *F.D. 1760* and *C.B. 1779;* they are most prob-ably Central Italian but there is insufficient evidence

239

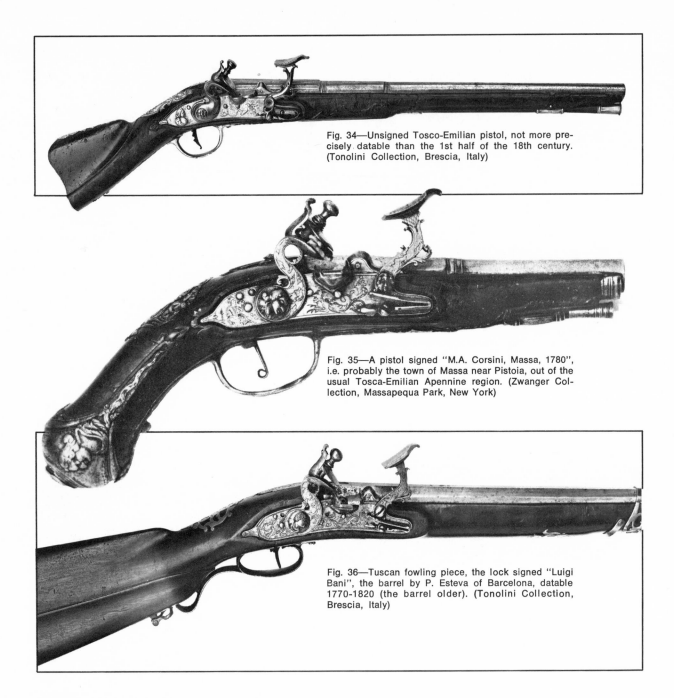

Fig. 34—Unsigned Tosco-Emilian pistol, not more precisely datable than the 1st half of the 18th century. (Tonolini Collection, Brescia, Italy)

Fig. 35—A pistol signed "M.A. Corsini, Massa, 1780", i.e. probably the town of Massa near Pistoia, out of the usual Tosca-Emilian Apennine region. (Zwanger Collection, Massapequa Park, New York)

Fig. 36—Tuscan fowling piece, the lock signed "Luigi Bani", the barrel by P. Esteva of Barcelona, datable 1770-1820 (the barrel older). (Tonolini Collection, Brescia, Italy)

to classify them as Tosco-Emilian. A flat lock in Keith Neal's Collection (Warminster, Wilts., England) is, on the contrary, so similar to the works of the late members of the Negroni family that it can be reasonably considered as coming from the Brento area; it bears the initials *P. M.* and the very advanced date 1828. Finally, a gunmaker who signs with the initials *F. A.* seems to have been the last to produce snaphaunce locks assignable to the Tosco-Emilian group; Fig. 37 is one example of his work, and another is a lock fitted to a pistol in the Tonolini Collection, Brescia, and dated 1845.

It is natural that Tosco-Emilian work, which had been widely popular and much appreciated for a long time and which was still being produced during the second quarter of the 19th century, had to adapt to the increasing popularity of the newly-developed percussion system. In some cases, the same gunmakers who had so far produced *alla fiorentina* locks turned to the new system and altered their traditional forms and patterns in consequence of an attempt to produce new and harmonious types of lock; this was true of a proportion of the makers in Anghiari. But in most cases, the change consisted simply of a conversion from snaphaunce locks to percussion: the cock was removed but the original screw was kept and the pan cover and steel were removed to make room for the nipple (e.g., Fig. 38).

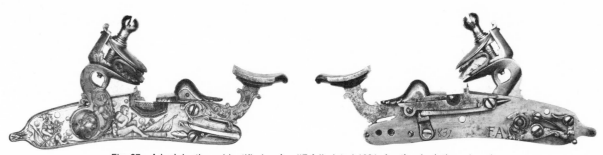

Fig. 37—A lock by the unidentified maker "F.A.", dated 1831. Another lock thus signed is dated 1845—"F.A." seems to have been the world's last snaphaunce maker. (S.V. Grancsay Collection, Brooklyn, New York)

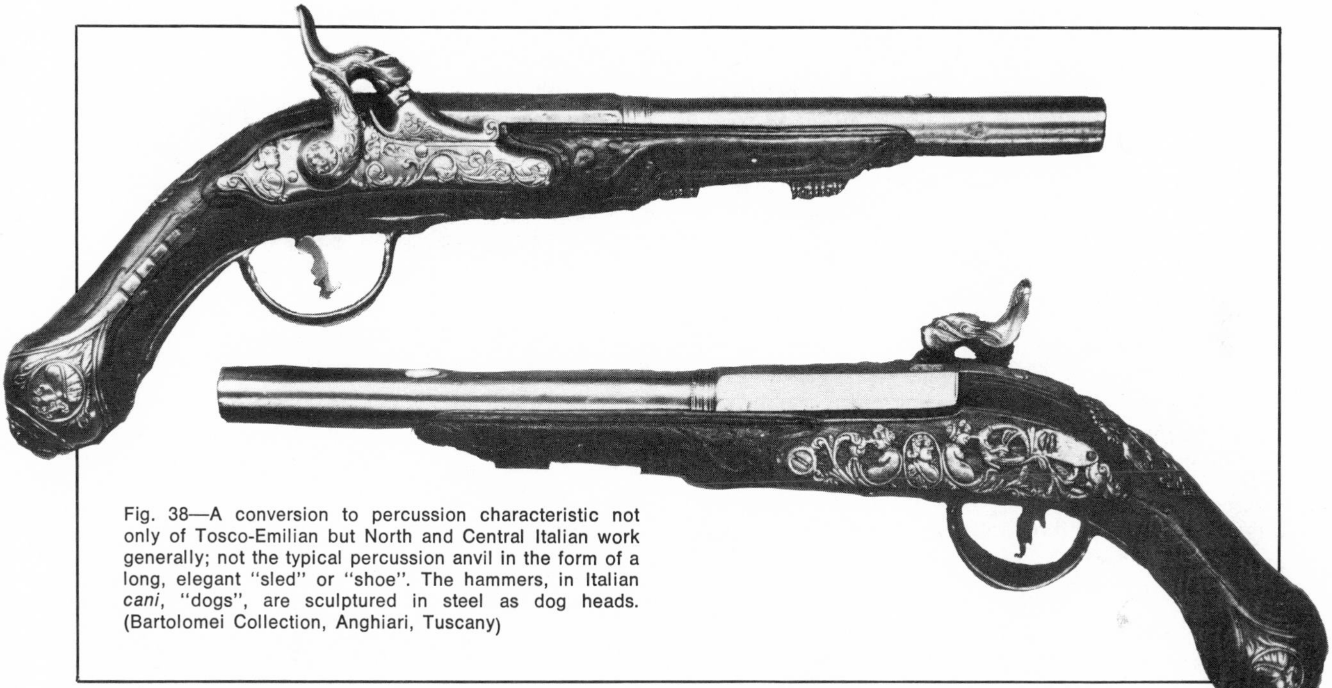

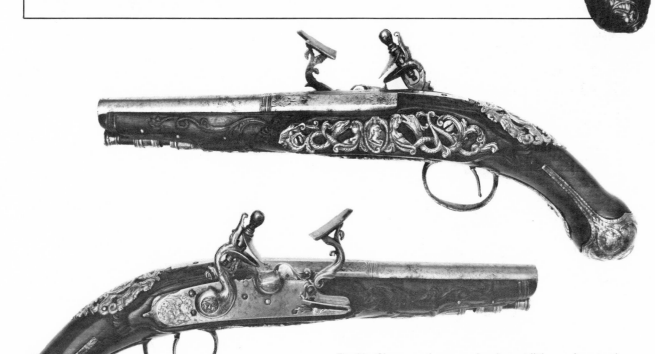

Fig. 38—A conversion to percussion characteristic not only of Tosco-Emilian but North and Central Italian work generally; not the typical percussion anvil in the form of a long, elegant "sled" or "shoe". The hammers, in Italian *cani*, "dogs", are sculptured in steel as dog heads. (Bartolomei Collection, Anghiari, Tuscany)

Fig. 39—Obverse and reverse of a pleasant little snaphaunce pistol signed "Aless.ro Ghini/Loiano;" first half of 18th century. The folksy lampooning of classical designs in the chiseled iron furniture, particularly in the escutcheon plate (not well discernible in the side views), is unusually vigorous and appealing. (Canepari Collection, San Donato Milanese, Italy)

EPILOGUE

In closing, then, this brief outline, let us summarize some conclusions. The production of firearms in the 18th century in the area of the Tosco-Emilian Apennines, together with that of the neighbouring town of Anghiari, assumed a strong individual character which not only differentiate it from that of other parts of Tuscany, but influenced the gunmakers of the surrounding regions of Central Italy (Emilia, Marche, Umbria). Some distinctions may be made of traits within this production. Two families of gunmakers seem to have adopted a comparatively independent style in the execution of their works: the Acquafresca of Bargi—not counting the superlative works of Matteo Acquafresca (1651-1738), which are among the finest weapons ever produced anywhere, anytime—and the Ghini of Loiano. The remaining production was wrought by other families of clever craftsmen, principally by the members of the Negroni family, scattered through the several little centres of this area (Brento, Sabbione, Casalecchio, Filigare) and by a certain number of independent gunmakers (Astolfi, Bani, Mazanti, etc.) whose dwelling places we do not know, at times even the men themselves being known only by their initials.

The locks were almost invariably snaphaunces *(alla fiorentina),* used on both longarms and pistols. A number of decorative and technical features clearly indicate Tosco-Emilian provenance and allow correct classification of many arms which until just a few years ago were generally considered Brescian, or, at best, "Central Italian" in a vague, sweeping notion.

Still, several problems are not yet solved. For instance, the various sources of ornamental motifs—French pattern books, Brescian models, local traditions and personal inventiveness—have not yet been exactly clarified. Nor do we know when, where and by whom were first carried out the two fundamental decorative schemes which were to become standardised for many decades with but slight variations in the interchangeable details: on round, chiselled locks, the more or less stylized masks at the rear end of the lockplate, the single or double-facing mermaids on the center of the lockplate, the battery arms in form of harpies or flower stems; and on flat, engraved locks, the interior or landscape scenes inhabited by a lady playing a harp, a gentleman playing a lute, a warrior fighting a lion or a dragon, and so on. There were hardly any changes in style or execution, only a timid, unpretentious mirroring of the general evolution of tastes in fourteen or fifteen decades from baroque to post-Empire neoclassicism. The decorative scheme for arms with round-faced, chiselled locks was apparently already settled by the 1730's and lasted till the end of the century (a great help in classification is the Tosco-Emilian custom of dating works—unlike, for instance, in Brescia). Flat locks engraved with scenes and figures, mostly in contemporary dress, though probably originating in some works of Matteo Acquafresca, apparently congealed in their conventions much later, not before the 1750's as far as we know, but then lasted well into the 19th century.

The continuation of research, the study of new specimens coming to light and the possible discovery of documents will help us to increase our knowledge of this interesting sector of arms history.

NOTES

1. M. Terenzi, Catalogue of the *Mostra dell Armi da Fuoco Anghiaresi e dell'Appennino Tosco-Emiliano,* Palazzo Taglieschi, Anghiari (Arezzo), 1968.
2. One of these was stolen in 1971 and has not been recovered.
3. L.G. Boccia, "Gli Acquafresca di Bargi", *Physis,* IX, Florence, 1967, pp. 91-160.
4. Arne Hoff, *Feuerwaffen,* Brunswick, 1969, Vol. II, p. 288, suggests that the maker of these guns was Sebastiano (1619-1692), Matteo's father.
5. S. Calindri, in his *Dizionario coregrafico, georgico ecc . . . degli Stati Pontifici,* I, 1781, p. 30, states "Bargi: for a long time this place has been famous for locks and mounts of steel, chiselled and engraved, produced by two expert gunmakers who live there." Also, in a diary kept by Pietro Antonio (1732-1809), grandson of the brother of Matteo Acquafresca, are noted the sales of complete firearms or, more often, of locks. The earliest date is 1752 and the latest 1800: see Boccia, *op. cit.,* p. 151.
6. Among the three Ghini families recorded by the census of 1632, the most important is that of Alessandro. He was, perhaps, the grandfather of the gunmaker of the same name working in the 18th century. Among the descendants of Alessandro there appears a Claudio mentioned in 1725.
7. One is in the Marzoli Museum, Brescia, No. 111, and another, probably forming a pair with it, was sold at auction in the Galerie Fischer, Lucerne, Switzerland, on 19th June, 1967, Lot 105. A third pistol which is quite similar to these two appeared at a Christie's Sale, London, on April 1st, 1969, Lot 116.
8. A lock signed *Giovan Battista Negroni di Loiano* is in the Terenzi Collection, Rome; see *Mostra* (note 1, above), No. 94. See also N. di Carpegna, "Armi da Fuoco dell'Italia Centrale", *Zeischrift für Waffen und Kostümkunde,* 1962, p. 123, Fig. 5.
9. The Negroni family appears in the Census of Brento from 1725. A Francesco Negroni is mentioned in 1750. He died before 1775 when two of his sons, Giuseppe and Antonio, appear to have been the proprietors of the house known locally as the *Ca' de' Mazza* ("the Mazzas' house," after the previous owners). No documents are available after that year.

"Negroni" is a North Italian name and there is documentary evidence that a Negroni family was active in the field of arms production and trade in Brescia in the 16th and 17th centuries. I owe this information to General A. Gaibi. It is possible that some members of this family moved South at the beginning of the 18th century and settled in a place for which they retained the name of the previous owners.

10. A pair of pistols, ex-Renwick Collection, Tucson, Ariz., sold at Sotheby's Sale of 17th July, 1972, Lot 29, has the following inscription on its locks: *Il Negroni Brento/Fecit l'Anno 1740*. In the Joe Kindig Jr. Collection, York, Pa., there is a gun with the barrel signed *B. Caltrani*, the lock of which is signed *Il Negroni 1761* (Fig. 6). In the Odescalchi Collection in Rome is a pistol, No. 89, signed *Il Negroni 1767*. The following undated pieces are known (all pairs of pistols): Brescia, Marzoli Museum, Nos. 209 & 264; Florence, Stibbert Museum, Nos. 754 & 756; Paris, de Lallemant de Liocourt Collection (pointed out to me by Col. Jacques Wemaere); Windsor Castle, Nos. 498/9; Sotheby's Sale of 18th July, 1966, Lot 202. All are signed *Il Negroni* on one lock and *Brento* on the other. One single pistol, signed *Il Negroni* near the pan, is in the R.W. MacWillie Collection, Lakewood, Calif.

11. This has led to some misinterpretation: see for example, the catalogue of the Loan Exhibition held in the Metropolitan Museum of Art, New York, in 1931, No. 428, where the name *Brento* is given as *Buenio* from the way in which it was written. In other cases—Marzoli Museum, Brescia, pistols by "Il Negroni" already mentioned; W. Scollard Collection, Anaheim, Calif., pistol (Terenzi, *Mostra*, No. 105)—the word *Brento* is written with the letter "m" replacing the letter "n" and the letter "r" has a peculiar form.

12. Other known works signed Brento which are not illustrated or mentioned elsewhere in this article are: Beckenham, Kent, England, P.A. Bedford Collection, a pistol; Brussels, private collection, a pistol; Burlington, Ontario, R.E. Egles Collection, a pistol; Florence, Stibbert Museum, No. 2934, a lock; Genoa, M. Barroere Serena Collection, a lock; London, Tower of London Armouries, No. XII, 1374, a lock; D.S.H. Collection, a pistol; New York, Metropolitan Museum of Art, No. 14.25.-1404.a,b, a pair of pistols, the barrels of which were made in Pistoia; Orangeville, Ontario, J.J. Wardlaw Collection, a pistol; Rome, S.L. Melandri Collection, a lock which, oddly, has the date 1755 inscribed on the inner edge of the pan, so that it can be seen only when the lock is dismantled; Turin, Royal Armoury, No. M.32, a gun, the barrel attributed to Manuel Deop of Ripoll, and the butt bearing the date 1785 and the signature of the Bolognese stockmaker Giuseppe Riccardi; Rothschild Collection, Waddesdon Manor, England, a pair of pistols, the barrels by *Lazarino Cominazzo* (information from Claude Blair); York, Pa., Joe Kindig, Jr., Collection, two pistols.

13. And not A.C., as stated in the Catalogue of the Peyron Collection to which it once belonged (No. 450). This pistol is now in the Joe Kindig, Jr., Collection, York, Pa.

14. Works by Ottaviano Pozzi include: Stibbert Museum, Florence, No. 753, a pistol, the barrel of which is inscribed *Fran.co M.a Bagnara feci*[*t*] and the lock *Il Pozzi Sabione* (Gaibi, *Armi da Fuoco Portatili Italiane*, 2nd Ed., Milan, 1968, Fig. 589; Terenzi, *Mostra*, No. 194) and No. 2939, a lock (Gaibi, *op. cit.*, Fig. 276a and Terenzi, *Mostra*, No. 195). Munich, Bayer. Nationalmuseum, W. 2664, a lock. Metropolitan Museum of Art, New York, No. 52.-208, 2/3 a pair of pistols, the barrels with the marks of Gardone, the lock inscribed *Ottaviano Pozzi Sabbione* (B. Dean, *The Collection of . . . R. Stuyvesant*, New York, 1914, No. 188, and Gaibi, *op. cit.*, Fig. 587 and caption 588). See also the Sale Catalogue of Salle Drouot, Paris, of 27th February, 1968: Lot 80, a pair of pistols with barrels by P. Pisinardo and Lot 81, a gun. A lock, once in the Peyron Collection in Florence and now in the Scollard Collection in Anaheim, Calif., is signed *A Sabione*.

15. See *Zeitschrift für Waffen und Kostümkunde*, 1962, p. 127, Fig. 13.

16. The earliest datable specimen containing a box-sear is a detached lock in the Keith Neal Collection, Warminster, Wilts., England, signed by Sebastiano Acquafresca (1619-1692). A pistol in the Tonolini Collection, Brescia, has a lock with the same contrivance, signed with the initials G.B.S. and dated 1715. Earlier examples may exist; all would have been produced in Central Italy.

17. Boccia, *op. cit.* (See note 3, above).

18. The question of the identification of this monogram has been dealt with by L. Boccia in his article in *Physis*, p. 115. See also Boccia's *Nove Secoli di Armi da Caccia*, p. 107 and N. di Carpegna, *Armi da Fuoco*, p. 110 (see below, note 20b). Boccia suggests that the monogram is composed of the letters *M* and *FF* and refers to Ferdinando de'Medici the son of Cosimo III (1663-1713). In fact, in some cases, but not as a rule, the horizontal bar of the letter which is supposed to be *A* is interrupted. What can be said is that all the firearms bearing this monogram, and about thirty have been noted so far, appear to be of Tuscan manufacture and date from between 1680 and 1720.

19. See the exhaustive and excellent volume by Marcello Terenzi, *Gli Armaioli Anghiaresi* ("The Gunmakers of Anghiari"), Rome, 1972.

20. Some works on firearms by N. di Carpegna, other than the Odescalchi Catalogue:

 (a) "La Collezione d'Armi Odescalchi", *in Zeitschrift für Waffen und Kostümkunde*, 1961, pp. 63-71.

 (b) "Armi da Fuoco dell'Italia Centrale", in *Zeitschrift für Waffen und Kostümkunde*, 1962, pp. 120-128.

 (c) *Armi Antiche dal sec. IX al XVIII, già Collezione Odescalchi*, Catalogue of the Exhibition, Rome, 1969.

 (d) *Antiche Armi dal Museo Civico L.Marzoli* (in collaboration with Francesco Rossi), Catalogue of the Exhibition, Brescia, 1969.

 (e) "Un Elenco di Armi da Fuoco del 1747", *Armi Antiche*, 1970, pp. 81-92.

 (f) "Notes on Central Italian Firearms of the 18th Century", in *The Journal of the Arms and Armour Society*, London, June 1971, pp. 17-48 (the second part now [May 1973] being readied for the press).

 (g) In preparation, with General Agostino Gaibi and Francesco Rossi: *Storia delle Armi da Fuoco Bresciane* ("A History of Brescian Firearms").

The First British Naval Uniforms

Text and drawings by
LAWRENCE KEEBLE

Lawrence Keeble is a frequent contributor to Tradition *Magazine, the well-known British monthly journal dedicated to military dress history. It may come as a surprise to many readers that the British Navy officer had no uniform before 1748 (the seaman not until 1857!). Here is a summary of how officers' dress began.*

In 1740, the composer Thomas Arne wrote an air for the play *Alfred* by James Thomson, the refrain of which went:
Rule, Britannia Britannia, rule the waves!
Britons never never shall be slaves!
For the next two hundred years this simplicism was to work an evocative spell in all British and some non-British hearts; almost at once it became a species of Sacred Command, with many able and willing executants in the Sea Service. But it was not until 1745 that the Officers' Club, formed to advance its sea-going members' interests, petitioned George II to grant them what other navies already possessed: the privilege of distinctive dress. The King, legend and tradition will have it, was asked to choose between variations of blue and red, and chose blue with white facings after a glimpse of the Duchess of Bedford attired for riding in a habit of these colours. Whatever its motivations, the decision was momentous: the time was to come when every maritime nation would dress its navy in attire based on it, i.e. fundamentally on the British style and colours.

In the eighteenth century, Britain's navy was commanded by two kinds of professional sea officers: first, those responsible for maintaining a ship to a proper standard of performance, rig, equipment, weapons and stores, meaning the master, boatswain, gunner, carpenter, sail-maker, master-at-arms, cook, purser, surgeon and chaplain (the last three were not "executive" but "civilian", though all were appointed on a permanent footing by Warrant from the Admiralty). Neither they nor their subordinates were to be given distinctive dress until much later (the seamen-ratings not officially until 1857). The second kind was the "military" fighting officer, whose duty was to direct the ship and her company as a weapon of war.

The ranks of the Royal Navy were: three Flag-Officers—Admiral, Vice Admiral and Rear Admiral; Captain (over three years post), Captain (under three years post); Master-and-Commander (not to be confused with warrant rank "Master"); and Lieutenant. Although holding no commission, Midshipmen were included in the Dress Order of 1748 and all thereafter.

But rank was not the same as "post". In all ships-of-the-line (vessels of 60 to 100 guns, fit to lie in the line of battle) and in frigates (smaller ships of 30 to 40 guns employed for scouting and communication), the *post* of commanding officer was filled by a man who held the title of "Captain, R.N." but this officer was not necessarily a Captain, R.N. by *rank* merely because he was "*the* captain" of a ship; officers of lower rank could be appointed to command certain types of ships. Moreover, a King's Commission authorised its holder to occupy one particular *post* and no other: the "general Commission" to hold *rank* as an Officer of the Royal Navy came much later, in 1860. Many vessels—sloops, bomb-ketches, cutters and the like—were too small for the services of a ranking Captain. In large ships, sailing and navigation was the master's duty, but he was not carried in small vessels. The rank "Master-and-Commander", intermediate between Captain and Lieutenant, was created for certain Commission officers skilled in navigation, to qualify them for these lesser commands. At a later date, when warrant masters were sent into small ships, the cumbersome rank-name was shortened to "Commander".

The Lieutenant, literally, was the captain's deputy, but the increasing size of ships and crews and the complexity of their organization required the services of ever more lieutenants. The senior Lieutenant was Second-in-Command—"first" of a group, with lower grades of Second, Third and so on: but these were distinctions of *post* in the ship, not of rank in the Navy. A Lieutenant could be promoted to Captain without passing through Commander's rank and, like the latter, could also assume command of small vessels. Midshipmen, traditionally youths drawn from all the middle classes, had become what they were to remain: officer-trainees, usually protégés of Captains or Admirals. But by the order of 1748, "Persons acting as Midshipmen should likewise have a uniform cloathing in order to distinguish their Class to be in the Rank of Gentlemen."

The Flag-Officer group subdivided into nine

Fig. 1—Captain (over three years' post).

stages of seniority. The Dutch wars of the late seventeenth century had gathered English sea forces into one huge fleet in home waters, tactically disposed in three squadrons: the Centre (red ensigns), Van (white ensigns), Rear (blue ensigns)—the Chief Command being exercised from the Centre, or Red Squadron. Next in command was the Admiral of the White, third the Admiral of the Blue. Each Squadron was a fleet in itself, with centre, van and rear divisions in charge respectively of Admiral, Vice, and Rear-Admiral. Hence nine Flag-Officers were present, their status defined by their tactical positions, a Vice-Admiral of the White being senior to his colleague of the Blue. There was no post called "Admiral of the Red"—the officer commanding the Centre was also the "Admiral of the Fleet".

By the first quarter of the eighteenth century, fleets had become smaller and more numerous, acting separately over wider areas; but the Flag List still allowed for only nine Admirals, in the former sense of appointments to one fleet (although more Captains were being promoted in rank). By this association of rank with non-existent posts, and the concept of senority which this implied, a Rear-Admiral of the Blue might have to spend the next

Fig. 2—Midshipman's all-purpose coat. Collars of 1748, 1758, 1767.

and the universal three-cornered hat. Military coats were sometimes worn, and buff or matching waistcoats and breeches. This garb in no way differed from that of all middle and upper-class European males, being an evolved form—shorter and fuller skirted—of the late seventeenth-century "Persian Vest." Its military undress version had an embryonic collar and wide lapels for buttoning over the chest if desired (see Fig. 1). The under or "waist" coat was sleeved but cuffless, with a hemline at mid-thigh.

Nothing could more extravagantly epitomise the freedom enjoyed in dress than Hogarth's celebrated picture at Greenwich of Captain Lord George Graham in his cabin (painted about 1754). His lordship wears a grey coat lined blue, grey breeches, and white waistcoat with very wide gold lace. A red cloak edged with thick grey fur lies nonchalantly about his shoulders and, in the absence of his wig—temporarily consigned for safe-keeping to the head of his pet dog—he sports a blue velvet cap, and smokes a long pipe.

Excepting Midshipmen, every officer was now to supply himself with two uniforms: a dress "sute" for formal wear, and a "frock" for more ordinary occasions, with appropriate waistcoats. The Order said nothing about breeches, hats, or swords. Sealed patterns of the coats were lodged at the London office and Plymouth Dockyard, for officers' guidance, but no patterns were sent to ships abroad, nor can a verbal description be traced. A covering letter instructed Commanders to follow the pattern suit for junior Captains "as it varies only in the manner of the lacing", but no details were vouchsafed, nor was any pattern for the "frock" for this rank, so far as we know. By happy chance, the two main sources of our knowledge are complementary. The Dockyard patterns for Midshipmen and Lieutenants, with waistcoats for both grades of Captain, are now in

thirty years of his life climbing the nine rank-steps of the List. The farce finally ended in 1864, when the three-colour system of squadronal seniority was abandoned, but in 1815 there were two hundred and twenty Flag-Officers in the Royal Navy!

Lastly, the "Commodore". This was a post, never a rank. When two or more ships acted in concert without benefit of a flag officer, the senior Captain could be appointed Commodore to underline his authority. This entitled him to fly a penant at his masthead, but not to wear a distinctive dress: he reverted to normal status when his special duty was over.

* * *

By an Order dated April 13th, 1748, the Admiralty announced that henceforth a "uniform cloathing" was to be worn by flag officers, Captains, Commanders, Lieutenants and Midshipmen of His Majesty's Navy. Before this date, sea-officers had pleased themselves about the colour and cut of their clothes: portraits and literary references suggest a preference for red, grey, blue, or brown, with gold or silver lace

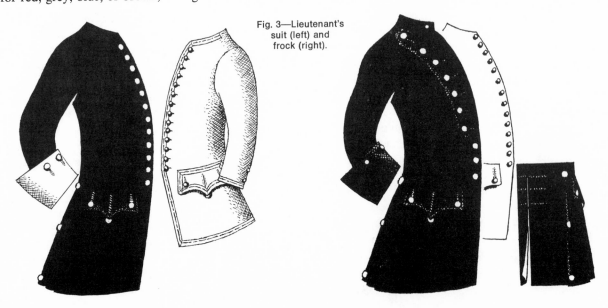

Fig. 3—Lieutenant's suit (left) and frock (right).

246

the Museum at Greenwich. A letter to London in 1780 reports the theft of the Captains' and flag-officers' patterns, but an Admiral's dress coat in the Scottish United Services Museum confirms contemporary paintings. With these and with the many portraits of Captains, our information would be complete but for the back and pocket lacing on flag-officers' uniforms, the Captains' back lacing on both uniforms, and the Commanders' dress.

The pattern coats are of fairly dark blue cloth, lined white. Portraits show a lighter blue, perhaps as a result of colour-loss in the exposed pigments or, no less plausible, of uncleanable penetrations of atmospheric soot in the surviving cloth specimens. This "navy blue" was to become darker still, a near black. The waistcoats, now yellowed with age, were originally white kerseymere. The lace was gold throughout and came in two patterns; flag-officers' were gold-embroidered. The frock was versatile, fitted inside the front edges with a buttoned flap for closing together, and when extra protection was sought, the lapels could be crossed over the chest. Buttons on suits other than flag-officers', and including the Midshipman's one-purpose coat, were convex, made of wood faced with brass, and quite plain (Figs. 12 a, b). Frocks of Captains and lesser ranks had slightly convex solid brass buttons, with an incised Tudor rose design (Fig. 12c), but for flag-officers the ornament was a small floral device within a circle, enclosed by an octagonal border figured with a centre row of small beads (Fig. 7). Suit buttons for flag-officers appear to be similar. A smaller size of each button was used on waistcoats and, in the case of the frocks, on collars.

The following notes on the accompanying drawings may be useful to the reader:

MIDSHIPMAN—All-purpose uniform (Fig. 2): Blue coat, single-breasted; 12 buttons front, black stitched holes; wide turnback of white lining at neck, small button right for turning-up and closing over throat. (On the pattern, this turnback is detached from the neckline in the front segment, either from intention or age.) Small cuffs turned-up white, with blue sash (lined white on reverse) with three buttons and black holes.

Pocket-flaps of this and both lieutenants' coats are identical. Outer buttons are practical; the middle one is below the point, its hole a dummy. Side-skirts divide from the tail in a plait, the tail is divided up the centre. The back has six buttons: one at the top of each plait, two on the outer edge of each half of the tail for fastening to the side-skirt. Of these the lowermost is at the hem, the second slightly higher than midway. Three rows of plain black button-hole stitching traverse the upper 5 in. of the tail, either side of the slit. Skirts and tail are amply folded at

Fig. 4—Captain's (over three years) frock (top) and suit (bottom). Three center inserts show modifications for under three years' post.

the plaits; this tailoring was, of course, standard for most coats of the time.

LIEUTENANT—Undress Frock (Fig. 3): Blue coat; short lapels faced blue, tops wide and triangle-pointed, tapering to waist, seven buttons aside with black holes (top hole sloped down); three single buttons below lapel, right front, black holes left front. Low collar (about 1 in.), small button right (missing on pattern, but shown in portrait); large blue round cuffs (about 6 in. deep in front, 8 in. at back), three *small* buttons and holes. Waistcoat plain white, small buttons (also for MIDSHIPMAN, but convex plain buttons).

Dress Suit: Blue coat, single-breasted, 11 buttons front, black holes; no collar; large round white cuffs, three full-size buttons, white stitched waistcoat white, gold-laced neck, front, pocket-flaps and hem as shown. 14 small buttons front, three to pocket.

MASTER-AND-COMMANDER—Undress Frock (Fig. 4?): Conjectural. Probably same as CAPTAIN

Fig. 5—Flag Officer's (all grades) suit (top) and frock (bottom).

rear buttons and down to hem of skirts, and tail-slit was laced both edges as shown. Waistcoat same as LIEUTENANT's Dress.

Frock (over three years Post) (Fig. 4): same as above, but additional row framing slashes and pockets of coat and waistcoat.

Reynolds' portrait of Alexander Hood, later Lord Bridgport, very clearly shows the junior CAPTAIN's frock, and a popular mode of wearing it with crossed lapels. There is some confusion about the frock lacing distinction between the two Captain's grades. Dudley Jarret reproduces a Gainsborough portrait of Howe to illustrate a senior Captain. This shows white lapels and *one* row of lace on cuff-slashes and pocket-flaps. But this is also true of the Hood portrait and of an unnamed Captain, both of which are described by the Museum authorities as "Captain (under three years)". It is worth while to refer to yet another Reynolds' portrait at Greenwich, of his friend Keppel as a Captain. Although representing him landing in France after his ship had run aground in 1747, the portrait was painted 1753-4. Keppel had been an advocate for a naval uniform. He is shown wearing a frock remarkably like the one adopted; the position of the arms obscures the lace on the cuff-slashes, but the waistcoat pockets are double-laced. It is not known whether Reynolds, who painted Keppel many times, used the new official uniform as a model, or the pre-1748 unofficial version worn by his subject on the occasion depicted. By 1774, senior Captains were wearing this additional lace framing the slashes and flaps: in the writer's view this was probably the case always, and he has so drawn it.

Dress Suit (under three years): blue coat, single-breasted, 9-11 buttons; large round white cuffs, three buttons; no collar; wide lace down front edges, one row; one row narrow lace round neck; wide lace two rows cuffs, one row flaps, pocket-frames and skirt-seams. Doubtless the back lace conformed to the manner of the frock. Waistcoat white, wide lace one row neck, front edges, hem, flaps and frames, 14 buttons front.

Dress Suit (over three years Post): as above, but fronts, cuffs, and flaps edged with additional one row narrow lace, and one row of the same lengthways between wide pocket-frame lace and lower edge of flaps. Back lacing assumed as above.

FLAG-OFFICER—Frock (all grades) (Fig. 5): Blue coat with short lapels faced white, seven buttons; three single buttons below; low collar, one button; large round white cuffs, three buttons. Laced two rows collar, one row lapels, pointed lace holes (back and front). Cuffs laced one row top, one row below joining outer laced holes. Widths as drawn. Skirt and pocket lace not clear—this and back lace inferred from "one-purpose" dress of 1767, a modifi-

(under three years) but blue lapels, as in later Orders. Logic would suggest lapels of the lower rank with the cuffs and lace of the higher. An alternative would be to add CAPTAIN's lace to a LIEUTENANT's coat, but subsequent uniform does not support this.

Dress Suit: even less certain; possible distinctions from CAPTAIN (under three years) could be: (i) narrow lace throughout, (ii) one row wide lace on cuffs, one row on flaps but not surrounding pocket, or (iii) some combination of these.

CAPTAIN—Frock (under three years Post) (Fig. 4): Blue coat; short tapered lapels faced white, seven buttons, white holes; three buttons below lapel, right front; low collar, small button right; small white cuffs, blue slashes, three buttons; all buttons *below* pocket-flaps; narrow lace, two rows collar, one row lapels (back and front), front coat-edges to hem only, cuffs and slashes, flaps and skirt-seams. By inference from later practice, the seam lace ran round the top

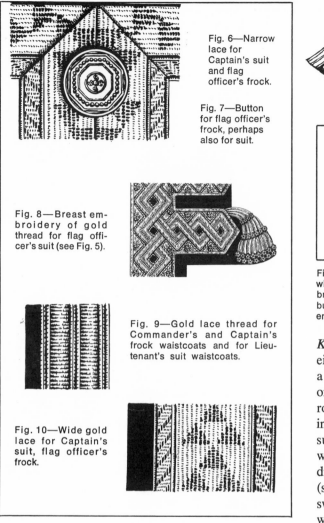

Fig. 6—Narrow lace for Captain's suit and flag officer's frock.

Fig. 7—Button for flag officer's frock, perhaps also for suit.

Fig. 8—Breast embroidery of gold thread for flag officer's suit (see Fig. 5).

Fig. 9—Gold lace thread for Commander's and Captain's frock waistcoats and for Lieutenant's suit waistcoats.

Fig. 10—Wide gold lace for Captain's suit, flag officer's frock.

Fig. 11—Lapel and hat of, presumably, a Commander.

Figs. 12 a, b, c—From l. to r.: small general button, all-purpose where not essential to decor; wood covered with brass and all-brass. Frock button, to Captain; wood faced with brass. Suit button, to Captain, wood faced with brass ornamented with an embossed Tudor rose. See Fig. 7.

Knots: with suit, a gilt or silver-hilted small sword, either *colichemarde* or triangle-bladed; with frock, a fighting sword, either double-edged military type, or shorter one-edged curved cutlass-type, both with round pommel and curved guard. Probably always in leather shoulder-belt (oblique frog-suspension) as suggested by the Serres plates of 1777, sometimes worn over the waistcoat or even over the coat in undress. Black leather scabbards, brass, gilt or silver (small-sword) mounts, blue and gold cord-and-tassel swordknots, usually for dress wear only. *Gloves:* white or light buff skin, usually for dress wear only.

The rough-and-tumble of sea life and the strong individuality of the age would have delayed adoption of the dress, with evasions of its use, despite the petition to have it granted. We may suppose quaint variations and interpretations to which official attention had to be called until a reasonable conformity was reached. Apart from the slight alteration to the Midshipman's white turnback in 1758, the Order was in force until January 23, 1767, when the suit was abolished and the frock modified to be a dress for all occasions.

cation of this suit. Waistcoat white, laced as shown.

Dress Suit (all grades): blue coat, single breasted, eight buttons front; large round white cuffs, three buttons; white waistcoat; ornate embroidery on both garments, as shown in drawing. A specimen survives (already cited), and numerous portraits, notably of Anson, after Reynolds, in the National Portrait Gallery, two at Greenwich of the ill-fated Byng by Hudson and an unknown, and of Tyrell also by Hudson. All evidence is consistent and leaves no room for doubt.

It remains to refer briefly to items not covered by the Order. *Breeches:* portraits confirm the adoption of matching blue for these, which fastened with four small buttons below the knee over the white stockings. *Hats:* black, gold-laced for all ranks (probably wide lace for flag-officers) with the usual Hanoverian black silk cockade, button and lace loop. *Neckcloth:* almost always white at this period. *Shoes:* black, with brass or gilt buckles. *Hair and Wigs:* senior officers appear in powdered full-bottomed wigs, younger men in the tie-wig and queue, or their own hair tied in a black bow. *Swords, Belts and*

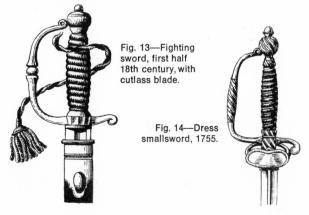

Fig. 13—Fighting sword, first half 18th century, with cutlass blade.

Fig. 14—Dress smallsword, 1755.

Napoleon Was *Not* Afraid of It

by *FRED H. BAER*

Fred H. Baer, born in Vienna in 1924, is a journalist serving American business and technical publications as foreign correspondent from Vienna, London and Bonn. He is also chief correspondent for McGraw-Hill publications in Austria and supervisor of McGraw-Hill's East European correspondents. Baer has written for the Gun Digest, *the* American Rifleman, Guns Magazine, The Gun Report *and* Diana Armi.

Most of his articles are based on his researches in the Vienna War Archives and are largely illustrated with his own weapons —he possesses what most visitors agree to be the most complete collection of Austrian Imperial-Royal Army long arms of the time span 1659 to 1918. His library includes arms manuals, official biographies and accounts of military engagements published throughout the same period.

People's habit of accepting everything they read as Gospel truth, as well as the lack of hard information based on original documents, have often brought about the birth of legends, sometimes perpetuated for commercial purposes. The story of the Austrian compressed air military rifle, best known at the *Girandoni System,* constitutes a typical example of this process.

Nearly everything that has ever been written about the Girandoni *Windbüchse* tells how Napoleon was so terrified—and outraged—by this weapon that he issued standing orders for the instant execution, without trial, of any Austrian soldier found with one. This apocryphal tale originated in an article by K. Maleyka published in Berlin in 1937, and has been revived indiscriminately many times since. Its repudiation was made possible only in the recent past.[1]

Nothing is known about when, exactly, the Austrian Imperial War Council first approached Girandoni, or he the A.I.W.C.; his name first appears in a document dated March 1, 1779, in which *Feld-*

---

[1] The investigators who have reconstructed the history of Girandoni and his rifles as completely and reliably as surviving documents permit are: Dr. Walter Hummelberger, Curator of Arms & Armor of the Historical Museum of the City of Vienna; Leo Scharer, restorer of arms, armor and military items at the same institute; Dr. Walter Wagner of the War Archive; Hans Nagl (photographs); and Marco Morin of Florence, whose biographical researches about Girandoni will be summarized at the end of the present exposition.

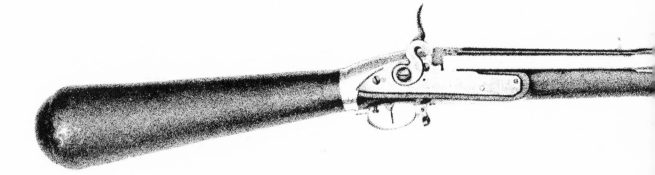

marschall-leutnant Theodor Baron Rouvroy submitted to Emperor Joseph II a project for a repeating flintlock carbine with a deeply rifled barrel. This weapon was proposed in the same year in which the world's first officially-issued breechloading military long-arm, the Crespi (copied some forty years later by Hall and adopted in 1819 in the United States, essentially unchanged), was being withdrawn from service after two years of trial use by three selected cavalry regiments. The Girandoni repeating flintlock rifle already possessed the system of an oscillating transverse breechblock also used on the *Windbüchse,* or air rifle, which was to become the dominant arm of the Jäger units between 1793 and 1801.[2] It differed considerably from the conventional military flintlock rifles of the period. An iron tube affixed to the left side of the rear one-third of the barrel contained twelve rounds of lead balls, while an identical cylinder fastened to the right side held the powder sufficient for loading and priming twenty shots. To load and fire the piece, the flashpan cover was first closed and the hammer half-cocked; priming of the pan was then brought about via a breechblock that

ran perpendicularly across the rear part of the barrel. When the piece was held muzzle-up, the movement of the breechblock towards the right permitted a given quantity of powder to fall from the right tube into a cavity in the breechblock and thence into the firing chamber; a movement of the breechblock toward the left permitted a ball to roll into another cavity in the block, the return action of which then carried the ball into a central position exactly in line with and in front of the powder load. Difficulties of manufacturing and maintaining the fine tolerance between breechblock and barrel required for free motion, yet preventing gas escape and pressure loss (with the consequent gradual erosion and deformation of the block), prevented the acceptance and diffusion of this interesting firearm. Only drawings of it survive and no examples. The story that Bartolomeo Girandoni fell victim to his own weapon owing to a powder magazine explosion, with a consequent amputation of an arm is incorrect; but his son Giovanni did in fact meet with such an accident while working on a project not related to the repeating rifle. Bartolomeo Girandoni must have realized the scarce practical value of his flintlock rifle, but he was eager to present simultaneously his project for an air rifle; the flintlock was not only the vehicle, so to speak, for the other, but a stepping stone to the highest authorities.

The air rifle was in fact capable of shooting twenty lead balls within a few seconds with a mean range of about 100 yards. On March 19, 1779, Emperor

---

[2] While the *Windbüchse* was the dominant, the most dramatic and of course the most interesting of the weapons of the Jäger of that period, their *basic* arms remained the *Jägersuzen* Model 1769, a deeply-grooved flintlock with a heavy octagonal barrel about two-thirds as long as that of an ordinary infantry musket's; in appearance it was quite similar to both the Girandoni powder-charged, breechloading repeaters.

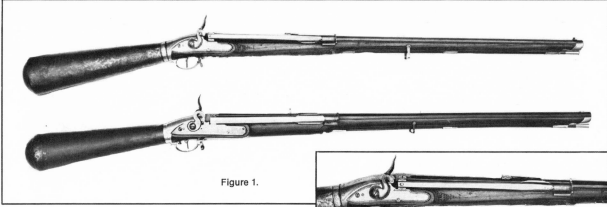

Figure 1.

Fig. 1—Two Girandoni air rifles, the upper one a richly ornamented civilian version, the lower one the standard military arm,
both datable in the 1790's. They differ only in decoration and
external refinements. The civilian one is of a quality that suggests
that it may have been destined for the Emperor himself. (In the
author's collection)

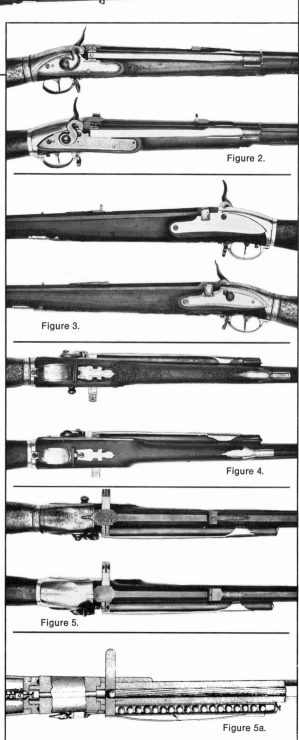

Figure 2.

Figure 3.

Figure 4.

Figure 5.

Figure 5a.

Figs. 2-5—Right, left, bottom and top views of the weapons in
Fig. 1. Diagram clearly shows all the essentials of the simple,
ingenious Girandoni principle.

Joseph II ordered Major General Johann Albert von
Schroeder to begin conducting exhaustive experiments with the two prototypes, flint and air. Shortly
after, in a report from *Feldmarschall* Franz Moritz
Count Lacy, dated July 13, 1779, addressed to the
Emperor, Lacy declared that both weapons tested
would be efficient in the open field as well as in
fortified zones, and proposed an order for one thousand flintlocks and five hundred air rifles. In about
nine months' time, Girandoni had been able to con-
vince the supreme military authorities, the Emperor
himself included, of the value of his projects.

Having obtained the *placet* of Joseph II, Girandoni returned to his native Cortina D'Ampezzo, then
under Austrian Crown Rule, only soon to journey
back to Vienna together with his family and with
Francesco Colli, his assistant in his watchmaker's
shop in the Alpine village. With the help of Colli
and that of two other workmen, Girandoni produced
274 air rifles in Vienna between 1780 and November 22, 1784, complete save for the conical air
reservoirs which constituted the butts. Moreover, he
produced all necessary constituent parts for another
16 air rifles, 105 tested air reservoirs and 50 to be
tested, and 111 flintlock repeating carbines. Monthly
production fluctuated between a mere six and seven
complete arms. In the course of these four years the
required materials were supplied according to Girandoni's precise specifications, but the slow pace of
production, and the rumors which accused him,
rightly or libellously, of detouring a goodly quantity
of ready pieces to the private arms market, imposed
some radical changes in the contract.

The next lot of 700 air rifles, produced between
January 1785 and September 1787, were consigned
to the State for the established price of 35 gulden
for a complete air rifle, 30 gulden for a repeating
rifle, 5 gulden for an air reservoir replacement and
3 gulden for a hand pump. From 1785 onward Giran-

Fig. 6—A close-up of the breech sections and cross-bolts, seen from the top.

Fig. 8—Crossbolt unfastened and displaced to extreme right, out of normal position, to show ball-receiving cavity (and a ball that would normally be in the magazine tube).

doni was required to provide all the necessary material himself, though he had the right to select those suppliers he considered best.

Only one contemporary description of the Girandoni air rifle has come down to us. It is an instruction booklet, dated October 24, 1788, printed for Austrian troops during the war with Turkey and now conserved in the Austrian War Archive in Vienna (on August 24, 1787, Turkey declared war against Russia and, for Continental political reasons, Austria was compelled to adhere to the Treaty of Alliance she had contracted with the Tsar in 1781).

Fig. 7—A light push with the thumb is all that is required to transfer a ball from the magazine tube at the right of the barrel to the firing chamber.

It gives the following specifications: Calibre 13 mm. (abt. .51 in.), weight loaded 4.23 kg. (abt. 9 lbs. 5 oz.) (unloaded 4.18 kg.), overall length 1.227 m. (abt. 48½ in.), length of barrel of octagonal form 834.06 mm. (abt. 32.8 in.); the forestock was walnut, while the butt constituted the air reservoir made of forged sheet iron in two symmetrical halves joined by eleven rivets and brazed all around for a hermetic seal, the whole being lastly covered with leather.

About two thousand strokes of a hand pump were required to bring the reservoir up to operative pressure, approximately 25-30 atm.; thereafter the shooter could count on thirty accurate and deadly shots, fired with astonishing rapidity but decreasing in range from 120 meters to about 75. After these, the air reservoir was still not completely empty. The muzzle velocity of a bullet was about 300 meters per second (about 985 feet)—about that of bullets fired from most European hunting rifles of the period. The energy was comparable to that of a Colt .45 automatic pistol bullet.

Firing procedure was as follows: with the rifle held muzzle-up, one pushed the transverse breech-block to the right, allowing a ball to fall and to lodge in an opposite cavity in the block, which returned to starting position by force of the long flat spring on the right side of the barrel and thus placed the ball into a species of firing chamber on axis with the bore. Next, one cocked the "hammer"—or, better, the cocking lever—which, upon the trigger being pulled, snapped in such a way as to open and close with lightning rapidity a small valve between reservoir and ball, thus releasing a quantity of air sufficient for propelling the ball. The blued octagonal steel barrel was deeply rifled with twelve grooves prescribing one turn in the length of the barrel. The front and rear sight, respectively blade and V, were fixed and unadjustable. The housing for the mechanism was cast brass, as was the conventional trigger

Fig. 9—Bottom view of barrel, showing cross-bolt, magazine tube and return spring.

guard; there were two sling swivels, one on the trigger guard and the other about halfway down the forestock.

In the middle of 1787, when more than a thousand rifles had been accumulated in the Vienna artillery warehouse, an unexpected order arrived from the Emperor to outfit each rifle with three air reservoirs. A quick survey by one Major General Franz Anton von Maurer reported that the execution of His Imperial Majesty's order would require 1600 additional reservoirs and 800 pumps; nonetheless, a first lot of two hundred rifles, each one outfitted

Fig. 10—A butt reservoir terminating in a valve and female thread, and the rear section of the brass receiver wih the male thread and the valve-opening plunger. Note interchangeability of parts: reservoir is numbered 822, rifle receiver 1010.

with three reservoirs and a pump in a compartmentalized leather case, was ready for shipment to Imperial troops in Hungary. Upon departure of these, the Emperor ordered that the 800 rifles remaining in Vienna be outfitted with *two* reservoirs each, while a spare-parts reserve of an additional ten per cent, i.e. of 160 more reservoirs, was to be set aside in the warehouses. On September 4th, 1787, Girandoni received a verbal rush order from the Emperor for 2400 more reservoirs and 400 hand pumps, but he pleaded that the bad quality of iron, and hence the need for vigilant selectivity, would make the consignment doubtful before March 1788. When Girandoni put forward this order as a valid excuse for a delay in the delivery of the previously-ordered 1600 reservoirs, which were to bring the total to

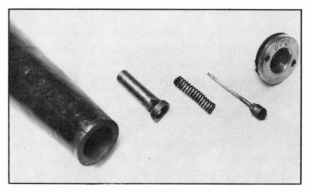

Fig. 11—The air release valve assembly in the butt reservoir.

two for each rifle, tempers ran hot in the War Council and only the unassailable supremacy of Imperial *fiat* cooled them. An Imperial Resolution dated November 17th, 1787, established definitely that *every* rifle was to be supplied with 3 reservoirs after all, without exceptions; simultaneously, the Emperor granted Girandoni's request to be relieved of the contractual requirements for further consignment of repeating flintlock rifles (about which, parenthetically, no records remain to show whether they were ever actually used in war).

On November 17, 1788, Joseph II, respecting his treaty obligations toward the Tsar of Russia, finally declared war on Turkey. Two days earlier he had issued orders for the distribution of arms to the troops. Each of thirty-four chosen battalions of riflemen was to be issued twenty-two air rifles, while twelve more battalions were to have twenty-one each. These weapons were destined for the air-rifle platoon in each battalion, commanded by an officer, generally a lieutenant, and consisting of twenty or twenty-two carefully selected marksmen, including two corporals. It was for these units that the manual of instructions had been printed. In the meanwhile, Girandoni faced continued troubles with his reservoirs. Owing to the poor quality of the iron, of the one hundred produced every week no fewer than twenty to thirty

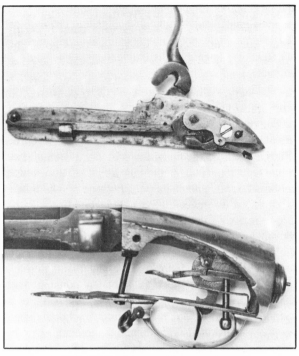

Fig. 12—Lock removed from receiver.

blew up during proof; hence the reservoirless rifles stored in the arsenal could be sent to the front only in small batches, as three reservoirs for each became available. Unfortunately, it is not known how many of these "noiseless, smokeless and flamless" wonder-weapons, which had so roused the enthusiasm of Emperor and War Council, actually saw action in the Austro-Turkish campaign. Documents report that twenty rifles were lost in battle, and that for the most part the rest were used by the advance guard to cover the movements of infantry and the artillery against the enemy's rear guard. On July 21st, 1789, Lieutenant General Joseph Maria Count of Colloredo reported to the War Council on the very modest results, mainly because ". . . it is difficult to prevent the troops from using the arm incorrectly and, as has actually happened, in a rough fashion incompatible with its delicacy." He went on to propose—Joseph II was not to approve—the creation of a corps of Light Sharpshooters armed with air rifles. In the meantime, air-gun platoons had been formed within ten battalions of Grenadiers. Moreover, a great change in policy came about when Leopold II succeeded his brother Joseph in 1790: on March 13th of that year, the new Emperor ordered the formation of a Special Corp armed entirely with air rifles. It was therefore decreed that the Jäger or riflemen should be joined with the recently-constituted corps of Tyrolean marksmen, all armed with the 1313 available air rifles together with a reserve supply of reservoirs, bandoliers and pumps. But apparently the rifles returning from the Turkish campaign were in such a sad state of disrepair and wreckage that,

according to a report of the Jäger Corps, none had as yet been issued as of December 16, 1792!

Leopold II died in 1792, and Franz II, his son and successor, did not show the same interest in air rifles as his uncle and father. Nonetheless, on December 16, 1792, he granted, reluctantly, a request by Captain Franz Philipp Fenner von Fenneberg, Captain in the Tyrolean sharp-shooters corps, for 40 air rifles to be issued to each of the companies of Tyrolean marksmen. Franz had no great faith in his own soldiers: hence his indifference about this assignment, and his opposition to the abolition of the bounty of one ducat paid to every air-rifle marksman who could show at the end of a campaign that his arm was still in fine condition! Still, the air rifle came into action repeatedly in the Wars of the First Coalition against revolutionary France, 1792-97, es-

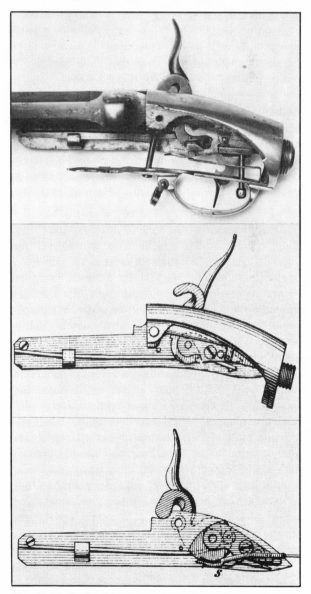

Figs. 13-15—Lock rejoined to receiver. The internal motion of the part that corresponds to the tumbler in conventional gunlocks causes a spring-loaded plunger to be driven against the valve stem of the butt reservoir, releasing the required blast of air.

255

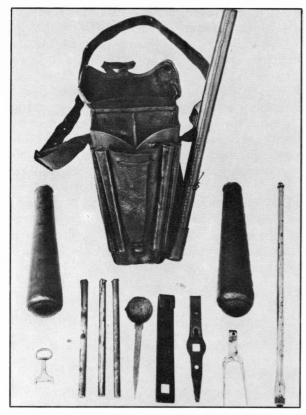

Fig. 16—A complete air-rifleman's accoutrements, including two spare reservoirs, lead-casting ladle and pump. (Courtesy of the Museo dell' Artiglieria, Turin)

pecially in the Rhinelands. Only about a hundred were left behind in the Vienna arsenals, some five hundred having been issued to the Tyrolean Jäger Corps alone, while other commanders requested smaller quantities for units of the advance guard. A request to the Emperor to obtain thirty for the corporals of the Jäger companies stationed in Luxembourg was denied, while a request for another thirty made on December 15th, 1796, by General Joseph von Alvintsy was granted.

Upon cessation of hostilities, a report from the War Council dated September 21, 1799, noted the loss of 308 of the 1500 air rifles produced: 1091 had been returned to the warehouses and 101 were still in service with the Tyrolean Jäger Corps (who were later on to be armed mainly with flintlocks). The last recorded policy decision bears the same date, September 21st, 1799; signed by Franz II, it ordered production to cease. A final lot of 41 rifles consigned in the Spring of 1800 brought the number in the Vienna warehouses to about 1150.

On January 20, 1801, the now-Col. von Fenneberg, reported that 399 of his 500 air rifles received since 1793 had been lost in battle and requested authorization to substitute the 101 remaining ones with an equal number of flintlock Jägerstutzen M. 1795. The grant of this plea on March 5, 1801, marked the end of Girandoni's rifles in the Austrian (and any other) army. The last document concerning them bears the date 1806; while Napoleon's forces were advancing menacingly on Vienna, the War Council ordered all the remaining rifles and their accessories (stored in the artillery warehouse) taken to the fortress of Komorn in Hungary.

Today, only a few examples exist in museums and private collections. But for these, the Girandoni air rifle has vanished from history. It constituted a revolutionary step toward the abolition of gunpowder for small arms, and if its performance on the battlefield failed to meet the great expectations entertained for it by emporers, generals and of course by the inventor himself, this seems to have been due to the delicacy of the mechanism, susceptible to disarrayment by dirt and unskilled useage, and perhaps to the weakness of the brass receiver housing. Had the weapon enjoyed a more normal course of evolution and perfection, unpressured by hostile gunpowder traditionalists in high circles and by the frenetic delivery schedules set up in times of war or of preparation for war, perhaps most of the faults could have been overcome; it would certainly seem

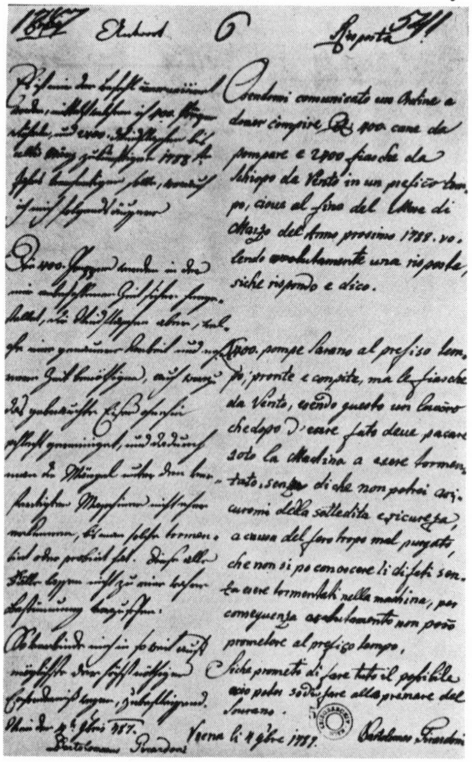

Girandoni comunicato un Ordine a dover compire 400 cane da pompare e 2400 fiasche da Schioppo da Vento in un prefisso tempo, cioue al fine del Mese di Marzo del Anno prossimo 1788. volendo assolutamente una risposta, siche rispondo e dico.

400. pompe saranno al prefiso tempo, pronte e compite, ma le fiasche da Vento, essendo questo un lavoro che dopo d'esare fato deue pasare soto la Machina a essere tormentato, senza di che non potrei assicuromi della sodedita e sicurezza, a causa del fero tropo mal purgato, che non si po conoscere li difeti senza esse tormentati nella machina, per conseguenza assolutamente non posso prometere al prefiso tempo,

Siche prometo di fare tuto il posibile acio poter sodisfare alla premure del Sourano.

Viena li 4 9bre 1787. Bartolomeo Girandoni

Fig. 17—A deposition by Girandoni—here signed "Girardoni"—in German and Italian, dated November 4, 1787, in which he states that he can supply 400 pumps by the required deadline, March 31, 1788, but that there can be no hope of his delivering 2400 reservoirs because "these must be tortured (i.e. proved) on the machine" to insure solidity and safety, but "owing to the too poorly-refined iron" many of them fail to pass because of flaws not detectable in any other way. Nonetheless, he will "do everything possible to satisfy the Sovereign's desire." (Courtesy War Archives, Vienna, and Sig. Marco Morin, Florence).

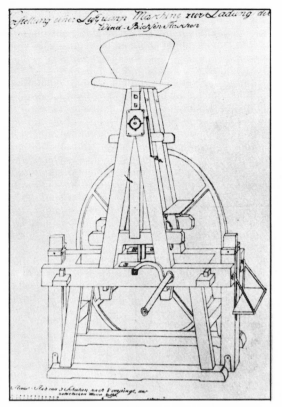

Fig. 18—"Representation of an Air-Pump Machine for Charging Air-Rifle Reservoirs"—a contemporary sketch. (Courtesy Sig. Marco Morin, Florence)

so, judging from the comfortable vantage point of hindsight. Very likely Girandoni did in fact have projects for improvements in mind and must have pressed these upon the authorities as long as he lived—without, alas, avail. He also made muzzle-loading air rifles and rifled carbines for civilian use —the collections of imperial arms now housed in the Kunsthistorisches Museum in Vienna number two of these, both marked "Girandoni" on the breech sections of the barrels.

A relative on the side of Girandoni's second wife, a certain Leopoldo Zana, produced single-shot muzzle-loading air rifles as well as the military version, both apparently for the civilian market, for a good long time after Waterloo: specimens of his work, richly ornamented, can be studied in Vienna's Hapsburg Collection. Later on in the nineteenth century, civilian air rifles and repeating air pistols were made by the famous Viennese gunmaker Josef Contriner (e.g., Military Museum, Prague). Other names associated with the production of air arms made in the Girandoni tradition are Friedrich Stuetsinger, Ignaz Senger and Philip Colnott; Marco Morin reports a rifle signed "Lancedelli—Ampezzo—1831".

It is interesting to note that an Imperial Edict prohibited unlicensed manufacture of compressed air arms in the Empire as early as 1766, the law's main worry having apparently been the favor such weapons found, for obvious reasons, among poach-

ers. A further edict of 1796 forbade the manufacture and/or carrying of air guns disguised as walking sticks, while still another of September 1802 specifically declared air guns "insidious arms" the construction of which—as well as of pumps and accoutrements—would henceforth be subject to police licensing and control. The official explanation was the rise of injuries from burst reservoirs, but the real reason was no doubt establishment fear of an armed proletariat, particularly one armed with an effective sniping rifle requiring no powder supply and able to deliver deadly shots noiselessly and smokelessly, rendering detection of the shooter's hiding place among the city's garretts all but impossible.

Most of the biographical material known about Bartolomeo Girandoni has been unearthed by Marco Morin and published in *Diana Armi* (Florence, 1969, No. 3, May-June). Morin discovered in the archives of Cortina d'Ampezzo that "Bartolamio Gilardoni" was born there on May 30, 1744. The name of the family was spelled in many ways, and even the adult Bartolomeo ("Bartolamio" is local dialect) was recorded as "Gilardoni," "Gilandoni," "Girardami," "Girandony," etc. No doubt Morin is right in suggesting that "Gilardoni" should be considered correct, but since the inventor was recorded in official documents as well as on his own weapons more often as "Girandoni" than in any other way, the present writer proposes to continue refering to him—perhaps imprecisely but conventionally—by that spelling. He was married, on November 16, 1762, to Catharina Barbaria, who died on April 20, 1775 after having given birth to four children between 1764 and 1772. A second marriage, on July 23, 1776, to Maria Eleonora Magerita de Zanna resulted in six children. There are still direct Girandoni descendants living in Vienna.

Girandoni acquired some property and died in prosperity. (Giuseppe Crespi died in poverty.) He left behind a small mansion, Penzing No. 12, near Schoenbrun Castle, as well as a farm in his native Cortina and several thousand gulden in cash—a small fortune. He died at Penzing, then a suburb of Vienna, on March 21, 1799.

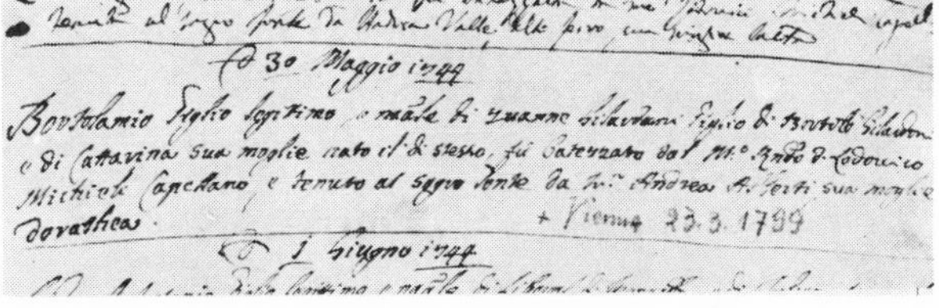

Fig. 19—Registry of Bartolomeo Girandoni's birth in Cortina d'Ampezzo on May 30, 1744, as "Bartolamio Gilardoni". Arms student Sig. Marco Morin who photographed this entry, says rightly that the inventor should logically be called Gilardoni, but by now the weight of tradition and Austrian documents seems to have immortalized him as Girandoni.

257

Trafalgar Swords of Honour

by DEREK SPALDING

Derek Spalding has been a student and collector of antique weapons since age nine (i.e. since 1950). As he matured, his main interests focused ever more on the English Middle Ages and on the Napoleonic/Regency periods, spheres in which he has researched extensively in hitherto unexplored documents. He has a marked preference for armor and edged weapons over firearms. Quite a few years ago he intended to teach applied arts, but after a brief career as a commercial artist-illustrator he decided to make weapons history his life's work, and toward that end joined the firm of Peter Dale, Ltd., London. Trafalgar Swords of Honour *is the first serious study of this absorbing epicycle of* armes-blanches *history.*

War was decreed by France against Great Britain on February 1st, 1793, and 'His Majesties Proclamation' for making reprisals was dated on the 11th of the same month. During this war, which was to last twenty-two years, the ancient custom of awarding swords to national military and naval heros was revived. The present notes deal with some of the most well-known swords-of-honour, those awarded by the Patriotic Fund at Lloyd's, particularly those awarded to officers who commanded ships at the Battle off Cape Trafalgar on the 21st October 1805.

The Patriotic Fund was founded at a meeting called at Lloyd's Coffee House, Royal Exchange, London, on July 20th, 1803. It was there decided that "to animate the efforts of our defenders by sea and land it is expedient to raise, by the patriotism of the community at large, a suitable fund for their comfort and relief, for the purposes of assuaging the anguish of their wounds, or palliating in some degree the more weighty misfortune of the loss of limbs, or alleviating the distress of widows and orphans, and granting pecuniary rewards or honourable badges of distinction for successful exertions of value or merit." The "honourable badges" took the form of superb neo-classical silver vases and handsome gilt sabres. Lloyd's were very up-to-date in choosing sabres, for the 19th century ushered in the curved-blade sword as the fashionable officer's sidearm; light cavalry regiments had adopted a new pattern sabre in 1796, and certain infantry officers were ordered to wear sabres in 1803.

The Patriotic Fund sabres were divided into three main grades, starting with a sword of £30 value for presentation to mates and midshipmen, and proceeding to a sword of £50 value for lieutenants and a £100 sword for commanders and captains. For their gallant services in the Battle of Trafalgar many of the officers who commanded ships were awarded a special "Trafalgar" sword, of which more anon. Although the majority of Lloyd's swords were awarded to Royal Navy officers, thirteen were awarded to officers in the Royal Marines and four swords went to army officers.

All but one of the existing Lloyd's swords are engraved on the scabbard top with the name and address of the London sword cutler and jeweller, Richard Teed of Lancaster Court in the Strand. Most £100 swords are signed "Richard Teed, Sword Cutler, Lancaster Court, London"; this inscription is engraved in Roman capital letters around the thickness of metal at the mouth of the scabbard. Early £50 swords were similarly signed, but after 1804 the majority in this value category were signed in the more usual place on the top rear of the scabbard. This change was probably due to the revised inscription "Richard Teed, Dress sword maker to the Patriotic Fund, Lancaster Court, London" being too long for the original position around the throat. The odd sword out, as previously mentioned, is the £50 sword awarded in 1805 to Lieutenant George Pigot; its scabbard is signed by another well-known London

cutler, J. Salter of 35, Strand.

The hilts of the sabres all take the same form, the design being inspired by classical mythology. A small printed card (Fig. 1) presented with each sword described the hilt's symbolism:

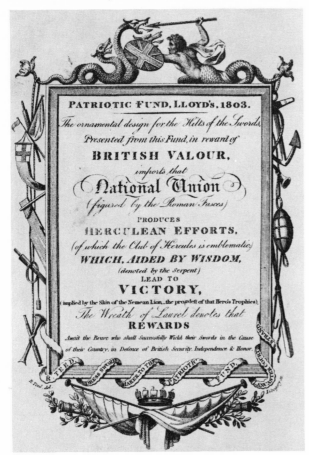

Fig. 1—Printed card explaining the symbolism of the sword hilt. Each sword was accompanied by such a card.

The grips are of checkered ivory and the metalwork of the hilt of mercury gilt copper or gilding metal. Some earlier accounts of Lloyd's swords have described the hilts and scabbard mountings as being of silver gilt, but such a sword has not yet come to light.

The blades varied a great deal; the more expensive the sword the more skill was lavished on the decoration and finish. All blades, however, were decorated with acid-etched motifs, mercury gilding and fire blueing, and had the presentation inscription in Roman capital letters. On most £30 swords the inscription is in capital letters raised slightly in relief against an etched and gilded background, while on £50 and £100 swords the inscription is in small gilt letters on a blued panel. On most blades the inscription is read when the sword is horizontal with the cutting edge downwards, but a few swords must be held with the cutting edge uppermost to read the inscription. Trafalgar blades had the recipient's initials etched within a gilded star together

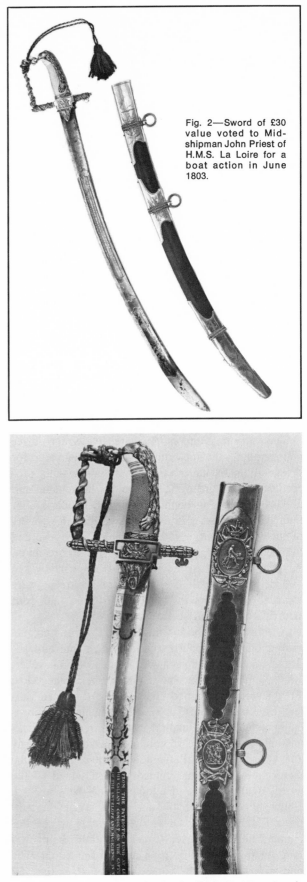

Fig. 2—Sword of £30 value voted to Midshipman John Priest of H.M.S. La Loire for a boat action in June 1803.

Fig. 3—Sword of £50 value showing in detail the hilt and scabbard mountings. Voted to James Boxer of H.M.S. Antelope for an action in March 1804.

Fig. 4—Sword of £50 value voted to Lieutenant G. A. Crofton of H.M.S. Cambrian for a boat action in September 1805. The portrait shows Lt. Crofton in later life (c. 1850) still proudly displaying his sword of honour.

with two mermaids each bearing a banner inscribed respectively "VICTORY" and "TRAFALGAR".

The major visual difference between the grades of swords was in the amount of decoration on the scabbards. £30 swords (Fig. 2) had scabbards of normal construction: the body was made of wood covered in blue leather, and the three mercury gilt mounts were entirely separate units, well engraved with non-classical naval motifs and emblems; each mount was encircled by two bands of gilt cable, the cable on the top two mounts being pierced by circular suspension rings. The £50 scabbards (Figs. 3, 4, 5 and 7) were more elaborate and the decorative theme was classical. The gilt mounts were no longer three separate units but were joined by decorative side pieces which also formed the borders of two oval shagreen panels on the front and rear of the scabbard. All these mounts were attached to the wooden scabbard body by small gilt screws. The decoration was both engraved and applied; each main section of mounting had a small applied oval cartouche depicting Hercules in the course of one of his Labours, usually in combat with the Nemean Lion or with the nine-headed Hydra or taming the three-headed dog-serpent Cerberus on a leash; each cartouche was surrounded by a trophy of naval arms. The sword was suspended by two circular rings of cable.

The gilt metal mounting of the £100 and Trafalgar scabbard (Figs. 6 and 9) was formed as one complete unit into which the wooden scabbard body was inserted. The two oval panels were now of dark blue or black velvet which was decorated further with applied gilt trophies. Two of the oval cartouches still depicted Herculean Labours but the top cartouche was replaced by a larger oval panel depicting a seated Britannia holding the Union Shield and a trident overlooking two ships at sea. The Trafalgar scabbard had a similar panel but now with Britannia holding a victor's laurel wreath and gazing out over the assembled fleets. On the highest grade scabbards the name of the recipient's ship appeared on a ribbon scroll above the top oval panel, and on the Trafalgar scabbard on drapes below this panel were the words "NELSON, TRAFALGAR, 21st Octr 1805." Scabbard suspension rings were replaced by ornate curling serpents, and the trail of the chape was of beaded form.

Lloyd's sabres were presented in a polished mahogany case the lid of which was fitted with an inlaid folding brass handle and a rectangular brass plate. The plate was engraved with the recipient's name, the date and brief details of the award. The case was lined with blue baize and Richard Teed's trade label was pasted to the inside of the lid; with each sword came a small printed card explaining the classical symbolism of the hilt (Fig. 1). Each sword had a sword belt and a knot. The belts were of two types: for the lower grades of swords they were of

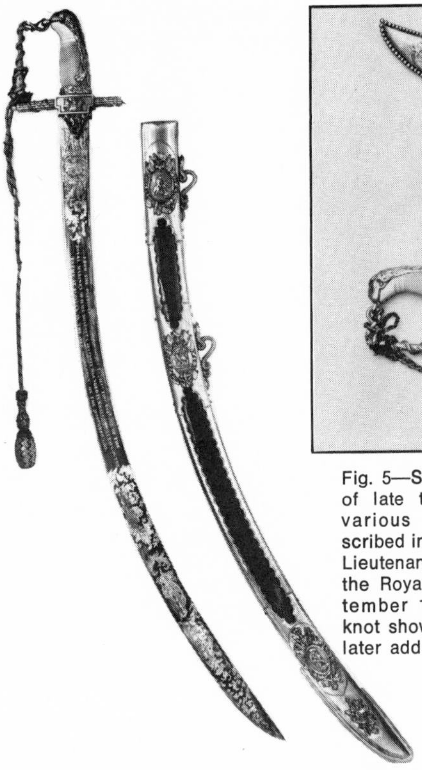

Fig. 5—Sword of £50 value of late type showing the various differences described in the text. Voted to Lieutenant Robert Pye of the Royal Marines in September 1809. The sword knot shown is an incorrect later addition.

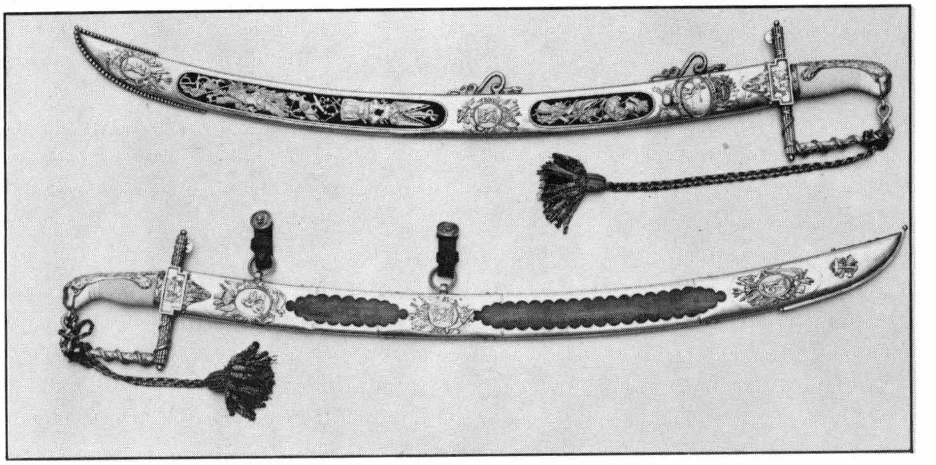

Figs. 6 and 7—Trafalgar sword of honour voted to Captain Robert Redmill of H.M.S. Polyphemus. Below is a standard £50 sword for comparison.

blue leather with gilt bullion edges and an ornate wavy gilt centre line; all the buckles and joint bosses took the form of gilt lion masks, and the clasp was a small gilt "S" snake between two lion masks. For the £100 and Trafalgar swords the snake was replaced by a circular clasp (Fig. 10) depicting Hercules in combat with the Hydra, in the exergue the words "Patriotic Fund 1803." The sword knots were of blue and gold twisted cord with a large blue tassel having gold bullions.

The Battle off Cape Trafalgar, fought on October 21st 1805, was the naval action for which the greatest number of Lloyd's swords were awarded at one time. In the past it has been assumed that each of the officers commanding a ship received a sword, but this was not the case. Some officers have been recorded as receiving a sword when in actual fact they received a silver vase. This mistaken impression of swords all-round (with notable exceptions) is continued in the latest publication on naval swords. The following list denotes wherever possible documentary evidence of the officer receiving either sword or vase (the ships are listed in the battle formation as they were on the 21st October):*

---

*The Editors recommend David Howarth's *Trafalgar: The Nelson Touch* (Glasgow, 1969, William Collins Sons & Co.; London, 1971, Fontana Books [paperback edition, richly illustrated]), for a gripping you-can't-put-it-down account of Trafalgar, its antecedents and consequences. Many of the officers in Mr. Spalding's tally of sword awards will come to life in Mr. Howarth's pages, and the positions and roles of their ships will be made clear.

WEATHER DIVISION

VICTORY (100 guns). Vice-Admiral Lord Nelson K.B. (killed). The Fund presented both his widow and his brother, William, Earl Nelson, with a silver vase value of £500. Lady Nelson's vase was not completed until January 1810 when it was sent to her in Bath, where she then lived. Although of £500 value when voted in 1805, when completed over four years later the actual cost of this vase was £650.

Captain Thomas M. Hardy was voted a silver vase of £100 value. This was probably the vase exhibited at the Royal Naval Exhibition at Chelsea, London, in 1891 as exhibit number 1935 (R.N.E.** 1935).

TEMERAIRE (98 guns). Captain Eliab Harvey is believed to have been voted a sword. No letter of thanks for a sword appears in Lloyd's Nelson Collection (L.N.C.) and as yet to the author's knowledge his sword is unrecorded.

NEPTUNE (98 guns). Captain Thomas Francis Freemantle was voted a £100 vase which was exhibited at the Royal Naval Exhibition in 1891 (R.N.E.-1966).

CONQUEROR (74 guns). Captain Israel Pellew was voted a sword. Upon his arrival in Plymouth in August 1806 he received the "very handsome sword which the Patriotic Committee have been pleased to present me." His letter of thanks to the Fund is in Lloyd's Nelson Collection (L.N.C.-P.179).

LEVIATHAN (74 guns). Captain Henry William Bayntun is believed to have been voted a sword.

AJAX (74 guns). Lieutenant John Pilford (acting Captain in the absence of the Captain) was voted a sword which is now in a private collection in the United States.

**Abbreviations Used in Text
L.N.C.—Lloyd's Nelson Collection (London), followed by the appropriate letter number.
R.N.E.—Catalogue of a Royal Naval Exhibition, Chelsea (London), 1891.

Fig. 8—Trafalgar silver vase designed by John Flaxman and made by Rundell, Bridge & Rundell of London.

ORION (74 guns). Captain Edward Codrington is believed to have been voted a sword.

AGAMEMNON (64 guns). Captain Sir Edward Berry was voted a vase of £100 value which was exhibited at the Royal Naval Exhibition in 1891 (R.N.E.-1928).

MINOTAUR (74 guns). Captain Charles John Moore Mansfield was voted a sword which is still in the possession of his descendants in England. The sword is complete with its case, belt, knot and symbolism card.

SPARTIATE (74 guns). Captain Francis Laforey is believed to have been voted a sword.

BRITANNIA (100 guns). Rear-Admiral Lord Northesk was voted a vase of £300 value.

Captain Charles Bullen was voted a sword. In a letter to Lloyds dated 6th September 1806 Captain Bullen states he had received the sword and "I beg you will be pleased to assure those Gentlemen who compose the Committee, how sensible I am of the Honour, they have confer'd on me, and my thanks for it." (L.N.C.-P.62).

AFRICA (64 guns). Captain Henry Digby was voted a sword. In his letter of thanks, 9th January 1806, the good Captain notes, "I have been given to understand that to wear it we have not the Sanction of thè Lords Commissioners of the Admty." (L.N.C.-P.272).

ROYAL SOVEREIGN (100 guns). Vice-Admiral Sir Cuthbert Collingwood was voted a silver vase of £500 value. Patriotic Fund Minutes, 3rd December 1805: "Resolved—That a vase of like value (£500) be presented to Vice-Admiral Lord Collingwood, who, after the death of the Commander-in-Chief in the hour of victory, so nobly compleated the triumph of the day."

Captain Edward Rotherham was voted a vase of £100 value which has now returned to its home and can be viewed in the Nelson Collection at Lloyd's. In a letter to Lloyds dated 5th February 1806 Captain Rotherham writes, "Understanding it to be the intention of the Committee to do me the honour of presenting me with a Sword of the value of one hundred pounds I inclose a letter to them on the subject which you will also be pleased to lay before them." It would appear that Rotherham asked the committee for a vase in lieu of the intended sword. (L.N.C.-P.44).

MARS (74 guns). Captain George Duff was killed early in the action by a shot which decapitated him. A vase of £100 value was voted to his son and widow, Sophia. Her letter of thanks dated 14th January 1806 for "the flattering gift of a piece of plate to myself and my son as a testimony of their regard to the memory of my beloved and lamented husband" is in Lloyd's Nelson Collection (L.N.C.-P.154).

Lieutenant William Hannah succeeded to the command on the death of his Captain and was voted a vase of £100 value. His letter of receipt and thanks for the vase is at Lloyd's (L.N.C.-P.161). It is dated 24th October 1806 and the Lieutenant states, "To say that I am proud of the honour, that I admire the Workmanship would be a very inadequate representation of my Feelings on such an occasion."

BELLEISLE (74 guns). "Captain William Hargood, H.M.S. Belleisle, who shared in the danger and glory of the memorable victory of Trafalgar, a vase of the value of £100."

TONNANT (80 guns). Captain Charles Tyler was voted a sword. In a letter of thanks dated 21st August 1806 he writes, "I have received the Sword ordered by the Gentlemen of the Committee of the Patriotic Fund to be presented me it is extremely handsome."

BELLEROPHON (74 guns). Captain John Cooke was killed because he refused to take off his gilt epaulettes. Lieutenant Cumby pointed out to his Captain that his epaulettes would make an excellent mark for snipers in the enemy's tops. Cook replied, "It is too late to take them off; I see my situation, but I will die like a man," which is unfortunately what he did. His last words were, "Tell Lieutenant Cumby never to strike." It was resolved that a vase of the value of £200, with an appropriate inscription, be presented to Mrs. Cooke, his widow.

Lieutenant William Pryce Cumby, who took command on the death of his Captain, was voted a sword. In a letter to Lloyd's dated 24th July 1806 he writes, "I beg to acknowledge the receipt of a most elegant Sword from Mr. Teed," and "that I

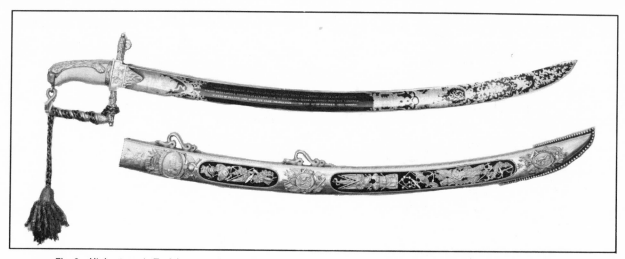

Fig. 9—Highest-grade Trafalgar sword, presented to the Honourable Henry Blackwood, Captain of H.M.S. Euryalus.

shall never disgrace the honourable weapon now entrusted to my care." (L.N.C.-P.235).

COLOSSUS (74 guns). Captain James Nicoll Morris was severely wounded and it was resolved that he be voted a vase of the value of £100.

ACHILLES (74 guns). Captain Richard King was voted a sword which is now in the Collection of the National Maritime Museum at Greenwich (Sword 123.)

POLYPHEMUS (64 guns). Captain Robert Redmill was voted a sword which was sold by auction at Sotheby's in London in March 1966.

REVENGE (74 guns). Captain Robert Moorson was voted a sword. He received it in August 1806 and in his letter of thanks dated the 12th of the same month he states, "I shall have great pleasure in preserving to my family, such a lasting and appropriate remembrance of the Battle of Trafalgar."

SWIFTSURE (74 guns). Captain William George Rutherford was voted a sword which was until quite recently exhibited at the Royal United Services Museum, Whitehall, London (No. 3105). This museum is now unfortunately closed and its contents dispersed.

DEFENCE (74 guns). Captain George Johnstone Hope was voted a sword. In a letter dated 11th June 1806 he writes, "Having this day the honor of receiving the sword voted to me at a special general meeting of the Committee for managing the Patriotic Fund, on the 3rd Decr last. I have to request you will assure the Committee how highly sensible I am of this honorable mark of their approbation of my conduct in the Service of my Country," (L.N.C.-P.219). Captain Hope's sword is now in a private house in Buckinghamshire, England.

THUNDERER (74 guns). Lieutenant John Stockham was in command at the battle owing to the absence of Captain Lechmere, who had returned to England to attend a Court-Martial on Sir Richard Calder.

Stockham's sword is now exhibited at the Victoria and Albert Museum in London, on loan from the National Maritime Museum (Sword 44). His letter of "warmest thanks and acknowledgements for the honor you have conferred on me" is at Lloyd's, (L.N.C.-P.265).

DEFIANCE (74 guns). Captain Philip Charles Durham was voted a sword. He is shown wearing it in a portrait of him painted by John Wood in about 1845. This portrait is now in the National Maritime Museum, Greenwich Hospital Collection.

PRINCE (98 guns). Captain Richard Grindall was voted a sword which has now returned home and is exhibited in the Nelson Collection at Lloyd's. In a letter to Lloyd's dated 1st September 1806 he writes, "I have to acknowledge the receipt of the Sword from Mr. Teed (the maker) this day, presented me, by the Committee of the Patrotic (sic) Fund, for which I beg leave to return my best Thanks," (L.N.C.-P.95).

DREADNOUGHT (98 guns). Captain John Conn was voted a sword. "I beg to inform you that I have this day recd the Sword which the Patriotic Fund did me the Honour to vote me." His letter to Lloyd's was from Liskeard in Cornwall and dated 6th December 1806 (L.N.C.-P.93).
His sword was sold by Spinks of London in 1970.

OTHER SHIPS

EURYALUS (36 guns). Captain Hon. Henry Blackwood was voted a sword. In a letter to Lloyd's dated 5th July 1806 he writes, "I must beg to acknowledge the receipt of the Sword sent to me by the Patriotick Fund; which I hope as long as I live I shall have frequent opportunities of turning to the Defence of my King and Country," (L.N.C.-P.284). Captain Blackwood's sword is numbered 171 in the Collection of the National Maritime Museum, Greenwich.

NAIAD (36 guns). Captain Thomas Dundas was voted a sword. His letter dated 30th June 1806 says, "On my return to Town, I found at my house a Sword

Fig. 10—Gilt bronze belt clasp worn with the £100 and Trafalgar swords.

you have done me the favour to present me with, I beg you will rest assured I shall ever consider it as the greatest possible honour in having so particular a mark of attention confered on me by so rispectable (sic) body as the Committee for the Patriotick Fund at Lloyds," (L.N.C.-P.286).

PHOEBE (36 guns). Captain Hon. Thomas Bladen Capel was voted a vase of £100 value which is now on exhibition at the Nelson Collection at Lloyd's. It was also exhibited as item 1919 in the Royal Naval Exhibition of 1891.

SIRIUS (36 guns). Captain William Prowse is believed to have been voted a sword.

PICKLE (10 guns) Lieutenant John Richards Lapenotière was voted a sword which is now at the National Maritime Museum, Greenwich (Sword 45). H.M.S. Pickle was sent home with Collingwood's Trafalgar dispatches.

ENTREPRENANTE. Lieutenant Robert Benjamin Young in a letter to Lloyd's dated 5th May 1805 asked, "Having heard since my arrival that your Board has liberally bestowed a Sword to each of the Commanders in the Trafalgar action, I hope to excite the munificence of the Committee to grant me the like," (L.N.C.-P.289). His cheek paid off for a sword was in due course awarded him.

Whether an officer received a sword or a vase would appear to have been a matter of individual choice, for if any officer had received a presentation sword before Trafalgar, a piece of plate may have been more acceptable than another sword. The answer may be found in a letter (L.N.C.—P.211) written by Captain Lawrence Halstead to the Fund in December 1806. "Having been informed that several of the Captains who had been voted swords for the action off Trafalgar and the action of the 4th Novr. under Sir Rich. Strachan, had been offered their choice, either to receive a sword or piece of plate of equal value, I shall be obliged By your giving me a line on the subject." Captain Halstead subsequently received a vase of £100 value for his part in the engagement off Ferrol.

The Patriotic Fund ceased awarding swords in May 1809, continuing to award both heroic deed and injury alike by a payment of money. Nevertheless, a few swords do exist which bear dates later than May 1809; it is possible that some officers used their cash payments to purchase suitable swords from Teed, who probably assembled them from parts he must have had still in stock. Indeed, these late swords do have the appearance of assembled pieces, differing in many ways from the standard sword. A £50 sword inscribed as voted to Lieutenant Robert Pye of the Royal Marines for an action in September 1809 has the following differences (Fig. 5): the blade, although curved, is unfullered, whereas the early blades had one broad fuller on each face; the etched decoration is inferior, lacking both in quality and quantity; and the scabbard, instead of having cabled rings for suspension, is fitted with the £100 curling serpents.

Another late £50 sword also to a Royal Marine officer, Lieutenant Thomas S. Cox, for an action in August 1810 is on exhibition at the Royal Marines Museum in Portsmouth.

Should any reader of this article know the whereabouts of any Lloyd's presentation sabres, especially those in America, the author would be delighted to know of them.

ILLUSTRATIONS ACKNOWLEDGEMENTS

Figure 1	Author's Collection
Figure 2	By courtesy of Wallis & Wallis, Lewes, Sussex, England
Figures 3, 4, 5 & 10	By courtesy of Peter Dale, Ltd., London
Figures 6 & 7	By courtesy of Christie, Manson & Woods, London
Figure 8	By courtesy of the Victoria & Albert Museum, London
Figure 9	By courtesy of National Maritime Museum, Greenwich, England

Hidden Marks on Boutet Firearms

by STUART W. PYHRR

Stuart W. Pyhrr is currently completing his candidacy for a Ph.D. in art history, with specialization in arms and armor, at New York University. He is holder of the C.O. von Kienbusch Fellowship for studies in the Department of Arms and Armor in the Metropolitan Museum of Art, New York, where he has been working under the tutelage of Dr. Helmut Nickel. The example of Mr. Pyhrr's scholarship that follows gives bright promise that its author will carry on the standards and traditions associated with the Metropolitan over the past half century and more. As a contribution to Boutet studies, the present piece is doubtless the most important to appear since before World War II.

In the summer of 1972 the Metropolitan Museum's collection of firearms made by and under the direction of Nicholas Noël Boutet (1761-1833) was dismantled, studied and cleaned. The large and varied collection includes a flintlock carbine *(carabine de luxe ordinaire),* two double-barreled flintlock fowling pieces *(fusils de chasse doubles),* three pocket pistols with folding triggers *(pistolets de poche à détente cachée),* and a garniture of arms comprising a carbine and two holster pistols. The cleaning process entailed not only the usual removal of the barrels and locks, but also—and perhaps for the first time since their manufacture—the removal of all major silver mounts, notably the butt-caps, trigger-guards, side-plates and ramrod pipes. This thorough dismemberment of the guns, a sound conservation technique when executed by a skilled restorer, yielded an unexpected hidden treasure of marks and inscriptions hitherto unnoticed. The results of this investigation are presented in the following notes.[1]

The most recent addition to the Museum's collection of Boutet firearms is the rare silver-mounted garniture complete with carbine, two holster pistols and full cleaning and loading accessories, all contained within the original blue-velvet-lined mahogany case (Figures 1-9).[2] The garniture has been preserved in pristine, unfired condition and evinces the technical perfection and artistic invention characteristic of the *Manufacture d'armes de Versailles.*[3] The slightly swamped octagonal barrels, rifled with 44 grooves for the carbine and approximately 100 for each pistol *(rayées cheveux),* are blued with mat finish and embellished with gilt floral designs at the breech and muzzle, the entire length *semé* with gold stars. The round-faced locks of polished steel are crisply engraved with swans, harpies, sphinxes and other fantastic creatures.[4] Framed by heavy silver mounts cast and chiselled with mythological and allegorical motifs appropriate to the prevailing neo-classical taste, the walnut stock itself is inlaid with silver sheet cut and engraved with designs of foliage, scrolls, serpents, trophies of arms, flaming grenades and fasces. The winged caryatid and monster beneath the stock are carved in ebony, a sculpture in miniature worthy of a master cabinetmaker of the eighteenth century. Boutet's name appears on all major elements: on the silver plaque adorning the case of the garniture, *Manu à Versailles Entrep^se Boutet;* beneath the barrels *Boutet Directeur Artiste Manuf^re à Versailles;* on the beveled edges of the locks *BOUTET à Versailles;* on the priming flask *Entreprise Boutet Manufac^re à Versailles.* Hall-marked for the period 1798-1809, the garniture probably dates prior to Napoleon's coronation in May, 1804, after which the Versailles factory assumed the name *Manufacture Impériale.* Contemporary government accounts contain numerous references to garnitures of arms ordered from Boutet between the years 1801 and 1804. One such order, placed in 1801 by M. de Champagny, Minister of Exterior Affairs, requests three or four *nécessaires d'armes, composés chacun d'une carabine et d'une paire de pistolets renfermés dans leur boîte d'acajou et dans le prix de 6000 fr. l'une,*[5] the type and value of which were probably very similar to the Museum's garniture.

The escutcheon of the carbine is engraved with the coat of arms of the owner surmounted by his name in Cyrillic, the transliteration of which is *Nicolai Pompeyevich Shabelski* (Figure 7). The name is repeated on the inside of the trigger-guards of the pistols, which also bear the interlaced monogram NS. Of Polish rather than Russian origin, only the name of the owner is certain, his personal history and political or military achievements having escaped our search.[6] Siebmacher's *Wappenbuch*[7] lists over twenty-five Polish families whose coat of arms are similar to Shabelski's, i.e., a crescent with a broken sword above and below, though Shabelski's family is not included among them. Perhaps a Polish *émigré* in the French military service or an Eastern European diplomat, Shabelski was undoubtedly a man of the moment, one whose recognition may never have exceeded the gift of these firearms and whose fame has not preserved his name for biographers.

Lacking adequate biographical data about Shabelski, we might never have known if he was the original recipient of the garniture or only its later owner—had it not been for the removal of the side-plate of the car-

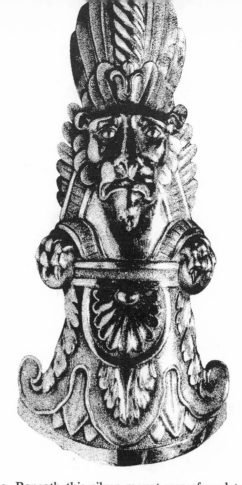

bine. Beneath this silver mount were found two inscriptions stamped into the wood in letters one-sixteenth-inch high: *NICOLAS DE CHABELSKY —ST RAPHAEL VAR FRANCE* (Figure 8). The first inscription is the same as that found on the escutcheon and trigger-guards, though with somewhat modified spelling. The second inscription probably represents the address or garrison of Shabelski in the town of Saint-Raphael, on the Côte d'Azur south of Cannes, which is in the *département* of the Var. Saint-Raphael was a port of significance in Boutet's era, Napoleon having landed there upon his triumphant return from Egypt in 1799 and, under less auspicious circumstances, having embarked there for Elba in 1814. In light of their concealment and the French orthographic interpretation of the Polish name, the inscriptions were most likely added before the carbine left Boutet's workshop.[8] They may have been applied in an atelier in which other carbines of similar type were in preparation, the stamps employed to distinguish the Shabelski carbine from the others. This appears to be the first recorded instance of the name and address of a recipient added in this manner to the stock of a Boutet presentation firearm.

Closer examination of the garniture also revealed a meticulous use of assembly marks, each individual part of lock, stock and barrel, down to the most insignificant screw, bearing either an X or ↓ (an arrow?). The marks, so thoroughly applied to the pistols, are less consistently used on the carbine, implying, perhaps, that the latter was made in a dif-

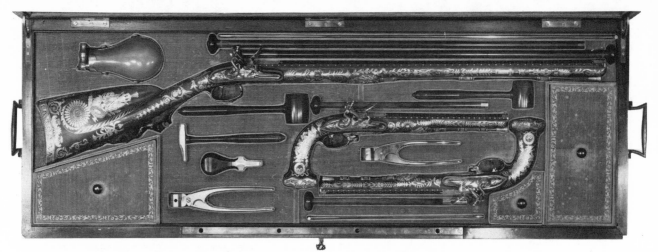

Fig. 1—Garniture of flintlock firearms with full accessories, by Nicolas Noël Boutet. Silver furniture hall-marked for 1798-1809. French (Versailles), c. 1800-1804. The Metropolitan Museum of Art, Rogers Fund, 1970. 179.1

Fig. 2—Detail of the lock of the carbine of the garniture.

Fig. 3—Side plate of the carbine.

Fig. 4—Ebony caryatid beneath the stock of the carbine.

ferent atelier or under the supervision of a different foreman. The suggestion gains credence in view of the fact that only upon the carbine were hidden inscriptions found, while the pistols alone reveal on the inside of their locks the mark of the yet-unidentified lockmaker *JQ*.

Little is know about the internal management and division of work within the *Manufacture d'armes de Versailles* beyond the name of a few inspectors.[9] Established by decree in 1793, the enterprise was housed in the Grand-Commun at 17 rue de la Union, in the south wing of the palace.[10] Designed by Mansard and built between 1682 and 1686, the building measured 83 x 76 meters and had a central court 46 x 39 meters, presenting a total surface area of 4514 square meters. At one time organized as a barracks, the interior had been divided into 1000 chambers lodging more than 2000 individuals. It was requisitioned by Minister Bénézech, the first administrative director of the Manufacture, as a structure suitable with regards both to space and light (it had over 500 windows) for the establishment of a national center for the fabrication of arms. Under the supervision of Bénézech and his *directeur-artiste*. Boutet, the cluttered interior was demolished and 40 ateliers established by 1794. Machines[11] and men, including gunmakers, mechanics, clockmakers and locksmiths exempted from mil-

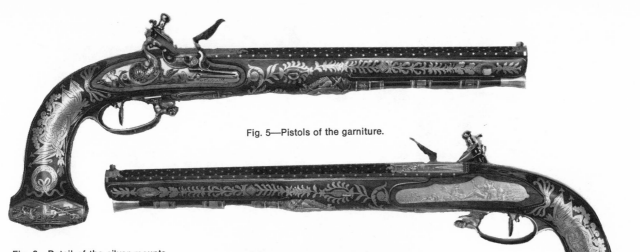

Fig. 5—Pistols of the garniture.

Fig. 6—Detail of the silver mounts beneath a pistol from the garniture.

Fig. 7—Escutcheon of the carbine.

Fig. 8—Inscription beneath the carbine's side plate.

itary service, were conscripted from nearby districts; a colony of skilled workers from Liège, the famous arms-making center in the Netherlands (Belgium having been annexed to France in 1792), was an important contingent of the work force. Of the 1200 craftsmen once employed at the manufactory, we are ignorant not only of their names but also of their individual contributions to the enormous output of Boutet's enterprise. Only in the subtlety of design and finesse of execution of the carved stocks and chiselled furniture can different hands occasionally be discerned.

The practice of hall-marking firearms mounts of precious metal is of singular importance in assign-

Fig. 9—Hall-marks found on the mounts of the garniture.

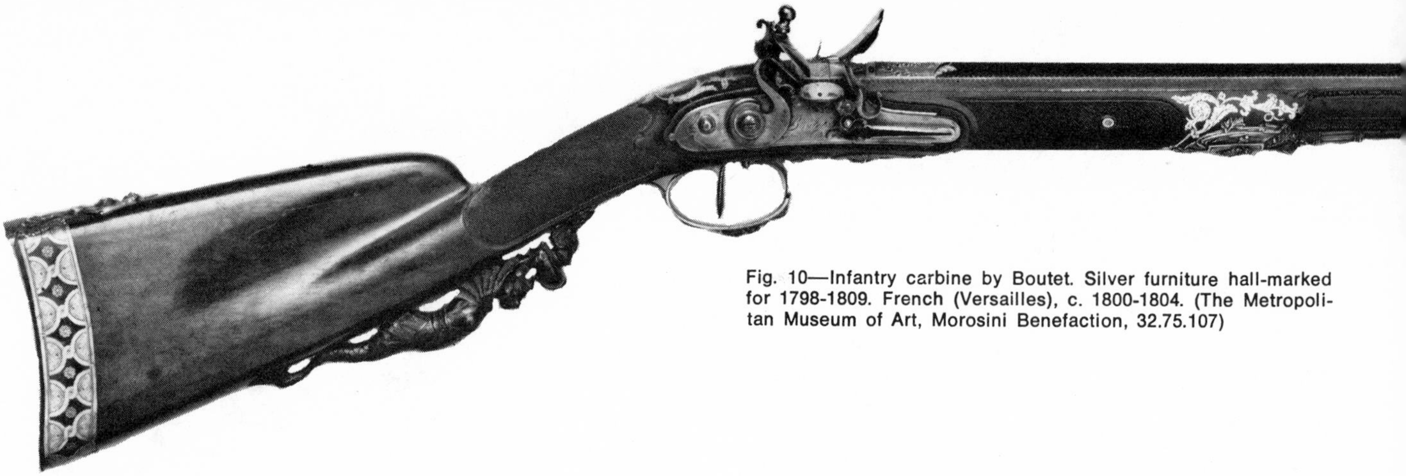

Fig. 10—Infantry carbine by Boutet. Silver furniture hall-marked for 1798-1809. French (Versailles), c. 1800-1804. (The Metropolitan Museum of Art, Morosini Benefaction, 32.75.107)

ing date and place of manufacture. The silver furniture of the garniture carries three hall-marks, the first two used exclusively for the period 19 June 1798 to 31 August 1809: (1) an octagon containing a cock with number 1 to the left, the *département* assay mark *(poinçon de titre)* denoting first standard silver; (2) an oval containing the number 88 separated by the head of an old man, the excise mark *(poinçon de garantie)* used in the Seine-Inférieure Département for large-sized work; and (3) a lozenge containing the initials JM separated by a pellet, a five-pointed star above, seven pellets below in the form of a grape cluster, the maker's mark (Figure 9).[12]

The recognition of the Seine-Inférieure excise mark raises speculation whether some atelier in or near Rouen, the ancient capital of Normandy and center for that *département,* was in fact responsible for the casting and chiselling of the silver furniture found on Boutet firearms. Bottet notes the dispersion of the elements of fabrication that greatly increased the cost of arms made under Boutet's direction, but he gives no details pertaining to the production of the furniture.[13] With the principal works of the enterprise located in the Grand-Commun, the *banc d'épreuve*[14] in the *Potager du Roi* in the park of Versailles, the grinding of barrels at Vert-Lepetit, the manufacture of certain carbine locks at Saint-Valéry-sur-Somme in Picardy, and the *magasin* of the Manufacture at 87 rue de Richelieu in Paris, the fabrication of mounts in the vicinity of Rouen is not implausible. Though renowned for textiles and soft-paste porcelain rather than silver wares, Rouen was, prior to the Revolution, a center for the production of export arms[15] and thus may have had a craft tradition of which Boutet could make use. Upon completion, mounts made at Rouen could have been sent down the Seine to Versailles, there to be stored and fitted to stocks as needed. The extensive use of standard patterns of ornament, repeated on even some of the costliest guns,[16] undoubtedly facilitated —and may have been engendered by—the separation of workshops and specialization of labor.

No doubt Master JM was an important member of the Seine-Inférieure silver atelier. His mark[17] occurs on the firearms as often as that of Boutet himself, so that we may assume he had an active hand in designing as well as executing the furniture. On a pair of 'Medusa-head' officer's pistols in the collection of C. O. von Kienbusch in New York, the mark of Master JM is found on the butt-caps while the trigger-guards are stamped with Boutet's own mark (a lozenge containing the initials NB separated by a pistol). Each master may thus have stamped the mounts of his own design, which, in this striking example, were later combined upon the same gun. Whatever his role, mounts bearing the mark of Master JM are by no means inferior to those with Boutet's mark. All are superbly designed, cast and finished, the multi-figured side-plate and the languid, elegantly proportioned figure of Diana before the trigger-guard of the carbine especially worthy of note (Figures 2 and 3). Emblematic of the care of the silversmith and his respect for the integrity of the designs, most hall-marks have been stamped on the interior surfaces of the mounts. As a result only one complete set of marks, on the unembellished rear portion of each trigger-guard, remains visible. It is useful to note that the concealed hall-marks tend to be punched deeper into the metal and are not as rubbed as those on the exterior, so that they are more easily identifiable for purposes of documentation.

The discovery of the hidden inscriptions, assembly- and hall-marks on the garniture raised hopes that additional marks would be found on other Boutet firearms in the Metropolitan Museum. An entirely different series of inscriptions and assembly marks did in fact appear, this time on the carbine formerly in the Morosini collection (Figure 10).[18]

Sparingly decorated with finely carved silver furniture, this rifle for infantry officers was known as a *carabine de luxe ordinaire,* one whose barrel was rifled with 33 grooves. It is contemporary with the garniture and bears identical hall-marks; the lock is signed *Boutet Directeur Artiste,* the top of the barrel similarly engraved, and marked *Manufacture à Versailles.* Beneath the barrel, near the breech, an

270

Fig. 11—Double-barreled flintlock fowling piece by Boutet. Gold furniture hall-marked for 1819-1838. French (Versailles and Paris), c. 1820. (The Metropolitan Museum of Art, Gift of Stephen V. Grancsay, 42.50.7)

octagonal mark is found containing the letters $B^{L.Y.}_{N•1}$. In addition, faintly visible on the side of the barrel near the touch-hole is the lightly scratched inscription *Pour Brouilly*. As Stephen Grancsay has observed, there is apparently a connection between the mark and the name.[19] But it is unlikely that either refers to the barrel-maker or to a proof mark, the inscription clearly indicating the barrel to have been made for *Brouilly*. Furthermore, scratched on the interior of no less than five silver mounts the name of Brouilly again is found, suggesting that the entire gun was made for him. All silver mounts, as well as lock, barrel and false breech, also bear a second mark, a stamped initial *B* (for Boutet or Brouilly?), not otherwise encountered on the Museum's Boutets. The identity of Brouilly, the intended recipient or perhaps an atelier foreman, is not known. The name is not found in the *Annuaire*.

A second name joins the first on the 'Brouilly carbine'. On the interior of the small silver mount supporting the forward side-screw (no single side-plate present) the tiny signature of *Leon Fletcher* was discovered. The name written in a delicate, florid script, may be English rather than French, possibly the *graffito* of an owner or the signature of a later gunsmith who cleaned or repaired the carbine, though no evidence of the repair is apparent on the weapon. He cannot be credited with the later addition of the silver mount inscribed with his name, for it too is stamped with the letter *B* as are the other original mounts. On the other hand, we have no way of knowing if Leon Fletcher was a member of the Boutet workshop. He certainly cannot be identified as the silversmith who signed his works JM. Only the discovery of a list of names of the workers employed by Boutet may provide some identification for these names recently brought to light.

Most striking of all the Boutet firearms in the Metropolitan Museum is the double-barreled flintlock fowling piece with the furniture of solid gold (Figures 11-14).[20] In contrast to the broad designs in cut sheet more common on Boutet firearms, the stock of this gun is inlaid with dense scrolls of delicate yellow-gold wire, punctuated with red-gold foil

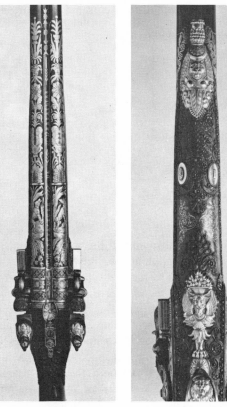

Fig. 12.—Gold-decorated barrels of the fowling piece.

Fig. 13—Detail of the underside of the fore-stock of the fowling piece.

Fig. 14—Tang of the buttplate of the fowling piece.

engraved with birds and squirrels, a rabbit and monkey, a cornucopia and sinuous dragon. The locks and barrels are of blued steel overlaid in gold; among the designs the archaic fox and dog motifs, still popular with Boutet and his contemporaries.[21] Said to have belonged to Napoleon—a palpable attribution if one judges by the value of the precious metal ornament—the gun bears neither initials nor iconographic features in the decoration to connect it with the Emperor. The small oval escutcheon, upon which an imperial monogram, emblem or coat of arms would have been engraved, is empty. It was hoped that a gun of this quality would bear some indication of the owner's identity, as did the carbine of

Fig. 15 — Silver-smith's mark found on the furniture of the firearms illustrated in Figures 11 and 16.

Fig. 16—Flintlock pistol (one of a pair), the barrel inscribed A PARIS and stamped with the mark of A. Rennette. Silver furniture hall-marked for 1809-1819. French (Paris), c. 1815. (The Metropolitan Museum of Art, Rogers Fund, 04.3.190-191)

the garniture. Unfortunately the major mounts, beneath which inscriptions might yet be concealed, proved impossible to remove because of the extreme contraction of the wood over the securing screws.

The gold furniture is hall-marked, however, and therefore can tell us something of its origin. Each of the individual mounts is stamped on the exterior with two marks: (1) an octagon containing a sphinx with the number 3 to the left, the Paris mark for third standard gold; and (2) an oval containing a profile mask flanked by the number 72, the Paris excise mark. Both were in use between 16 August 1819 and 9 May 1838, a period considerably later than the usual date of c. 1810-1815 assigned to the gun in recent literature.[22]

The hall-marks suggest the fowling piece to be of Paris manufacture, perhaps the richest and most beautiful gun to distinguish the last phase of Boutet's working career. Following the pillage of his factory by the Prussians in 1815 and the loss of his concession in Versailles (1800-1818), Boutet moved to Paris, to the former *magasin* on the rue de Richelieu. There he had to compete with his Parisian rivals, LePage, Gosset, and Manceaux, all of whom had once worked at the Versailles factory under his management.[23] According to Bottet, the former *Directeur-Artiste* continued to sign these late works *à Versailles,* an evocation of the success and fame he had enjoyed in his native city.[24] To this effect, the

locks of the fowling piece are signed in gold *BOUTET à Versailles,* the barrel inscribed *Manufacture de Versailles.* We know Boutet maintained some workmen and storehouses in Versailles after moving to Paris, but the exact nature of these establishments, or their significance for Boutet's late work, is not clear. On the other hand, in light of the stockpiling of elements practiced within Boutet's workshop, and the escape of some deluxe arms from the destruction of 1815,[25] some—if not all—of the barrels and locks marked *à Versailles* may date prior to 1818 or even 1815, and may simply have been added to later stocks.

Previously unnoticed, though not actually hidden, a third and fourth mark appear on the exterior of a small gold mount beneath the stock of the fowling piece. One is obliterated, making it impossible to decipher its shape and character, but the other is recognizable as a maker's mark of lozenge shape containing the letters LB separated by a cross and pellet (Figure 15). The same silversmith's mark, together with Paris hall-marks for 1809-1819, are found on a pair of pistols in the Metropolitan Museum (Figure 16).[26] The mounts of the fowling piece and pistols share in common heavy, space-filling floral and scroll ornament and both have stocks combining inlays of metal foil and wire. Only a few pseudo-Egyptian creatures (Figures 13, 14), vestiges of the Neoclassical style that had reached its zenith a decade earlier, distinguish the otherwise non-commital decoration of the fowling piece. Bottet observed that, while rare, the late Boutet firearms were easily recognizable by their decoration, *le mauvais goût qui présida au style de la Restauration.*[27] The fowling piece dates c. 1820, certainly before the death of Boutet's wife (1822), which precipitated a final, ruinous bankrupcy case brought against Boutet by his creditors.

The fowling piece having been made at so late a date, the attribution of ownership to Napoleon is no longer tenable, the deposed Emperor having lived in exile on the island of St. Helena from 1815 until his death in 1821. But the decoration may yet hold a clue to the identity of the person for whom this costly weapon was created. In addition to the gold inlays of oriental dragon and crescent motifs, a large gold mount beneath the stock (Figure 17) displays a heavy, sprawling panoply of crescent-headed standards and a turban-like hussar's cap, implying a Near Eastern or East European owner, perhaps of Polish or Russian nationality. The provenance supports this hypothesis, as the gun purports to have come—as does the garniture—from Prince Osten-Sacken in Russia.

The interpretation of the newly discovered signatures, inscriptions and marks can only be conjectural for the present, as they are unique and otherwise unrecorded. They imply a highly developed organization of ateliers with division of labor and specialization of surprising modernity, reminding one of the system of marks employed at the *Manufacture Royale de Porcelaine de Sèvre,* where a factory mark, letter date, and initials of the painters and gilders are found in addition to the *marques en creux* of the *tourneurs, moleurs* and *répareurs.* Of particular historical importance, the marks on the arms suggest a practice, however occasional, of marking the arms with the names of the intended recipients. Only with the thorough examination of many more Boutet firearms will the full significance of the hidden inscriptions become clearer. In the absence of documentary evidence elucidating the atelier practices of the Versailles factory, we welcome the increasing importance of the guns themselves as primary sources of information in this neglected area of study.

Fig. 17—Gold mount beneath the rear-stock of the fowling piece illustrated in Figure 11.

NOTES

1. I wish to thank Dr. Helmut Nickel, Curator of Arms and Armor, for his generous advice and encouragement, and Mr. Robert Carroll, Restorer, for his able technical assistance.

2. Acc. no. 1970.179.1. Rifle: length 43-5/16 inches, caliber .63; Pistols, each: length 17-1/8 inches, caliber .51. Previously the garniture was part of the Gustave Diderrich Collection and was exhibited at the Metropolitan Museum in 1931. Stephen V. Grancsay, *Loan Exhibition of European Arms and Armor,* New York, 1931, no. 390, ill. After the dispersal of the Diderrich collection, the garniture disappeared from sight until sold by Christie's in London on July 8, 1970, lot 81, ill. Some confusion still exists concerning the provenance of the garniture prior to its inclusion in the Diderrich collection. It was exhibited at the Exposition Universelle in Paris, 1900, an inscription to that effect having been added to the butt plate of the rifle. Maurice Bottet, *La Manufacture d'Armes de Versailles,* Paris, 1903, plate LIII, published detailed photographs of the garniture, noting that it had been lent by Prince Osten-Sacken to the Pavillon de la Chasse of the Exposition. The official catalogue, *Musée retrospectif de la class 51; armes de chasse . . . rapport du Comité d'installation,* Paris, 1900, mentions the name of Osten-Sacken only in connection with the garniture of rifle, two pistols and sword given to him as military governor of Paris in 1814. The garniture was property of M. Bidal; *Nécessaire acajou contenant* to the Exposition. The only other garniture men-

tioned in the catalogue is described (p. 15) as the property of M. Bidal: *Nécessaire acajou contenant une carabine et une paire de pistolets de la manufacture de Versailles, garnitures argent ciselé trés riches.* It seems likely that Bottet confused the Osten-Sacken garniture lent by the czar with that lent by the otherwise unknown M. Bidal.

3. The fundamental documentary study of Boutet and the Versailles factory is the work by Maurice Bottet, *op. cit.* The *Annuaire* or almanac of the Manufacture, a manuscript detailing the number and type of arms produced in the Versailles workshop and now in the library of the Musée de l'Armée in Paris, was published as "Manufacture Impériale d'Armes de Versailles Année 1800," *Bulletin de la Société des Amis de Musée de l'Armée,* no. 25, April 1927, pp. 28-57, and no. 26, August 1927, pp. 18-46. While not complete, the *Annuaire* is of particular importance for deluxe arms, the name of the customer or recipient having been listed opposite the weapons made for him. Among the studies of the firearms themselves the most important for the present work is that by Stephen V. Grancsay, "Napoleon's Gunmaker," *The American Rifleman,* XCVI, July 1948, pp. 35-38, in which most of the Boutet firearms now in the Metropolitan Museum are discussed.

4. The cock of one pistol has completely cracked while the other shows fissures in the narrow bend of the neck. This damage, found on other Boutet firearms with swan-neck cocks, is caused by the crystalization of the extremely hard steel used in the Versailles

factory. To prevent further splitting the mainsprings have been removed. Interestingly, cocks of the reversed-C shape, which more evenly distributes the shock of the flint's impact against the battery, do not exhibit similar damage.

5. The letter continues: *Je vous prie de vous occuper immédiatement de ce travail et de donner tous vos soins pour sa promte exécution. Vous n'épargnerez rien, sans doute, pour que ces ouvrages, par leur richess et leur perfection, remplissent les vues que je me propose et ajoutent encore à la reputation de votre établissement.* Alphonse Maze-Sencier, *Les Fournisseurs de Napoléon Ier,* Paris, 1893, p. 144. In connection with this last statement, a reflection on the high esteem enjoyed by Boutet's enterprise, we read in *Le Cicerone de Versailles,* ed. J. A. Jacob, Versailles, 1804, p. 147, that in the ninth year of the Republic (1800-1801) the Jury of Arts awarded Citizen Boutet a silver medal for *avoir formé cette belle Manufacture au compte du Gouvernement* and for *l'avoir maintenue dans sa splendeur, depuis qu'elle est à son compte particulier.*

6. The staff of the Slavic Division of the New York Public Library has very kindly helped me in search of biographical references to Shabelski but without success. Shabelski's name does not figure in the *Annuaire,* nor could it be found in the standard French biographies and encyclopedias of the nineteenth century.

7. J. Siebmacher, *Wappenbuch,* IV, Teil 14, 1905, p. 34-35.

8. The side-plates of the firearms, as well as the locks, are secured by hidden screws; in the case of the former, a screw vertically descends through the false breech, in the latter the screws are hidden behind the side-plate. When partially unscrewed, the side-plate is ejected by a serpentine spring attached to the stock beneath the plate. Prior to its recent cleaning the side-plate was firmly wedged into the stock by accumulated dirt, evidence of its long undisturbed condition. The photographs of the silver mounts of the rifle, published by Bottet on plate LIII, were taken with the mounts still attached to the stock and not dismantled as were those of the pistols.

9. The following details concerning the Manufacture are found in *Le Cicerone de Versailles* of 1804. The *Cicerone* was the first general guidebook of Versailles published after the Revolution, a symptom of the restored order in France and the renewal of travel and tourism within her borders. Boutet's enterprise, famed throughout Europe for its extravagant luxury weapons, was a central attraction in the city, second only to the palace and its gardens. As early as 1795 Boutet began to decorate the great hall, ordering from the chateau a bust of Alexander and several cardboard armors with heads of warriors in plaster (P. Fromageot, "Le Chateau de Versailles en 1795, d'apres le journal de Hugues Lagarde," *Revue de l'Histoire de Versailles et de Seine-et-Oise,* 1903, p. 232). This central area was set aside as a showroom which "especially excited admiration by the tasteful display of an infinite number of splendid arms disposed in a variety of elegant forms." (*Versailles and its Historical Museum,* Paris, n.d.).

10. The Manufacture remained in the Grand-Commun until about 1809-1810 (Bottet, p. 28) when, according to the *Cicerone* published in 1813, *cet important établissement vient d'être transféré rue de la Prompe no 24, dans l'ancien hôtel de Noailles, dont MM. Boutet pére et fils ont aquis la propriété.*

11. Among the tools employed in the Manufacture were those that once belonged to Louis XVI, an amateur *serrurier,* a locksmith and metal worker. The extensive equipment that once furnished the royal laboratory and that was valued at nearly 2000 livres, was ceded to Boutet in 1793. H. Lemoine, "Les outils de Louis XVI," *Revue de l'Histoire de Versailles et de Seine-et-Oise,* 1931, pp. 87-94.

12. Master JM is not the same person as J. Martin of Lyon, as suggested by the Christie's sale catalogue. According to E. Beuque and M. Frapsauce, *Dictionnaire des Poinçons de Maîtres-Orfevres Français du XIVe siécle à 1838,* Paris, 1929, p. 314, no. 2797, the mark of J. Martin consists of a lozenge containing the initials JM separated by a pellet, a six-pointed star above and below.

13. *La Manufacture de Versailles,* p. 26.

14. *Le Cicerone de Versailles,* 1804, mentions the *banc d'épreuve,* where *les armes à feu . . . sont éprouvées par des doubles et triples charges, en diregeant le coup sur un terre-plein, préparé en face.*

15. Aristide Guilbert, *Histoire des Villes de France,* Paris, 1848, V, p. 481****.

16. A cased pair of pistols almost identical to those of the garniture are found in the National Museum, Cracow. They are accompanied by the original bill of sale, made out on 12 March 1803 to the account of one M. Stagenski for the sum of 2640 francs. This transaction is recorded in the *Annuaire.* Adam Labinowicz, "Les Produits de la Manufacture de Versailles de Nicholas Noël Boutet dans les Collections de Cracovie," (French title only), *Studia I Materialy Do Dziejow Dawnego Uzbrojenia I Ubioru Wojskowego* (Muzeum Narodowe W Krakowie), III, 1967, pp. 27-38, ill.

17. Unlike the personal marks employed by gunsmiths upon their mounts of silver and gold—marks distinguishable by the inclusion of a gun—Master JM's mark appears to be exclusively that of a silversmith. The article "Arquebuserie" in Diderot's *Encyclopedie,* Paris, 1751, I, p. 704, notes that gunmakers were allowed to make their own mounts in precious metal: *les statuts de la communauté permettent aux maîtres de travailler, & d'appliquer ces ouvrages de gravure & de cizelure, de quelque métal qu'ils veuillent les faire.*

18. Acc. no. 32.75.107; length 40-1/2 inches; caliber .60.

19. "Napoleon's Gunmaker," p.38.

20. Acc. no. 42.50.7; length 47-3/8 inches; caliber .61. A second set of barrels (not illustrated) by Leopold Bernard of Paris and locks by G. Zaoue of Marsailles, were later commissioned to allow the owner to convert his flintlock fowling piece into one of the more modern percussion system.

21. A.V.B. Norman, "Decoration for the Chase," *Country Life,* September 22, 1966, pp. 692-694.

22. The late date of this weapon was recognized years ago by Stephen Grancsay, "Napoleon's Gunmaker," p. 37, but the information has subsequently been overlooked.

23. Bottet, *La Manufacture de Versailles,* p. 35.

24. *Ibid.,* p. 45.

25. *Ibid.,* p. 30.

26. Acc. no. 04.3.190-191; length 21-3/8 inches; caliber .64.

27. Bottet, *La Manufacture de Versailles,* p. 35.

William Parker and Parker Field, Gunmakers

by FREDERICK WILKINSON

Frederick Wilkinson was for many years Honorary Secretary of the Arms and Armour Society of London and is now its President. A school teacher by profession, he became interested in arms and armor during the course of his history studies. He has written a number of books on various aspects of arms and armor and has contributed to specialist magazines in Europe and America; he also lectures extensively.

His main works in book length are Swords and Daggers *(1967),* Small Arms *(1965),* Edged Weapons *(1970),* Guns *(1970) and* Arms & Armour *(1971).*

During the Middle Ages London was crowded within its protective walls; at the eastern corner stood the massive fortress of the Tower of London, begun by William the Conqueror and destined to become the arsenal of England. Within its walls were lodged the officers whose job it was to ensure a steady supply of arms for the English army. Such a center of demand was inevitably bound to attract suppliers, and gradually a colony of gunsmiths grew up in its vicinity. During the latter part of the 16th and early part of the 17th centuries, the majority of London gunmakers were to be found within the local parishes, especially in the area of the Minories, a road which still runs from Aldgate down to the Tower. When the Great Fire of London (September, 1666) was spent at last, it had destroyed not only architectural monuments but the homes and shops of many London tradesmen. When these men sought to rebuild their lives they felt themselves restricted, physically and commercially, by the city, and there was a move to rebuild outside the walls. In the northwest, passing through Newgate, ran the road which went on to Oxford and traversed, in contrast with the crowded, bustling squalor of the city, a pleasant countryside. Speculators like the Earl of Southampton and Praise-God Barebones saw the advantages of creating new homes in this area, and soon the road running from Newgate—known as Holborn—was a bustling thoroughfare lined with shops. Along this road passed the criminals from Newgate gaol on

275

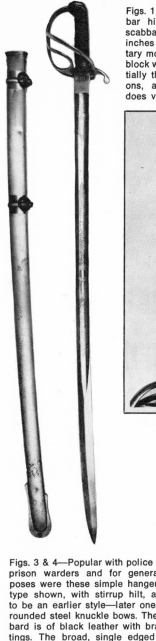

Figs. 1 & 2—Officer's sword with three-bar hilt, pattern of 1822, with steel scabbard. The slightly curved blade, 35 inches long, is etched with typical military motif including "V.R.". The etched block with the name of the firm is essentially that found on most edged weapons, although the decorative border does vary somewhat.

Figs. 3 & 4—Popular with police forces, prison warders and for general purposes were these simple hangers. The type shown, with stirrup hilt, appears to be an earlier style—later ones have rounded steel knuckle bows. The scabbard is of black leather with brass fittings. The broad, single edged blade has *W. PARKER WARRANTED* etched on it, but similar swords will be found with variants, including the full address. Length of blade 24 in., width 1⅜ in.

their way to the gallows at Tyburn, near the site of the present Marble Arch. Public hangings were popular spectacles that attracted large crowds, perhaps another factor which encouraged tradesmen to move into this area.

Roughly half-way along Holborn, as it runs from Newgate to St. Giles Church, stood No. 233, destined to become the home of one of the most prolific and versatile of London gunmakers. In 1789 the *London Directories* record that these premises were occupied by Field and Clarke, Silversmiths; in 1790 the *Universal British Directory* records only John Field, Silversmith. *Kent's Directory* for 1792 lists the premises as being occupied by Field & Co., Goldsmiths and Gunsmiths, whereas the *London Directory* for 1793 and 1794 records Field and Clarke, Silversmiths. *Kent's Directory* for 1794 and 1795 lists Field and Parker, Goldsmiths and Gunsmiths (the first use of the name of Parker). The *London Directory* for 1797 lists William Parker, Gunmaker, 233, High Holborn. Since there was always considerable delay in the production of a directory, it is unsafe to rely upon them to establish a precise date. Far more reliable are the local Rate Books: in London, money to pay the costs of the local administration were raised by means of "rates," a sum levied on every householder, and fortunately the Rate Books for this period for the churches of St. Giles in the Fields and St. George's, Bloomsbury, Holborn, have survived. In them, John Field first appears at 233 Holborn in 1783 and he continued to pay rates until 1790. The entry for 1791 lists John Field, but the word John is underlined and "widow" written above it, indicating that John Field died during the year. For 1792 the entry reads "Widow Field" and this, in turn, has been underlined and the name "William Parker" added in pencil above it. Written on a sheet of blotting paper facing this page is "William Parker paid £1. 6.3", a sum which is half the year's rates of £2.12.6. due on the value of the house, which was £42. It seems reasonable to assume that William Parker took over occupancy of the house during the second half of 1792. What connection, if any, he had with the Field family is unknown.

The entries for Parker which subsequently appear in the directories are of some interest, for they indicate the gradually expanding markets of this very prolific maker.

Date	Source	Description
1798	Kents Directory	Goldsmith
1798	London Directory	Goldsmith
1799	London Directory	Gunmaker
1800	Kents Directory	Gunsmith and Sword Cutler
1800	New Annual Directory	Goldsmith
1801	Kents Directory	Gunsmith and Sword Cutler

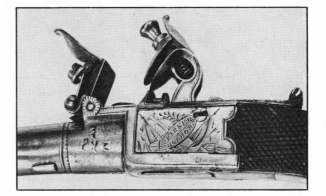

Figs. 5 & 6—Small pocket pistol with folding trigger and sliding top safety catch. Silver butt cap bears an engraved number 63; barrel has post-1813 Birmingham view marks. Marks on the breech indicate a sometime Indian proprietor. Overall length 5.7 in., barrel 1.5 in., calibre .40.

1802	Holdens Triennial Directory	Gunmaker to His Royal Highness the Duke of Kent
1802-1818	Various Directories	Gunsmith and Gunmaker
1819	Robson's New London Directory	Gunmaker to his Majesty (William IV)
1819	Post Office Annual Directory	Goldsmith
1820-1829	Various Directories	Gunmaker and Sword Cutler
1829	Post Office London Directory	Gunmaker to His Majesty
1834-1838	Post Office London Directory	Gunmaker to His Majesty, The Hon. Board of Ordnance and the Hon. East India Company
1839	Post Office London Directory	Gunmaker to His Majesty, The Hon. Board of Ordnance, The Hon. East India Company and Armourer to the Police

Presumably the increasing length of the entries indicates a proportionate expansion of Parker's business, and in the *Piggot Directory* of 1839 he is listed as owning property at 10, Chamber Street, Leman Street, near the traditional home of the gunmakers, not far from the Tower of London. An interesting variation occurs in *Robson's New London Directory* of 1839, which shows that in Leman Street, at the address given above, the property is owned by John Field, Gunmaker; in *Kelly's Directory* of 1842, 233 High Holborn appears as the property of "Parker Field and Sons, Gunmaker and Cutler to H.M. Board of Ordnance, the Hon. East India Company, The Hudson's Bay Company and Armourer to the

Police." Referring to the Rate Books of St. Giles in the Field and St. George, Bloomsbury, the entry for 1841 for the Poor Rate reads "Parker, William", but this is crossed out and written above is "Field John, Field John and William Parker and Field John William Shakespeare". Entries remain as Parker Field & Son in various forms until 1877, when the entry at Michaelmas shows "Field John William Parker", but next to it is a pencilled note which says "left at Michaelmas" (September 29th).

The reason for the change of name in 1841 is not far to seek, for on the 25th of August of that year the last will of William Parker was proved. This will makes clear a number of points concerning the relationship of Parker and Parker Field. The opening statement reads "This is the last Will and Testament of me William Parker of High Holborn"—a small but interesting point since, so far, only three items (other than the will and the 1797 *London Directory* entry) that give Parker's address at 233 *High* Holborn have come to light—all others make it 233 Holborn.* His first bequest in the will is to "give and bequeth the several legacies following (that is to say) To my son-in-law John Field my gold watch and Chain and Seals—The Silver Snuff Box presented to me by the Fish Club—the Portrait of myself and my late dear Wife and my fine China Jars. To Mary Field the Wife of the said John Field my late Wife's Diamond Ring . . . To the Reverend Mr. Tyler the highly esteemed and respected Rector of

*Editor's note: A silver plaque inside the lid of the case of a pair of French napoleonic-period pistols is engraved "Transformed from Flint-Lock by Wm. Parker, High Holborn, London, February 1828" (until 1969 in a private collection in Aarhus, Denmark; present location not known, but photographs exist). In addition to this, there are the two styles of case labels illustrated in the present article. — R.H.

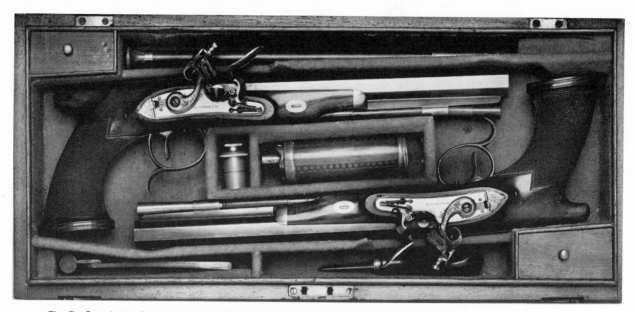

Fig. 7—Cased set of saw-handled dueling pistols of very high quality, c. 1810-20, in original case with accessories. These represent Parker at his best and show that when he wanted to, he could rank among London's very best—but he wanted to only infrequently: for the most part, his production is exemplified by very good, solid, highly serviceable commercial weapons like the traveling or officer's pistols in Fig. 8. See trade label from inside lid in Fig. 9.

the Parish of Saint Giles in the Fields and also to The Reverend Mr. Pratt the Curate a mourning Ring". This last bequest is in keeping with the character of William Parker, for he was apparently a reasonably steady churchgoer and served as Church Warden for a number of years at St. Giles. It would also appear that he was very proud of his family name, for his nephew and nieces all used the name Parker: there was a Thomas Parker Speary, a Ruth Parker Speary, a Sarah Parker Porch and a Thomas Parker Porch, to each of whom he left 19 guineas. Parker also left to John Field all his "household goods, chattels and effects of every description which

at the time of my decease shall be in my house and premises at Finchley" (North London). To the sons of John Field, namely John William Parker Field and William Shakespeare Field, "the two eldest children of the said John Field", Parker left all his household goods and furnitures, pictures, prints, plate, linen, books and other household effects "which, at the time of my decease shall be at said dwelling house in Holborn." Nor did he forget his workmen: "I give to each of my workmen, David Lock, Joseph Lock, Francis Whitehead, Henry Barberick Senior and Henry Barberick Junior, if they shall be in my service at the time of my decease, a

Fig. 8—Cased set of bag-grip so-called traveling or officer's pistols, c. 1805-15, in original case. Case lining is velvet of a light military blue, flask is covered by red morocco leather, giving a marked military flavor which is strengthened by the regulation caliber. Quality is very good but not of the very best. See trade label from inside lid in Fig. 10.

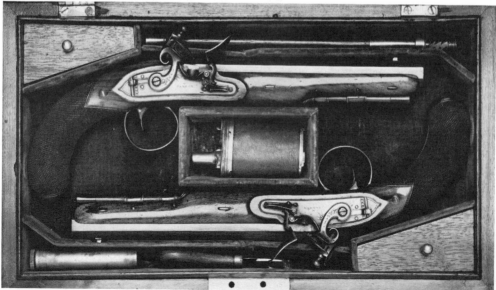

Figs. 9 & 10—Two slightly different Parker trade labels, the one on the left from the saw-handled dueling pistols in Fig. 7, the right one from the traveling or officer's pistols in Fig. 8. Background scene, around circular legend space, is almost identical, but in left label the dog carries a dead bird in his mouth, in the right he does not; but the right one bears a miniscule engraver's signature and date in the lower right corner, "S.N. [or L.N.] 1806," which does not appear on its companion. The central legends vary considerably: left label says "W. Parker," right "Wm. Parker;" left advertisement says "Merchants, Dealers and others supplyd with all kinds of Fire-arms, of the best Quality, on the Lowest Terms, and shortest Notice," while right one announces "Fire-arms of the best Quality:— Guns, Rifles and Pistols of all bores always in Stock, or made up to Gentlemen's orders on the shortest Notice." Very likely the right label is the earlier version, since the dead bird in the dog's mouth could have been added to the plate but not easily subtracted, and the inscription still employs the long "s"; date "1806" was probably smoothed out of plate to make label seem less of a tired old stock item.

Suit of Mourning, and it is my wish and request that they do attend my funeral and place my remains in the same Grave where my beloved wife now rests". Parker's prosperity is evidenced by the bequests of money he left to various members of the family, which come to a considerable total. The remainder of the estate was divided giving one half share to John Field and a quarter each to John William Parker Field and William Shakespeare Field. Family pride again asserts itself, for the will continues: "I declare that it is my particular wish and desire and intention that as early as possible after my decease my said Executors shall for their mutual benefit engage in, carry on and continue my said business of a Gun Maker under the name, style or firm of W. Parker Field and Sons". This plea was honoured by his son-in-law.

There is little reason to doubt that John Field was as hard-working and ambitious as his father-in-law, for he produced a wide range of articles. On occasions he was, perhaps, a little over emphatic, for in the *Kelly's Directory,* of 1865 an advertisement appears on page 2642 which states that Parker Field and Sons "are now manufacturing the Enfield Rifle and Carbine for Her Majesty's War Department, also double-barreled rifles and rifled carbines carrying the Government ammunition, improved revolving pistols, improved breech loading guns and rifles of all descriptions, air guns. Gunmaker to Her Majesty, the Hon. East India Company, Rifle maker to his Royal Highness the late Prince Consort." Manufacturing premises were given as 58 Mantel Street, Minories, and it was stated that Parker Field & Sons were also contractors to the Police for truncheons, cutlasses, pistols, handcuffs and other law-enforcement gear. This account of their products—

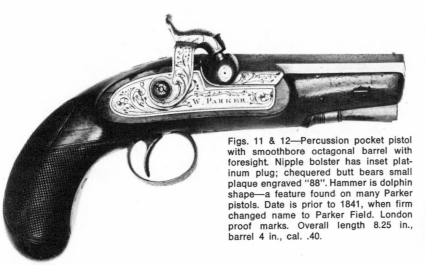

Figs. 11 & 12—Percussion pocket pistol with smoothbore octagonal barrel with foresight. Nipple bolster has inset platinum plug; chequered butt bears small plaque engraved "88". Hammer is dolphin shape—a feature found on many Parker pistols. Date is prior to 1841, when firm changed name to Parker Field. London proof marks. Overall length 8.25 in., barrel 4 in., cal. .40.

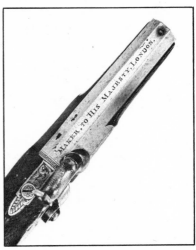

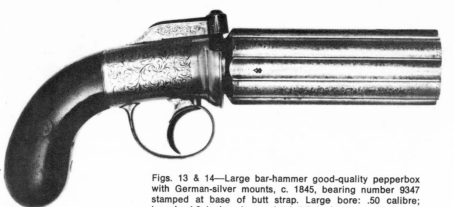

Figs. 13 & 14—Large bar-hammer good-quality pepperbox with German-silver mounts, c. 1845, bearing number 9347 stamped at base of butt strap. Large bore: .50 calibre; barrels 4.6 inches long, pistol 9.5 inches overall; weight 2.5 pounds.

no doubt factual—was followed by the claim "Established for 100 years", an overstatement by more than 25 years!

Why the firm of Parker Field quitted the premises at 233 Holborn is unknown; the Directories of 1877 record them as being then at 59 Leman Street, and those of '79, '80 and '81 at 122 Leman Street, although an advertisement of 1880 also gives No. 59. In 1882 it changed to 82 Tavistock Street, Covent Garden, and the firm was described as an Army Contractor. The same advertisement was repeated in 1884-86, but not in 1887. Occasional advertisements and Directory entries gave other addresses, such as 62 Tenter Street in South Goodmans Field, which apeared in 1871.

During its working life of some 80 years, the firm of Parker and its successor, Parker Field, produced an enormous range of items. They were not inclined to be selective: their name appears on small pocket pistols, officers' pistols, cased duelling pistols, long arms, swords, bayonets, pepperboxes, percussion revolvers, tipstaves, truncheons, handcuffs and rattles; at least one small cannon in a private collection bears Parker's name. As supplier to the Hudson's Bay Company Parker provided trade muskets and, no doubt, accessories as well. In his will he mentions a total of five workmen but there is no way of knowing whether these were the total of his forces or only a select few faithfuls. Judging by the volume of his

output one may assume that he obtained at least some of his components ready-made and in bulk, and merely finished and assembled them before adding his name. In general, the quality of workmanship is good and the engraving on his pistols is conventional but, on the costlier products, of a high standard. On balance, he must be judged as a safely orthodox worker, for there are no noteworthy features which distinguish his work from that of most of his colleagues, although many of his percussion pistols are fitted with dolphin-shaped hammers.

A turning point in Parker's career may well have come when he became one of the suppliers to the London Police. In 1792, the year in which Parker started work in Holborn, an Act of Parliament was passed which set up eight Police Offices, each with a complement of eight paid constables. To each was allocated a certain sum of money, the disbursement of which was left to the discretion of the two presiding magistrates. Surviving accounts show that from 1792 onwards, each Office purchased pistols, truncheons and cutlasses from several suppliers, but from 1803 onwards Parker seems gradually to have pulled ahead into the Number One position. He not only supplied swords and pistols but also repaired, cleaned and refurbished weapons and other equipment. A statement of charges for April-May, 1810, to the Thames Police Office, illustrates his typical activities as well as his fees:

Figs. 15 & 16—Percussion holster pistol with nicely chequered butt, steel furniture, browned barrel, swivel ramrod. Round barrel has flat top rib with fore and back sights, is numbered 8767 (repeated on trigger guard). Note dolphin-type hammer (cf. Fig. 11). Overall length 13 in., barrel 7.7 in., cal. .65.

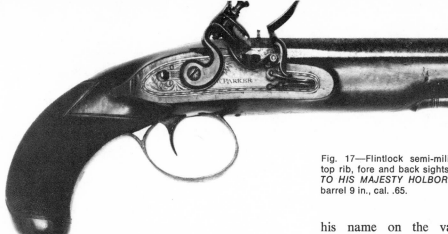

Fig. 17—Flintlock semi-military pistol with round barrel (flat top rib, fore and back sights) inscribed *W. PARKER GUNMAKER TO HIS MAJESTY HOLBORN LONDON*. Overall length 14.5 in., barrel 9 in., cal. .65.

Dr. to W. Parker Gunmaker Holborn

1810			
April 6	To 2 new Cutlasses	£ 1.19.	0.
	To repairing a cutlass	7.	6.
	To new scabbard and mounting to a Cutlass	7.	6.
24	To 3 new side nails to pistol locks	3.	0.
	To 6 new rods and worms to pistols	9.	0.
	To 2 Cocks to locks	7.	0.
	To 2 Cock nails	3.	0.
	To 5 new sears to locks	15.	0.
	To repair 3 tumblers	2.	6.
	To 2 sear pins	1.	6.
	To 2 new hammers	6.	0.
	To Smoothing 8 barrels	8.	0.
	To Browning 8dᵒ	12.	0.
	To Cleaning 9 pistols	13.	6.
	To new pipe to pistol	1.	6.
	To mending tang[?]britch	2.	6.
	To 2 side screws	2.	0.
	To Britch nail	1.	0.
	To pistol key	1.	6.
	To Cleaning and hardening 9 locks, 9 Breeches, fryzins, etc.	18.	0.
May 16	To 4 new Cutlasses	3.18.	0.
	To 10 Powder flasks & Pouches	2. 5.	0.
		£14. 4.	0.

The Police Offices were of limited value but survived until 1829 when, in September of that year, Home Secretary Sir Robert Peel managed at last to persuade, cajole and bully Parliament into setting up the Metropolitan Police Force. Applications for contracts to supply the new police with their various needs were invited (the contract for swords was given to Henry Tatham of Charing Cross, a well-known cutler who, however, for unknown reasons, seems not to have taken it up, no police sword bearing this maker's name having thus far come to light). Parker's position seems to have been quite an entrenched one from the very start, for when the Metropolitan Police held their inaugural parade on an open space not very far from Parker's shop on September 29th, 1829, Police Orders stated that he would be present to issue equipment. It seems unlikely that he had the facilities to produce all the items supplied; it is probable that he merely stamped

his name on the various handcuffs and truncheons before passing them on to the police, but no doubt the gear he delivered was of good standard, for he and his successor held the monopoly of supplying the police for many years. He was also a competitive retailer: Mr. William Day, Secretary of State Office Keeper of Criminal Records, stated in a report (p. 34) to the Select Committee on the Police of the Metropolis, published on July 17th, 1822, that the Mounted Patrol officers who patroled the roads leading into London carried the same equipment as cavalry regiments. Day was then asked "In what manner do you provide the arms?" and he replied "The man who has supplied the police for some years, Parker of Holborn Hill, still supplies". "Do you take care to ascertain his charges are not too high?" "Yes, I have generally had reason to believe that they are under what their price may be."

When Parker died in the summer of 1841, his good will and reputation carried over to his son-in-law and to the firm of Parker Field, for they continued to satisfy police requirements. In general, Field honoured his father-in-law's wishes with respect to the name of the firm, although a number of items bearing the address 233 Holborn carry only the name Field or Field & Sons.

The firm kept abreast with developments in the firearms industry, converting flintlocks to percussion as well as supplying new percussion weapons. Parker Field offered percussion revolvers, on both Tranter and Adams licenses. Parker had made the acquaintance of Samuel Colt in 1835 when the "Colonel" was visiting London to acquire his British patent and was staying near Ludgate Circus; on his way around London he came upon the shop at No. 233 Holborn. W. Edwards in *The Story of Colt's Revolver* (Pennsylvania, 1957) quotes Colt as saying that he found the shop of a "Mr. Palmer" [*sic*] and there had his pistol polished, blued, hardened and engraved."

Parker was not an innovator. There are no recorded patents in his name, though John Field had at least two ideas translated into practical realizations: on June 14th, 1852, a Registered Design (No. 3300) was recorded in his name; it was for a spring-operated rammer, fitted to the side of percussion re-

Fig. 18—Typical 19th century handcuffs. Upper pair is stamped *PARKER HOLBORN,* lower *FIELD AND SONS.*

Fig. 19—Police rattles, used to call assistance in same way as later whistles. Larger one may have been carried by a Watchman of London, but lower is stamped PARKER HOLBORN and POLICE, and has division letter and number N39. Dates 1829-41, i.e. between formation of Metropolitan Police and Parker's death. Both have lead insets to give body some weight for swinging.

Fig. 20—*Left:* Truncheon of Hatton Garden Police Office; black with gold lettering; base of grip is stamped *PARKER HOLBORN.* Length 20.5 in.
Center: Metropolitan police truncheon, finely painted with the Royal Arms. Overall length 12.5 in. This shorter type was carried by inspectors and plainclothes detectives.
Right: Brass and ebony tipstaff stamped *PARKER FIELD & SONS LONDON.* These were badges of office, not weapons.

ideas was a "quick draw" truncheon case. Up to the 1860's, London's policemen carried their wooden truncheon in a tubular leather case suspended from the belt. Field placed a spring in the bottom of the case and covered it with a leather pad. The truncheon was pushed down into the case, compressing the spring, and the top flap was then closed and secured. As soon as the flap was undone the spring pushed the truncheon up to present the grip well clear of the top of the case.

Field played a part in the Volunteer movement of the mid-19th century and supplied Long Enfield rifles with bayonets (both spike and yataghan type); all bear the firm name and address. In the Great Exhibition held in London in 1851, Parker Field & Sons had Stand No. 224 and displayed many of their products.

After Field left his old premises in Holborn in 1877, they continued to be used as a shop and remained largely unchanged, at least externally, until the early part of this century. In the Holborn Public Library there is a photograph of part of Holborn which, though it bears no date, seems to stem from 1890—1910 (judging by costumes and other details); it shows the shop front of 233 essentially unchanged from the way it appeared in the engraving by John Tallis in his *London Street Views* of 1839. In the 1930's the site was cleared to make way for the present office block.

A reference by sporting-book author Thomas Johnson, writing in 1816, places Parker in the top rank of gunmakers, but he seems never to have attracted the approbation of other contemporary writers the way Manton, Mortimer, Egg, Nock and others did. But Johnson's remark notwithstanding (it may have been motivated by something less than perfect impartiality), it seems more objective to classify Parker as a thoroughly competent commercial gunmaker who on occasion could and did produce prestige weapons such as the superb cased saw-handled flintlock dueling pistols shown in Fig. 7, but more generally was the author of solid upper-middle-level but undistinguished arms like the cased general-purpose flintlock "officer's" pistols in Fig. 8 and the other hand-arms here illustrated. He was obviously more concerned with widening his general trade than in limiting himself to producing top-grade pieces. The majority of surviving specimens of even his run-of-the-mill production bear good and often fine engraving, and a finish of above-average standard. Parker's work tends to be more individualistic than that of his son-in-law, but one must bear in mind that by the time Parker Field & Sons were in production, industrial standardization and mechanized mass-production were rapidly reducing, at times even eliminating, the component of individuality in artianship.

volver barrels, which had a spring housed in a cylindrical fitting and a rod with a T-shaped flap at the end which folded down when not in use (most examples are found on Lang revolvers with long spurred hammers and fluted cylinders). Field also claimed credit for a type of revolver which gave a gas-tight seal between cylinder and barrel (see A. W. F. Taylerson, R. A. N. Andrews & J. Frith, *The Revolver, 1818-1865* [London, 1968]). The other of Field's

The Development of Percussion Primers

by S. JAMES GOODING

S. James Gooding, still another contributor in little need of introduction to gun collectordom, is Editor-in-Chief of The Canadian Journal of Arms Collecting *and Director of the arms books publishing house* Museum Restoration Service, Ottawa *(Ont.). He has spent "nearly all" of his 43 years as a student of firearms history, with special interest in the evolutionary phases of new systems and the transitions from one system to another. He was responsible for the management and organization of the Arms & Armour section at the Royal Ontario Museum from 1949 to 1957. He has published articles in all major arms periodicals; his* magna opera *are the books* Canadian Gunsmiths *and* An Introduction to British Artillery. *A resident of Ottawa, he is married and has two children.*

The present article is serving Mr. Gooding as the basis for a much enlarged future edition, to appear in book or monograph form.

I.

When in 1807 the Rev. Alexander Forsyth of Belhelvie Parish in Scotland patented his invention for the ignition of gun charges by shock- or blow-sensitive explosive compounds, he triggered, as it were, a long succession of developments which culminated in the rim- and centerfire cartridge primers in use today.

The explosive, blow-sensitive properties of many substances, in particular of the fulminates of gold, mercury and silver, had been known in the early seventeenth century and most likely in the sixteenth and even before, but there are no records of any successful harnessing of their forces—their explosions were too powerful to allow them to serve as propellants, and no one prior to Forsyth seems to have thought of any other use. (The word "fulminate" is often but erroneously used to describe any substance that will explode or detonate when struck sharply, but, properly speaking, fulminates are salts of fulminic acid, $C:N.OH$, and nothing else; a detonating compound that is not a fulminate should not be called one.) Forsyth's experiments seem to have begun around 1800, resulted in a prototypal but workable detonator lock in 1805, and were continued in 1806 and after in the Tower of London under the patronage and encouragement of Lord Moira, Master General of Ordnance. On April 11th, 1807, Forsyth was granted Patent No. 3032, which covered all forms of percussion locks using detonating substances. Forsyth's principles proved successful not only owing to his particular detonating compound itself—the basic ingredient was chlorate of potash, not a fulminate—but also to the very tiny quantity used per priming and to the effective lock for containing, applying and detonating it. Almost at once, many gunmakers all over Britain and elsewhere came forward with adaptations, imitations and modifications of this system, but all were judged —in Britain—infringements on Forsyth's patent, so that he continued to enjoy protection—at least where British law obtained—until 1821. But thereafter the field was legally clear for all comers, and an avalanche of real and fancied improvements swept through the gun trade.

Throughout the period under consideration—say, 1821 into the 1860's—there appears to have raged a fashion at times bordering on the maniacal for securing patents for inventions both petty and great, foolish and enduring, often for prestige more than for any serious hopes of production and profit—a circumstance of considerable usefulness to modern research-

ers in nineteenth-century industrial history, and in particular to arms and ammunition students. The British Patent Office records abound with a wealth of information, for patents were issued for detonating devices in all shapes, sizes and materials: there were proposals for pellets, tubes and caps, for discs, mushrooms and tapes; for caps of two-piece construction, false-bottom caps, caps of gutta-percha, metal caps lined with gutta-percha, and caps of woven fibrous materials such as calico; for alloys of zinc, tin, silver and other metals; for single-priming tubes of copper, of softened leather and of gutta-percha and for continuous tubes of pewter; for rolled strips of paper, thin metal and collodion; and the whole vast lot of these were designated by the all-embracing term "primers." But of course the issuance of a patent by no means insured manufacture. To cite but one of scores of citeable examples of an impractical notion protected by patent but obviously never destined to leave the drawing board: one savant thought it brilliant that percussion caps should "be formed by gentle pressure on the copper *after* the detonating charge has been inserted!" In addition to Patent Office records, the designs registered under the *Non-Ornamental or Useful Act* of 1843, which gave three years' protection, and the *Designs Act* of 1850, which gave one year, have proven useful sources.

As to contemporary books and articles, far and away the most informative is Lt. Col. Peter Hawker's

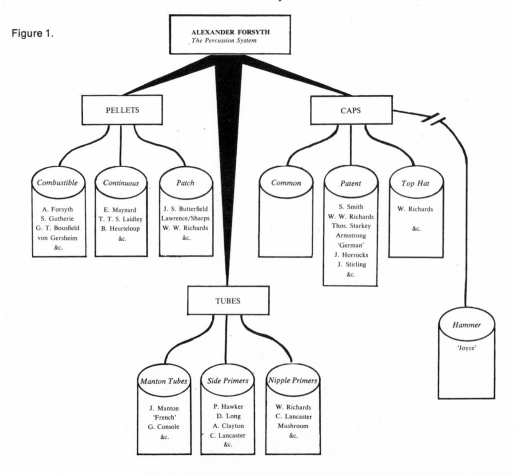

Figure 1.

famous *Instructions to Young Sportsmen in All that Relates to Guns and Shooting,* which ran through ten more British and one American editions after the first one of 1814, the subsequent ones appearing in 1816, 1824, 1825, 1826, 1830, 1833, 1838, 1844, 1846 (American) and, posthumously and edited by his son Major P.W.L. Hawker, 1854 and 1859. At first, Hawker was not enthusiastic about the percussion system, though he soon became an avid devotee of it and described new developments as his book progressed through the various editions.

Yet in spite of the importance of the subject and the availablity of study materials, arms scholarship to date has not published any really adequate account of percussion primer development, perhaps because so much of the work was experimental and ephemeral and therefore—patent records notwithstanding—received little or no publicity of the sort destined to arouse passions and polemics in the contemporary sporting, military and scientific press, nor, consequently, among future students. It is in the hope of filling this void to some extent that these present observations are submitted to the reader's consideration. (For further reference, the following are to be recommended: *Early Percussion Firearms,* by Lewis Winant; *The Rise and Progress of the British Explosives Industry,* edited by E.A. Brayley Hodgetts; and "The Coming of Percussion," by G. Charter Harrison in No. 46 of *The Gun Collector).*

II.

The following account is divided into three sections that follow the overall schema shown in Fig. 1: PELLET PRIMERS, TUBE PRIMERS and PERCUSSION CAPS.

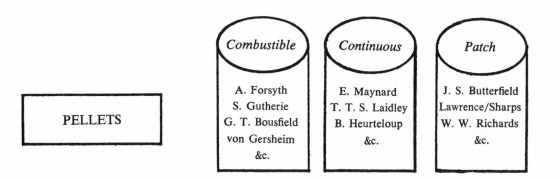

PELLETS	Combustible	Continuous	Patch
	A. Forsyth	E. Maynard	J. S. Butterfield
	S. Gutherie	T. T. S. Laidley	Lawrence/Sharps
	G. T. Bousfield	B. Heurteloup	W. W. Richards
	von Gersheim	&c.	&c.
	&c.		

Pellet or **Pill Primers** were tiny agglomerates of detonating substance employed in three main ways:

Combustible pellets, not wrapped in paper or anything else, were pressed into any of many shapes required to fit the percussion receptacle on the barrel breech and sometimes coated with collodion, resin or varnish; examples are pellets used by A. Forsyth, S. Guthrie, G.T. Bousfield, von Gersheim and others.

Continuous pellets were sandwiched between paper, metal or other strips, much like today's toy caps, an advancing mechanism bringing each one into line with the vent and hammer; examples are the systems by E. Maynard, T.T.S. Laidley, B. Heurteloup *et al.*

Patch primers were pellets sandwiched between paper, metal or other discs individually, not in tapes; examples are J.S. Butterfield's, Lawrence-Sharps' and W.W. Richards' systems.

The small, gold-colored pills shown here were identified on the label of the round tin as "Dr. Guthrie's Patent," made for the revolving rifles produced by William Billinghurst of Rochester, N.Y., in the 1830's —though they served equally well in punch-lock weapons and in the Jennings repeating rifle (predecessor of the Volcanic-Henry-Winchester succession). They differed from Forsyth's pellets only in being slightly larger.

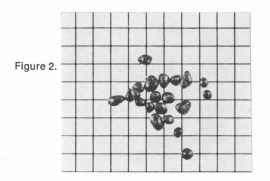

Figure 2.

Figure 3.

Figure 4.

Fig. 4 shows George Tomlinson Bousfield's primers, Patent No. 2882, November 17, 1857. The specifications say: "This improvement in priming consists in making a compound and in forming the same into small cylindrical, prismatic or other convenient elongated pieces. These pieces are formed of the fulminate of mercury or other detonating compounds used for priming and mixing with collodian or dissolved guncotton . . . instead of the collodian, guncotton may be used to enclose the fulminate and form spindles, caps, or other formed fillings, and then coated with collodian to form the priming. To employ the new priming, I omit the cones [nipples;—Ed.] and form a recess at the touch-hole of the firearm."

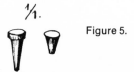

¹⁄₁.

Figure 5.

In 1850, according to Thierbach, a certain von Gersheim invented a primer composed of detonating compound in the shape of a tack or nail which was waterproofed with lacquer (Fig. 5). A gun was made for it by "Winiwater in Gumpoldskirchen near Vienna." A larger size was made for cannons.

Figure 6.

The only illustration available of W.W. Richards' patch primer is that in Greener's *The Gun and Its Development* (Fig. 6). It consists of a pill of detonating compound sandwiched between two pieces of thin paper; it was pressed into the percussion receptacle and there struck by the hammer.

The specifications for Westley Richards' Patent Patch Primer (Fig. 7), No. 9177, December 14, 1481, say:

> And secondly, in enclosing the priming or detonating composition by which the gunpowder is to be ignited in a small water proof frame or case of pasteboard, milled board, papier-maché or other suitable material, which can with the greatest facility be slid or pressed into, or otherwise attached to a suitable holder contiguous with the touch-hole of the gun . . . The form in

which I proposed to make my improved primers is shown in figures 8, 9 and 10. A piece of milled board, papier-maché, or other light suitable material is cut out to the slightly wedged form shown, about an inch long, and a sixteenth of an inch in thickness. The middle of this piece is perforated which perforation or hole is to receive the percussion priming matter. The frame or case of the primer could be made firm which

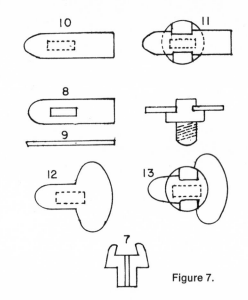

Figure 7.

may be done by rolling or pressing the millboard or other material. Figure 8, represents the flat side of the case; figure 9 is its edge view. One side of the case is to be first covered with tinfoil, or other thin water proof material, stuck on with shellac or other adhesive material matter not liable to be affected by water. Into the recess in the case the detonating firing composition is then to be introduced, and the other side of the case covered with tinfoil, or other suitable thin water proof material, as before, which will enclose the priming and keep it secure and dry, as at fig. 10, or the priming may be made secure in the recess without a covering. In priming the piece one of these cases so charged is to be slid in sideways into the holder M, as at figure 11, the folding lips being dovetailed to retain the priming case more securely . . . Figure 12 is another form of holding the detonating composition, which is to be made and prepared in the same way as before described in reference to figures 8, 9 and 10.

Figs. 8, 9 and 10 show Maynard's Tape Primer. Dr. Edward Maynard, an American, patented a tape primer in the United States (No. 4208) and in England (No. 1078) in 1845. The drawing is taken from his British patent specifications issued (to Joseph Washington Tyson) on June 19th of that year. The tape shown in Fig. 9 is the regular brown production

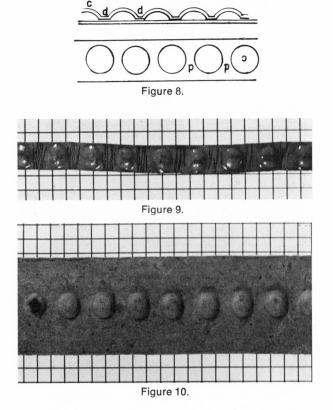

Figure 8.

Figure 9.

Figure 10.

compounded detonating powder. The inventor stated: "I shake [the detonating powder] into small soft metal drawn tubes of pewter or other soft metal, of about one tenth of an inch in diameter, [which are] closed at their lower ends by being pinched which keeps the powder from running out . . . After filling . . . the tubes are . . . pressed through a pair of rollers, which will flatten them, and cause them to assume the form of tapes." The tubes described were used in an under-hammer gun with a knife in the nose of the hammer which cut off the required amount of the tube without detonating the remainder. The Baron, whose "commoner" name was Charles Louis Stanislas, received earlier patents in England, France and the United States for the same basic idea.

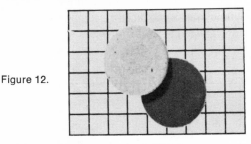

Figure 12.

Fig. 12 shows two cardboard primers, red on one side and white on the other. They are 11/32nds in. in diameter and allegedly came from a package marked "Butterfield Primers" handwritten in old ink on the wrapper. This may be true, but their diameter is too large to fit any of the Butterfield magazines that have been observed by the present author. It is more likely that the Butterfield that was patented in 1885 used a primer similar to the Sharps' primers.

Tube primers fell into three main groups:

Manton and *Manton-type primers* were little metal tubelets inserted sideways and perpendicularly into a touchhole, the projecting part resting on a small flashpan-like anvil onto which it was clamped by a hinged, spring-loaded holder and then struck by the dull-blade nose of the hammer. The earliest of these devices were open at both ends, the detonating compound inside being kept in place by its expansion upon drying after having been filled into the tube; but since the tube was struck by the hammer nose in the middle, as much fire spewed outward from the lock as inward into the charge—a discomfiting circumstance for bystanders, and of course dangerous in the proximity of open powder flasks and of guns being loaded. As we shall see, many attempts were made to solve this problem.

Side primers were not fundamentally different from the Manton-types but rate being classified by themselves because of the various built-in holding, clamping and end-closing gadgets with which they were fitted.

Nipple primers were inserted vertically into vents, "cones" and nipples of various shapes.

version of Maynard's tape, but green and red versions have also been observed—their significance is not known. Fig. 10 shows a section of tape obtained by Col. B.R. Lewis, author of *Small Arms and Ammunition in the United States Service,* from the reference collection assembled by Dr. Maynard. It is 11/16ths in. wide and is said to have been part of the tape submitted with Maynard's original patent application in 1845.

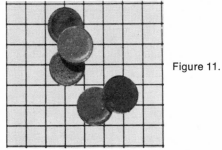

Figure 11.

In Fig. 11 we see Christian Sharps' pellet primers, patented in the U.S. on June 28th, 1853. They were designed to be used in a magazine fitted to the Sharps rifle. They were made of two small copper cups with the detonating compound sandwiched between them. Col. B.R. Lewis reports (op.cit.,cf.Fig.10) that an earlier type had foil on one side.

No illustration is available for Heurteloup's Continuous Tube, but from the description of British Patent No. 9084, issued to Charles Baron Heurteloup on September 9th, 1841, the invention appears to have been a continuous tube filled with a specially

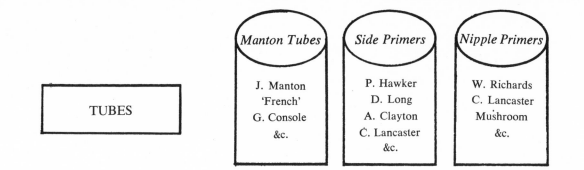

```
                    ┌──────────┐  ┌──────────┐  ┌──────────┐
                    │Manton Tubes│ │Side Primers│ │Nipple Primers│
```

	Manton Tubes	Side Primers	Nipple Primers
TUBES	J. Manton	P. Hawker	W. Richards
	'French'	D. Long	C. Lancaster
	G. Console	A. Clayton	Mushroom
	&c.	C. Lancaster	&c.
		&c.	

Although Joseph Manton obtained his first patent on a percussion tube in 1818, his patent No. 3985, obtained February 29, 1816, was for a lock which used a form of tube as the means of ignition. Actually, the 1816 tube was a movable steel one which was loaded with a pellet and placed in the nose of the hammer. He wrote:

. . . that part of the cock which holds the flint in common locks is made with the proper aperture to receive and hold a small tube which contains a minute quantity of some of those substances which will produce fire and explosion . . . and the flame produced by the explosion issuing with violence from the perforated end of the tube

Figure 13.

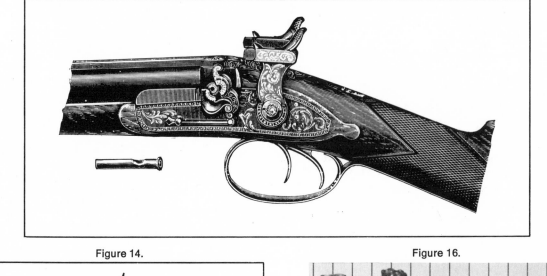

Figure 14.

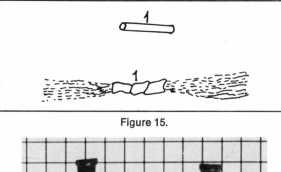

Figure 15.

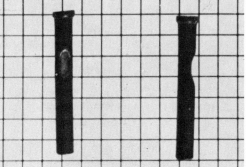

Figure 16.

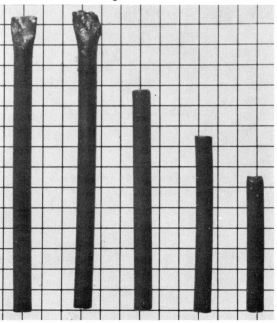

288

passes through the touch-hole or passage into the barrel of the piece . . . When the piece is reloaded the said tube which contained the detonating substance can be readily detached from the cock and replaced by another . . . and the perforated end of the tube and touch-hole may be covered with as much bees wax or any such substance as will completely exclude damp air.

Manton's second patent, No. 4285, enrolled on February 2, 1818, covers the tubes illustrated in Figs. 15 & 16. The drawings which he included with the specifications are a little confusing but they are included here (Fig. 14) for the information that might be derived from them. He stated in the specifications:

My primers for firearms are small hollow tubes made of very thin metal or other suitable substance. The dimensions of the tube must be according to the size of the piece to which they are to be applied as primers, but for a musket or fowling piece they should be from half an inch to three-quarters of an inch in length, and from one-tenth to one-eighth of an inch in diameter, and open at both ends . . . the open ends of the primer are stopped with bees wax to retain the fulminating substance in the tube, and preserve the same from damp . . . I confine my claim to the invention of primers or detached tubes as I have described.

Many variations of Manton's tube primer will be encountered and it is now difficult to determine how the first ones were made. It is likely though that they were simple tubes like those illustrated in Fig. 16, for Hawker mentions that they were drilled from solid metal rods. Those shown are approximately .10 inch diameter and from .62 to 1.45 inches long.

The earliest illustration that has been found which identifies a tube as "Manton's, is that used by W.W. Greener in *The Gun and Its Development*, first published in 1881. He illustrated the same primer as that shown in Fig. 13.

Figure 17.

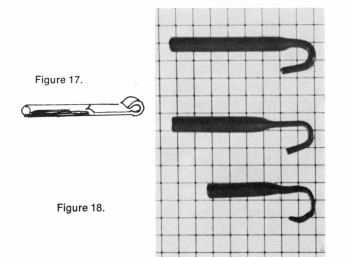

Figure 18.

In the 9th (1844) edition of *Instructions to Young Sportsmen,* Hawker illustrated the primer shown in Fig. 17, which is very similar to those in Fig. 18. He stated "a gentleman in a two-handed punt can have which he pleases—either a light (80-90 lb.) stanchion flint, or a heavy (120 lb.) one with the copper primer of Joe Manton: the only detonating ignition that I could ever depend on, and that will safely hold the primer, with very large guns." .

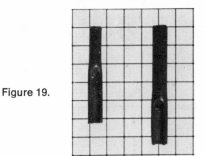

Figure 19.

The crimped tube primers shown in Fig. 19 probably stem from the 1820s. They have been called "French" because the first of this species was found in a cased pair of pistols by D. Ancion & Fils of Paris —though of course this does not insure French primacy of the invention.

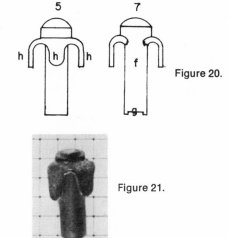

Figure 20.

Figure 21.

The primer patented by Westley Richards on February 11, 1831, is now often called a "mushroom primer," but it was known by many names during the period that it was popular. In the patent specifications it was called simply "Primers for Firearms." The first known writer to give it a name was Hawker in *Instructions to Young Sportsmen;* he called it the "new steel primer" in 1833, and the "hermetically sealed primer" or "solid brass primer" in 1844. A bag of the primers manufactured for the "agent in London," William Bishop, 170 Newbond Street, well known at the time as "The Bishop of Bond Street," identified them as safety primers." The detonating substance was held in .15 inch diameter brass tubes which were inserted into the hole of the nipples or touch holes (as they were called in the patent specifications). Judging from the name, the primer was probably of all-steel construction as originally made, but all those examined by the author have brass tubes, tinned iron flanges and a red-colored waterproofing over the end. In the patent papers it was noted that the primer could be "recharged with percussion powder as often as required."

Figure 22.

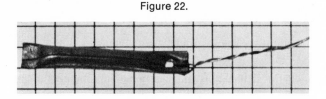

Giuseppe Console, a Milanese gunmaker in the service of the Imperial Austrian Military Government, came up with a percussion system in the early 1830's specifically designed for easy conversion of flintlocks. He cut the frizzen off the flashpan cover, leaving only the hump-backed cover, brazed up the flashpan flush to the top but with a little groove running from the touchholes outward to the end of the pan, and sometimes also brazed a convex protruberance to the bottom of the pancover. Into the flint cock's jaws was fitted a downcurved nose long enough to strike the pancover on the hump. A primer like the one in Fig. 22 was inserted into the touchhole, the pancover was closed down onto it, the hammer's nose struck the top of the hump, the blow was transmitted to the primer, the primer flashed and the shot went off. For easier extraction of the spent tube, a small pull-wire was attached to each. Later, this system was much perfected and refined, especially as the famous Model 1854, but the principle of the cover-transmitted blow remained always. A considerable quantity of 1854 and later Console muskets were imported by the Union during the American Civil War.

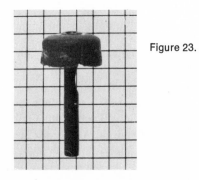

Figure 23.

Charles Lancaster, the famous and excellent London gunsmith, designed a variant of the tube primer which was popular for a time. Hawker described it in 1844, together with Long's primer (see below), as "best for single guns because they (being side primers) do not obscure the line of sight." Lancaster's tube was inserted laterally into the primer hole, after

which the umbrella, made of thin tinned iron, was pressed over a steel bolster designed for it. The exact date of introduction of this "umbrella primer," as it is sometimes called, has not been established, but about 1840 would seem right.

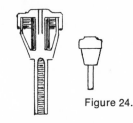

Figure 24.

In the same 1844 edition of *Instructions,* Hawker describes Long's primer as:

> this new invention [which] has all the advantages of the preceeding one [Lancaster's 'umbrella']; and here the tube is placed so close to the charge that the smallest quantity of detonating powder is sufficient to insure instantaneous ignition, with the least possible report from the primer. All below is lined with platina, so that the largest grained, and consequently the strongest powder may be used without the risk of missing fire.

Daniel Long & Son were London gunsmiths working at 8 Old Cavendish Street, and there was a John Long at 8 Allsop Place, Regent's Park. Hawker does not state which Long was the inventor, but since he had high praise for Daniel, it would appear that it was his design.

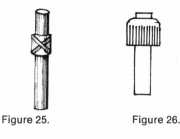

Figure 25.   Figure 26.

The only information available on the tube illustrated in Fig. 25 comes from Greener's *The Gun and Its Development,* where it is described as a "priming tube, the one end being inserted into the touch-hole and the other struck by the cock," It appears to be a nipple primer (for upright insertion), judging from the description and from the appearance. As to the device in Fig. 26, to the author's knowledge it has never been accurately identified, although it is quite common. Herschel C. Logan in his work *Cartridges* calls it "the mushroom primer—another of the hooded tube primers," while Lewis Winant in *Early Percussion Firearms* refers to it simply as "one of the tube primers." It is probably related to Westley Richards' "All-Steel Primer" (Figs. 20 & 21).

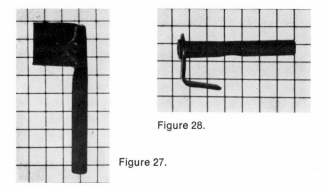

Figure 27.

Figure 28.

Two other unidentified tube primers are the flag-shaped one in Fig. 27 and the hooked one in Fig. 28. The first is possibly a side-primer tube; all specimens found have turned up in England and may be dated 1830-40. The tube section of the hook-shaped device is identical to that in Fig. 15, and may be an adaptation of Hawker's side primer (see Fig. 30, below). Enough have been found in England to indicate that they were commercially produced, not privately made by a gadgeteering sportsman.

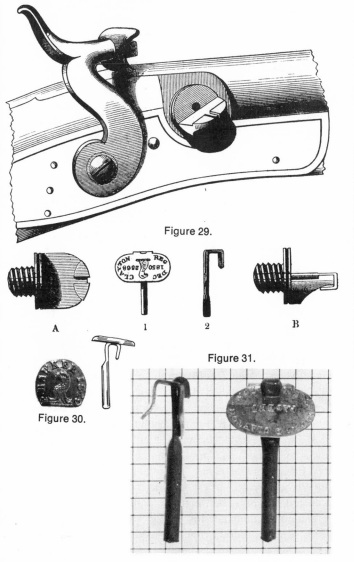

Figure 29.

Figure 31.

A   1   2   B

Figure 30.

In 1848-49, Peter Hawker developed what he called his "saucer-plug and side-primer ignition." It consisted of a shelf-like plug threaded into an enlarged vent (Fig. 29). The tube primer had a hook to be clamped over the edge of the shelf, and a three-fourths-circular brass end platelet (soldered on) embossed with the inscription "P. Hawker" around the head of a hawk (Fig. 30). He conducted field trails at Keyhaven on June 4, 1849. A variation of Hawker's primer was registered by Alfred Clayton, a gunmaker of Lymington, in December of 1850, Reg. No. 2486. It was described in *The Practical Mechanic's Magazine,* January 1, 1851. The Clayton primer shown in Fig. 31 is marked *Alfred Clayton—Patent—Southampton,* but this was probably an illegal use of the word "Patent," since no such patent has been found; the primer should have been stamped "Registered." The similarity between Hawker's and Clayton's systems—indeed, the near-identity—raise some unanswered, and probably unanswerable, questions. Was there close cooperation between the two men? Hawker's son, Major P.W.L., chose to publish Clayton's rather than his father's version when he edited the 11th and posthumous 1859 edition of *Instructions* (Fig. 29); did he do so on his father's advice, or on a basis of extant correspondence and notes? Had Peter honorably yielded place because he had known Clayton's system to be better? The hawk's head embossed on the Clayton primer as reproduced in the 11th edition is particularly intriguing!

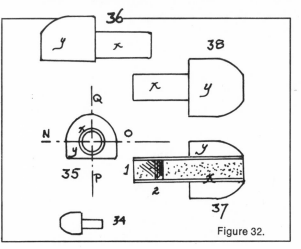

Figure 32.

The last of the major tube primers to be considered is Charles Lancaster's of 1850. His patent, No. 13161, July 3rd of that year, covers many aspects of weaponry, especially artillery; we are concerned here solely with Part Three, *Improvements in The Manufacture of Percussion Tubes,* for the dimensions of the primers under this heading indicate that they were intended for small arms. The specifications say that his invention consisted in:

. . . wholly or partially covering such tubes with leather or some other material possessing the

291

same or similar amount of compressibility, and also in filling such tubes partly with gun powder and partly with detonating powder. I have . . . exhibited several views of the said percussion tube and tools for forming the same. Figure 34 exhibits the percussion tube, drawn to the natural size, and as it would appear when formed; Figure 35 is an end view thereof, drawn to a scale 6 times the natural size; Figure 36 a side elevation of the said percussion tube; Figure 37 a longitudinal and vertical section thereof taken through the line n, o, at Figure 35 . . . X marks a piece of copper tubing, around one part of

edition must have taken place in 1816 or shortly after, judging from the reference to Manton's detonators and Davies Street, from where Manton moved to Hanover Square in 1819:

> The copper cap is now in general use all over the world, and therefore many gun-makers attempt to claim its invention as their own. I do not mean to say that I was the inventor of it—probably not; but this I must beg leave to state:—When Joe first brought out his detonator in Davies Street, he made the most perfect gun I ever saw; and doubting whether such another

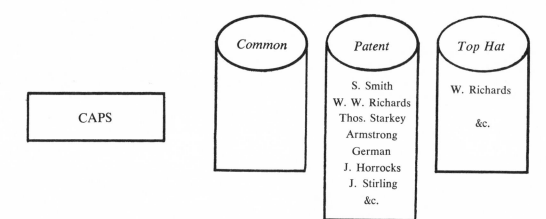

which a piece of leather y or other suitable elastic substance . . . in the following manner . . . take a piece of leather and steep it in a solution of soda and water or other of the known means for softening the same and when fit for use I place it between the dies z, z′ . . . I fill the tube between the points 1 and 2 with detonating powder, and the remaining part of the tube between points 2 and 3 are filled with gun powder, and I finally cover both ends and other parts with varnish so as to retain the powders in the tube [and] to protect them from damp or moisture.

Percussion caps, too, lend themselves to division into three main overall categories:

Common caps

Patent caps, for example those of S. Smith, W.W. Richards, Thomas Starkey, Armstrong, "German", J. Horrocks, J. Stirling *et al.*

Top hat caps, e.g. those of W. Richards, &c.

The invention of the percussion cap is surrounded by controversy and confusion. A number of men have claimed the honor, but even as early as 1840 it was already impossible to single out one individual who could say with certainty to have been the inventor.

The most famous claimant was Joseph Manton. Hawker promoted himself for the laurels, suggesting that in fact the idea was his, Manton's only the execution—the incident he described in the 7th (1833)

could be got, I set my wits to work in order to simplify the invention. At last the plan of a perforated nipple, and the detonating powder in the crown of a small cap, occurred to me. I made a drawing of it, and took it to Joe. After having explained it, he said he would show me something in a few weeks' time, when, lo and behold! there was a rough gun altered to precisely my own plan—his factotum, poor Asell, informing me that the whole job was done from my drawing. Thus Joe, who led the fashion for all the world, sent out a few copper-cap guns, and I know with some degree of reluctance. The trade, finding he had then deviated from his own patent, adopted this plan, and it proved to answer so well that we now see it in general circulation.

Since Manton felt free to "send out a few copper-cap guns," presumably without fear of prosecution by Forsyth (who succeeded in getting Manton's 1818 tube primers declared an infringement until April 11, 1821, the date of the Forsyth Patent expiration), and since "the trade . . . [found Manton] had then deviated from his own patent," a statement implying presumed validity of that patent, the incident must have occurred sometime between 1816 and 1818.

The great gunmaker Joseph Egg engraved on many of his superb products that he was the inventor of the percussion cap, but his claim is not nearly as sound as either Manton's and/or Hawker's. Several other English claims stand up even less firmly. On the Continent, the Parisian gunmaker Prelat actually received a French patent for a cap lock in 1818. But Prelat, a prolific patentee and thoroughly unscrupulous plagiarist of other people's inventions, cannot be given serious consideration. Prelat, of whom practically nothing is known beyond some signed, very good-quality guns and pistols and his patent mania, was associated with S.J. Pauly in a shop on rue des Trois Frères, Paris.

The variations found in the common cap are limited to size and materials, the shapes and principle being the same for all. The earliest, if one accepts the claims of one Joshua Shaw of 1816, were iron and reloadable, but even in the initial period of cap evolution tin, pewter, silver and other metals were used in addition to the most prevalent one, namely copper. Differences in manufacturing techniques by various cap makers led to slight differences in appearance, and every producer had his "secret formula" for creating a cap superior to all others. The most typical species had ribbed sides to help control fragmentation when fired, but they were also available smooth. The better caps had ground edges, but cheaper versions, often of Continental manufacture, were supplied with untrimmed, irregular edges, just as they came out of the machines (See Fig. 34, bottom left).

Figure 33.

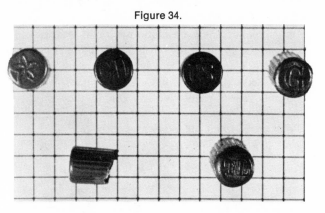

The size of percussion caps was coded to a number of scales, the most common having been the London and Birmingham Standards. Cap sizes were the same, but the numbers differed. Caps of United States manufacture followed the London standard. Fig. 33 shows a sample kit with twelve sporting and six military caps produced by G. Kynoch & Co., Birmingham, in the 1880's. It bears the rubber stamp of the gunmaker who used it, W. Richards of Liverpool. There are minor differences among the caps, and No. 1 Sporting are divided into red, white and yellow waterproofing codes. All others, except Nos. 5 & 6 Sporting, LM and Chassepot, are foil-covered.

Figure 34.

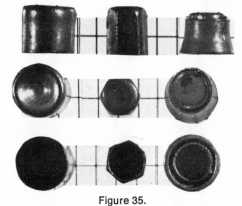

Various headstamps will be found on the common cap of Continental origin. Shown in Fig. 34 are a star, *GD, US, G* and *TL*. The cap on the lower left has an untrimmed edge. Headstamps were trade marks, one of the most familiar being the *GD* of French manufacture. Headstamping or otherwise trademarking caps was not a common, although not an unknown, practice in the United States or in England.

Figure 35.

Fig. 35 shows a trio of exotic caps that have not yet been identified. They were collected in Continental Europe. The one on the left is smooth-sided but has a slightly dished top, much like the Ely dished-base cartridge. The one in the center is hexagonal. The one on the right is a two-piece specimen, similar to, but not exactly like, W. Richards' patent (Figs. 42 & 43, Nos. 5 & 6).

Figure 36.   Figure 37.   Figure 38.

Each maker used a distinctive label, some of which —there were hundreds—are shown in Figs. 36-38. Occasionally caps were made for, or at least advertised for, a specific gun (Colt caps are the most frequently encountered of this type—they were supplied with cased Colts and also sold in gunshops to highly exigent Colt owners, but of course they worked equally well on any weapon of that nipple size, and Colts worked well with other caps).

Westley Richards: the top is checkered and the undersides of the flanges or wings are marked *W R & Co.* The cap in the upper left corner is marked J. Goldmark, an American cap maker who in 1867 patented a detonator with a sulphocyanite of a metal or other base in combination with chlorate of potash.

Figure 39.

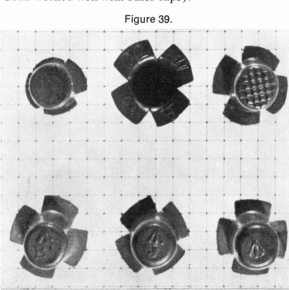

Figure 40.

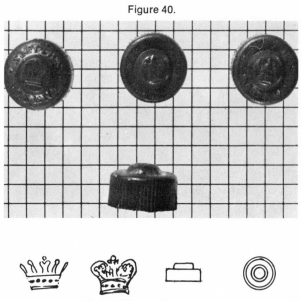

Figure 41.

The musket, military or "top-hat" cap (as it is generally known today) was invented at an unknown time and place by an unknown inventor in the second decade of the nineteenth century. Lewis Winant, in *Early Percussion Firearms,* illustrates the French patent drawings of Prelat, but here as in the case of other Prelat claims, extreme caution is in order. Although top-hat caps are usually thought of as military munitions designed for easier handling with gloved hands, they were available in many sizes for sporting use, too. Three British military headstamps have been identified: the government broad arrow over *BO* (the mark of the Board of Ordnance, which ceased to exist in 1855); the arrow over a *J,* indicating a government contract issued to Frederick Joyce and Company; and the arrow alone. Two caps shown in Fig. 39 are by

Samuel Smith's patent, No. 5978, of August 7th, 1830, was for "a new nipple or touch-hole" and "a new cap and primer." The nipple was of a considerably larger diameter than usual. "The cap," said the specifications, "that it may be easily handled, is made large to correspond with the nipple, and the priming is placed in a small cup in the center thereof." The primers illustrated are marked *Smith's Patent* in raised letters around a central embossed crown. The label of a tin of Smith caps found in a cased gun calls these devices *Smith's Patent Imperial Cap and Nipple,* and explains that "the Patent Imperial cap corresponds with its nipple and has the detonating powder placed in a small cell in the centre. The advantages derived from it are, that its increased size make it easier to use in gloves or cold weather; and from the diameter of the cap being so much larger than that the priming powder, the explosion is not near so much confined and thus removes all chance of the cap being blown to pieces." Three variations of Smith's cap have been observed: two with domed central sections and the crowns, the other with a flat central detonator receptacle, more like the patent drawing.

The drawings for Thomas Starkey's patent, No. 9188 of December 16, 1841, are missing, but from the wording used in the specifications it appears that caps were in production under the patent. The inventor states: "My improvements consist in depositing the fulminating powder between the caps, the one placed within the other, the end of the inner cap being perforated with a small hole, exactly coincident with the touch-hole in the nipple or cone of the gun, . . . waterproofing by a disc of tinfoil or instead of tinfoil a round piece of oiled silk or other water proof material may be used . . ."

Figure 42.

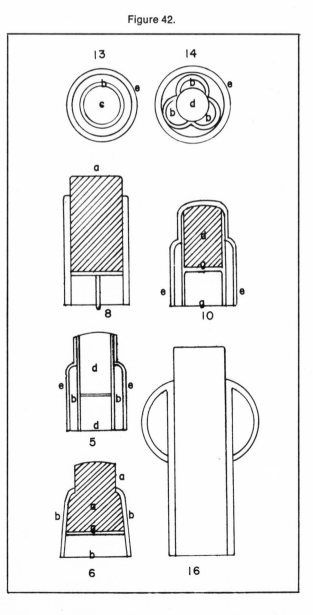

W.W. Richards' patent, No. 7041 of March 22, 1836 (Figs. 42 & 43), called for "making the primers much larger than the ordinary copper caps . . . And my improvements consist, first, in removing or transferring the percussion or detonating powder of the primer from immediate contact with the inside of the head, or top, of the cap or primer, and placing it nearer to the mouth thereof, so that the explosion or firing of the detonating primer shall not take place at the bottom of the interior or the cup of the primer but nearer to its mouth . . . I shall describe several different methods of constructing these improved primers." Figure 43 shows the simplified external view of each of the variants of this "improvement,"

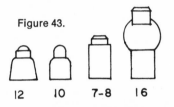

Figure 43.

12   10   7-8   16

the numbers corresponding with those of the sectionalized views in Fig. 42. The specifications explain that the detonating powder had been "removed from the top of the cap into its novel position, nearer to the mouth thereof. Letter *a* is the top of the cap, *b* the sides, *c* the position of the priming or detonating powder, . . . the space between *a* and *c* being occupied by a piece of any kind of hard metal, *b,* soldered or otherwise fastened into the cap . . . by placing the priming material into a shallow cup or dish, fixed into the end of a piece of hard metal."

Figure 44.

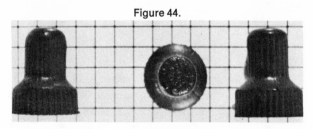

W.W. Richards' "two-step" cap (Fig. 44) is known to have existed in three different lengths, from .375 to .425 in., the diameters remaining equal. The middle size is made of considerably heavier copper than the other two. The shortest is marked *Registered March 9, 1849* in raised letters on the top, indicating registry under the *Non-Ornamental or Useful Act* of 1843 (Reg. No. 1806).

The specifications from W.W. Richards' patent, No. 14027 of March 28, 1852, state that:

Figures 16 and 17 represent my improved percussion cap. It consists of a tube of Gutta Percha, in the upper part of which a percussion cap of the ordinary form and construction is inserted as shown in the section, Figure 16. In putting my

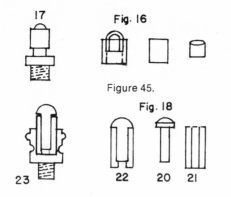

Fig. 16

Figure 45.

Fig. 18

17

23 · 22 · 20 · 21

improved cap on the nipple of the gun (see Figure 17) the lower part of the gutta percha tube in which the common cap is fixed fits the said nipple so tightly that access of water to the said cap is prevented. Figure 18 represents my improved primer, and Figure 19 [it appears that the drawing was incorrectly numbered 23;— S.J.G.] represents the same applied to a suitable touch-hole. The said primer consists of a tube of gutta percha or other elastic or flexible material of about half an inch long, and having an external diameter of a quarter of an inch, and internal diameter of about one eighth of an inch . . . a steel or iron peg, having the shape represented at number 20, Figure 18, is inserted in the said tube and fits tightly. The peg 20 being somewhat shorter than the tube 21, there is left at the bottom of the said tube a vacant space 22, which is filled with detonating composition. I insert in the gun with which my improved primer is used a touchhole of the form represented in Figure 19 [i.e., 23].

The patent of John Davies Morries Stirling, No. 66, January 10, 1853, claimed that while:

...heretofore percussion caps have been made of copper, which has been sometimes coated with silver, [the patentee has] found that by employing a zinc coated with tin not only is the cost of production reduced, but this manufacture is greatly improved. My invention consists in substituting zinc covered or plated with tin, Britannia metal, and other ductile alloys of tin, and zinc covered with silver, for copper and alloys of copper at present employed in the manufacture of percussion caps; and I employ zinc so covered or plated with tin and ductile alloys of tin or zinc plated with silver, in the same way as copper and its alloys are at present employed . . . I prefer zinc . . . as described in my patents on 31st day of January 1851 and the 22nd December 1851.

The patent of John Horrocks, Jr., and James Dunlop Horrocks, No. 1404, June 8, 1853, specified that:

The object of the invention is to manufacture percussion caps in such a manner that the interior faces or lining may be flexible or elastic, in order that a cap might tightly and closely fit different nipples, though they may somewhat differ in size and shape, and also fit each nipple in a manner to be waterproof . . . Parts of woven or suitable fabric are cut into crosslike forms, and the gutta percha is used in the form of short cylinders cut from a sheet of gutta percha. The fabric is placed over a perforated plate or dye, each perforation having a forcer, which, descending into the dye, by which each dye produces a cap, into which the detonating material is placed and then a sheet of very thin metal (copper) is placed over the dye and by the descent of a cutting tool to each dye, a disc of copper is cut out and the same is forced into the cap of gutta percha and the perforation of the metal disc will be so raised in contact with the interior gutta percha as to render the whole waterproof . . . In place of metal, calico or other woven fabric, or other material may be used for the outside covering of caps.

Figure 46.

It is unusual that the provisional specifications of a patent should have drawings, but in the case of the patent of Charles Clarke Armstrong and William Pursall, No. 157, January 23, 1854, they appear in both the provisional and in the entered specifications. Since there are some differences, both are here shown. The provisional specifications, illustrated by the three views in Fig. 46, explain that the inner copper cap *b*, on the right, which has a little depression on the top for the detonating substance, fits inside the outer cap *a*, to form the double-cap shown in section in the middle. The entered specifications go into considerable details, verbally and graphically (Fig. 47), of the proposed manufacture of the two types of caps shown in the top row, Nos. I and II. The objects in second row are:

blanks of sheet metal but we prefer to use a blank of the form figure 5 for the outer cap, and a blank of the form figure 3 for the inner; . . . we press or raise the said blank by means of ordinary pressing machinery into either of the forms represented in figures 6, 7 and 8. That is to say, if we wish to make a percussion cap of the form represented in figure 1, we get the blank form represented in figure 8; if we wish to make a percussion cap of the form represented

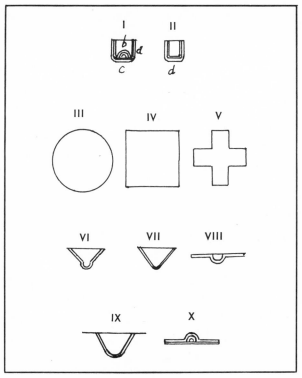

Figure 47.

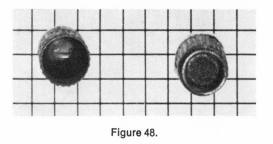

Figure 48.

Our account closes with an unidentified cap bearing a raised *J* on the inside (indicating manufacture by Frederick Joyce & Co.) designed to be fitted by its *deep* aperture, i.e. what would seem to be the opening to fit over the nipple, over the nose of the hammer, while the shallow aperture, i.e. what would seem to be an indented or slightly dished top of a common cap, held the detonating substance and was slammed downward onto a suitably-sized nipple. The date appears to be in the 1855-65 span. No name has been associated with this invention.

The packaging of percussion primers will be the subject of a future article. There were as many variations in use as there were of primers—round, square and oval, metal, cardboard and leather, sacks, cups and special dispensers; all were tried and marketed. At the same time, it is hoped, a lengthy list of percussion cap manufacturers will be published. The author would be grateful for any new information sent to him to P.O. Box 2037, Station D, Ottawa, Ontario, Canada, or to the editorial offices of the ARMS AND ARMOR ANNUAL.

ACKNOWLEDGEMENTS
This article would not have been possible without the assistance of many collectors, to whom I express my sincere appreciation. Particular thanks are due to D.M. Blyth, G. Buller, J.A. Dron, R.J. Dynes, Alex Glendinning, David C. Haas, Ray Hanning, John Hintlian, T.L. Johnson, B.R. Lewis, Stu Miller and James C. Tillinghast. The tin of Billinghurst primer pellets in Fig. 3 has been reproduced with the kind permission of Ray Riling of Philadelphia.

in figure 2 we get the blank of either the forms represented in 6 and 7 . . . we take a second flat blank and combine it with one of the partially raised and charged blanks, figures 6, 7 and 8, in the manner illustrated in section figures 9 and 10. In making the percussion cap figure 1 we place the partially raised and charged figure 8 upon the second flat blank in the manner shown in figure 10 and in making the percussion cap in figure 2 we place a second or plain blank upon the partially raised and charged blanks, figures 6 and 7, in the manner shown in figure 9. We then subject a pair of blanks, figure 9, and a pair of figure 10 to the action of the press such as is represented partially in section figure 11.

Sabretaches

by Lt. Colonel
J. B. R. NICHOLSON (retired)

Lt. Col. Nicholson, born in London in 1915, is a retired officer of the British Army in India. He is widely known in Anglo-American circles for his studies of uniforms, accoutrements and insignia of the past, in particular of Britain's but also of other nation's forces. He is editor of Tradition Magazine, *dedicated to uniform studies, and author of many articles as well as the books* Military Uniforms *and* The British Army in Crimea *(both London, 1973). He is also his own illustrator, rendering in watercolors and pen sketches his reconstructions of uniforms and pertinent objects, and often also of scenes showing their employment. He is married and has a son who is studying at Oxford.*

The sabretache is one of those strange pieces of military equipment the use or purpose of which often appears incomprehensible to the layman. It was in fact an eminently practical, even essential item in its earliest form, having been neither more nor less than a plain pouch or haversack worn on the left side by Hungarian horsemen, alongside the sabre. The German word for pouch is *Tasche.*

With the widespread demand for light cavalry in Europe during the eighteenth and nineteenth centuries, the Hungarian Hussar became the accepted model upon which most European powers based at least a part of their cavalry establishment; and since according to contemporary thinking no cavalryman could possibly function as a hussar if wearing anything other than the full Hungarian costume, this was duly adopted, with such minor local variations as were considered appropriate. The full regalia was not always designed, adopted, manufactured and issued in one single governmental spending spree, although this was *sometimes* the case. The British Light Dragoon dress, for example, became gradually closer to the Hungarian fashion until, in a final spurt, four regiments were converted to Hussars in 1807, fur cap and all.

Officers of Light Dragoons had begun to adopt the sabretache in the 1790's, and it had already become a flat map and writing case, far less bulky than its ancestors. At this stage it was still most useful, but was already becoming decorative as well, and very shortly the structural quality, elegance and beauty, and consequently the expense, of officers' sabretaches—laced, embroidered with monograms, battle-honours, mottoes and insignia of one sort or another—rose so vertiginously that plain leather models, with perhaps a simple metal badge, were taken into use for daily and campaign wear. The decorative dress models were reserved for occasions of pomp and circumstance, and were seldom and perhaps never opened. The collector, however, who has the good fortune to find one should always look inside as sometimes the name of the former owner or his visiting card may be found, or at least the name of the manufacturer. (I do not wish to try the reader's credulity, but I once found a two-shilling piece in a Highland sporran . . .) Sometimes a sabretache was provided with an oiled silk cover as a protection against wear and tear, but these rarely survive and should not be confused with the well-made leather cases lined with velvet which were often supplied by manufacturers for storing the sabretache when not in use.

Amongst the earliest British examples is that worn by officers of the 26th Light Dragoons. It is covered entirely with leopard skin except for a circle of red cloth in the centre upon which are the numerals "26" in silver; it was worn upon three straps. An even more elaborate model, shaped like a shield, was worn by officers of the Governor General of India's Bodyguard in 1791. It was also covered with leopard skin, but was edged with wide silver lace and had a large blue-edged silver star in the centre, and was worn on two short straps not more than four inches long. By the 1800s most officers of Light Dragoons appear to have adopted sabretaches, usually faced with red or blue cloth with gold or silver embroidery and laced edge according to regiment. The usual device at this period was the letters G R for *Georgius Rex* (George the Third having been King of England at the time), this being surmounted by a crown which was usually of gold embroidery, the "jewels" in the crown often rendered in coloured silks and the top of the crown showing a crimson velvet lining. Later on, when battle-honours such as "Waterloo" were added by way of commemorating a regiment's presence at the battle, these were usually embroidered upon a scroll of contrasting colour.

With the introduction of the full Hussar costume, all ranks in the regiment adopted plain black leather sabretaches, officers having in addition a dress model; in 1812, when new uniforms were introduced throughout the British cavalry, all regiments followed suit. General Officers of Hussars or Light Dragoons wore scarlet-faced, gold-laced sabretaches with the royal cipher, a crown and the crossed-sword-and-baton insignia of their rank. The exam-

ple illustrated (Fig. 1) is exceptionally fine, but it was more usual to have simple gold lace round the edge. General Officers of Heavy Cavalry may have adopted some similar pattern, but the writer does not recollect ever seeing one in any portrait. The Household Cavalry, that is to say the Life Guards and the Royal Horse Guards, had plain black sabretaches with extremely decorative patterns for officers before Waterloo in 1815. They were worn close to the waist-belt on short straps, and not at calf length as in the light cavalry. They were worn for only a few years and had disappeared by the Coronation of Queen Victoria in 1837.

In the Royal Horse Artillery and Rifles, whose officers and artillerymen wore a uniform similar to Hussars, the sabretache was also used. The artillery eventually prescribed them for all officers, and there survives an interesting letter from one Captain Dyneley of the Horse Artillery written after escaping from the French in the Peninsula, he having been taken prisoner and plundered of all his belongings: "I shall want directly a sword and sabretache complete; tell Hawkes to let the sabretache to be of his last pattern, lock and key, inkstand, etc." It is interesting to note that the tailors referred to, Hawkes, are still in business in Savile Row, London, and could doubtless supply a similar sabretache today.

After Waterloo, regiments which had been present there lost no time in having the word embroidered on standards, saddlecloths or sabertaches—a useful pointer in identification. At the same time four

Fig. 1—Dress sabretache of a General Officer of Hussars, c. 1815, scarlet cloth face embroidered with gold and sequins. Note the crossed-sword-and-baton insignia of rank. The special uniform authorised for Hussar Generals was last worn in the 1860's. Size 10 by 15 inches.

Fig. 2—Officers' dress sabretache, 5th (Princess Charlotte of Wales' Own) Dragoon Guards, c. 1815. This sabretache has a dark green velvet face with gold lace and embroidery; parts of the crown are silver, as is the bottom scroll with the gold-embroidered battle honour "Peninsula." All the scrolls are outlined with gold wire.

Fig. 3—Officers' undress sabretache of the 1st (Royal) Regiment of Dragoons, c. 1820. This sabretache is of plain black leather with gilt metal badges. Note that the bottom edges are straight as in Fig. 2, a style which later disappeared in favour of the shape seen in Fig. 1.

Fig. 4 — Officers' dress sabretache of the 6th (Inniskilling) Regiment of Dragoons, c. 1830, of black leather without any facing cloth, gold lace border and gilt metal insignia and wreath. Note the battle honour "Waterloo" under the castle, and the rounded bottom.

Fig. 5—3rd Bengal Irregulars, C. 1845. This splendid officer's sabretache has a black velvet front with gold lace and embroidery. Notice the technical excellence of the monogram I.C. intertwined and wrought in bright and dull contrasting threads. The native ranks did not wear the sabretache in Irregular cavalry. The matching belts have gold lace with a black stripe.

regiments were converted to Lancers on the Polish model, and as usual the rank and file had plain black leather sabretaches, officers having a decorative dress pattern.

Immediately after the Crimean War, 1854-5, when so much finery was swept away, the sabretache suffered a temporary eclipse, surviving only in the Hussars and Artillery, although officers of Engineers had what was called a "sketching case", never worn in dress uniform. It is described in the 1857 Dress Regulations as "black patent leather fitted up to contain drawing materials . . . regimental badge, gilt." In fact it looked exactly like a plain sabretache. Later in the century the sabretache returned to favour, although not issued to the ranks (in the Hussars they were retained by non-commissioned officers). Amongst commissioned officers they proliferated, and in the 1894 Regulations, the last to be issued before their final abolition, the following instructions appear:

"*Sabretaches.* Staff officers will wear when mounted, Russia leather taches with three slings of staff pattern." (This was of crimson leather with gilt *VR* and crown badge.—*Author*)

"Officers of Household Cavalry, Dragoon Guards, Dragoons, Lancers, Mounted Officers of Royal Engineers, Foot Guards, Rifles and Departments, wear, when on mounted duties, black leather sabretaches of similar pattern, with three slings, 1 inch wide, of patterns to match their sword-belts. Metal ornaments of regimental patterns, or of departmental patterns, will be worn on the flaps. Mounted Officers of Infantry will also wear sabretaches of the pattern described above, but without metal ornaments."

The Royal Artillery are not mentioned; neither are the Hussar regiments, as details appear in their own sections of the regulations. These were the only Regular Army units to retain the embroidered sabretache at the end of the century, when it was abolished, never to return. The Artillery pattern for dress wear had the Royal Arms of England elaborately embroidered in gold over a gilt metal gun and

Fig. 6—Officer's sabretache of the 12th (The Prince of Wales') Royal Regiment of Lancers, c. 1845. This very fine sabretache has a scarlet cloth face with gold lace and embroidery. The crown is lined crimson velvet, the base being represented by silver embroidery with black "ermine" tails. The upper part of the lance penants are embroidered in silver, as are the backgrounds of the two battle honour scrolls. The beautifully carved, if somewhat overpowering, frame of mahogany is the only one of its kind known to the author.

Fig. 7—Officer's dress sabretache of the Northumberland Hussars, c. 1890. This was one of the County regiments of Yeomanry, Cavalry, who were part-time volunteers and not regular soldiers. The face is scarlet cloth with all gold lace and embroidery, except for the castle, which is silver. The scroll is of dark blue velvet.

Fig. 8—Officer's dress sabretache of the 11th (Prince Albert's own) Hussars, c. 1869. This sabretache is of great magnificence. The face is crimson cloth and the lace and embroidery of gold, the scrolls being blue ribbed silk. Note how beautifully the cypher *VR* is worked in sequins and dull and bright threads. The sphinx badge is of metal.

Fig. 9—This is an undress sabretache of an officer of the Royal Artillery, c. 1890. It is plain black leather with gilt-die stamped badge, and is typical of the pattern used also in the Royal Engineers and Infantry until the sabretache's abolition in 1900. This pattern in crimson leather with a gilt *VR* and crown was worn by staff officers.

scroll with the motto *Ubique*. Where this is all in silver, not gold, it belonged to a Volunteer Artillery unit.

Unfortunately the perishable nature of patent leather together with the vandalism of some collectors who do not hesitate to rip badges and buttons off uniforms and accoutrements, afterwards consigning the denuded carcasses to the trash can, have combined to make the plain sabretache rare and the embroidered models rarer.

One of the problems in identifying the elaborate patterns is the lack of detailed descriptions. Regulations usually refer to "regimental devices", and it is therefore often necessary to identify specimens by a process of elimination: the colour of the face and lace, numerals, mottoes and battle-honours are the best indicators, but dating may well require considerable knowledge of regimental history. Sometimes the knowledge of County insignia may be called for; thus on the officers' sabretaches of the Yorkshire

Hussars Yeomanry the White Rose of York is embroidered in silver thread, a symbol dating back to the Wars of the Roses in the fifteenth century. On the plain black 'tache of the East Kent Mounted Rifles Yeomanry appeared the White Horse of Kent, a badge of far greater antiquity. (It should perhaps be explained that Yeomanry cavalry were volunteer cavalrymen raised in the various counties, and formed no part of the Regular Army.)

Currently sabretaches are one of the most sought-after pieces of militaria. This is scarcely surprising since they appeal not only to the military collector but to many who have no interest in things military as such but are attracted by the beautiful embroidery, the elegant design and potential for interior decoration. They were so used even in Victorian times. I have seen them mounted as firescreens; the lancer 'tache illustrated in a mahogany frame (Fig. 6) is an early example of conversion to a wall decoration.

DESCRIPTION OF SABRETACHES :—

1. FOR OFFICERS WEARING THE UNIFORM OF "COLONEL ON THE STAFF."
2. ALL MOUNTED OFFICERS EXCEPT AS ABOVE.* (ROYAL ARTILLERY AND HUSSARS FOR UNDRESS ONLY.)

Dimensions are subject to reasonable manufacturing toleration.

(1) OFFICERS WEARING UNIFORM OF COLONEL ON THE STAFF.

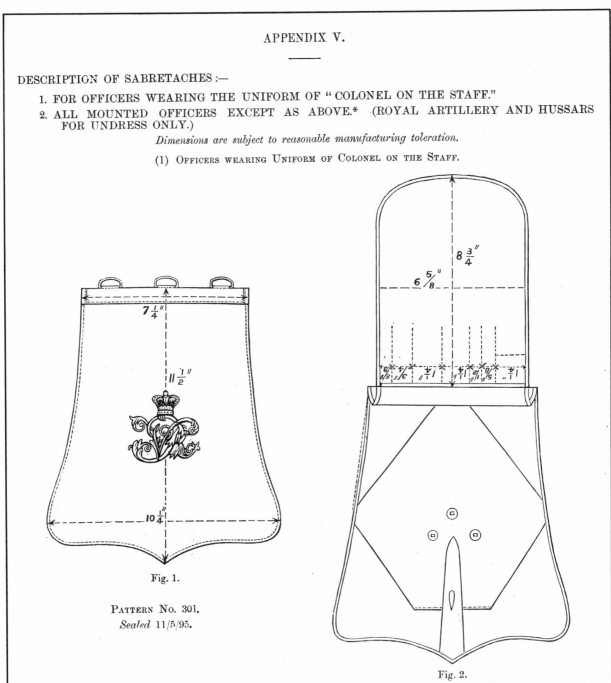

Fig. 1.

PATTERN No. 301.
Sealed 11/5/95.

Fig. 2.

Flap.—Front, as in Fig. 1, made of millboard, covered back and front with red Russia leather. The front part is turned over the edge so as to form a binding, and is sewn all round with silk to match. Three gilt metal dees $\frac{3}{4}$ inch wide are attached to the flap at top by means of leather chapes sewn on to the back. The centre part of the pocket comes over the top, forming a binding through which the chapes for the dees pass.

Ornament.—Gilding metal, "V.R." and Crown above. It is fastened through the flap by means of fixed screws and small nuts.

The back of the flap is covered with red Russia leather, having extra pieces on the corners, as in Fig. 2, which shows the sabretache opened. A tab is fitted at the bottom to fasten the pocket down.

Pocket.—The pocket is double, one compartment being on either side of the centre piece. This, as above stated, passes over the top of the flap and forms a binding.

The gussets are made in one piece for each of the two compartments, and are sewn on to the centre piece; each gusset is $1\frac{3}{8}$ inches wide when made up.

The inner compartment is shown in Fig. 2. It is a plain pocket without flap, bound all round. Inside the top on the front part is attached a piece of elastic webbing $1\frac{1}{2}$ inches wide, sewn down at intervals to form loops for pens &c. In the centre is a small leather inner pocket for safety ink bottle, $1\frac{1}{8}$ inches wide, and 2 inches deep.

* Regiments of Cavalry having special regimental patterns are allowed to retain them.

Fig. 10—Excerpt from British Army dress regulations, 1900.

Both compartments, except the gussets, are lined with red skiver.

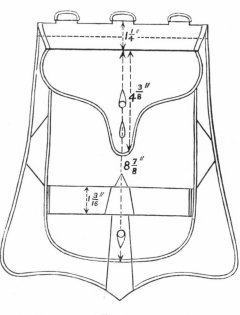

Fig. 3.

Fig. 3 shows the back of the pocket when closed. There is a sword loop across the bottom of the pocket $1\frac{3}{16}$ inches wide, with a loop in the centre for the tab to pass through. The pocket and flap thereof are bound all round. The flap is sewn on from the inside and is turned over. Two studs are sewn in as shown.

The centre piece is bound on each side above the pockets.

(2) PATTERN FOR MOUNTED OFFICERS EXCEPT THOSE WEARING (1).

This is the same as Fig. 1, in shape, make, and size, with the following exceptions :—

The front is of solid black patent leather. It is unlined, but has corner-pieces at the back (as shown in Fig. 2), and is not bound, but is stitched round the edge.

The pocket is made as in pattern (1), except that it is of black enamelled horse hide, lined with black roan and the gussets are of black roan.

No ornament is worn on it by Mounted Officers of Infantry except in Rifle Regiments.

Departmental Officers wear the same device as shown in Fig. 1.

In other branches regimental devices are worn as authorized.

Body Armor in the American Civil War

by HAROLD L. PETERSON

It is about as necessary to introduce Harold L. Peterson to readers of arms literature as Big Ben to Londoners. The same process of metonymy that has made Webster's *synonymous with "dictionary" and* Baedeker *with "tourist guide" may some day give the English language* a Peterson *for books on arms and armor—if not, it won't be for want of effort on the part of Chief Curator of the United States National Parks Service Harold L. ———, author of (we won't even mention the scores of articles and monographs— just the very good, thick, well-researched richly illustrated books)* Arms and Armor in Colonial America *(1956),* American Knives *(1958),* The Treasury of the Gun *(1962),* The Encyclopedia of Firearms [as Editor and contributor] *(1964),* The Continental Soldier *(1968),* Fighting Knives *(1968) and, as co-author with Robert Elman,* The Great Guns *(1971). He is now readying for publication in 1974 (Charles Scribner's Sons, New York)* How Do You Tell the New From the Old?, *a study of—and defense against—fakery. Mr. Peterson lives with his wife and two children in Arlington, Va.*

To the average modern American, the word "armor" immediately calls forth a picture of European knights in full battle array. It is definitely associated with other ages and other lands. Yet body armor has played a part in every major conflict in American history, from the full suits of the early colonial wars to the helmets and flak suits of World War II and the nylon and fiberglass armor of today.

The Civil War was no exception, and the outbreak of hostilities in 1861 brought a rash of inventions and proposals for body armor which continued through the early years of the war. Portable shields, which an infantryman could carry before him, were proposed on several occasions and received some support. A variety of breastplates were developed and tested; and one interested individual suggested to Secretary of War Stanton in 1862 that all artillerymen should be equipped with half armor consisting of helmet, cuirass and vambraces.[1]

Most of these proposals were ignored despite enthusiastic support in the newspapers. The breastplates, however, received a kinder reception than the others. They were tested and seriously considered by the Army, and they enjoyed a brief but widespread popularity through private purchase by individual soldiers.[2]

The breastplates worn by the Union soldiers fall into two principal types. The most popular of these, the "Soldiers' Bullet Proof Vest", was manufactured by G. & D. Cook & Co. of New Haven, Connecticut.

It consisted of a regular black military vest, containing pockets into which were inserted two thin pieces of spring steel, one on either side of the chest. When the vest was buttoned, the plates overlapped in the center. The standard infantry vest weighed three and one half pounds, while a much heavier model for cavalry and artillery weighed six pounds. Some attempt was made to secure an individual fit by issuing the vest in three sizes, small, medium and large. The price of the complete infantry vest for a private was five dollars; for an officer, seven dollars. An almost identical vest was manufactured by M.A. Benjamin, also of New Haven.[3]

The second most popular type of breastplate was made by still another New Haven firm, the Atwater Armor Company. It was a far more complicated product than the Soldier's Bullet Proof Vest and cost about twice as much. The main body of the armor consisted of four large plates held together by a key-hole and rivet system. To the bottom of the cuirass formed by these plates were attached hinged tassets of two lames each. These could be easily detached by extracting the pins from the top hinges. The inventor, J.J. Atwater, even provided against the loss of these removable pins by chaining them to the plate above. When worn, the armor was held in position by broad metal hooks over the shoulders and a belt around the waist fastened by buckles on both sides. For ease in carrying, the whole cuirass could be quickly dismantled into six pieces of a relatively small and uniform size.[4]

In addition to these two primary types, there were also a variety of home-made specimens. An illustration of such a product is in the armory of the Washington Light Infantry of Charleston, South Carolina. It consists of two pieces of iron fastened together by metal straps at top and bottom. Two more crude straps supply support by hooking over the shoulders. In addition there is a third plate designed to be suspended beneath the others as a protection for the lower abdomen. This vest was reportedly taken from the body of a Union officer at Gaines Mills.

Comparatively few breastplates were manufactured in the Confederacy. Metal was scarce, and manufacturing facilities were distinctly limited. What armor was worn was either captured from Union troops or produced by local blacksmiths. An example of the workmanship of one such Southern smith is in the collection of the Chicago Historical Society. It is a simple rectangle made up of four layers of lightweight sheet iron riveted together and bent to a slight convexity, the better to fit the body's contour. Six straps are provided for attachment.

The body armor of the Civil War was highly effective in protecting the wearer from wounds in the area covered. G. & D. Cook & Co. maintained that their vest would resist pistol balls at ten paces and musket

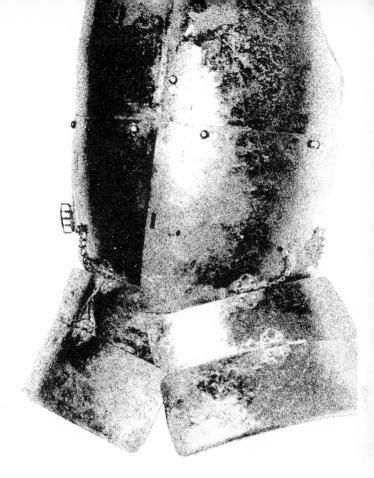

balls at forty rods. Their claim was later supported by Army tests. More recently the Atwater Armor Company's plate was tested by the late Dr. Bashford Dean of the Metropolitan Museum of Art. He found that it would resist a jacketed bullet with a muzzle velocity of 800 foot seconds fired from a .45 Colt automatic pistol at a distance of only ten feet, a really remarkable performance.[5]

There is only one instance on record in which the death of a soldier was caused by a missile penetrating one of these armor plates, and that was under most unusual circumstances. At the second battle of Corinth in the Fall of 1862, Colonel William P. Rogers of the 2nd Texas led one of the most gallant charges of the war against the Union troops in Battery Robinett. As if on parade, he rode at the head of his men across the open ground, threaded his way through the abatis, and jumped the ditch in front of the battery. Here his horse was killed beneath him, but he disentangled himself and continued on foot right up the embankment to the muzzles of the defending guns. There he received point-blank the last charge of canister in the possession of the Union gunners. Nothing could have withstood canister shot at that range, and with his death the spirit of the Confederate attack was broken. Colonel Rogers' spectacular bravery drew praise from all sides, and General Rosecrans, commanding the Union army, ordered that he should be buried with full military honors.[6]

The breastplate worn by Colonel Rogers is now in the possession of the Wisconsin State Historical

305

Fig. 1—Metal plates from a G. & D. Cook Co. breastplate taken from a Union private near Kinston, N. C. (Courtesy Museum of the Confederacy, Richmond).

Fig. 2—Newspaper advertisement for the Cook breastplate showing the cloth vest. From the *Boston Daily Evening Traveler,* March 21, 1862.

Fig. 3—Paper label from a Smith breastplate made by Cook. (Private collection)

Fig. 4—Atwater Armor Company breastplate taken from a major of the 5th N. Y. Cavalry at the battle of Winchester. (Courtesy Museum of the Confederacy, Richmond)

Figs. 5 & 6—Front and side views of one of the plates worn by Col. Rogers at Corinth. A number of Cook breastplates have been found with shoulder straps riveted on for extra support. (Courtesy State Historical Society of Wisconsin)

Fig. 7—Breastplate taken from the body of a Union officer at Gaines Mills. (Courtesy Washington Light Infantry Armory, Charleston, S. C.)

Society. The jagged hole made by the canister shot is two inches across at its narrowest point, and the metal is greatly bent and torn, mutely attesting the force of the blow. Of particular interest, however, is a dent in the lower portion of the plate, indicating that one other shot had actually been stopped.

In contrast to the Rogers incident stand hundreds of accounts in which soldiers' lives were saved by these pieces of armor. Memoirs of the period and contemporary newspapers are filled with such stories. A typical experience was that of General Nathaniel Wales of Jamaica Plain, Massachusetts, at the battle of Antietam. Advancing with the 21st Massachusetts to meet a Confederate charge, he was struck just below the heart by a bullet at close range. The force of the blow knocked him down, dented the steel and bruised the flesh beneath. Had he not been wearing the armor he would unquestionably have been killed. The plate worn by General Wales in this instance was made by the Atwater Armor Company. The bullet struck where the four plates come together in the center, structurally the weakest spot in the vest.[7]

During the brief period of their popularity, steel breastplates were made and worn by the thousand, although they never became regulation in either army. The first advertisements appear in the newspapers of early 1862, and the regiments fitting out at that time supplied a ready market. Over fifty per cent of some organizations were equipped with these devices. In one day an agent of the Atwater Armor Company recorded two hundred sales. Throughout the year breastplates were worn in all theaters of the war. They were most prevalent in the Peninsular campaign, but their appearance is also recorded at Shiloh and Corinth. After the second battle of Corinth there is no more mention of body armor in either memoirs or newspapers.[8]

There were several reasons why the practice of

wearing armor did not continue. The infantry soldier particularly objected to the extra weight and bulk. The 15th Connecticut Volunteer Infantry wore their vests as far as Washington and then threw most of them into the Potomac as they crossed into Virginia. Officers and cavalrymen had facilities for transporting their baggage and so were less troubled by the weight. Consequently they continued to wear armor long after the infantryman had thrown it away. Probably the chief factor in discouraging the officers and cavalry was the ridicule to which they were subjected by comrades who did not avail themselves of the extra protection. There were several standing jokes about the "man in the iron stove" which never seemed to grow stale.[9]

It was the combination of inconveniences and ridicule that brought an end to the practice. Unable to combat the declining market, the breastplate manufacturers were soon forced out of business. The brief boom was over, and armor once more disappeared from the American scene, not to reappear in quantity again until World War I.

NOTES

1. Stephen A. Whipple to Cameron, July 29, 1861, *Letters Received, Secretary of War,* War Records Division, National Archives, W114. L.W. Finelli to Cameron, September 10, 1861, *ibid.,* (irregular file), F136. N.D. Ferguson to Cameron, July 3, 1861, *ibid.,* F85. N.D. Sperry to Cameron, December 25, 1861, *ibid.,* S977. George Rogers to Stanton, April 19, 1862, *ibid.,* R260. Hereafter this set of papers will be cited as LRSW.

2. *Philadelphia Inquirer,* July 17, 1861; January 18, 1862. *New York Times,* January 18, 1862. *Frank Leslie's Illustrated Newspaper,* March 8, 1862. *Richmond Whig,* March 27, 1862. One source states that greaves were also manufactured, though they were never very popular. John D. Billings, *Hardtack and Coffee, or the Unwritten Story of Army Life,* Boston, 1887, 275. No corroboration can be found for this statement. Billings also maintains, p. 278, that the brass shoulder scales first worn by the light artillery and then by enlisted men in all branches of the army were originally designed to ward off saber strokes from enemy cavalry. This is logical since the shoulders are a particularly exposed portion of the body and the brass would afford some protection, but no official substantiation for this statement has been located.

3. *Leslie's,* March 8, 1862, 252, 254. *The Scientific American,* October 26, 1861, 264, 344. Advertisements for these vests appeared frequently in *Leslie's* and *Harper's Weekly* during the spring of 1862. Specimens of the plates from these vests may be found in a number of museums. However, a prolonged search has revealed only one specimen in which the cloth vest is still intact. This piece is in the museum of the First Corps Cadets, Boston.

4. N.D. Sperry to Cameron, December 25, 1861, *LRSW,* S977. Sheldon B. Thorpe, *The History of the Fifteenth Connecticut Volunteers,* New Haven, 1893, 15.

5. *Leslie's,* March 8, 1862, 252, 254. *Harper's,* March 8, 1862, 160. *Daily Richmond Whig,* March 27, 1862. *New York Times,* January 18, 1862. *Philadelphia Inquirer,* January 18, 1862. Bashford Dean, *Helmets and Body Armor in Modern Warfare,* New Haven, 1920, 58n.

6. There is a somewhat gory photograph of Col. Rogers' body in Francis Miller, *Photographic History of the Civil War,* 10 vols., New York, 1911, II, 145. He is lying at the foot of the embankment of Battery Robinett. His clothing has been opened and the breastplate removed, revealing the hole caused by the canister shot. There is also one recorded instance at Williamsburg in which a soldier was killed by a bayonet thrust which struck one of the G. & D. Cook & Co. vests at just the right angle to separate the two plates where they overlapped in the center. Martin A. Haynes, *A History of the Second Regiment, New Hampshire Volunteer Infantry in the War of the Rebellion,* Lakeport, N. H., 1896, 78.

7. Statement by General Wales, Dean, *Helmets and Body Armor,* 58, 59, 60, n. Statement of Fred W. Cross in possession of author. Mr. Cross was a friend of General Wales and had often seen the vest. Other interesting instances of the saving of life by these breastplates can be found in *Daily Richmond Whig,* April 25, 1862; New York *Daily Tribune,* June 28, 1862; W.D. Whetstone, "Notes from Battlefields," the *Confederate Veteran,* XIX, no. 9 (September, 1911), 433. One instance worth recording is given in Harry Gilmor, *Four Years in the Saddle,* New York, 1866, 35. In describing a cavalry skirmish near Front Royal, Virginia in 1862, Gilmor, a Confederate colonel of cavalry, reported, "It was then that I captured Adjutant Hasbrouck. The adjutant had on, as I afterward found, a steel breastplate underneath his clothing, rendering him bullet proof to some extent. I fired twice at him, and he three or four times at me. At length I got up close to him and fired. Great was my astonishment that he did not fall. This was my last load; so, drawing sabers, we closed for a hand-to-hand fight."

8. McHenry Howard, *Recollection of a Maryland Confederate Soldier,* Baltimore, 1914, 120, 120n. William Leroy Broun, "The Red Artillery" in Thomas L. Broun and Bessie L. Broun, *Dr. William Leroy Broun,* New York, 1912, 217. *Daily Richmond Whig,* April 25, 1862. New York *Daily Tribune,* June 28, 1862. W.D. Whetstone, "Notes from Battlefields," *loc. cit.,* 433. Charles D. Rhodes, "The Federal Cavalry, Its Organization and Equipment", in Miller, *Photographic History,* IV, 64. Dean, *Helmets and Body Armor,* 58n. Haynes, *Second Regiment, N. H. Volunteers,* 78. Thorpe, *Fifteenth Conn. Volunteers,* 15. Billings, *Hardtack and Coffee,* 275. The highest serial number found during this study was 18383.

9. Thorpe, *Fifteenth Conn. Volunteers,* 15. Rhodes, "Federal Cavalry", *loc. cit.* 64. Billings, *Hardtack and Coffee,* 275.

Substantial portions of this article appeared in the May-June 1950 issue of *Ordnance* and in the June 1952 issue of the *Military Collector & Historian.* These portions have been reprinted by the gracious permission of the American Ordnance Association and The Company of Military Historians.

The Final Word on the Venditti-Volcanic Controversy

by EMANUELE MARCIANÒ

One of Europe's two finest monthly magazines dedicated to arms studies, antique and modern—and probably one of the four best in the world in any language— is Diana Armi, *published in Florence under the strong-willed, demanding and creative editorship of Emanuele Marcianò. Born in 1935, sig. Marcianò studied engineering and geology but in mid-course changed to mathematics, a field in which he took his degree and which he taught for seven years. His involvement with arms goes back to his adolescence and centered first on modern military weapons, then expanded into all firearms of the period 1850-1918—a sphere in which only a few men can vie with him for knowledge. He left the academic world in 1968 to take over* Diana Armi *and has since elevated it to a publication of international stature.*

Naples has been the birthplace of a remarkable number of equally remarkable contributions to mankind: to its honour redound not only the pizza pie and the music of Pergolesi but also, among other things, the first railway in Italy (Naples-Portici, 7½ kilometers, 1839). Hence there is no need to try to make it the cradle of the Winchester as well—as some of my fellow-citizens and colleagues have recently endeavoured, in print and in addresses to important collectors' conventions in Italy and abroad. Let's examine briefly why they have done so, and why it has become necessary to refute them *una volta per sempre*—once and for all.

In Italy, interest in the history of weapons—particularly of firearms—is currently in a phase of rapid, indeed frenetic development, a phenomenon of the past ten and especially the last three or four years. But when students and collectors seek to get on with serious, hard-core source research, they encounter all but insurmountable barriers, chief among which is the inaccessibility of documents: either these are immured behind forbidding, at times downright hostile, bureaucratic procedures that little or nothing can accelerate, or else they are contained— or may be reasonable supposed to be contained—in that mountainous millennial mass of unexplored records reposing and slowly decaying in thousands of more or less forgotten archives throughout the peninsula. [Editor's Note: Compare this with Claude Blair's comments at the end of his article on wheel-locks, p. 28!—R.H.] Though much has been and is

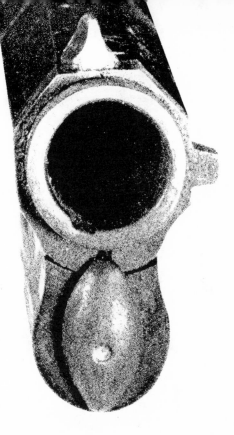

constantly being done, this is but a scratch on the surface of the unexplored that lies ahead.

Since active arms collecting and academic arms studies are developing at an even pace, the still-booming Italian collecting boom (focused mainly on two centers of gravity: the Golden Age 1600-1700, and the *Risorgimento* c. 1820-70) has rendered access to studiable specimens difficult and costly. If, then, to the difficulties of source research and specimen procurement we add a lively interest in American frontier arms, it is not hard to understand why the existence of an Italian 19th-century pistol—the Venditti—extremely similar to the Volcanic repeaters should have engendered the patriotic legend that *here* was to be found the true ancestor and prototype of the carbines of Buffalo Bill and Sitting Bull. It would probably prove amusing for the reader to glance through the arguments adduced by some Italian arms historians in "support" of this thesis; but the present page is not the place for polemics of that sort, and we shall keep ourselves strictly to recounting the true and documented story of "our Volcanic" and of its "inventor" Pietro Venditti (whom some would present as Jennings, Hunt, Smith, Wesson, Henry, King and Winchester rolled into one—and von Braun, too: rocket balls).

To begin with, there is no justification for the mystery that has hitherto shrouded the identity of Pietro Venditti, said by many men to have been many men—some would have him a Swiss engineer! But in fact, the record of his birth is available to all for the trouble of searching (a trouble few have ever taken): he was born at one o'clock in the afternoon of February 9th, 1828, in the township of Cerreto, province of Naples. His father was a scissors maker specialized in sheep-shearing tools; perhaps the son acquired a mechanical bent in his father's workshop, and when the father moved to Sala in 1843, his son came along (a good many 15-year olds left home before that age in those days). Some time later Venditti Jr. moved to Atripalda near Avellino, earning his bread now as a weaver of monks' cloth. Though this occupation should have imbued him with Christian meekness, his fiery temperament seems to have flamed unabated, for he killed a co-worker in a quarrel and was condemned to indefinite forced labour—to the chain gangs; but in 1860 a certain *Cavaliere* Giuseppe Biondi—apparently the prison doctor—managed to get him reprieved. Free once more, he found a job in the state arsenal at Lancusi, where he won quick promotion to foreman. So far as we can ever hope to know, this was the first time in Venditti's life that he took an interest in firearms —six years after the appearance of the first "Venditti-type" Smith & Wesson, and exactly in the year of the effectual demise of Volcanics and their evolution into the Henry.

Not until fully eleven years later, in 1871—having apparently become proficient in the arms crafts— did Venditti, now aged 43, emerge into the public limelight: viz., as an exhibitor in the International Maritime Exhibition at Naples, displaying a cannon model and small breech-loading pistols and a long arm—but *not* repeaters: *single*-shot breechloaders! On February 8, 1872, the first patent bearing the name Pietro Venditti was registered (Fig. 3); it covered a small double-barrelled breech-loading pistol with barrels that swung horizontally about a vertical pivot to allow loading with . . . obsolete, ineffectual rocket balls! Evidently it had been pistols of this sort that he had exhibited at Naples the year before; one of them was destined to be presented to the Countess of Mirafiori, mistress and confidante of H.M. Victor Emanuel II. In 1873 Venditti took part in the International Exhibition in Vienna with two cannons. Then, on February 27th, 1875, he obtained registry of a three-year patent, No. 77, for "a new system for the Venditti pistol, a twenty-six shot repeater with a moving bolt with a firing-pin, also applicable to long arms by means of the same mechanism"—"*Nuovo sistema della pistola Venditti, a ripetizione a ventisei colpi con l'otturatore mobile ad ago, applicabile anche a fucili con lo stesso meccanismo*" (Fig. 4).

The specifications for Patent No. 77 are perfectly clear in their description, in word and diagram, of the Volcanic mechanism, except for a few minor details. Let us examine these differences rather than

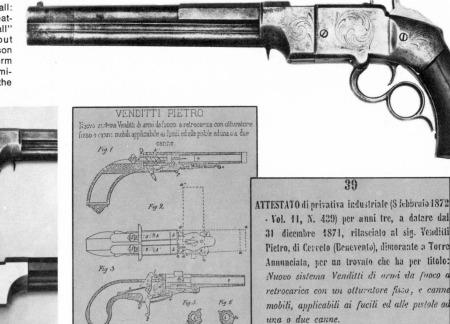

Fig. 1—The grandfather of them all: a Smith & Wesson Volitional Repeating Pistol of 1854-55 for "rocket-ball" caseless ammunition, often but wrongly called "the Smith & Wesson Volcanic." In this arm lay the germ of a descendancy destined to terminate in the Winchester '66 and in the Vendittis.

Fig. 2—In 1855, Smith & Wesson became the Volcanic Arms Company and this, in 1857, under the administration and manipulations of Oliver Winchester, the New Haven Arms Company. Both firms produced weapons essentially identical to the Smith & Wessons though modified in several details—and, like Smith & Wesson, failed to sell them because of the woefully ineffectual ammunition. The photograph compares the toggle links of the Smith & Wesson pistol in Fig. 1 with those of a Volcanic carbine.

Fig. 3 — Venditti's Kingdom of Italy patent specifications for single-shot, double-barreled breechloading pistols using rocket-ball ammunition.

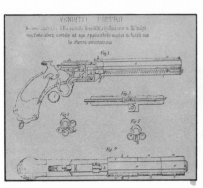

Fig. 4—Venditti's Kingdom of Italy patent specifications for the First Series or rocket-ball repeating pistols, Feb. 27, 1875, under the title "a new system for Venditti pistols, a twenty-six shot repeater with a moving bolt with a firing pin, applicable also to long arms by means of the same mechanism." No prior Kingdom of the Two Sicilies patents are known, and may be assumed nonexistent by virtue of the logic of events (see text).

the similarities, on the assumption that the reader is familiar with the essential workings of the Smith & Wesson, Volcanic, Henry and Winchester '66 mechanisms, all fundamentally the same. The most obvious variant is the presence of two tubular magazines parallel to the barrel on the right and left side—or rather, two tubular containers for rocket balls from which the true magazine, situated under the barrel, might be refilled by rotating the muzzle block to align the true magazine muzzle section with first one, then the other of the container tubes; if the pistol was held first muzzle-down, then muzzle-up, gravity would feed the balls from the tubes into the magazine via the muzzle block extension tubes. This was Venditti's only original idea; it was also an absurd and impractical one. Another difference was

Venditti's use of a hollow bolt containing a sliding firing pin instead of a simple, solid bolt (actually two-piece, but in effect a solid rod) with an integral firing pin at the end, as in the Volcanics. No judgement of quality or efficacy can be passed on this: probably it is an indication that the detonators were seated farther inside the base cavity of the Vendittis' projectiles than in the Volcanics'.

Pistols of this type (Fig. 5) constitute the First Series—if one may designate them in so formal a vein—and are marked on the top barrel flats "Sistema Venditti", together with a small circular mark (Fig. 6) containing a crown, a sword, a star and the letters "T.A."—not unreasonably supposed to have been a proof stamp of the arsenal of Torre Annunciata, near Naples, where, after the Unification of

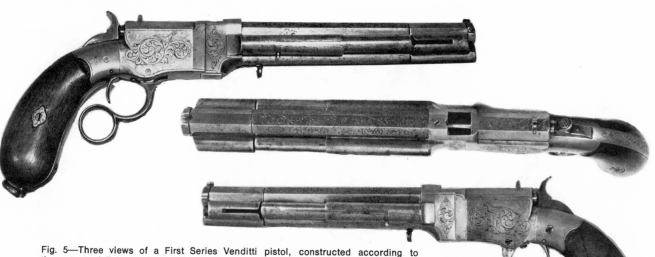

Fig. 5—Three views of a First Series Venditti pistol, constructed according to the patent of Feb. 27, 1875 (Fig. 4). These weapons were marked "Sistema Venditti." The lateral "magazines" are really containers for spare rocket balls that can be transferred into the true magazine under the barrel via the rotating muzzle block. Aside from this impractical encumbrance, Vendittis differed from Volcanics only in the use of a separate firing pin which passed longitudinally through the obturator bolt—in Volcanics the bolt served both as obturator and firing pin.

Fig. 6—Inscription on top barrel flat of the First Series Vendittis. The circular stamp with a crown, dagger, star and TA is thought to be a proof mark of the government arsenal at Torre Annunciata.

Fig. 7—Muzzle views of a Henry rifle (left) and a First Series Venditti (right).

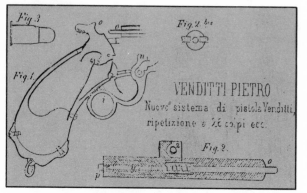

Fig. 8—Venditti's Kingdom of Italy patent specification of March 15, 1877, for the curious cartridge and striker thereafter to be used in what have come to be called Second Series Vendittis.

Italy in 1870, civilan arms were probably proved and thus stamped (though the exact meaning has not yet been absolutely established; but that has no bearing on the discussion at hand). Like the Volcanics, First Series Venditti pistols have iron barrels made integrally with the magazine out of a single piece, and brass receivers; but the Venditti sideplates are of steel, while those of the Volcanics are brass. Venditti ammunition consisted of Volcanic-type *rocket balls,* i.e. the so-called "self-propelling" (they weren't) hollowed-out ogival-conical bullets whose base cavity contained the propellent powder, without the aid of a cartridge case; proof of this lies in the Venditti's lack of an extractor, in the short length of the elevator and in the equally short firing chamber (which was just the bore without rifling lands).

On March 15th, 1877, Venditti secured Patent No. 105 (Fig. 8), valid for an initial period of three years (it lapsed in 1880 for default of payment of the renewal fee); it specified "improvements" consisting of the adoption of a strange brass- or copper-cased cartridge that constituted a sort of compromise between center-fire ignition and Dreyse-Chassepot needle perforation, and hence necessarily the inclusion of extractors placed at 3 and 9 o'clock of the bolt face. In other respects this "Second Series" weapon differed from the First in the absence of the lateral container tubes and in a longer elevator and firing chamber to accommodate the longer projectile and its case. The markings were changed to "Venditti e Cⁱ Lancusi", the "& Company" ("e Cⁱ") suggesting the presence of financiers or partners (Fig.

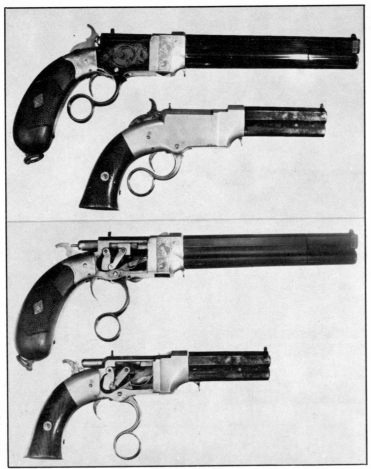

Figs. 9a & 9b—Two views, closed and open of (top) a Second Series Venditti, 1877 and after, and (bottom) a pocket-model Volcanic with a four-inch barrel, about 1856. These Vendittis, marked "Venditti e Ci—Lancusi" ("Venditti & Company, Lancusi"), used a strange copper- or brass-cased cartridge, a compromise between center-fire and Dreyse needle-perforation, calibre 9.5 mm. Little comment is required on the virtual identity of the mechanisms. But the Venditti's side plates are steel, the Volcanic's brass.

Fig. 10—Inscription on barrels of two Second Series Vendittis.

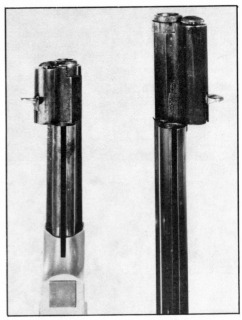

Fig. 11—Another—but negligible—difference between Volcanics and Vendittis is the opposite rotation of the muzzle blocks: Volcanic at left, Venditti at right.

10). To this very day there is a gloomy watchmaker's shop in Lancusi (which is not far from Salerno) whose proprietor, well up in his eighties, has clear memories of his father working with Venditti—and in fact, he keeps in the shop a blank casting from which Venditti levers were machined, as well as a die for drawing the barrel-cum-magazine units (Figs. 16 & 17).

The several Italian arms students who have hitherto preached the priority of the Venditti can be pardoned for their inexactitudes by the almost total lack of readily available documents. The laurels for passionate and difficult researches splendidly absolved go to signor Francesco Denaro, a summary of whose findings was published in *Diana Armi* [See introductory note at head of this article—*Ed.*] in 1971 and 1972; but for his work, even the present article would necessarily have been speculative.

Nonetheless, a few die-hards still plead Venditti's case. It should be sufficient to remind them that if the Kingdom of Italy patents here cited had indeed been transfers of pre-Unification (i.e. pre-1870 Kingdom of the Two Sicilies) patents, it is strange indeed that Venditti should not have exhibited his repeaters in the Naples International Maritime Exhibition of 1871 or at Vienna in 1873. Stranger still that he should have waited five more years, until February 27th, 1875, before requesting the protection of a Kingdom of Italy patent—five protection-less years in which anyone anywhere would have been free to capitalize on his (hypothetical) generation-old invention! Still another plank in support of the Volcanic's priority is the existence of the Volcanic's predecessors, the Smith & Wesson pistols of 1854-56 (Fig. 1), which differ from both Volcanics and Vendittis only in some minor mechanical solutions, in outline and in the use of a steel receiver instead of brass. It is quite absurd to think that if

312

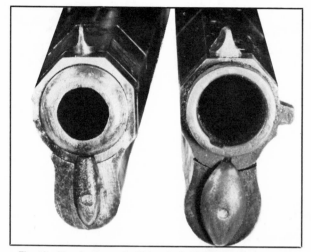

Fig. 12—Muzzle views of a Volcanic (left) and a Venditti (right).

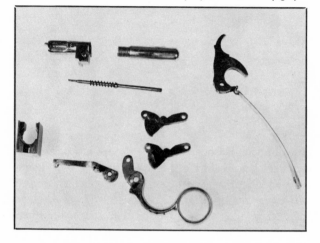

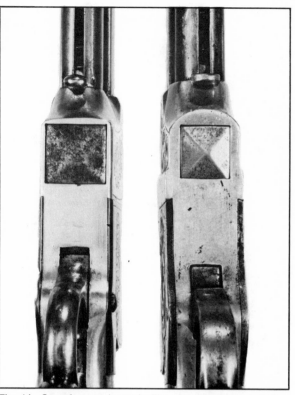

Fig. 14—Seen from underneath: The elevator of the cartridge-using Second Series Venditti at the left is by necessity larger than that of the First Series rocket-ball version.

Fig. 13—The components of a Second Series Venditti. Note the long, spring-loaded firing pin that travels through the two-piece bolt, and the ejector prongs on the front of the bolt secured by screws.

PRINCIPAL DIMENSIONS OF VENDITTI PISTOLS

First Series, Patent 1875: Self-propellent "rocket ball" ammunition, no extractors on bolt face, lateral spare ammunition tubes on left and right.

Second Series, Patent 1877: Pseudo-centerfire copper or brass cartridge, extractors on bolt face, no spare ammunition tubes.

	FIRST SERIES		SECOND SERIES	
Calibre	10.0 mm.	.394 in.	9.1 mm	.358 in.
Overall Length	31 cm.	12.2 in.	33 cm.	13.0 in.
Barrel Length	15.5 cm.	6.1 in.	17.5 cm.	6.9 in.
Weight	830 gms.	1 lb. 13 oz.	760 gms.	1 lb. 12 oz.
Ammunition length	14.0 mm.	.55 in.	15.0 mm	.59 in.
Magazine capacity	9 balls in main mag.		9 cartridges in mag.	
	1 ball in chamber		1 cartridge on elevator	
	8 balls in left tube		1 cartridge in chamber	
	8 balls in right tube		10 in true lever-action repetition.	
	26 shots			
	of which two-times-ten and one-times-six in true lever-action repetition.			

These figures apply to the two main models, or perhaps it would be better to say the two most frequently encountered. There appear to have been quite a few variations, produced in limited or very small quantities, e.g. a flat-butted Second Series version, (see Fig. 15), and others not yet catalogued; but some of these may be patent invasions or franchise products.

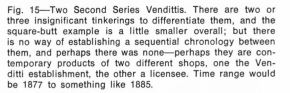

Fig. 15—Two Second Series Vendittis. There are two or three insignificant tinkerings to differentiate them, and the square-butt example is a little smaller overall; but there is no way of establishing a sequential chronology between them, and perhaps there was none—perhaps they are contemporary products of two different shops, one the Venditti establishment, the other a licensee. Time range would be 1877 to something like 1885.

Fig. 16—Keyhole die for drawing Venditti barrel-and-magazine units in a single piece, found together with the lever blank shown in Fig. 17.

Fig. 17—This rough forging of what was to become a Venditti lever was recently found by arms student signor Francesco Denaro in a watchmaker's shop in Lancusi, home town of Venditti production, whose 80-odd-year old proprietor remembers his father working with Pietro Venditti.

Messrs. Smith and Wesson had indeed been out to pirate an Italian archtype, they would have first produced a considerably changed version that would not, however, have constituted any improvement over the supposed Neapolitan "original". More absurd still is the notion that in intensely industrialized America, well into the early cartridge phase of history and in need of powerful firearms, a manufacturer would not only have copied a type of projectile incapable of penetrating a stout winter overcoat at ten steps' distance, but reduced its caliber and therefore efficacy even more. He might have toyed with such an invention in its original, untried state and then promptly discarded it, as in fact Oliver Winchester did between 1857 and 1860 with Smith & Wesson/Volcanic "rocket balls", but he would never have initiated production of a known and proved failure. This of course leads fairly to the question why Pietro Venditti should have done such a foolish thing; and the answer is in part that as a matter of fact he sought to augment calibre and hence efficacy of rocket balls, alas to no avail, and in part that in the Southern Mediterranean climate of Venditti's market the kind of winter clothing which afforded adequate protection against Volcanic balls was just not worn.

Nor must one overlook the other "inventors" of the Volcanic immemorialized in Italian patent files: Lorenzo Salvatore, Vincenzo d'Amore, Giacomo Sabatini and Luca de Carluccio all staked their claims to inventions with essentially Volcanic and Venditti characteristics between 1877 and 1888. A certain firm of Bodeo & Micheloni for a time assayed an ugly smoothbore shotgun version of the Henry.

Venditti pistols were probably produced in terms of a few hundreds, not thousands. In good, clean condition (the same standards that gauge Volcanics are applicable), they are now rather valuable, the three-magazine version being worth more than the cartridge model, but both being much sought-after in this country. They constituted one more case of famous established arms imitated elsewhere, like the "Henries" made in Bavaria and the innumerable more-or-less 1851 Navy "Colts" and more-or-less "Adams" and "Tranter" revolvers produced all over the world in qualities ranging from splendid to wretched. (By way of balancing our ledger of national honour, be it remembered that the Lorenzoni-Berselli repeating system was copied by everyone everywhere for 160-odd years, right up to London's Mortimer in the 1820's [see the article by Dr. Thomas T. Hoopes in the present volume—Ed.], and that the American Hall breechloaders were thinly-disguised re-hashes of the Milanese Antonio Crespi's design of the 1780's, tried and quickly abandoned by the Austrian army.) Both the Vendittis and the Volcanics were blind alleys in arms history; to own one specimen of each should be a goal for many collectors. The fact that signor Denaro's publications as well as these present lines should silence forever the claims of Italian priority does not rob these rather endearing, somewhat hapless weapons of their just historical and collecting merits.

314

A Unique Trio of Winchester 1866 Carbines

An Editorial Presentation
by ROBERT HELD

The photographs accompanying these observations show in some detail what appears to be the only trio of Winchester '66's ever to have come to light. There is no indication of anything similar in all of Winchester literature.

The known history of these pieces is brief. They were bought in 1968 in Santiago, Chile, by a European businessman and three years later traded with an American collector for several pairs of high-quality French, Dutch and Italian late-seventeenth-century flintlock pistols. In April, 1973, they returned to Europe, having been acquired for an undisclosed sum by a leading Continental collector. It is said that until just before the Chilean purchase in 1968 they had been stored in the original two-tier, brass-mounted mahogany case bearing the trade label of a St. Louis retailer in the lid, but that the last Chilean owner, finding so sturdy a chest much more useful than three old guns for which no ammunition would ever again be available, ripped it to pieces and made it over into a household tool chest—a hideous tale, and a beweepable pity if true, as it probably is.

In briefest terms, we have here three 1866 carbines bearing serial numbers 47830, 48505 and 49157, which dates them 1870, quite probably September-October. The distances in production units are 675 and 652, a total of 1,327 between the extremes, equal to a span of about twelve or fourteen working days at the factory. *Note, please, that all the photographs show the weapons arranged in serial number sequence from top to bottom and from left to right, i.e.*

4	4	4		4 7 8 3 0
7	8	9		———————
8	5	1	or	4 8 5 0 5
3	0	5		———————
0	5	7		4 9 1 5 7

Their condition is far above average for '66 carbines. 47830 has extensive remains, thin but uniform, of original blue, going over into brown; 48505 has traces of blue but is mainly brown; 49157 is down to white iron, spotted but smooth. There is no pitting or corrosion anywhere. The nickel plating varies but is present to about 85-90% as an average for all three pieces, being virtually intact on 47830 and most worn —but still 75% present—on 49157. There are not signs of any repairs or restorations save three small screw replacements.

Their most striking quality is, of course, the threesomeness. Inspection under various magnifications from 10X to 35X suggests very strongly that all three were engraved at the same time by three different hands sharing some common tools, and that this was done very shortly after the date of manufacture; the nickel-plating was done without any doubt *after* the engraving. The evidence of tool marks and hand motions is easily enough established under the microscope; the conclusion of the engraving and plating date is prompted by the fact that the microscopic patina of

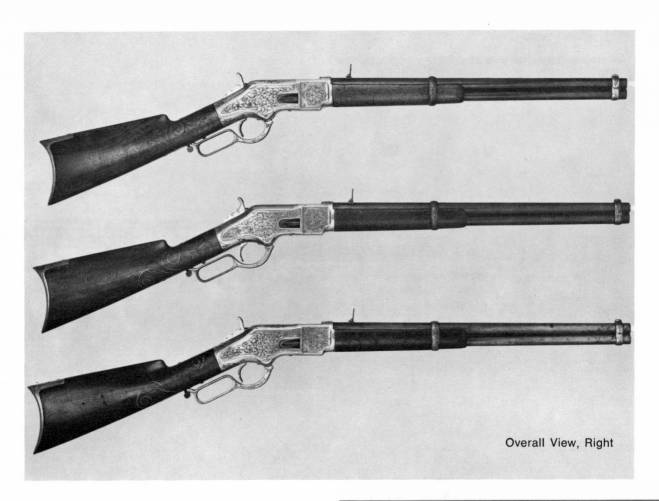

Overall View, Right

surface abrasion and oxidation is equal on the flat, un-engraved nickeled surfaces, in the engraving grooves, on the edges of transition between unengraved and groove, and on the hard-steel surfaces. All of the veteran Winchester students who have examined these arms agree that "collector's instinct," even in the absence of microscopes, leaves little doubt about the simultaniety of manufacture, engraving and plating ("simultaneity" in the sense that all three of these processes were completed by the time of the original purchase).

Nonetheless, the "trioness" is somewhat impaired by the fact that only 47830 and 49157 are absolutely identical, 48505 differing in several respects (cf. photographs): its left side is a contracted and modified—or perhaps initial tryout?—version of the design which thereafter remains identical on all the other *five* sides, including the *right* side of 48505 itself; moreover, 48505 bears a very delicate and decorative but a typical design on the butt plate tang and on the underside of the cartridge elevator, as well as other minor variations in details. Yet these divergences notwithstanding, one cannot consider these weapons anything but a *trio*. They share what is essentially the same design, variations or no variations; they share the very rare and completely identical silver inlay on the stocks and forearms—now largely missing, but the grooves are

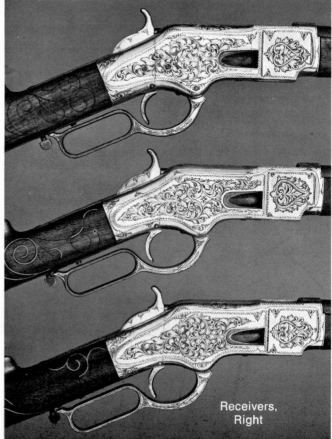

Receivers, Right

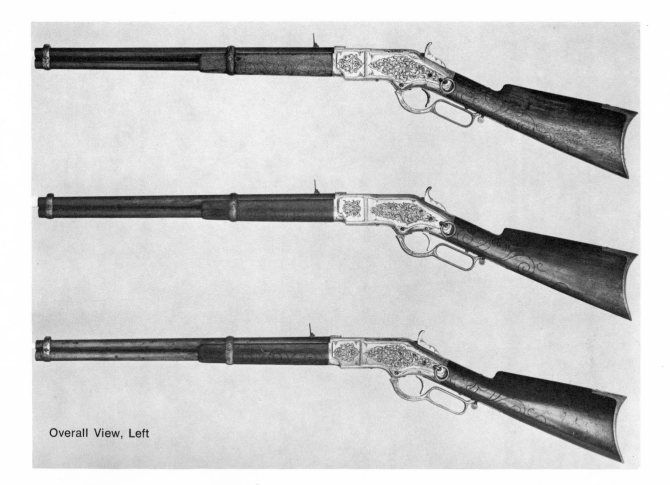

Overall View, Left

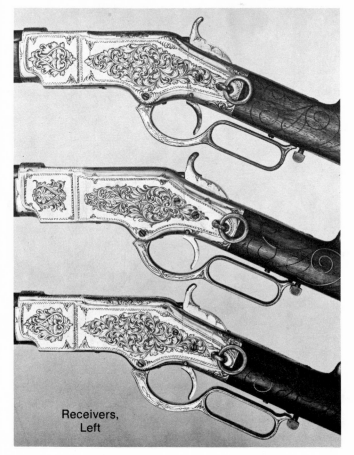

Receivers, Left

sharp and deep; they share the unusual lush coverage not only in engraving but in plating on the butt plates, hammers, levers, triggers and barrel bands!—even the undersides of the levers, i.e. the surfaces facing the serial numbers, are well engraved! They share the same special-order, rifle- or Henry-style, very high-combed butts, and the unusually high-quality wood (though not burl or deluxe) of which these are made. They were "born" in the course of a very short production run—twelve or fourteen working days, sometime in late 1870. Finally, they have come down together for 103 years. Hence they constitute a trio.

As to the style of the engraving, the hands at work were German or German-schooled, heavily influenced by the London-Birmingham traditions still prevailing in America in the 1850's and 1860's but already well on the way toward a new American idiom that begins to disown both the German and the British parentage. Louis Nimschke and his followers continued to hew most closely to the European models, while the Ulrichs and their imitators abandoned them almost entirely and the Young school weaved an uneven course between loyalty to the old and enthusiasm for the new. Diligent comparison of the pieces under discussion with the recently-published Nimschke engravings—not only with his work on Winchester '66s but on walking sticks, doorbells, shotguns, dentist's plaques,

317

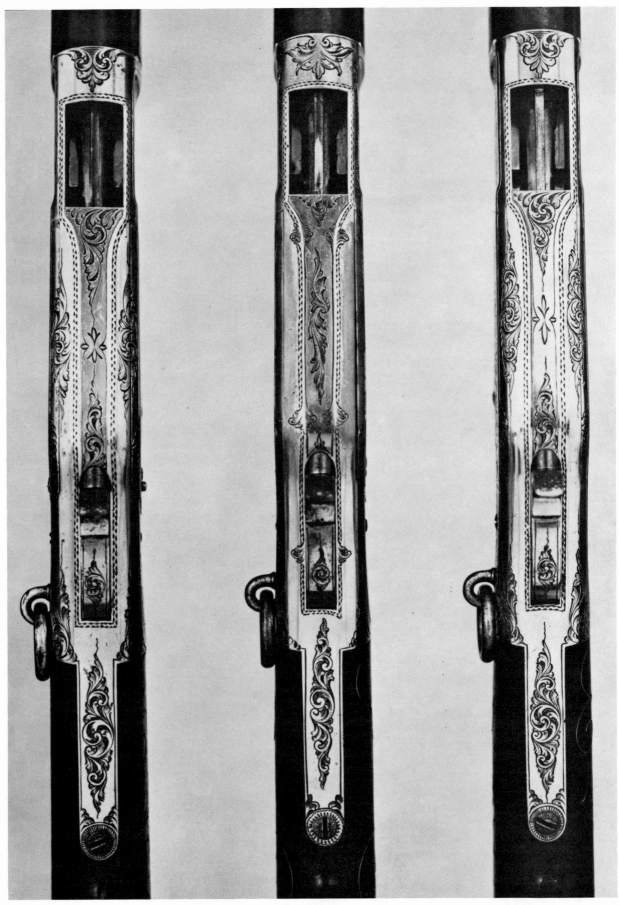

Top View

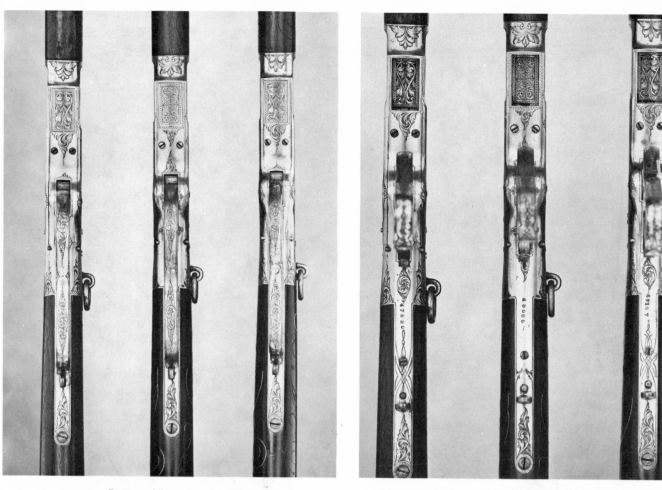

Bottom View, Levers Closed   Bottom View, Levers Open

dozens of every-day metal utensils—will leave little doubt that the trio's provenance is rooted in the Nimschke-Young ambience. But they are neither Nimschke nor Young products: not Nimschke because the scrolls are two-dimensional, without any under- or over-crossing (a monoplanar approach found, in fact, in Young's work but never in Nimschke's); and not Young because the containment of the designs within the spaces they fill are too free, too flowing, and not sufficiently fixed, stable and defined. It is interesting to note that the quiet, conservative character of the silver-wire inlay in the wood (one must imagine it complete) meshes well with that of the engraving.

Three artisans were at work in this production. Each one did one complete carbine by himself, and some burins seem to have been shared—judging by enlargements of tool traces. But they were far apart in skill. 48505 is executed with the highest degree of competence—the shading, cross-hatching and uniformity of curves is equal to anything ever done by Nimschke, Young or the Ulrichs. Next comes 49157, which is neat, crisp, done by a polished professional but not as imaginatively or conscientiously as 48505.

Finally, 47830 is the most summary, a good pro job, better by far than all but the most luxurious Winchester factory work, but not up to 48505 or 49157. It is remarkable that none of the background is stippled but rather cross-hatched—by far the more arduous technique of filling-in.

Rather as an anticlimax, all this leads to no defensible conclusion. Very *likely,* but not demonstrably, these splendid specimens of Americana passed from the factory directly into the riotous arms trade along the Mississippi, from St. Louis all the way down to New Orleans, and were engraved, plated and cased by a dealer somewhere along the route, more likely than not nearer the St. Louis environs, and still more likely on order for a customer, perhaps the rich Chilean *haciendero* who took or shipped them home, perhaps some *Yanqui* who used them long and hard before they eventually drifted down to Santiago.

But their uniqueness and, hence, importance in the study of Winchesters is unassailable. Should any reader be able to connect their school of decoration with any similar specimen elsewhere, please let us hear.

——*Ed.*

319

Upper Sides of Levers, i.e. Surfaces
Against Serial Numbers.

Butt Plate Tangs

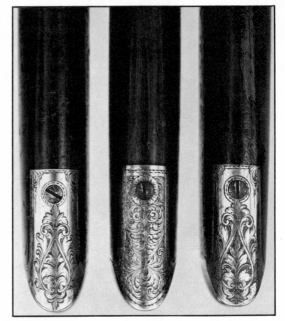

Barrels with Engraved and Plated Bands, Right and Left.

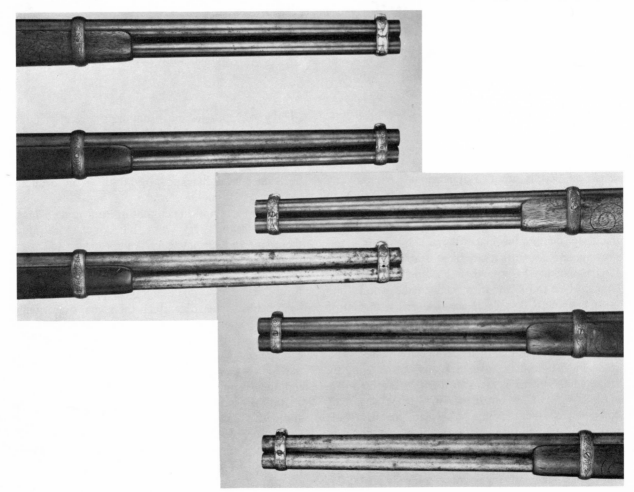

EPILOGUE

Dear Reader:

On this page and the following page you will find a brief questionnaire. Your completing it and mailing it to us will be of great help in planning an even better second issue of the ANNUAL. Please note that the page can be cut at the dotted line without damaging the rest of this edition. The completed questionnaire can be sent either to our U.S. publishing offices or to our European editorial office.

Thank You!   —R.H.

Please mail this questionnaire to:
ARMS AND ARMOR ANNUAL
Digest Books, Inc.
540 Frontage Road
Northfield, Illinois 60093

or

Editorial Office
ARMS AND ARMOR ANNUAL
Piazza Santa Maria Sopr'arno 1 R
Florence, Italy

Name and Address (entirely optional—omit if you wish):

_____

_____

_____

For those not wishing to identify themselves, please give city, state and country of residence) for our distribution statistics) :

_____

Your Age: _____

Your Occupation or Profession_____

1. How did the ARMS AND ARMOR ANNUAL first come to your attention?
   ☐ Through the recommendation of a friend.
   ☐ In a bookshop or sporting goods store display.
   ☐ In/Through (explain briefly) :

2. Please list in order of preference, by their authors' last names, the five (5) articles you found most interesting *solely for their subject matter,* without regard to style of writing or quality of illustrations:

_____   _____   _____

_____   _____

3. Now, again in order of preference and by authors' names, the five (5) articles you judge best for *style and clarity of writing,* without regard to their subject matter:

_____   _____   _____

_____   _____

4. For the dark end of the scale, which are the five (5) articles you found most boring *solely for their subject matter?*:

_____   _____   _____

_____   _____

5. And which five (5) are the dullest, most tedious, judged solely for style and clarity (or muddiness) of writing?:

_____   _____   _____

_____   _____

6. On a scale on which Zero (0) equals *Terrible, No Good At All*, Fifty (50) equals *Good But Undistinguished* and One Hundred (100) equals *Superb Beyond All Expectations*, please rate the ANNUAL for all factors taken together —e.g., chronological and geographic scope, aptness of subjects covered, quality of illustrations, layout—everything that makes up the totality of the book (feel free to add a verbal evaluation, too!) : _____

7. The ANNUAL is based on an editorial policy of presenting for the most part highly compact subjects in unusual depth and detail—for example, specifically *French* royal armor as reflected in the designs of *one* famous artist, swords of honor awarded only to veteran officers of *Trafalgar*, or the function of solely the *Lorenzoni* repeating flintlock system *in its perfected state,* and so on. Please indicate with which of the following two evaluations of this policy you tend to agree most, or, if you agree with neither, write your opinion separately:

☐ The policy is essentially a good one; it sets the ARMS AND ARMOR ANNUAL apart from most other periodicals in the field and endows it with the attributes of a much-needed, adult-level forum of international compass. The policy, although it may be relaxed now and then must not grow inflexible, should not be compromised in principle.

☐ The approach is excessively restrictive because it presupposes too much background study on the reader's part and hence renders the ANNUAL esoteric. It should be replaced by a policy for greater width and less depth—for example, articles on royal and parade armor of *various* nationalities and design schools, on presentation and honor swords of *all* British napoleonic campaigns, or on the function of most of the "Lorenzoni"-type repeating flintlock systems in use for almost 150 years, et cetera.

☐ (Use additional paper for still another point of view.)

8. Should future issues devote a fair amount of space to the Near and Far East, Africa and Oceania? (Japanese swords, pole arms and armor excluded—they consitute a special category of study.)   ☐ Yes   ☐ No

9. Which *four* of the following twelve main divisions of arms studies would you like to see noticeably emphasized in the next issue? Please indicate your order of preference by writing "1", "2", "3" and "4" in the brackets in the front of the appropriate division; if you have no preferences, just mark all four with a check or an X. Then please add after each selection the historical time span that interests you most, either in terms of from-to (e.g., "1750-1785"), "early 16th century" or similar, or with a word or two of common arms and armor jargon that closely defines an established era (e.g., "Early percussion," "Maximilian," "Rapiers"). Feel free to indicate your preferred periods for *all* the divisions, even those you did not mark for future special emphasis!

☐ Armor _____
☐ Edged Weapons _____
☐ Pole Arms _____
☐ Portable Firearms _____
☐ Artillery _____
☐ Crossbow & Catapults _____

☐ Militaria & Accoutrements _____
☐ Military Architecture _____
☐ Naval Architecture _____
☐ Military Strategy & Tactics _____
☐ Naval Strategy & Tactics _____
☐ Flags, Standards & Heraldry _____

10. The ANNUAL's content reflects still another editorial policy, namely to devote comparatively little space to Americana, since American weaponry and everything pertaining to it directly or remotely is profusely and competently covered in the many U.S. and Canadian monthly and bi-monthly gun magazines and in the many collectors clubs' news-letters, circulars, journals, etc. In view of this, it is felt that American subjects can be limited (in the present issue, to three articles out of thirty) and that most of the space should be given over to themes rarely, if ever, presented in these same publications. Which of the following comes closest to summing up your opinion on this?   ☐ The decision is wise and should stand.   ☐ It is all right in principle, but three American topics out of thirty are too few.   ☐ Poor reasoning —in view of its undeniable importance, American weapons history should constitute at least a quarter of the contents.

11. Do you think that the next issue of the ANNUAL should include one or two works of fiction, either commissioned specifically for the purpose or a reprinted classic, whose plots closely involve some unusually interesting aspect of arms and armor studies?

☐ Yes, definitely!   ☐ Let's try it.   ☐ Doesn't seem right.   ☐ Absolutely not!

12. Would you pay a reasonable increase in the ANNUAL's price for the inclusion of a hefty and well-chosen color section?   ☐ Yes   ☐ No

Thank you for the trouble you've taken.